COMMENTARY
2021–2022
VOLUME 115

ISBN: 978-1-6816/7-773-6

This commentary is based on the International Sunday School Lessons and International Bible Lessons for Christian Teaching, copyrighted by the International Council of Religious Education, and is used by permission.

Entered according to Act of Congress in the Office of Librarian of Congress in the year 1903 at Washington, DC, by R. H. Boyd, D.D., LL.D.

R. H. Boyd, D.D., LL.D., Founder (1896–1922)

H. A. Boyd, D.D. (1922–1959) • T. B. Boyd Jr., D.D. (1959–1979) • T. B. Boyd III, D.D. (1979–2017)

LaDonna Boyd, EdD
President/CEO (2017–Present)

LaDonna Boyd, EdD
President/CEO

David Groves, DMin, PhD
Director of Publications

EDITORIAL STAFF
Olivia M. Cloud, MRE
Associate Editor

Landon Dickerson, MTS; Monique Gooch, BA; Joseph Tribble, MDiv;
Brittany Batson, BA; Sinclaire Sparkman, BS; Freida Crawley, BS; Carla Davis, BA

Dr. Barry Johnson • Dr. Napoleon Harris
Rev. Melvin Guest • Dr. Bernard Williams
Writers

Jasmine Cole
Cover Design

Cover Photo by: LaDonna Boyd, EdD
Photo taken in Chamonix-Mont-Blanc, France (2018)

R.H. BOYD
EST. 1896

www.rhboyd.com

R.H. Boyd Publishing Corporation
6717 Centennial Blvd.• Nashville, Tennessee 37209-1017

A WORD FROM THE PUBLISHER

Greetings,

This is our 125th year of existence as a Christian publisher in the Lord's vineyard. One hundred twenty-five years of God's providence and of our labor to bring you the best in Christian resources. *Boyd's Commentary for the Sunday School* has been a staple in Christian Education throughout that time. This year's book has been thoughtfully and prayerfully prepared. It is our hope that as you walk through this year's lessons it would aid you along with the direction of the Holy Spirit. This commentary is for anyone who wants to deepen his/her spiritual walk before God and deepen his/her understanding of the Bible and practical life application. As you walk through four quarters of biblical insights while preparing to share the Gospel with those who will hear your voice, be blessed. As you enjoy this resource, consider visiting our website www.rhboyd.com and following us on social media to stay abreast of all the Christian resources we are bringing to you at R.H. Boyd Publishing.

Onward,

LaDonna Boyd, EdD
Fifth-generation *President/CEO*

A WORD FROM THE DIRECTOR

Greetings!

This year marks the 125th anniversary for Boyd Publishing and for well over a century, Boyd's Commentary has been a reliable resource for those who desire in-depth theological and biblical exposition. You can be sure that this commentary has been developed by people of faith who take seriously the task to rightly divide the Word of God. The texts used within this resource have been prudently investigated using the appropriate exegetical skills and tools to develop a proper hermeneutic that is relevant to modern-day believers. Our goal is to provide you with a commentary that will give you the added depth that you need to make the biblical text come alive to your congregations, small group classes, other Christian education gatherings, and discipleship ministries. Thank you for your continued patronage of our products and visit our website www.rhboyd.com to see how we might help you strengthen your Christian journey.

Yours in Christ,

Rev. David Groves, DMin, PhD

NOTES FROM THE EDITOR

The layout of the *2021–2022 Boyd's Commentary* has been formatted for easy use in the classroom. In keeping with our rich history of publishing quality Christian literature, we have added the Unifying Principle as a feature that will enhance our commentary. Listed below is an explanation of each feature and the intended use of each.

Lesson Setting: Gives the basic time line and place for the events in the lesson.

Lesson Outline: Provides the topics used in the exposition of the lesson.

Unifying Principle: States the main idea for the lesson across age groups. This feature allows the teacher to understand exactly what each lesson is about.

Introduction: Gives the thesis and any background information that will be useful in the study of the lesson.

Exposition: Provides the exegetical study done by the writer, breaking down the text for discussion.

The Lesson Applied: Provides possible life applications of the biblical text for today's learners.

Let's Talk About It: Highlights ideas from the text in a question-and-answer format.

Home Daily Devotional Readings: Located at the end of each lesson, the topics are designed to lead into the following lesson.

Know Your Writers

Dr. Barry Johnson

Dr. Barry C. Johnson, a native of Louisville, serves as the Pastor of the Southern Star Baptist Church of Louisville, Kentucky. Dr. Johnson holds the Bachelor (BM) and Masters Degrees (MM) in Music Composition from the University of Louisville, Doctor of Musical Arts (DMA) degree in Music Composition from the University of Kentucky, Master of Theology (M.Div) and Doctor of Ministry (D.Min) degrees in Black Church Studies from the Southern Baptist Theological Seminary, in addition to Post-Doctoral studies at Berklee College of Music. Previous teaching assignments were at Savannah State University, Western Kentucky University, and Kentucky State University, where he retired as a Full Professor of Music. An avid musician, scholar, and composer, Dr. Johnson is the owner of TNT Productions and Recording Studios and teaches part-time at the University of Louisville in the School of Music.

Dr. Napoleon Harris

Napoleon Harris is the proud pastor of the First Baptist Church of South Inglewood in Nashville, TN. He has a passion for helping people realize the fullness of God's love. His amazing wife is the former Sherma Nyasha Douglass of Kingstown, St. Vincent, together they have two wonderful daughters. Dr. Harris attended Vanderbilt University Divinity School and earned a doctorate from the illustrious Tennessee State University, where he currently works in the Division of Student Affairs. Dr. Harris is a proud member of the Omega Psi Phi Fraternity Incorporated, and is affiliated with a barrage of social/political justice seeking organizations.

Rev. Melvin D. Guest

Melvin D. Guest, Jr. was born on August 16, 1988, in Nashville, Tennessee, to Melvin Guest Sr. and Angela Jones. He is the third of Six Children. Melvin received a high school diploma from Pearl-Cohn High School, an Associate's degree in Applied Science from Daymar Institute, a Bachelor of Arts degree from Tennessee State University, a Master of Divinity degree from Vanderbilt University, and now pursuing a Master of Arts degree in Hebrew Bible in the Graduate Department of Religion at Vanderbilt University. As an active member, he is currently listed as Young Adult & College Ministry President and Adult Sunday School Class Teacher at Olivet Baptist Church in Nashville, Tennessee.

Dr. Bernard Williams

Dr. Bernard Williams is a native of Nashville, Tennessee. He has pastored churches in Tennessee and Florida. He is a graduate of the University of Tennessee Knoxville and The Southern Baptist Theological Seminary in Louisville, Kentucky. He also holds a Ph.D. in homiletics and church and society. Dr. Williams is a great proponent of small-group Bible study and serves as a teacher in Christian education. He holds numerous revivals, conferences, workshops, and seminars each year. He is a member of the American Academy of Religion and the Academy of Homiletics.

2021–2022 LESSON OVERVIEW

The Fall Quarter (September–November 2021) focuses on acts of worship and praise that celebrate both God's divine attributes and God's actions on behalf of the whole created order. The first unit, "God's People Offer Praise," has four lessons focusing on examples of God's people in praise. Unit II, "Called to Praise God," contains five lessons exploring psalms that call God's people to celebrate what God has done. "Visions of Praise," the third unit, presents four lessons that share John's visions of celebration for God's ultimate victory in establishing a realm of justice.

The Winter Quarter (December–February 2021/22) traces themes of justice in the Old Testament. Unit I, "God Requires Justice," presents four lessons exploring how leaders must rely on God's Law as they administer justice. Unit II, "God: The Source of Justice," has five lessons that focus on God's justice in the lives of God's people. Genesis has the stories of Cain and Abel and Hagar and Ishmael. Exodus seeks justice for everyone, even one's enemies. Deuteronomy directs judges, officials, and priests to administer justice for God's people, especially the marginalized. Unit III, "Justice and Adversity," consists of four lessons that deal with situations where justice seems absent. David's injustice to Uriah the Hittite, Bathsheba's husband, is condemned in 2 Samuel. Ezra seeks to restore respect for God's Law. And Job tells of his faithfulness to God following the tragic events in his life.

The Spring Quarter (March–May 2022) examines the nature of God through the lenses of liberation and Christian freedom. Unit I, "Liberating Passover," has four lessons exploring the liberating event of the Exodus. Unit II, "Liberating Gospels," uses four lessons to explore the liberating freedom from Jesus' triumphal entry into Jerusalem through his death and resurrection. Unit III, "Liberating Letters," presents five lessons based on the letters to the Romans and Galatians that explore a Christian understanding of the radical nature of Christian freedom.

The Summer Quarter (June–August 2022) looks at ways believers partner with God through Christ in redeeming all creation. The four lessons of Unit I, "God Delivers and Restores," draw from the Book of Isaiah and examine the prophetic message warning of Babylon's destruction and inspiring hope for Israel's deliverance. Unit II, "The Word: The Agent of Creation," uses five lessons from John's Gospel to look at how the Creating Word became flesh, healed the sick, saved the lost, resurrected the dead, and granted peace. "The Great Hope of the Saints," Unit III, is a four-lesson study from Revelation. It helps learners envision the new home and city God has prepared for the redeemed, including the new water of eternal life.

● ●

Boyd's Commentary for the Sunday School (2021–2022)

Copyright © 2021 by R.H. Boyd Publishing Corporation

6717 Centennial Blvd., Nashville, TN 37209–1017

PREFACE

The *2021–2022 Boyd's Commentary* has been formatted and written with you in mind. This format is to help you further your preparation and study of the Sunday school lessons.

We have presented a parallel Scripture lesson passage with the *New Revised Standard Version* alongside the *King James Version*. This allows you to have a clearer and more contemporary approach to the Scripture passages each week. This version is reliable and reputable. It will bless you as you rightly divide the word of truth (2 Tim. 2:15, KJV).

These lessons have a new look, but they still have the same accurate interpretation, concise Christian doctrine, and competent, skilled scholarship.

The abbreviations used throughout the commentary are as follows:

KJV — King James Version
NIV — New International Version
NKJV — New King James Version
NLT — New Living Translation
NRSV — New Revised Standard Version
RSV — Revised Standard Version
TLB — The Living Bible
NEB — New English Bible
JB — Jerusalem Bible
ESV — English Standard Version

To the pastor: Our hope is that this commentary will provide context and insight for your sermons. Also, we hope this commentary will serve as a preparatory aid for the message of God.

To the Bible teacher: This commentary also has you in mind. You can use it as a ready reference to the background of the text and difficult terms that are used in the Bible. To be sure, this commentary will provide your lesson study with the historical context that will enable you to interpret the text for your students more effectively.

This text is for anyone who wants to get a glimpse at the glory of God. This commentary seeks to highlight and lift the workings of God with His people and to make God's history with humanity ever present.

We hope and pray God will bless you and keep you as you diligently study His mighty and majestic Word. Remain ever steadfast to our one eternal God. Keep the faith, and pray always.

CONTENTS

CONTENTS

SECOND QUARTER

CONTENTS

CONTENTS

FOURTH QUARTER

FIRST QUARTER

September

October

November

MOSES AND MIRIAM PRAISE GOD

| ADULT TOPIC: CELEBRATING WITH SONG | BACKGROUND SCRIPTURE: EXODUS 14:1–15:1–21 |

EXODUS 15:11–21

King James Version

WHO is like unto thee, O LORD, among the gods? who is like thee, glorious in holiness, fearful in praises, doing wonders?

12 Thou stretchedst out thy right hand, the earth swallowed them.

13 Thou in thy mercy hast led forth the people which thou hast redeemed: thou hast guided them in thy strength unto thy holy habitation.

14 The people shall hear, and be afraid: sorrow shall take hold on the inhabitants of Palestina.

15 Then the dukes of Edom shall be amazed; the mighty men of Moab, trembling shall take hold upon them; all the inhabitants of Canaan shall melt away.

16 Fear and dread shall fall upon them; by the greatness of thine arm they shall be as still as a stone; till thy people pass over, O LORD, till the people pass over, which thou hast purchased.

17 Thou shalt bring them in, and plant them in the mountain of thine inheritance, in the place, O LORD, which thou hast made for thee to dwell in, in the Sanctuary, O LORD, which thy hands have established.

18 The LORD shall reign for ever and ever.

19 For the horse of Pharaoh went in with his chariots and with his horsemen into the sea, and the LORD brought again the waters of the sea upon them; but the children of Israel went on dry land in the midst of the sea.

20 And Miriam the prophetess, the sister of Aaron, took a timbrel in her hand; and all the women went out after her with timbrels and with dances.

New Revised Standard Version

"WHO is like you, O LORD, among the gods? Who is like you, majestic in holiness, awesome in splendor, doing wonders?

12 You stretched out your right hand, the earth swallowed them.

13 "In your steadfast love you led the people whom you redeemed; you guided them by your strength to your holy abode.

14 The peoples heard, they trembled; pangs seized the inhabitants of Philistia.

15 Then the chiefs of Edom were dismayed; trembling seized the leaders of Moab; all the inhabitants of Canaan melted away.

16 Terror and dread fell upon them; by the might of your arm, they became still as a stone until your people, O LORD, passed by, until the people whom you acquired passed by.

17 You brought them in and planted them on the mountain of your own possession, the place, O LORD, that you made your abode, the sanctuary, O LORD, that your hands have established.

18 The LORD will reign forever and ever."

19 When the horses of Pharaoh with his chariots and his chariot drivers went into the sea, the LORD brought back the waters of the sea upon them; but the Israelites walked through the sea on dry ground.

20 Then the prophet Miriam, Aaron's sister, took a tambourine in her hand; and all the women went out after her with tambourines and with dancing.

MAIN THOUGHT: Who is like unto thee, O LORD, among the gods? who is like thee, glorious in holiness, fearful in praises, doing wonders? (Exodus 15:11, KJV)

EXODUS 15:11–21

<table>
<tr><td>King James Version</td><td>New Revised Standard Version</td></tr>
<tr><td>21 And Miriam answered them, Sing ye to the LORD, for he hath triumphed gloriously; the horse and his rider hath he thrown into the sea.</td><td>21 And Miriam sang to them: "Sing to the LORD, for he has triumphed gloriously; horse and rider he has thrown into the sea."</td></tr>
</table>

LESSON SETTING
Time: 1250 BC
Place: The Red Sea

LESSON OUTLINE
I. Praise For God's Awesome Character (Exodus 15:11)
II. Praise For God's Awesome Past Activities (Exodus 15:12)
III. Praise For God's Anticipated Future Activities (Exodus 15:13–19)
IV. Praise God: The All Inclusive Nature of Praise to God (Exodus 15:20, 21)

UNIFYING PRINCIPLE
People compose poems and songs for different celebrations. How can songs and poems express thankfulness and rejoicing in victory? After their deliverance from Egyptian slavery, Moses and Miriam composed songs and led the people in praising God.

INTRODUCTION
Enthusiastic appreciative response to a grand performance is normative behavior in many of life's grand arenas. From concert halls to sports auditoriums, grand performances elicit enthusiastic, appreciative responses like applauses, cheers, and high fives. The same holds true for believers when we see God's miraculous performances in the arena of our lives. Moses, Miriam, and the whole of Israel reiterate this reality. In our lesson today we observe Israel's response of enthusiasm and appreciation for God's miraculous liberating deliverance from the oppressive, life-denying, God-dishonoring slavery imposed on them by Egypt. More specifically, Israel praises God for the jaw-dropping act of God's eradication of the Egyptian army by drowning them in the Red Sea. The printed text of our lesson begins mid praise and unfolds in several stanzas. It begins by noting and celebrating the character of God, then moves into extolling God's immediate past activity. Praise is then extended for God's anticipated future activities, and finally Prophetess Miriam concludes the praise break that is this lesson in a manner that suggests the inclusion of praise.

EXPOSITION

I. PRAISE FOR GOD'S AWESOME CHARACTER (EXODUS 15:11)
The first cause for praise in this passage is the character of God. This suggests that our praise and worship should be done in accordance of what we know about God. Interestingly enough the etymology of our English word for worship is derived from the Old English word *weorthscipe* which means worth-ship. Thus, worship is an act in which we ascribe value or worth to the recipient of our adoration. If our worship is to be accurate and effectual, we

must know about God in order to properly ascribe the right amount of worthiness.

Moses and company have just had a unique upfront and personal view point of God's miraculous power, as God wrought a series of devastating plagues on Egypt, and then finally drowned the army of Egypt in the Red Sea. Should questions arise with regard to the plausibility and placement of this miracle it is helpful to remember that miracles are in fact miracles. They are divine acts on the stage of human experience and by very definition their explanations often escape rational thought. Thus, the characters in our lesson, have experienced the unexplainable and in their gratitude and reflection they extol God's character. Specifically, they delight in the uniqueness of God.

This may seem sophomoric because most of us today have had the benefit of being born in regions where monotheism (the belief in one God) is standard and taken for granted. This was not so in the case of our lesson's heroes. The Israelites have been tabernacled in Egypt for long enough to multiply and prosper for the exploits of Joseph to have been forgotten. In Egypt monotheism was not the norm. Although the pharaoh, *Akhenaten*, introduced monotheism to Egypt, it was not at all accepted and he along with the concept was eradicated from the nation's collective memory. The Egyptians maintained that there was a pantheon of gods. Thus, the Israelites exclamation in verse 11 is profound. They ask the question who is like our God? Therefore, maintaining that their God is unique! Moreover, the term gods used here in the lesson text is literally translated as "celestials." In the ancient near eastern mind this was a term used to refer to gods which were often associated with celestial bodies like the moon, stars, or sun. Hence the Hebrews are professing that God is more significant than any other being, god, celestial body, or spirit. *The Expositor's Bible Commentary* states "the defeat of the Egyptians is simultaneously a defeat of their gods..." thus God is not just unique, but in a class all by Himself. God is not just the greatest God of all time, but God by definition is the only God.

The basis for God's uniqueness is a theme that truly unfolds throughout the rest of the song namely God's powerful acts to and on behalf of Israel across time. Verse 11 instructs that God is unique because God is "majestic (glorious/foremost) in holiness." Holiness is uniqueness, to be holy is to be set aside, made and or treated as special. Hence God is chief in holiness-uniqueness. God is in the words of Black Thought, a poet from the Roots "neighbor less for a ten-mile radius" meaning incomparable to anyone else. In a league by God's own self! Moses and company continue with their ode to God's character by singing that God is "awesome in splendor" (Jewish Study Bible) but "fearful in praises" (KJV). The meaning here is that God, due to God's uniqueness, is worthy of the highest praises. Again, we return to the point that it takes a healthy understanding of God to truly praise God. In essence, what one knows of God will turn up in worship by what one shows.

Finally, Moses and company demonstrate that God does awesome deeds/ wonders. Again, this praise of God is rooted in their knowledge and first-hand experience of God. They know from experience that God does awesome/wonderful deeds because they have witnessed it firsthand. It is important to remember that this portion of praise is for God's character. God is unique, holy and worthy of praise for God's uniqueness, holiness, and wondrous capacity for awesome works. Our worship should show that God is most important and superior to anything and anyone else in our lives!

II. PRAISE FOR GOD'S AWESOME PAST ACTIVITIES (EXODUS 15:12)

In this verse Moses and the Israelites begin to praise God for His past activities, namely God's amazing display of strength in their deliverance from Egypt. They state how God stretched out His right hand, the hand of strength. God does not have to bear arms to bring about the change He intends for the world. God is so good that He can merely stretch out God's divine and everlasting arm to bring about change. What is perhaps even more remarkable is that the earth's geological makeup responds to the gesturing of God. They praise God for God's activity at the Red Sea. Although they remark about the land responding to God's outstretched hand, the thought is that the sea is encompassed by the land and thus the parting of the Red Sea is an extension of God's handling of the land.

This passage reminds us that praise is due to God for God's powerful past activities. We should remember what God has done and remember to give God the appropriate thankful response. These past activities are not just limited to what we ourselves have seen, but also the past actions of God that predate us.

III. PRAISE FOR GOD'S ANTICIPATED FUTURE ACTIVITIES (EXODUS 15:13–19)

In these verses Israel directs the ensuing praise party in the direction of God's anticipated future actions. On the basis of God's character and God's past activities, they extend forward to God confidence and boastful praise in faith. Faith reviews God's past history of goodness and unmatched holiness, praiseworthiness, and wondrous works and extends forward to praise. This praise is rooted in anticipatory hope for God's continued work in the future. In the same way that lenders view our credit (past performance) to determine our loan worthiness, we should appraise God on the basis of God's character and powerful past actions and extend forward praise. Simply stated, because of God's past we can trust God for our futures. This is exactly what we discover in these verses.

In verse 13, we find the word "mercy" (KJV), "unfailing love" (NIV) or "loyalty" (CEB). The key word in this passage of Scripture is 'hesed' in Hebrew. It is a word that translates roughly to mean faithfulness and according to the Jewish Study Bible it "refers to acts of kindness that are expected between parties in a relationship-husband and wife, parents and children, relatives, and allies, and to reciprocation of kindness." It also refers to God's covenant and His relationship with God's people. Thus, the key to Israel's ability to look forward and praise God for God's anticipated acts is mercy—the doggedly determined loving-kindness and faithfulness of God.

The song continues that in God's faithful love, the kind that does not wear off, God led or will lead (depending on the Bible translation) His people ultimately to His holy habitation. What's important to note here is that the saints count God's future activity as done. They embody Hebrews 11:1 "Now faith is the assurance of things hoped for, the conviction of things not seen." They account God's future activities as already done. Faith counts God's promises as done deals. In addition, the saints praise God for God's leadership, God's redemption or saving activity and finally that God has led them into the promised place of God's holy dwelling/ habitation. It is the latter that demands our attention, Israel honors God for God's original promise to Abraham. It is also important to note that the reference to God's holy abode may also be an instance of an anachronistic insertion to the forthcoming temple, tabernacle, or even Mount Sinai itself. Textual criticism aside, what is teach-worthy is the anticipatory praise. Israel's praise looks forward to being with God again. This is something every child of God should take note of, our praise ought to signify that we look forward to being with God again, especially united in God's holy abode here on earth and God's holy abode beyond the earth (heaven).

Verses 14–16 continue the theme of anticipation. Here in these verses the Israelites praise God and boast that the powerful work of God against Egypt will make its way into the ears and psyches of neighboring Canaanite peoples. They belong to God and God alone is their sole proprietor. They may have been slaves in Egypt, but they were never the possession of Egypt, they always belonged to God.

In verses 17–18 we see the saints praising God for the future activity of establishing (planting) them. A vivid agricultural image that suggests God's future act of establishing Israel as a citadel and a nation, the fulfillment of God's promise to Abraham to make his seeds a great nation. Moreover, they also anticipate and accept as done the establishment of the temple. The temple mount is God's own mountain. Here the Israelites give a nod to God as the divine monarch and the cosmic king— after all the place where God resides (initially the Ark of the Covenant and eventually the temple) is the place where God is enthroned. Hence, they reify that God is the ultimate power. Remarkably, the Israelites who initially sang this were granted only partial fulfillment of this reality. They saw shades of this reality in the tabernacle and at Mt. Sinai. They thanked God for what they had yet to see, and in their lifetime, they were the partial recipients of what they forecast in praise.

IV. PRAISE GOD: THE ALL INCLUSIVE NATURE OF PRAISE TO GOD (EXODUS 15:20, 21)

In these verses Miriam the prophetess gathers the women (in keeping with the tradition of celebrating victory), grabs a tambourine, and together they raise their own hymn (although this was possibly a refrain of the larger hymn). Two things are noteworthy. The first is that Miriam is called a prophet. While the capacity for women to lead and respond to God's call to minister is still sadly hotly debated in some churches the Bible is not mute at all on the matter. Miriam is clearly labeled a prophetess in the lesson and proof of her leadership is also recorded in part in Numbers 12:2. Here Miriam initiates a lineage of other women leaders who too will sing songs of praise to God such as Deborah (Judges 4) and Huldah (2 Kings 22:14). The point here is not about whether or not women should lead or preach, but that all people should be actively involved in praising God. Miriam leads the women of Israel in praise not to make history, but rather in appropriate response to God's amazing character and activity in their lives. Regardless of church politics, or dogmatic understandings of Scripture, there is always room for praise and God's activity elicits a response—an all included and all-inclusive response from all of us!

THE LESSON APPLIED

We return to the applause analogy from our introduction. Think of an instance in which you applauded loudly. Perhaps it was at a concert? Maybe it was on a dance floor when a particular song came on. Whatever the scenario, you were responding to an incredible feat. Now think of the wondrous works you have seen God do in your life, in the life of your congregation, in the lives of our ancestors. Think of the ways in which God has kept you safe and spared your life in the midst of a global pandemic, and ask yourself— have

you responded accordingly? Take into consideration that Israel's praise in our lesson takes place on the shore of the Red Sea—no where near the Promised Land. This suggests that we do not have to be in the sanctuary to respond to God's wonderful character and wonderful acts appropriately. Nor do we have to wait until God has made good on all that we hope for. Thus, be sure to give God your best praise.

LET'S TALK ABOUT IT

Why do you think we all cherry pick passages to form and inform our own understanding of the world?

Miriam is labeled a prophetess, elsewhere Deborah is listed as a leader, so is Huldah, and quite a few other women are depicted in Scripture as leaders. Nonetheless, some feel as if women should not lead or preach with their sentiment based on their reading of Scripture. Regardless of your opinion or the teaching of your church—the point of this discussion is on the importance of interpretation. It is highly possible for two people to read the same passage and come up with divergent understandings. This is why it is so important to allow the Holy Spirit to guide our reading. Scripture reading should result in life, and transformed lives that glorify God.

HOME DAILY DEVOTIONAL READINGS
SEPTEMBER 6–12, 2021

MONDAY	TUESDAY	WEDNESDAY	THURSDAY	FRIDAY	SATURDAY	SUNDAY
David Prepares to Transport the Ark	The Holiness of the Sanctuary	Uzzah Disregards the Ark's Holiness	The House of the Lord!	Go to God's Dwelling Place	The Ark in the Heavenly Temple	David Dances Before the Ark
2 Samuel 6:1–5	Hebrews 9:1–7	2 Samuel 6:6–11	Psalm 122	Psalm 132:1–12	Revelation 11:15–19	2 Samuel 6:12–19

DAVID DANCES BEFORE THE ARK

ADULT TOPIC: CELEBRATING WITH ENTHUSIASM	BACKGROUND SCRIPTURE: 2 SAMUEL 6

2 SAMUEL 6:1–5, 14–19

King James Version

AGAIN, David gathered together all the chosen men of Israel, thirty thousand.

2 And David arose, and went with all the people that were with him from Baale of Judah, to bring up from thence the ark of God, whose name is called by the name of the LORD of hosts that dwelleth between the cherubims.

3 And they set the ark of God upon a new cart, and brought it out of the house of Abinadab that was in Gibeah: and Uzzah and Ahio, the sons of Abinadab, drave the new cart.

4 And they brought it out of the house of Abinadab which was at Gibeah, accompanying the ark of God: and Ahio went before the ark.

5 And David and all the house of Israel played before the LORD on all manner of instruments made of fir wood, even on harps, and on psalteries, and on timbrels, and on cornets, and on cymbals.

• • • • • •

14 And David danced before the LORD with all his might; and David was girded with a linen ephod.

15 So David and all the house of Israel brought up the ark of the LORD with shouting, and with the sound of the trumpet.

16 And as the ark of the LORD came into the city of David, Michal Saul's daughter looked through a window, and saw king David leaping and dancing before the LORD; and she despised him in her heart.

New Revised Standard Version

DAVID again gathered all the chosen men of Israel, thirty thousand.

2 David and all the people with him set out and went from Baale-judah, to bring up from there the ark of God, which is called by the name of the LORD of hosts who is enthroned on the cherubim.

3 They carried the ark of God on a new cart, and brought it out of the house of Abinadab, which was on the hill. Uzzah and Ahio, the sons of Abinadab, were driving the new cart

4 with the ark of God; and Ahio went in front of the ark.

5 David and all the house of Israel were dancing before the LORD with all their might, with songs and lyres and harps and tambourines and castanets and cymbals.

• • • • • •

14 David danced before the LORD with all his might; David was girded with a linen ephod.

15 So David and all the house of Israel brought up the ark of the LORD with shouting, and with the sound of the trumpet.

16 As the ark of the LORD came into the city of David, Michal daughter of Saul looked out of the window, and saw King David leaping and dancing before the LORD; and she despised him in her heart.

MAIN THOUGHT: And David and all the house of Israel played before the Lord on all manner of instruments made of fir wood, even on harps, and on psalteries, and on timbrels, and on cornets, and on cymbals. (2 Samuel 6:5, KJV)

2 Samuel 6:1–5, 14–19

King James Version

17 And they brought in the ark of the LORD, and set it in his place, in the midst of the tabernacle that David had pitched for it: and David offered burnt offerings and peace offerings before the LORD.

18 And as soon as David had made an end of offering burnt offerings and peace offerings, he blessed the people in the name of the LORD of hosts.

19 And he dealt among all the people, even among the whole multitude of Israel, as well to the women as men, to every one a cake of bread, and a good piece of flesh, and a flagon of wine. So all the people departed every one to his house.

New Revised Standard Version

17 They brought in the ark of the LORD, and set it in its place, inside the tent that David had pitched for it; and David offered burnt offerings and offerings of well-being before the LORD.

18 When David had finished offering the burnt offerings and the offerings of well-being, he blessed the people in the name of the LORD of hosts,

19 and distributed food among all the people, the whole multitude of Israel, both men and women, to each a cake of bread, a portion of meat, and a cake of raisins. Then all the people went back to their homes.

LESSON SETTING

Time: 993–994 BC
Place: From Baale-Judah/
Kiriath-Jearim and
Jerusalem

LESSON OUTLINE

I. The Recipe For Wrong Praise
(2 Samuel 6:1–5)
II. The Recipe For Proper Praise
(2 Samuel 6:14–17)
III. The Results of Proper Praise
(2 Samuel 6:17–19)

UNIFYING PRINCIPLE

Celebrations can be diverse in form and include various actions. How do we celebrate great events in our lives? King David expressed his joy and celebration of God by leading God's people in music and dance.

INTRODUCTION

In our society, parades are thrown to celebrate incredible victories, or festive occasions. HBCU's (Historically Black Colleges and Universities) are renowned for their amazing homecoming parades, as are championship sports teams. All over this great country prior to the social distancing of COVID-19, citizens lined the streets to celebrate everything from Justice for MLK to the revelry of St. Patrick's Day to freedom on the July 4th to various ethnic pride parades, and of course the Macy's Thanksgiving Day parade.

In our lesson today we will discover an ancient parade that rivaled any of our modern parades. A parade led by King David to inaugurate his new capital city Jerusalem as the religious and political capital of Israel. This parade was more than just a typical procession. It was a parade in which God served as the grand marshal! Can you imagine the splendor, decadence, and opulence of a parade fit for God?

As grand as that parade surely was, we do well to remember the truth that whenever we worship, God is in the midst (Matthew 18:20). Hence every worship service should entail careful planning. As we will discover in our lesson today, there is a recipe for the type of worship—the parade of praise God deserves. Likewise, there is also a recipe for the wrong parade of praise—one that meets with disaster and danger. Finally, in this lesson we will also explore the fruitful results of when we worship and praise God accordingly.

EXPOSITION

I. THE RECIPE FOR WRONG PRAISE (2 SAMUEL 6:1–5)

Doing the right thing in the wrong way makes it wrong. This holds true for worship. In these first verses we discover the formula for fraudulent praise and worship. The passage resumes with David who now has established Zion as his capital city desiring to centralize the city's importance by crowning it as the religious epicenter of the nation. In order to do this, David would need to recapture the Ark of the Covenant. The Ark had been previously captured by the Philistines because the Israelites foolishly tried to use God's presence as a good luck charm on one hand, and as a firearm with which to fight their own battle (1 Samuel 4). After direct intervention by God, the Ark was ultimately sent away by the Philistines to a border town of Israel, which sets up our lesson today.

David sets out with a band of mighty men of valor-soldiers (30,000 in total) to go and return the Ark of the Covenant to Jerusalem. The Ark was literally a chest in which the stone tablets that codified God's covenant with Israel were kept. It was also the place where God's presence was made manifest (see Exodus 25). The text states that David and military company have acquired a "new cart" with which to transport the Ark. In addition, we also discover that David has assigned some specific individuals to guide the cart and to walk in front and behind the Ark's cart. Finally, David has arranged for a multitude of musicians to play while he and the procession celebrated with all their strength.

Verses 6–8, disclose David's praise party was absolutely disastrous and dangerous. David approached worship from the wrong perspective. Ultimately David and his comrades lost the appropriate reverence and awe of God. They came to gather the Ark with a military convoy as if God was business as usual. In addition, David placed the Ark on a cart. God gave specific instructions as to who could handle the Ark, and how it should be handled. Thus, in very real sense David's error was that he had the wrong perspective, which likely resulted in him placing the Ark in the wrong place, and using the wrong people.

Ultimately, through this barrage of missteps David completely struck out. The end result of such a haphazard treatment of God's presence was death. We do well to remember this and make it our business to avoid mistreating God, and God's presence. Many professed believers and many churches have succumbed to spiritual death because of a cavalier attitude toward God and the presence of God in worship as well as the presence of God in other people. Notice in verse five that David, who completely disregarded God's commands and attempted to wrap his wrong in worship and praise, did so to no avail. His good intentions and good effort had no bearing on his fate. The same holds true today. Worship is not about us, neither our intentions nor our effort. Worship is about God. Proper and acceptable right worship is not a praise centered on our intentions so much as it is praise centered on God's instruction. Real and rightful worship is not about our sentiment but about doing what God has said with excellence. Opulence does not beat out obedience (1 Samuel 15:22).

II. THE RECIPE FOR PROPER PRAISE
(2 SAMUEL 6:14–17)

Initially distraught David hears about how the Ark of God's presence has been beneficial to Obed-Edom's house (its current location) (v. 12) and he decides to revisit his plans to bring the Ark to Jerusalem. This time around David again makes elaborate plans. He begins by sparing no expense with regard to worship, he orders that the chest be carried (apparently by Levites according to God's command 1 Chronicles 15:11–15) and that an ox and fat-ling calf be slaughtered after every six steps (v. 13). Although not mentioned in our printed text, vv. 12–13 give us important context. They infer that worship must be intentional. David further demonstrates this in v. 17, when he places the Ark in a prepared place. He is intentional. He understands that God cannot and should not be taken lightly. He has erected a special tabernacle for it. Proper praise and worship must never be an afterthought. Moreover, that it ought to align with what God commands. Since God is the object and recipient of our praise and worship our praise and worship must align with and mirror what God has already requested in God's Word to us.

In v. 14 we note David adorns an ephod, a priestly garment. David suggests to us a critical component of proper praise and worship, namely that we must have the right perspective regarding worship. In his initial attempt David attended to the Ark as king, but in this second attempt he has set aside his kingship and approached God as a priest-one assigned to minister to God. Hence, we learn the right perspective regarding worship. To truly praise God we must be willing to set ourselves aside, assume the role of priest, and serve God with self-less praise. This change in perspective would no doubt shift our praise and worship in the sanctuary. When believers understand themselves as priests, it altars their praise. Beloved, the next time you attend worship remember you are not king or queen standing by an attender or assessor of praise, No! You are a priest, one who has been charged with performing praise and worshipful acts before God. This is the change in perspective David demonstrates, and it causes him to become so involved in praise that he worships with what can only be described as reckless abandon (more on that later). This is the behavior that will ultimately earn him the ire and contempt of his wife Michal, who protests that David was not acting like a king at all (v. 20). She was right he had graduated from reigning king to ritual priest by changed his perspective, which culminated in a change in behavior. David was selfless in his show of appreciation, so much so that the Bible tells us he danced with all of his might (v. 14) with leaping and dancing (v. 16). David worships with what can only be described as reckless abandon. Beloved, David thus teaches us that proper praise requires a physical response to God. There are many who feel that worship and praise can be reserved, truthfully sometimes they can be, however, this text teaches us that in the same way we show enthusiasm for anything else we also are obligated to show enthusiastic physical response to God. At the least Samuel's descriptor of David's praise as "with all his might" should be our litmus test. However we praise God be it with dance, song, wave, run, Baptist Fit, or whatever we ought to embark on it with all of our might!

Thus, in these verses we glean a recipe for right praise. It requires strategy-intentional thoughtfulness. It requires we set ourselves (ego, class, and stature) aside, that we minister and praise God with all of our strength, and that we adhere to the principles and precepts of what God has already said to us.

III. The Results of Proper Praise (2 Samuel 6:17–19)

In the final verses of our lesson, we are presented with the wonderful residuals of worship and the payoff of praise. We begin by noting verse 16. David's wife Michal despises him because of his behavior (while he was not the only one dancing, he was the only king dancing, a feat that was reserved for regulars not royalty).

Many commentators make great assumptions about Michal, however we do well to remember that at one point she really loved David, so much so that she lied to her father Saul who initially gave her away as a political trophy (1 Samuel 18) and saved his life. Bear in mind that the Bible never hints that Michal's love for David was ever reciprocated, it only suggests that David saw her as a political advantage-a political pawn. In fact, while they were originally married (Saul withdrew her marriage to David and gave her away to Paltiel (1 Samuel 25:44) who loved her and wept when David took her away to further solidify his reign as Saul's successor (2 Samuel 3:13–16).

In fact, Paltiel was so in love with Michal that he is ordered by a military general to give up his efforts of protest through tears. So, when we see this story, we see a sister who has quite the right to be angry at David, however, not for this cause. The lesson here thus is twofold. One worship and praise does not necessarily undo the past, nor does it protect us from ire and harsh feelings from others.

Truth be told, we cannot praise our way out of every situation, and even after giving God our best praise at church we may arise and meet the worst problem at home. In addition, we should also learn from Michal, not to be so consumed with the perceived wrongs or past actions of a person that we can not see the good they may do. While it is apparent Michal may have had good reason to think of David as no good, she was blinded to the reality that on this occasion he was doing good. Real worship which posits us in the presence of God ought to allow us to see the good in others too.

In addition, proper praise should result in service. David in the culminating verses renders service to God and service to others. David offers appropriate sacrifices to demonstrate thanksgiving to God and well wishes for others. His burnt offering is a testament to his devotion to God and his awareness of his own sinfulness. The well being or peace offerings were a testament of his gratitude to God, but also his fellowship and interconnectedness with the people. It was a festal act that demonstrated a shared hope for mutual prosperity. In this regard David demonstrates to us that proper praise pays out dividends in service. Service that is rendered to God and to fellow humans. Verse 19 concludes with a beautiful image of truth and an aim for us to embark toward. Samuel records essentially that everyone left the praise parade with something! What a goal, we will know that we have performed praise in a God honoring way when we can say as the people of Israel did on that day that everyone can return home with something beneficial, and nourishing.

THE LESSON APPLIED

In our current cultural context churches have been engulfed in worship wars for years. Complicated by COVID-19, the expectations and demands of praise and worship are ever increasing. This lesson challenges us to regard our praise differently. It can no longer be relegated to appeasing our personality but must instead look to honor God. Moreover, we are challenged by this lesson to be intentional in our praise. While this certainly doesn't call for the eradication of extemporaneous moments of worship, spontaneity (i.e., we must always leave room for the Holy Ghost). It does call for us to approach God with excellence in mind. Perhaps those who prepare sermons and offer prayers can learn deep lessons from David's experience. Finally, this lesson causes us to ask, are we like David praising God with all of our might? We must all look to find ways to give God our best and our all. As we ask the perpetual question, is your all on the altar? Let us pause and consider our honest response and do better.

LET'S TALK ABOUT IT

What do you think caused Michal's and David's relationship to break down in the manner in which it did?

Michal and David have a very interesting relationship. What things persist in our world that causes love birds to become war hawks? Perhaps if Michal would have joined David in the celebration things would have been different. While praising God together may not be the sole guaranteer of staying together, it is true that couples who praise and prays together are able to stay together and in love. Might it be that praise posits us as vulnerable before God, and the ability to be vulnerable is a critical key to maintaining any successful relationship.

MONDAY	**TUESDAY**	**WEDNESDAY**	**THURSDAY**	**FRIDAY**	**SATURDAY**	**SUNDAY**
Blind Eyes Shall Be Opened	Declare God's Glory Among the Nations	Glory to God's Name Alone	Only God Is Good	Greatness through Servanthood	Praise the Lord, O My Soul!	Praise God for Healing!
Isaiah 35:1–6	Psalm 96	Psalm 115:1–3, 9–18	Mark 10:17–22	Mark 10:42–45	Psalm 146	Mark 10:46–52

GLORIFYING GOD

MARK 10:46–52

King James Version	*New Revised Standard Version*
AND they came to Jericho: and as he went out of Jericho with his disciples and a great number of people, blind Bartimaeus, the son of Timaeus, sat by the highway side begging.	THEY came to Jericho. As he and his disciples and a large crowd were leaving Jericho, Bartimaeus son of Timaeus, a blind beggar, was sitting by the roadside.
47 And when he heard that it was Jesus of Nazareth, he began to cry out, and say, Jesus, thou son of David, have mercy on me.	47 When he heard that it was Jesus of Nazareth, he began to shout out and say, "Jesus, Son of David, have mercy on me!"
48 And many charged him that he should hold his peace: but he cried the more a great deal, Thou son of David, have mercy on me.	48 Many sternly ordered him to be quiet, but he cried out even more loudly, "Son of David, have mercy on me!"
49 And Jesus stood still, and commanded him to be called. And they call the blind man, saying unto him, Be of good comfort, rise; he calleth thee.	49 Jesus stood still and said, "Call him here." And they called the blind man, saying to him, "Take heart; get up, he is calling you."
50 And he, casting away his garment, rose, and came to Jesus.	50 So throwing off his cloak, he sprang up and came to Jesus.
51 And Jesus answered and said unto him, What wilt thou that I should do unto thee? The blind man said unto him, Lord, that I might receive my sight.	51 Then Jesus said to him, "What do you want me to do for you?" The blind man said to him, "My teacher, let me see again."
52 And Jesus said unto him, Go thy way; thy faith hath made thee whole. And immediately he received his sight, and followed Jesus in the way.	52 Jesus said to him, "Go; your faith has made you well." Immediately he regained his sight and followed him on the way.

LESSON SETTING
Time: AD 27
Place: Jericho

LESSON OUTLINE
I. The Components of Call
   (Mark 10:46–48)
II. The Call: A Surprising
   Reciprocation (Mark 10:49)
III. An Adequate Response
   (Mark 10:50–52)

UNIFYING PRINCIPLE
People respond to life challenges and victories differently. How can we respond in ways that are encouraging for ourselves and others? Bartimaeus' boldness and faith

MAIN THOUGHT: And Jesus answered and said unto him, What wilt thou that I should do unto thee? The blind man said unto him, Lord, that I might receive my sight. (Mark 10:51, KJV)

in Jesus gave him the courage to ask for and receive his sight from Jesus.

INTRODUCTION

One of the hallmarks of the Black church worship experience is call and response. It traces back to the worshipful play and banter of our West African ancestors. It survived and recapitulated itself in the face of slavery, and today finds itself at home in both the church, and at home across the street corners where bold believers fight for justice and chant "No justice, no peace!"

It proves its intersectionality, as it is home across all forms of Blackness and musicality. Perhaps the best example of call and response is experienced in the lining of Dr. Watts hymns wherein one person calls out the stanza and the rest of the saints moan/sing the response. That is call and response. It is bold and boisterous. It is praise. It is Black and beautiful.

In our lesson today we will explore another experience of call and response that is instructive for us in praise too. We will discover that in order to celebrate God with expectation it will require that we first respond to God with anticipatory recognition, make bold requests, be resilient, and ultimately respond to Christ's call with haste and honesty. Moreover, we will also learn that Jesus' call like the call and response in church is dualistic in an exciting way.

EXPOSITION

I. THE COMPONENTS OF CALL (MARK 10:46–48)

In these brief verses we are introduced to some profound and immeasurable truths of the continued walk with Christ we are called to, hence we are introduced to the components of call. In these verses we are introduced to Bartimaeus and his sterling faith. The Bible lets us know that Bartimaeus is blind. We are not informed of how Bartimaeus has come to be blind, nor how long he has been blind. To Mark it matters not when, how, why, or where Bartimaeus became blind.

Despite his limitation in sight, we note that he makes full use of his other senses. He hears that Jesus is passing through. Bartimaeus informs us that praise and other forms of participation in the Christian walk are not limited by what we cannot do, they are unlocked by doing what we can do. To be clear no aspect of our walk with Christ (including praise) need be impeded or limited by our limitations, instead we should be resourceful and use what God has graciously blessed us with. As the saints of old would say "If I couldn't say nothing, I'll just wave my hand."

Bartimaeus though blind, sees an opportunity in Jesus for wholeness and healing. Bartimaeus thus demonstrates that true faith in Christ calls us to see in Christ possibility and opportunity. The call to Christ, then begins by the acknowledgment that in Christ lies opportunity and possibility. The call to Christ is the recognition that hope, life, joy, peace, and the whole of humankind's needs are located in Christ and come to fruition in Him! The call to Christ begins with the acknowledgment that we need Him. Bartimaeus sees Christ and anticipates that Christ can improve his lot in life. He anticipates that Jesus is compassionate, and will help him, and he anticipates and recognizes that he needs Jesus. All who will be saved must likewise come to this conclusion. In fact it is a conclusion we must continually come to, we must all say in the words of the song writer, "I need thee oh, I need thee, every hour I need thee." In every aspect of life, we, like Bartimaeus, need Jesus.

Seeing that Bartimaeus although blind saw Jesus clearly, he does what any rational being would do, he asks for help! He cries out, "Jesus Son of David have mercy on me." Before we attend to the boldness of his request, we must attend to the literary context of this story—namely that it is a bridge between discipleship, what it means to follow Jesus and His opposition in Jerusalem. The irony should not be missed by the careful expositor that Bartimaeus, though blind, could see Jesus clearly and engaged Christ with a fitting Messianic title, whereas those who should have been able to see (indeed foresee) Jesus, the priests and temple officials, do not. They will go on later in the week to chant, "crucify Him", and indeed even cheer on His state sponsored lynching/execution (The officials and priests helped, but Jesus was ultimately and officially killed by the Roman government).

Bartimaeus, however sees Jesus and thus cries out to Him, his request is for mercy. The word for mercy that appears here is the complex Koine Greek word *eeleo* (εελεω). The term is described as having compassion—active loving compassion. Bartimaeus is not asking for pity. Pity would say, "I feel sorry for you, but glad I am not you." Pity would praise God for not being blind. Bartimaeus has likely been pitied before, Mark tells us his livelihood (a beggar) is attached to pity, but when he encounters Jesus, he anticipates and feels more than pity. He sees the opportunity for mercy. Mercy is not pity, it is empathy infused with love. Because of love's presence, it is an action! According to *The Holman Treasury of Key Bible Words: 200 Greek and 200 Hebrew Words Defined and Explained* mercy is "a blessing that is the act of God's favor."

Hence, we begin to see the boldness of Bart's faith and the boldness of the faith we are called to. It is one that says, "Jesus overlook what ails me, what I lack, instead empty out the reservoirs of heaven's best blessings and divine favor on me." That is boldness. To request God's best interest for us despite what life may presently be showing is boldness. To hope in God and request more than what the present hands us is bold. Making an expectant request is thus a bold act.

Bartimaeus' bold act was met with resistance. He was hindered and shushed by some of the people in the crowd. Much can be made of the bizarre request from Bartimaeus to cease and desist from participating in his own healing.

In our present day, local authorities have attempted to hush those who recognize the potential and possibilities of participating in their own healing and deliverance too. Shushing has been present when believers have shouted, "Black Lives Matter" and there has always been a menacing crowd shouting, "All Lives Matter." More notoriously governors, and other officials have enacted heinous laws that attempt to hush the righteous voice of activism and the holy quest for justice, restoration, and mercy through new and nefarious legislation that makes protest felonious for some, but permissible for others—as the January coup of our nation's capital demonstrated.

However, Bartimaeus' legacy of resilience lives on! Despite the contempt laden calls to be silent, Bartimaeus, like the proceeding prophets of the Old Testament and the bold activists of today persisted.

In fact, Mark says Bartimaeus, undaunted, gets even louder! This is the resilience we are called to do. In the face of opposition believers are called to find ways to let our light shine brighter, to blow our trumpets in Zion even louder. It is our prerogative, to try new ways to exclaim Christ's glorious Gospel even louder in a world that is all too ready to hush and shush our efforts! We must say as Bartimaeus showed and our ancestors sang "ain't gonna' let nobody turn us 'round."

II. THE CALL: A SURPRISING RECIPROCATION (MARK 10:49)

The lesson proceeds, we begin with Bartimaeus' recognition of Jesus as his situation's solution and Savior which led to his resolve to reach out—literally call out to Jesus. This was met with resistance and rebuke from members of the crowd. Nonetheless, Bartimaeus was persistent, he persevered with resilience. In this verse we see Bartimaeus' recognition and resilience warrants an incredible result—namely reciprocation. Here's the scene—Bartimaeus is busy calling Jesus, and Jesus gets busy calling him. This is the duality of our life walk with Jesus. It is a life of surprising reciprocity, we do not solely call on Jesus, Jesus also calls on us! Jesus calls us to participate in our own healing, our own deliverance, our own miracles. As we call on Jesus, Jesus too calls on us!

Jesus enlists the help of the crowd. He stops and orders that the crowd, "call him forward." The careful expositor should not miss the chance to enumerate on the glorious reversal underway here. Some of the same people who only a verse ago were trying to hinder Bartimaeus were now under divine orders to help him. Mark informs us that those who once were castigating Bartimaeus have now become his cheerleaders, they exclaim "take heart"— literally be encouraged or cheer up. What a difference it makes when Jesus stops and calls us! This is why one must never grow weary in well doing, because those who in one moment may stand as enemies of our healing and flourishing, may in the next become emissaries in our righteous cause.

This gives us good reason not to burn bridges in our pain and rejection. Bartimaeus when initially hushed by the crowd had the opportunity to lash out at the crowd. Bartimaeus could have told them where to go and how to get there, however, he chose to focus on Jesus. His focus kept him from choosing to make enemies of his detractors who now become his encouragement. Whereas, they do not do anything to help the blind man, their words certainly helped to give him confirmation of the startling reciprocation from Jesus. Which would have most likely been surprising to him as it undoubtedly was for others who were onlooking in the crowd at Jericho.

III. AN ADEQUATE RESPONSE (MARK 10:50–52)

Bartimaeus calls to Jesus, Jesus responds by calling to Bartimaeus. Bartimaeus thus responds to Jesus, and in his response teaches us what an adequate response to a call of unlimited possibility and wholeness in Christ looks like. It is one that is firstly expectant. We have already discussed Bartimaeus' expectancy, but we see it again here. Mark does not report that Bartimaeus is shocked that Jesus is calling him. An adequate response to Jesus is one of expectancy. When we pray, we pray expecting a response from heaven. When we teach or preach we do so with the expectancy that God will stop and shower our efforts with the mercy of His love to the sinful soul.

Moreover, Bartimaeus responds with haste. Mark says he immediately throws off his cloak and begins to make his way to Jesus. This is an act of immediacy. It is haste, but not hastily. Bartimaeus' response is as rational as it is rapid. With intentionality he removes whatever may trip him up, or hinder him on his way to wholeness in Christ. Are we not likewise encouraged in Hebrews to lay aside every weight and sin that readily trips us up (Heb. 12:1)? We absolutely are. Our response to Christ must be made in haste, rapidly with no hesitation, but it must also be an intentional one, wrought with thought. This is the paradoxical nature of what it is to respond to Christ's call.

We must be ever ready, ever careful, and ever mindful—yet ready to move with reckless abandon.

There is a third element of an adequate response to Christ available for our consumption in this lesson. In verse 51, Jesus asks Bartimaeus, "what do you want?" To which Bart aptly and honestly responds I want to see. Here he demonstrates that our response to Christ must be one of honesty. We must boldly, with expectancy, let our requests be made known (Phil. 4:6). More disciples should emulate Bartimaeus and be honest with God vulnerably confessing the desires of our hearts to God in prayer with praise.

We also do well to note that this question echoes Jesus' inquiry in response to the pressing and self-exalting inquisition of James and John (v. 35–36). In fact, the Bartimaeus narrative stands as a corrective—again the irony that a blind outsider gets this question right should not be lost to the careful expositor. Rather than asking for power, or the capacity to reign selfishly, Bartimaeus asks for perception and to be made whole. John and James want to sit, Bartimaeus wants to see. Thus, we discover that an adequate response to Jesus is righteously honest. It seeks righteousness (right-ness in the world) and wholeness. The prayer life of disciples is not for power but for perception to see the world through the crimson-stained lens of God's love at Calvary. Disciples opt for righteousness and restoration not the ability to reign.

As this story acts as a corrective to the James and John narrative a few verses earlier, it fits in with a larger motif in Mark's Gospel where those who should not get it, understand with greater clarity than those who have been given the keys to the Kingdom.

As an example, Jesus is unable to perform many miracles and acts of power in His hometown because of the people's lack of faith (6:5). Clearly, those with whom Jesus was reared should have been able to perceive His greatness and ability to help those in need. However, they along with others in this Gospel are hapless failing to recognize the Christ for who He is.

Finally, the lesson concludes with Bartimaeus' sight restored, the evidence is seen in that he begins to follow Jesus along the way. Beloved, this is the culminating act of a right and adequate response to Christ's call; it is following Him, and following Him to the cross where we die to self and sin. The best praise and worship is walking in pace with Jesus. Our lives are our instruments of praise. In so doing we live out the words of Scripture that tell us to let others see our works that God may be glorified. It is what lifting the Savior up looks like, when we follow properly the Excellence of God is exalted.

THE LESSON APPLIED

As we continue to explore the praises of God's people in this quarter, we would do well to note that in the story of Bartimaeus we see a higher form of praise. In one sense we admire his desperation and persistence in calling Jesus. Likewise, we also do well to note and celebrate his honest and quick response to Jesus. Yet the highest form of praise is seen in the final words of this story it is to follow Jesus.

True praise is not measured by what we do in the sanctuary or during virtual worship, it is what we do after the benediction. The highest praise is not shouting hallelujah, it is in being surrendered to Him—Jesus. In this we are reminded that our lives are to praise God. We not only praise God with our mouths or demonstrative acts but through the fiber of our daily existence. Bartimaeus understood this as one whose life had been impacted immensely by the Christ. As the saying goes, the highest form of flattery is imitation. Imitation is the basic idea of discipleship. We follow Jesus but more importantly we begin to behave like him as well. In so doing our lives become praise for our wonderful awe-inspiring God.

LET'S TALK ABOUT IT

Why do you think the people in the crowd opted to silence Bartimaeus? Have you seen instances in your church that mirror the silencing of the crowd?

Most likely they thought Jesus too important to be bothered with a blind beggar. Rather than judge them for their actions, we do well to explore the ways in which we silence people who may only be trying to get the very things we take for granted.

Let us imagine ways that, rather than putting the needy on mute, we can live out our call to be microphones, amplifying their pleas for restoration and healing. Let us resolve to be mediators of healing and restoration, after all that is what Jesus does in this lesson.

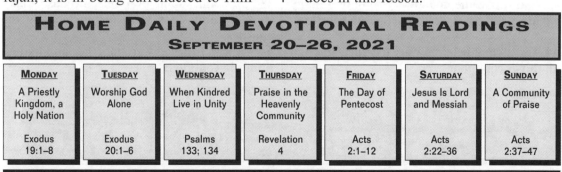

HOME DAILY DEVOTIONAL READINGS
SEPTEMBER 20–26, 2021

MONDAY	TUESDAY	WEDNESDAY	THURSDAY	FRIDAY	SATURDAY	SUNDAY
A Priestly Kingdom, a Holy Nation	Worship God Alone	When Kindred Live in Unity	Praise in the Heavenly Community	The Day of Pentecost	Jesus Is Lord and Messiah	A Community of Praise
Exodus 19:1–8	Exodus 20:1–6	Psalms 133; 134	Revelation 4	Acts 2:1–12	Acts 2:22–36	Acts 2:37–47

BELIEVERS PRAISE GOD

ACTS 2:32–33, 37–47

King James Version

THIS Jesus hath God raised up, whereof we all are witnesses.

33 Therefore being by the right hand of God exalted, and having received of the Father the promise of the Holy Ghost, he hath shed forth this, which ye now see and hear.

• • • • • •

37 Now when they heard this, they were pricked in their heart, and said unto Peter and to the rest of the apostles, Men and brethren, what shall we do?

38 Then Peter said unto them, Repent, and be baptized every one of you in the name of Jesus Christ for the remission of sins, and ye shall receive the gift of the Holy Ghost.

39 For the promise is unto you, and to your children, and to all that are afar off, even as many as the Lord our God shall call.

40 And with many other words did he testify and exhort, saying, Save yourselves from this untoward generation.

41 Then they that gladly received his word were baptized: and the same day there were added unto them about three thousand souls.

42 And they continued stedfastly in the apostles' doctrine and fellowship, and in breaking of bread, and in prayers.

43 And fear came upon every soul: and many wonders and signs were done by the apostles.

44 And all that believed were together, and had all things common;

New Revised Standard Version

THIS Jesus God raised up, and of that all of us are witnesses.

33 Being therefore exalted at the right hand of God, and having received from the Father the promise of the Holy Spirit, he has poured out this that you both see and hear.

• • • • • •

37 Now when they heard this, they were cut to the heart and said to Peter and to the other apostles, "Brothers, what should we do?"

38 Peter said to them, "Repent, and be baptized every one of you in the name of Jesus Christ so that your sins may be forgiven; and you will receive the gift of the Holy Spirit.

39 For the promise is for you, for your children, and for all who are far away, everyone whom the Lord our God calls to him."

40 And he testified with many other arguments and exhorted them, saying, "Save yourselves from this corrupt generation."

41 So those who welcomed his message were baptized, and that day about three thousand persons were added.

42 They devoted themselves to the apostles' teaching and fellowship, to the breaking of bread and the prayers.

43 Awe came upon everyone, because many wonders and signs were being done by the apostles.

44 All who believed were together and had all things in common;

MAIN THOUGHT: And they continued stedfastly in the apostles' doctrine and fellowship, and in breaking of bread, and in prayers. (Acts 2:42, KJV)

ACTS 2:32–33, 37–47

King James Version	*New Revised Standard Version*
45 And sold their possessions and goods, and parted them to all men, as every man had need.	45 they would sell their possessions and goods and distribute the proceeds[b] to all, as any had need.
46 And they, continuing daily with one accord in the temple, and breaking bread from house to house, did eat their meat with gladness and singleness of heart,	46 Day by day, as they spent much time together in the temple, they broke bread at home and ate their food with glad and generous hearts,
47 Praising God, and having favour with all the people. And the Lord added to the church daily such as should be saved.	47 praising God and having the goodwill of all the people. And day by day the Lord added to their number those who were being saved.

LESSON SETTING
Time: AD 30
Place: Jerusalem

LESSON OUTLINE
I. **Penitence: The Key To Celebrating In Unity (Acts 2:32–33; 37–41)**
II. **Partnership: The Key To Celebrating In Unity (Acts 2:42)**
III. **The Praiseworthy Results Of Celebrating In Unity (Acts 2:43–47)**

UNIFYING PRINCIPLE
Celebrations bring about unity and a new way of seeing and being in the world. How can our celebrations unify a divided community and world? The first Christian community heard the Gospel, was inspired by the Holy Spirit to see the world differently, and united to live, worship, and evangelize together.

INTRODUCTION
In our world today diverse people come together to celebrate a sports team winning a championship. In these occasions all manner of people from all walks of life readily come together, meet at a given place, and in merriment embrace and make quite a raucous. As an example the city of Cleveland, which is typically geographically separated by ethnicity and social status, was on one accord and united because LeBron James had made good on his promise to bring a championship home to Cleveland.

This is the same euphoria and unity we will discover in our lesson today. In fact, the saints were even more jovial and ecstatic, because their king Jesus—the King of Kings had just defeated death and made good on His promise of sending forth the Holy Spirit. In our study today we will explore the characteristics of this united and praise worthy congregation and discover ways to praise God through our unity.

EXPOSITION

I. PENITENCE: THE KEY TO CELEBRATING IN UNITY (ACTS 2:32–33; 37–41)
The first step to becoming a unified praiseworthy community that is able to praise God in a unified way is being born again, which starts with penitence (repentance) in the heart. Our lesson opens

with a fiery sermon (v. 14-37). Under the unction of the Holy Spirit Peter arises and preaches with power and conviction. The effects of such preaching is seen at the beginning of our lesson. Luke testifies that many who heard were "picked/pierced in the heart" (v. 37). The Common English Bible translates this response as "deeply troubled." However we read this passage and translate the word *katanyssomai* (κατανυσσομαι) we do well to note it relays the feeling of being agitated. In this case the soon to be saints were agitated and moved to action. This is where true repentance begins, it begins with an unsettling of the heart. As careful teachers and expositors of God's Gospel we must at all times remember that the Gospel is not always meant to make us feel good, so much as it is to make us be good. The Word of God is at times like castor oil and cod liver oil, they do not taste good, yet they are very profitable to our well-being.

Preaching should elicit a response, a transformational response. In verse 37, the soon to be saints say, "What should we do?" Peter's response in verse 38 warrants our attention. He says "repent and be baptized." Repent is a complex word that essentially has a dual meaning. On one hand repentance means we must change our actions. The first step to repentance is changing our praxis. We must cease our sinful habits and practices. The second critical component of repentance is perhaps more important-it is to change our hearts. Luke elsewhere informs us that the heart is the catalyst for our actions (Lk. 6:45). Repentance begins in the heart. In the early church converts had to be born again in the way God would have it!

Peter teaches that repentance is followed by baptism. We see clearly the importance of our Lord's ordinance (order) for the early church. Once a saint decided to live for Jesus they had to go public. Baptism is an initiation ritual. For the early church, baptism was not done in the comfort of a sanctuary, it was done in bodies of water and with procession. It was a public announcement that an individual belonged to Jesus the Christ.

Note this baptism prescribed by the apostle is done in the name of Jesus. In the ancient near east, when a task was done in the name of a person meant that was a means of signifying that the task had been done under the authority of said person. Baptism is thus done in Jesus' name because Jesus alone has the authority to forgive sin (Mark 2:1–12).

Note with attentiveness the words in verses 38–39. Peter prescribes a definitive order. Repent—Be baptized—Receive the Holy Spirit. Verse 39 notes a faithful promise, a promise available to those who hear Him, and anyone they come into contact with who is outside of the ark of safety. What wonderful news! If we repent, we can be baptized and identified with Christ, forgiven by Christ, and once cleansed we are free to receive the gift of the Holy Spirit! Remember the Holy Spirit is a gift from Christ. Peter here teaches that the Holy Spirit is a gift whom we can enjoy and experience once we repent and are baptized.

Peter persisted in his exhortation to leave and part ways with the present perverted and perishing generation and the final result was an addition of 3,000 people joining the new Jesus movement community. The Church is to be different from the present age. We are radically different because we are a repented—penitent people. Penitent hearts are a powerful praise to a powerful God. Penitent people can offer unified praise.

II. PARTNERSHIP: THE KEY TO CELEBRATING IN UNITY (ACTS 2:42)

There is another aspect of this united and praiseworthy community. As noted in verse 40, this community was ontologically different than the other communities of the world. Other communities are regarded and stamped as "perverse" (CEB) or "untoward" (KJV). Luke uses the word *skolias* (σκολιας), a word which means crooked and implies a kind of derangement rooted in evil or wickedness to define and characterize the communities of the world. On the contrary we learn in verse 42 the major defining characteristic of this redeemed and repentant community is not perversion but partnership.

Here we find the components of a five-star five-fold ministry/church. The saints partner with the disciples and God by gathering daily to learn. By gathering to learn we invoke an invisible yet irrefutable contract with those God has placed in our lives to teach us. We promise to learn as they promise to teach. In addition, we also have a covenant with God to participate in our own continued sanctification and transformation by learning, literally renewing our minds (Rom. 12:2). Hence, we see what is praiseworthy about this community they were devoted to discipleship, to learning how to live out their faith!

These saints were also devoted to each other. This is noteworthy because we are informed that this community is a hodge-podge of various cultural demarcations, they were all different (v. 7-12). Yet they were devoted to each other! We see the ways in which this unified praise worthy community praised God thought their devotion to each other, to their fellowship.

Now fellowship is a word we use in our modern era with modern error. Fellowship has been greatly reduced to afternoon worship services, but in fact the word connotes something much more splendid. Fellowship is common regard and common concern for the common welfare of the community. It is mutuality and mutual concern and care for each other. This beloved, is precisely what the saints show for each other. They are "down" for each other. There is concern that everyone is able to eat. They also hold each other in prayer faithfully. When taken with verses 45–46, we further note that this mindfulness and concern was not just daily but was also exercised beyond the walls of the church. This mindfulness and sensitivity to the needs and concerns of others made its way from house to house. In fact the saints were so ingrained together and so devoted to each other that Luke says they sold their possessions to make provisions for those who may not have any. What a picture of devotion and commitment.

Thus we see that unity is to be celebrated because it is supported by a Christlike selflessness that allows us to be concerned and mindful about others! Surely, this type of behavior is Holy Spirit birthed. It is not natural and according to this world. Whereas, the outside world is perverse and crooked-bent inwardly on their own self-interest, the church is different. The church is a community of partner-a community of concern, a community of mutuality (equals), a community of the Spirit, a community able to be together and thus able to celebrate together.

III. THE PRAISEWORTHY RESULTS OF CELEBRATING IN UNITY (ACTS 2:43–47)

The final verses of our lesson depict the wonderful and praiseworthy results of unity in this praiseworthy community.

Luke begins by telling us that while the surrounding community may be perverse—crooked in their practices there is nothing wrong with their perception. He notes that they look upon this community of the Spirit with awe. Luke says a "sense of fear" overtakes the larger outside community. Fear here is *phobos* (*φοβος*), the root we associate with phobia or fear. The word is complicated, on one hand it does mean to be afraid and on the other hand it means reverence. Both instances of use abound in the New Testament. Careful expositors can connect the dots to show how both responses are appropriate. On one hand this kind of concern for all people surely scared the powers that be that profited from the exploitation of some. Likewise, seeing such selflessness surely was a marvel worth astonishing over for others. Moreover, Luke says that God performed many wonderful acts and miracles were done through the church's leaders as signs to the rest of the world. We are not told the nature of these acts only that they were miraculous and that they were signs meant to convince the world of the reality of God's Spirit and kingdom initiation.

As already discussed, this community embodied and uncanny unbelievable unity! We have already noted the selfless sharing. The results of which was that everyone had something. In our world today if we would share, everyone would likewise have something too. If only the wealthiest would share and pay fitting taxes, all would have something. It is worth noting that money is called, currency. In nature currents are meant to travel, to move.

Take water for instance it is also discussed as a current. Water does not become problematic until the current becomes stagnant, when it does it begins to stink. Perhaps this is the pungent smell poverty makes in God's nostrils. Finally, we note the euphoric utopian society created by God. A utopia is derived from the Greek phrase literally meaning "no place" it is used to discuss a place that is unlike any place else, a desirable and almost unreal paradise like place. The early church was a utopia indeed. It fits the bill because it was a society in which all of its participants are reported as being glad. A community in which God was praised and glorified regularly. A community in which the goodness of God was showed through mutuality, mindfulness, and concern; finally, it was a community taken care of and populated by God. The early church was a community far removed from our experience of life today in our communities where so many people's needs are unmet. God is frequently not regarded in policy or praxis, and COVID-19 and other sicknesses threaten our populations. Luke tells us alas that it is God who adds to this community (v. 47)! Indeed, this is a community God blesses. This is a community that literally showers God with praise and shows the goodness of God in praxis and for their efforts is sustained by God who continues to add to their ranks. What a community!

THE LESSON APPLIED

Unity is a word used regularly in our modern society. As a concept, unity is a virtue praised and celebrated in our society. It is well sought after in our church communities both locally and globally.

However, unity often escapes us because while we love to celebrate it, we often are not led to pursue it. In our lesson today we see the prerequisites and payoffs for unity.

The early church was a unified church. Their success was knotted to their unity, as is ours. Their unity was birthed by the Holy Spirit which was received freely as a gift accompanying repentance and baptism. This suggests to us that our world and our churches cannot be truly united in any praiseworthy way until we align our hearts with God through penitent, changed lives through changed hearts and transformed minds. Once we seek Christ and His kingdom as our primary objective (Matthew 6:33)—evidenced through baptism we are then free to receive the Holy Spirit.

True praiseworthy unity is unattainable without the power of the Holy Spirit who grants us the necessary fruit to live in harmony and unselfishness.

Certainly, in our lesson today we see a cause to celebrate unity. It is what allows church leaders to display the full-on power of God. It allows church members to commit to God's Word and each other. It allows us to be persistent in our praise and powerful in our witness. All hail to godly unity. Blessed be the tie that binds.

LET'S TALK ABOUT IT
Did the early church really hold all things in common?

"All the believers were united and shared everything. They would sell pieces of property and possessions and distribute the proceeds to everyone who needed them." (v. 44–45, CEB) In this text today we see a type of true and conceptual idealized commune in the ways the saints in the early Jerusalem church held all things in common. While some scholars feel this was only a one time affair and done only to be hospitable for those travelers who were in the holy city for the feast days of Passover and Pentecost, others hold this was the divine ideal model for Jesus' movement. Whether the latter is so or not, we cannot truly determine. However what can be determined is that one of the central defining aspects of the early church was a willingness to share an uncanny generosity. Perhaps self-interest and selfishness are the latches, which when unattended jeopardize the buoyancy of unity in the Old Ship of Zion.

HOME DAILY DEVOTIONAL READINGS
SEPTEMBER 27–OCTOBER 3, 2021

MONDAY	TUESDAY	WEDNESDAY	THURSDAY	FRIDAY	SATURDAY	SUNDAY
Praise the Rock of Our Salvation	Stones Shout Out!	Indescribable and Glorious Joy	Sing to God a New Song	A Continuous Sacrifice of Praise	Rejoice in God's Mighty Rule	Enter God's Courts with Praise
Psalm 95	Luke 19:28, 36–40	1 Peter 1:3–9	Psalm 98	Hebrews 13:12–16	Psalm 66:1–7	Psalm 100

MAKE A JOYFUL NOISE

| ADULT TOPIC: "ONLY YOU" | BACKGROUND SCRIPTURE: PSALM 100 |

PSALM 100

King James Version	*New Revised Standard Version*
MAKE a joyful noise unto the LORD, all ye lands.	MAKE a joyful noise to the LORD, all the earth.
2 Serve the LORD with gladness: come before his presence with singing.	2 Worship the LORD with gladness; come into his presence with singing.
3 Know ye that the LORD he is God: it is he that hath made us, and not we ourselves; we are his people, and the sheep of his pasture.	3 Know that the LORD is God. It is he that made us, and we are his; we are his people, and the sheep of his pasture.
4 Enter into his gates with thanksgiving, and into his courts with praise: be thankful unto him, and bless his name.	4 Enter his gates with thanksgiving, and his courts with praise. Give thanks to him, bless his name.
5 For the LORD is good; his mercy is everlasting; and his truth endureth to all generations.	5 For the LORD is good; his steadfast love endures forever, and his faithfulness to all generations.

LESSON SETTING
Time: Unknown
Place: Unknown

LESSON OUTLINE
I. The Praise God Deserves Should Be Intense (Psalm 100:1–2)
II. The Praise God Deserves Should Be Informed (Psalm 100:3)
III. The Praise God Deserves Requires Initiative (Psalm 100:4)
IV. Only God Deserves Such Praise Because of His Incentives (Psalm 100:5)

UNIFYING PRINCIPLE
Life provides us with many opportunities to praise and find delight in people and things. How do we decide what has more value and is more worthy of our praise? Psalm 100 highlights that God is the object of the earth's praise and joy.

INTRODUCTION
It was a common occurrence among African Americans for generations to have separate clothing designated as "church clothes". Our ancestors maintained the practice of having "Sunday-go-to-meeting-clothes." This practice was our ancestor's way of aesthetically

MAIN THOUGHT: Know ye that the LORD he is God: it is he that hath made us, and not we ourselves; we are his people, and the sheep of his pasture. (Psalm 100:3, KJV)

designating top priority to God. It was a way of saying that God deserved our best. The notion that God is exclusive and exceptional thus deserving our best is the underlying theme of this week's lesson. While historically we have regarded God in this way in terms of aesthetics and clothing, this week's lesson challenges us to regard God with the same exclusionary excellence with our celebratory actions. In our lesson this week we are thoroughly reminded that God deserves our best efforts in worship, and we are challenged to adjust our behavior. This means our active participation in worship and praise to God should be more enthusiastic than our participation in anything else (sports, dancing, family gatherings, etc.).

Our lesson explores Psalm 100 as a primer about the kind of celebration due only to God, namely that it should be intense, informed, requires initiative, and pays immeasurable incentives.

EXPOSITION

I. THE PRAISE GOD DESERVES SHOULD BE INTENSE (PSALM 100:1–2)

This Psalm begins calling for an intense response to God. In the opening line we are told to "Make a joyful noise..." The actual Biblical word used here for joyful noise *ruwa*. *Strong's Dictionary* defines this word as deriving from an earlier word meaning "to mar (especially by breaking); to split the ears (with sound), i.e. shout (for alarm or joy); blow an alarm, cry (alarm, aloud, out), destroy, make a joyful noise, smart, shout (for joy), sound an alarm, triumph." Right away we get the image of a loud-ear splitting noise. The Psalmist says we must render this loud and boister-

ous ear-splitting action to God. The Bible directs us to truly worship and praise God in a grand and noisy fashion. The Psalmist states God deserves the same revelry typically found at the sports stadiums of the world. Biblically speaking God's worship and praise is not supposed to be somber. It is supposed to be celebrative. On-lookers should want to draw nigh, they should know a celebration is underway.

The command to make such ear-splitting noise is an open invitation to "all the lands." Literally to the whole earth. Hence we see that praising God is a universal experience and obligation. No one is left out, no one is excluded, all people and all parties are invited to participate in the holy earth-shattering act of praising God.

In verse two, there is further instructions with regard to the intensity owed God in worship and praise. The psalmist writes to "serve the LORD". Two things deserve our attention. Firstly, the word LORD. Throughout this Psalm the word is capitalized (written in small caps). In the Bible there are a plethora of names and terms for God. Lord is one and LORD is another. Whenever the writers use the all-capitalized LORD, the writer is indicating that the word used in the text is Yahweh. Yahweh is God's specific and personal name, it is the tetragrammaton so-called because it is transliterated (translated) from four Hebrew letters (*YHWH*). Hebrews understood this to be the name communicated to Moses when he asked God for a name (Exodus 3:14). Yahweh, is Israel's personal name for God. In fact, it was regarded as so holy, that the name was not even written in full or even spoken, a tradition that still persists in some Jewish and Christian sects to date. One may thus translate this LORD as the God we know, the God we've known, the God we are known by, and the God of our yesterday—our God through and through.

We are thus encouraged to "serve" this God. The word serve here is `abad a Hebrew word which means to work, to labor. The word's connotation is anchored in servility and bond slavery. The image for this word brings to mind hard, laborious, tedious work. Hence the Psalmist reminds us that praise and worship are tasks of volition, work of human will.

Moreover, it is a task that demands effort. Biblically speaking worship is work. It is not a passive or spectator activity; the Bible teaches that praise and worship are active participatory activities that we must will ourselves to do. "Amens" are therefore not optional they are obligatory. The worship leader's directive "to praise the Lord everybody" is not just conjecture, it is not just church talk, it is our biblical responsibility. We are to oblige and celebrate God even when we do not feel like it. The Psalmist states that this is our job.

Thus, in the same way we report to work despite how we may feel about the jobs we hold, we too must report to the sanctuary to work, that is serve God through worship. Worship is intense work, but alas there is a caveat, a nuance to the usual understanding of hard work; when we worship God, we are to do it with "gladness." The word used here literally means bliss and glee. Thus, worship and praise are intense, it involves ear-splitting noise, and volition, but it is not a task to dread, but rather is a task in which to find delight. Try it yourself, see if passionately praising

God to outpouring of praise will come an adequate outpouring of endorphins, the feel-good enzymes. Hence intense praise is deserved for only God, because God is able to repay our praise in kind with gladness.

II. THE PRAISE GOD DESERVES SHOULD BE INFORMED (PSALM 100:3)

As intense and raucous as the Psalmist dictates the worship reserved only for the true and living God is deserving, the writer also reminds us that this loud and boisterous celebration is not done in ignorance, it is reflective and insightful.

Hence the worship only God deserves is an informed activity. Throughout the Psalm the Psalmist maintains it as a cognitive ordeal, thus there are some things we should know. Proper praise requires pondering the right things. Worship and praise are thus actions that involve the intellect as well.

We are told to "know that the LORD" is God. This means essentially to know full well. It is used to describe a variety of ways in which one can come to an understanding or perceive a matter—i.e., literally, figuratively, and even through inference. Thus, we can understand the Psalmist's directive here to mean we must know without a shadow of a doubt—know in our hearts—know from experience—that the God we know, the God of our people, *Yahweh* of Israel is God. To give over oneself to this type of knowledge is to understand that the God of Israel is the one and only true and living God.

Moreover, to know this is to show this. This can be likened to school aged children, most teachers can typically tell when children know (or at least think they know) an answer to a question. Their bodies show it, their eyes light up and their hands instantaneously go up. When you know, you show. This holds true with worship—when we know, we show. If we in fact know God is real, then our praise will show it. Our amens will announce it, our shouting will confirm it. When we know, we show.

We are also to know and understand that God made us—we did not make ourselves. The image is illustrated aptly within the context. Sheep were cared for by their shepherds, the needs of the sheep were the concerns of the shepherd, the enemies of the sheep were the enemies of the shepherd. Hence, the Psalmist is essentially reminding us that proper praise requires that we remember that we belong to God.

Which means we are God's responsibility. God is responsible for taking care of us. We belong to God; our concerns are God's; our issues are God's; our battles are God's. To give God the proper praise that only God deserves we must be mindful and informed of who God is and that we belong to God!

III. THE PRAISE GOD DESERVES REQUIRES INITIATIVE (PSALM 100:4)

God's deserved praise is an exercise involving initiative. In verse 4 we receive the directive to "enter into" God's gates.

This can be rightly presented as a reference to the reign and kingship of God who was thought to be enthroned in the praise of His people, and specifically enthroned in the Ark of the Covenant, housed beyond the veil in the holiest of holy sites in the temple. Thus, the Psalmist invites us to approach God as King—King of all kings in a befitting manner. In antiquity (and presently) one did not just approach a king, one had to be invited. However, the Psalmist implies that we have been summoned by God as King and are thus, through worship, permitted to approach God's throne. It is also worth noting that the undertones of a vassal approaching a king are also present in v. 2 of our lesson.

We are to approach God; this speaks to the initiative required in worship. The point is demonstrated above that worship is an act of the will. We have been invited to approach the holy God through praise.

This is the only motivation ever needed for praising God. We have thought it as a response to an anointed act like a particular song, a powerful sermon, or an enthusiastic appeal to praise the Lord, when biblically speaking praise should not require any of that. Praise is an act of initiative. Response is not to a person's performance, but to God and does not need any prodding through song, sermon, or soundbite. We are invited to show initiative to come before our King. In fact, we have the obligation to praise simply because we have been extended the opportunity.

The mention of "gates" and "courts" further reminds us of the setting in which this Psalm was sung. The image here is of sojourners joyfully entering into the gates of the temple into the courts (wide open public spaces of the temple mount).

The Psalmist also implores us to show further initiative not just by approaching God but being active before God with the specific tasks of "thanksgiving, praise, being thankful and blessing" God's name.

The first word thanksgiving, is a word that suggests a specific act of offering. The word is *todah*—it is the thanksgiving offering, the word literally means thanksgiving. The thanksgiving offering was typically offered by a person to whom God had delivered from a great danger and was typically accompanied with a song or praise as our lesson posits. Here again the Bible is informative, the Psalmist reminds us that offering is a time of reflection. We are to reflect on how God has provided for us and protected us. It is also a time in which we should be joyful and celebrative.

We are also informed that we should show initiative by being thankful—that is appreciative and grateful to God for all that God has done! Appreciation always has a way of making itself known. When one is truly grateful, one will find a way to show it! When we worship and praise God, we should do it in a way that demonstrates our appreciation and gratitude. Moreover, the Psalmist says we should "bless" God.

The word bless is a loaded word. On one hand it has to do with bowing or saluting, which speaks to the posture of the heart and body in worship, we should be surrendered to God. However, on the other hand the word also conveys the connotation of being good to another. Hence the writer is suggesting that intense praise is the act of being good to God! Here is why that is noteworthy and indeed shout-worthy, it is clear that God has been good to us. Without a doubt this is true, however how is it possible that we may be good to God?

We as mere mortals are limited to truly do anything for God—we have nothing God needs, and nothing of our own anyway (Psalm 24; 1 Chronicles 29:14), yet God is indeed God enough to find a way to allow us to be good to Him. Perhaps God views our praise through the same loving lens as a parent views young children's works of art, although they do not qualify to adorn any art gallery they hang honorably in home simply because we love them!

Could it be God has allowed us through praise to be good to God simply because God loves us? That beloved is all the more reason to bless God! Through praise we have the chance to return to God some of the good God has poured out on us.

IV. Only God Deserves Such Praise Because of His Incentives (Psalm 100:5)

The Psalmist concludes this Psalm by giving us a rationale for our praise and worship, in short God's performance and characteristics are the only incentive we need. Here the Bible states that we do not praise God because we are looking to get anything from God (deliverance, breakthrough, etc.,) but rather because God is "good"—beneficial, pleasant, a joy.

To know the Lord God is to love God! Furthermore, His great "mercy" *hesed*—faithful/steadfast love never runs out. This alone is a reality that should prompt our praise. If God's ability to love had an expiration or a limit all would have exceeded it. God's love and kindness have no limit.

Finally, the Psalmist reminds us we praise God as only God deserves because God's "truth" endures to all generations. This literally means God's covenant and Word are intergenerational and never expire. Intergenerational meaning that God will be the same God to us today as God was to our ancestors of yesterday. The same miracle working God of the Bible is the same miracle working God of today. God who placed an air conditioner in the fiery furnace of Daniel's time has placed a brown skinned woman into the White House in our time. Moreover, God's truth, God's promises have no expiration date.

They are as good and as valid today as they were when they were written. God's covenant promises are valid, still paying, and are still yet to pay!

We do not need any more reasons to praise God, God's character and past performance have provided us all the incentive we need. We need only the chance.

THE LESSON APPLIED

In the same way that COVID-19 has changed the way many of us do things, this lesson should change the way many of us praise God. When we praise God we should give to God the energy and enthusiasm due God. We should praise God with intensity—it should be loud and boisterous. We should praise God with determination, having a mindfulness about God's presence in our lives. We should praise God with initiative—not waiting for any special feeling, song, or other outside agitation, we should praise God because God is good, God is ever loving, and God's promises hold true. The next worship service you participate in, be sure to bring the same enthusiasm of a political rally or sports event because God deserves our best, and our best energy should be relegated only for God. All the doxology says, "Praise Father, Son, and Holy Ghost. Amen."

LET'S TALK ABOUT IT

Serving the Lord will pay off after while... or does it?

Many people have advanced a faulty ideology that performing praise in the sanctuary will instantly transform our reality outside the sanctuary, and after experiencing such carnival trick theology many believers are wondering does praise really pay off? It is worth noting however, that to serve the Lord is to commit to God our whole heart and our whole life. We do well to remember the words of Jesus that no one can serve two masters (Matt. 6:24), and while Israel was at home in Egypt serving Pharaoh they could not worship-serve God. Their liberation was tied to worship (Ex. 3–4). Thus the idea of serving God is squarely tied to belonging to God wholly in mind, emotion, soul, and body. To belong to God is to serve God in worship and work, with gladness-eagerness and never reluctance.

This is the sort of service to God that pays off after a while, by and by, and instantly. This type of service reminds us that if we in fact belong to God, so do our battles, and God is yet undefeated.

HOME DAILY DEVOTIONAL READINGS
OCTOBER 4–10, 2021

MONDAY	TUESDAY	WEDNESDAY	THURSDAY	FRIDAY	SATURDAY	SUNDAY
Where Is Justice?	A Prayer for Justice	Let Justice Roll Down	God's Servant Proclaims Justice	God Has Executed Judgment	Jesus Pronounces Release and Recovery	God Judges with Righteousness
Ecclesiastes 3:16–22	Psalm 7:8–17	Amos 5:21–25	Matthew 12:14–21	Psalm 9:13–20	Luke 4:14–21	Psalm 9:1–12

PRAISE GOD FOR JUSTICE AND RIGHTEOUSNESS

ADULT TOPIC: BACKGROUND SCRIPTURE:
"BALL OF CONFUSION"   PSALM 9; ECCLESIASTES 3:16–22

PSALM 9:1–12

King James Version

I WILL praise thee, O LORD, with my whole heart; I will shew forth all thy marvellous works.

2 I will be glad and rejoice in thee: I will sing praise to thy name, O thou most High.

3 When mine enemies are turned back, they shall fall and perish at thy presence.

4 For thou hast maintained my right and my cause; thou satest in the throne judging right.

5 Thou hast rebuked the heathen, thou hast destroyed the wicked, thou hast put out their name for ever and ever.

6 O thou enemy, destructions are come to a perpetual end: and thou hast destroyed cities; their memorial is perished with them.

7 But the LORD shall endure for ever: he hath prepared his throne for judgment.

8 And he shall judge the world in righteousness, he shall minister judgment to the people in uprightness.

9 The LORD also will be a refuge for the oppressed, a refuge in times of trouble.

10 And they that know thy name will put their trust in thee: for thou, LORD, hast not forsaken them that seek thee.

11 Sing praises to the LORD, which dwelleth in Zion: declare among the people his doings.

12 When he maketh inquisition for blood, he remembereth them: he forgetteth not the cry of the humble.

New Revised Standard Version

I WILL give thanks to the LORD with my whole heart; I will tell of all your wonderful deeds.

2 I will be glad and exult in you; I will sing praise to your name, O Most High.

3 When my enemies turned back, they stumbled and perished before you.

4 For you have maintained my just cause; you have sat on the throne giving righteous judgment.

5 You have rebuked the nations, you have destroyed the wicked; you have blotted out their name forever and ever.

6 The enemies have vanished in everlasting ruins; their cities you have rooted out; the very memory of them has perished.

7 But the LORD sits enthroned forever, he has established his throne for judgment.

8 He judges the world with righteousness; he judges the peoples with equity.

9 The LORD is a stronghold for the oppressed, a stronghold in times of trouble.

10 And those who know your name put their trust in you, for you, O LORD, have not forsaken those who seek you.

11 Sing praises to the LORD, who dwells in Zion. Declare his deeds among the peoples.

12 For he who avenges blood is mindful of them; he does not forget the cry of the afflicted.

MAIN THOUGHT: And he shall judge the world in righteousness, he shall minister judgment to the people in uprightness. (Psalm 9:8, KJV)

LESSON SETTING
   Time: 1056 BC
   Place: Unknown

LESSON OUTLINE
   I. **How the Psalmist Resolves How to Praise God: Whole-hearted Praise (Psalm 9:1–2)**
   II. **The Psalmist Resolves What to Praise God For (Psalm 9:3–12)**

UNIFYING PRINCIPLE

People choose to praise and have joy in particular things that may not be the best for them. Why do we choose those things that may harm us or others? Psalm 9 proclaims that God will bring justice and this is cause for our joyful praise.

INTRODUCTION

David once said that he would "bless the Lord at all times" (Psalm 34), Paul instructs the saints at Philippi to rejoice in the Lord always (Philippians 4:4). The notion that we should always be grateful and maintain a praise and worshipful disposition is clearly outlined in Scripture. Surely it is understandably clear that we should thank God for good times. We teach this explicitly and implicitly through teaching children to say grace (give thanks) for meals. However what is not so clear, is how to maintain a praise filled disposition when life presents itself as challenging as it often times does.

It is one thing to thank God for a meal of sustenance, it is a whole entirely different task to thank God when life seats us at a table of mess or misery. This Psalm has a superscription to *Muthlabben*, which the Hebrew, although uncertain, is thought to mean "over the death of the son" (which helps explain why some scholars believe this Psalm correlates to the defeat and subsequent death of Absalom). Whether or not this Psalm was written in response to the defeat of Absalom or not we cannot know, but what can be determined is that this is not a Psalm written without regard for human suffering. This is a Psalm composed through reflection. It is precisely because of this, that this Psalm creates the perfect point of departure for our lesson, because this Psalm gives us a contemplated—well thought out rationale as to why we can still render God praise even when it appears our world has fallen apart or presents itself as a ball of utter confusion.

EXPOSITION

I. HOW THE PSALMIST RESOLVES HOW TO PRAISE GOD: WHOLE-HEARTED PRAISE (PSALM 9:1–2)

In the opening verses of this Psalm, the Psalmist identified as David, declares that he will "praise the Lord". The Psalmist is referring to Israel's God *Yahweh*. *Yahweh* is the personal name of God assigned to Israel's personal and experiential understanding of God through history. Hence, the Psalmist maintains that He will praise the God he knows, the God of his ancestors and what is more, David says he will do this with "his whole heart." The Hebrew word used here is "*leb*" a word that refers to the seat of thought, human volition/will, and emotions; essentially the Psalmist is saying that he will praise God with the entirety of his being. This is a prevailing theme throughout our quarter, true praise and worship is not an afterthought.

It is an intentional, enthusiastic, intense, and determined response to the persona and performance of God.

The Psalmist uses the Hebrew word "*saber*" here to discuss his first means of praising God with his whole heart. The KJV translates this word as "shew forth" other translations render it as "talk" and both are appropriate. The word in the biblical language has scribal connotations of proclaiming-making public, counting or tallying. Thus we can understand David's words here as his statement of resolve to remember and count the good deeds of God and to make the list public. There are two takeaways here for the careful expositor to replicate and embody in their life. The first is that in confusing times, we can find comfort and certainty in the past activity of God. In tougher times it is helpful to count as a scribe our blessings one by one in an effort to see what the Lord has done. Secondly, as we live in the information age where scores of information is readily available at the click of a computer key or mouse, David challenges us to be scribes, adding to the information available by detailing God's wondrous deeds in our life and in the life of our community.

Here David uses two distinct words to capture how he resolves to praise God even in troubling times. David says he resolves to "be glad" and "rejoice" in God. These two words in the biblical language are *samach* and *'alats* respectively. Samach meaning essentially to brighten up, and *'alats* meaning rejoicing or being jubilant, the word is also used to depict the joy of triumphing, especially over one's enemies. Hence David is stating that he chooses to allow God's presence to bring him up from his despondency. God's presence brings him up in the same way the thought of a special love interest does.

It follows to reason that when we resolve to count and vocally document God's goodness to us such activity brings us into God's presence (Psalm 22:3) which inherently brings us up. In fact, David seems to suggest that not only will we brighten but we will boast. He uses the word *'alats* a word for rejoicing or excitement that can be experienced from winning.

Finally David discusses that he will also sing God's praises. The word *zamar* sing for the Hebrews derives from a compound understanding, on one hand the word has connotations of striking with the fingers, and on the other it has to do with voice. Hence taken together the ancient Hebrew understanding of singing was very literal—to play the vocal chords something like an instrument. Now it is important to remember, that while we should give God our best efforts, being the best is not a prerequisite for excelling in praise. So long as we have vocal cords and we are able to move them, then as far as this passage is concerned we are well able to sing God's praises. Moreover, because worship is an act performed for an audience of God alone, God our loving parent enjoys hearing the unique sound of our voices.

II. The Psalmist Resolves What to Praise God For (Psalm 9:3–12)

Having already told us how he praises God, David discloses the reasons he praises God in the remaining verses.

David begins in verse three by thanking God for his anticipated protection. David here is not thanking God for a past event, he is anticipating God's forthcoming protection. He speaks in the affirmative, forecasting God's intervention in his affairs. This is a luxury that praise affords us, it gives us a confidence in God's forthcoming activity. This confidence works to comfort us even in the midst of peril and confusion. Also of interest for us is the nature of David's anticipated protection of God. David anticipates that God will turn back his enemies. David says our enemies will not prevail against us, but that they will not even succeed in retreating. He notes that his enemies will fall and perish. Indeed God specializes in enemy removal.

In verse 4 David continues documenting why he praises God. He notes God's posterity, that is to say God's long lasting work of justice. David now recalling a specific act in his life reflects on a time when God moved on his behalf to institute righteousness. Perhaps David is recalling an instance in which an enemy unjustly attacked him, notwithstanding God maintained, preserved and kept him safe.

In the second part of verse 4, David rejoices in the reality that God is seated or poised upon a throne from which God administrates justice rightly. Worth pointing out is that David is delighted in the fact that God is seated. The seated posture of God reminds David that whatever dilemma that may have gotten him or the nation riled up, has not so ruffled his all-powerful God. Additionally, David notes that God administers righteousness or justice from the vantage point of fair King and Righteous Judge. Moreover, God does this correctly. While the judges and nations of the world have their shortsighted and wrong sighted understandings of what is right, David praises God because His understanding of rightness is truly correct.

In verses 5–10, David lists a battery of ways in which God provides. He begins by noting that God has removed His enemies (v. 5–6). To begin with, David reminds us that God is not on the side of evil or oppression. The Psalmist notes that God opposes them or denounces them. God is not an idle observer in history. No, God takes sides, God sides against evil. David says God is in the business of eradicating the enemies of righteousness. It is worth noting the comprehensive manner in which God expels the Psalmist's enemies.

On one hand God vanquished his enemies, physically removing them. However, now the Psalmist ups the ante, by disclosing that God is also responsible for the erasure of their cities, even their names. God removes all marks of their existence.

In essence the Psalmist is informing us that God is well able to even extinguish the artifacts which may tarry as emotional and psychological scars of an enemy.

Moreover, David also discloses that God also provides righteousness, or a right way within the world. David has already elaborated on this theme, here he reiterates that God's reign is a righteous reign and God's ruler is predicated and substantiated by righteousness and justice. Moreover, the Psalmist adds, that God rules for the sake of righteousness (v.7). We as believers must therefore, strive to elect leaders who mirror God's commitment to righteousness. Moreover, in our churches and in our homes, we too must make those same commitments and mirror God by mobilizing to assume vantage points from which to administer righteousness, God's desires for the world. David, continues to inform us that God provides a respite of righteousness for the oppressed. David, not to be outdone, writes on a much earlier occasion teaching us that God is literally home for the oppressed (v.9). The Psalmist posits one final provision as a rationale for praising God, namely that God has been a reliable aid and ally. The Psalmist exclaims in verse 10 that God has not forsaken or abandoned those who maintain an unwavering trust in Him.

The Psalmist also states in verse 12 that God reigns forever, a fact already celebrated, but here David nuances it by locating the everlasting existence of God in the holy city Zion. To say God is present in Zion is to say that God is with His holy people. In history God's holy people were the Israelites, currently it is us who profess hope in Christ. Meaning God is always with God's people.

Finally, David asserts that he will praise God because God is in the business of paying back. God will fight the battle of justice and He will secure retribution.

Thus we have no need to sully our hands with revenge. We instead can resolve as the Psalmist does to fill our hands and hearts with praise.

The Lesson Applied

Praising God in perilous times can very well seem like a tall order, but the Psalmist in our lesson today gives us some concrete ways and reasons to praise God in the midst of uncertainty, when life feels like a ball of confusion. In short, in moments where we may not know what is happening, we can rejoice in what we do know, and that is God, and God's goodness.

Let's Talk About It

Have you seen or heard the new wave mantra, "I am not my ancestors"?

The sentiment of this new catch phrase is that, unlike the sage African-American ancestors, contemporary and present-day African Americans stand ready to accost any wrong doers.

In our lesson today the Psalmist boasts repeatedly about God as a righteous judge, so much so that David concludes our lesson with the reminder that God makes inquisition or avenges blood. In our lives we have seen so many miscarriages of justice that African-American communities are collectively traumatized. Nonetheless we as a whole have not revolted in large scale. Perhaps it is because the God of our ancestors has passed down an unimaginable peace called, hope? We believers, would certainly do well to remember that God is the final authority and vindicator on all matters. This is not to conveniently divorce us from civic responsibility, but to emphasize that vengeance belongs to God and Him alone.

Home Daily Devotional Readings
October 11–17, 2021

Monday	Tuesday	Wednesday	Thursday	Friday	Saturday	Sunday
Delivered from Hunger and Thirst	Delivered from Darkness and Gloom	Delivered from Storms	Delivered through Jesus Christ	Delivered from Sin	Delivered and Reconciled	Delivered by God's Steadfast Love
Psalm 107:1–9	Psalm 107:10–22	Psalm 107:23–32	Ephesians 1:3–14	Ephesians 2:1–10	Ephesians 2:11–22	Psalm 107:33–43

GIVE THANKS FOR DELIVERANCE

ADULT TOPIC:	BACKGROUND SCRIPTURE:
"I SHALL BE RELEASED"	PSALM 107

PSALM 107:1–9, 39–43

King James Version

O GIVE thanks unto the LORD, for he is good: for his mercy endureth for ever.

2 Let the redeemed of the LORD say so, whom he hath redeemed from the hand of the enemy;

3 And gathered them out of the lands, from the east, and from the west, from the north, and from the south.

4 They wandered in the wilderness in a solitary way; they found no city to dwell in.

5 Hungry and thirsty, their soul fainted in them.

6 Then they cried unto the LORD in their trouble, and he delivered them out of their distresses.

7 And he led them forth by the right way, that they might go to a city of habitation.

8 Oh that men would praise the LORD for his goodness, and for his wonderful works to the children of men!

9 For he satisfieth the longing soul, and filleth the hungry soul with goodness.

• • • • • •

39 Again, they are minished and brought low through oppression, affliction, and sorrow.

40 He poureth contempt upon princes, and causeth them to wander in the wilderness, where there is no way.

41 Yet setteth he the poor on high from affliction, and maketh him families like a flock.

42 The righteous shall see it, and rejoice: and all iniquity shall stop her mouth.

43 Whoso is wise, and will observe these things, even they shall understand the lovingkindness of the LORD.

New Revised Standard Version

O GIVE thanks to the LORD, for he is good; for his steadfast love endures forever.

2 Let the redeemed of the LORD say so, those he redeemed from trouble

3 and gathered in from the lands, from the east and from the west, from the north and from the south.

4 Some wandered in desert wastes, finding no way to an inhabited town;

5 hungry and thirsty, their soul fainted within them.

6 Then they cried to the LORD in their trouble, and he delivered them from their distress;

7 he led them by a straight way, until they reached an inhabited town.

8 Let them thank the LORD for his steadfast love, for his wonderful works to humankind.

9 For he satisfies the thirsty, and the hungry he fills with good things.

• • • • • •

39 When they are diminished and brought low through oppression, trouble, and sorrow,

40 he pours contempt on princes and makes them wander in trackless wastes;

41 but he raises up the needy out of distress, and makes their families like flocks.

42 The upright see it and are glad; and all wickedness stops its mouth.

43 Let those who are wise give heed to these things, and consider the steadfast love of the LORD.

MAIN THOUGHT: Then they cried unto the LORD in their trouble, and he delivered them out of their distresses. (Psalm 107:6, KJV)

LESSON SETTING
   Time: Unknown
   Place: Unknown

LESSON OUTLINE
   I. Praise God For Deliverance
      (Psalm 107:1–3)
   II. God Delivered Us From
       Wandering (Psalm 107:4–9)
   III. God Rights Wrongs
        (Psalm 107:39–41)
   IV. Praise, Pause, and Consider
       (Psalm 107:42–43)

UNIFYING PRINCIPLE
People seek deliverance when they are in trouble. How should we respond when we are delivered? Psalm 107 encourages us to be thankful to God for God's deliverance.

INTRODUCTION
The term deliverance has emerged in our modern era with popularity. Deliverance is defined as the act of being set free or rescued from a situation or ordeal. Many people have experienced deliverance from any number of adversities, from the cornucopia of addictions to arraignments. In our lesson today Israel reflects and renders God praise and thanksgiving for God's continued deliverance. The entire Psalm is centered around the various scenarios in which God has delivered His people. Our lesson however, explores two types of deliverance thus giving the reader an enveloped and overarching understanding of God's powerful capacity to deliver. Our lesson opens with an overture of God's deliverance which is why the Psalmist gives thanks as praise and offers the thanksgiving offering. It then narrows its focus to a specific way in which God delivers namely from wandering in the wilderness to finding community. Next, our lesson skips down toward the end of this Psalm into verses 39–41 to explore another way in which God delivers, namely in the righting of wrongs. Finally, the lesson concludes with the Psalmist inviting us to praise, pause, and consider the wonderful deliverance of God.

EXPOSITION

I. PRAISE GOD FOR DELIVERANCE (PSALM 107:1–3)
The Psalmist begins this song of thanksgiving by stating that one should thank God because God is good (*tob*). *Tob* is a Hebrew word which according to the *Complete Word Study Dictionary* means "good", "well, pleasing, fruitful, morally correct" and "describes that which is appealing and pleasant to the senses."

Surely God fits the bill of being good. Moreover, the Psalmist exclaims that God's mercy (*chesed/hesed*), God's faithful, steadfast, covenant, promise keeping love lasts or "endureth for ever." Endureth, from the KJV, is etymologically linked to endure, and endure is a fitting word for the perseverance of God's promise keeping love. God's commitment to the covenant with Israel (God's people) is an enduring one. It bears all things (1 Corinthians 13) and holds on even when God is not necessarily held to. Hence the Psalm is a Psalm of thanks, in which Israel is summoned to celebrate the faithful love of God and God's faithfulness to His covenant.

This phrase "Let the redeemed of the LORD say so," states that God's people are those who have been redeemed agree with and echo verse one. However, in the tradition of the Black church, this phrase has taken on an additional and nuanced meaning. We use this phrase in regards to bearing witness that God has been good.

For the Psalmist, those who belong to God understand that God is good and should demonstrate a proper response.

The word redeemed here means *saved* or *rescued* in the context of this Psalm. God has redeemed Israel from the hand of its enemy. There is a lot of speculation as to whom the unnamed foe is in this Psalm.

The anonymity of the enemy here works in the favor of the interpreter as it makes God's deliverance universal. Hence the Psalmist says that those whom have been saved should let it be known that God is a promise keeping God who is faithful to His Word and covenant rescuing those whom He is in relationship.

Verse three continues the theme of universal rescue for God's covenant people. The Psalmist boasts that God is able to redeem with far reaching arms. God's long reaching arms of deliverance are both ambidextrous and omnidirectional. Thus God can deliver from any place.

II. GOD DELIVERED US FROM WANDERING (PSALM 107:4–9)

In the next section the Psalmist is specific. The Psalmist thanks God for deliverance from the wilderness and to civilization and community.

Some commentators hold that the Psalmist is referring to the Exodus and the establishment of Israel in the promised land. Others hold that the Psalmist is commemorating Israel's return from Babylonian exile. Neither is wrong. During the exilic period many Israelites began to envision their return to Israel as a type of second Exodus, hence the frequent use of the term wilderness as an image in exilic and post exilic works. It is also worth noting that even as the Psalmist speaks of God's deliverance in more specific terms, there is still a universal nature to God's rescue.

In verse four, the Psalmist notes that some wandered in the wilderness. As a living word this speaks to the plight of modern humanity. The concept of wandering can suggest a deed of one's own volition.

In the case of Israel, all of their collective wandering in the wilderness experiences were the result of their own error. We in this present age resonate with this concept as we know what it is to err and have to live with its consequences.

The Psalmist makes it plain that this wandering was done in a wilderness. This is a wasteland, an unsettled and undesirable place. In verse five we are given another detail that further highlights the misery of the wilderness sojourners, they have no food or drink, painting a universal image of desperation. Even worse, as a result of not having access to a city or habitation where they can harvest food or raise livestock these pilgrims were on the verge of exhaustion. In fact, the Psalmist says their souls "fainted in them" (KJV) expressing that they were exhausted and at the point of giving up. They had reached a place of desperation and discouragement.

At the conclusion of verse five, we are left with an image of a people who have hit rock bottom. We side with Israel, because we too have felt the pangs of desperation associated with rock bottom. Hoping to garner help. They begin by lifting their voices up in earnest prayer. The Psalmist says they "cried unto the Lord" in their desperation. This act is worthy of further exploration. First they call/cry out to God from the midst of their affliction. They do not try to wait until they get better or until better comes, they cry out right in the midst of their affliction. This reminds us that God is not offput by our difficulties, trials, or afflictions even when they are self-imposed troubles. No not at all, God delivers them from their distress. God is able to delver us from the very same places and atrocities in which we entreat Him in prayer.

In verse seven, the Psalmist devotes his attention to detailing the nature of God's deliverance. He iterates that God led them to community, to human habitation, and what's more that God leads them directly there. Contextually speaking, we understand that God indeed leads Israel to the promised land. This is true in the exodus as well as in their return from exile.

The Psalmist concludes this section of his Psalm with an invitation and plea for Israel and all people to celebrate what God has done. In these summary verses the Psalmist invites us to thank God for answering prayers and changing circumstances. Surely a God who rescues wanderers, delivers drifters, and satisfies empty stomachs is worthy of praise.

III. God Rights Wrongs (Psalm 107:39–41)

In this pericope, the Psalmist begins to discuss another way in which God provides deliverance. He sets his pen to celebrate God's ability to deliver from circumstances brought on through the evil and impiety of others. We will explore God's ability to deliver in the face of the communal ills of injustice and oppression.

Beginning in verse 37, the Psalmist discusses God's ability to bless and deliver His people while they are in the land of promise. This Psalm celebrates God's comprehensive aptitude for deliverance. God delivers by land and by sea (v. 23–32). In verses 33–35, God is depicted as siding with the poor/oppressed. These verses provide an important context for our lesson, particularly v. 38. In verse 38, the Psalmist discusses how God can prosper His people. In verse 39, the Psalmist states that even if God's people should diminish due to the ill treatment of oppression, sorrow, trouble or grief, God would deliver them.

With the conditions of deliverance laid out the Psalmist now begins illuminating on the nature of God's deliverance. He says that God would side with His people by pouring contempt on their oppressors (v. 40). God sides with His people as a vocal and visible ally by standing against the force(s)/entity that opposes His people's flourishing and well-being. This is great news particularly for us today, as we live in a world in which people are afraid to stand up and denounce evil, yet we can take solace that God is not such an ally. The Psalmist says God pours contempt on their leaders because they are at the helm of oppression or injustice. God will cause the oppressors to wander in the wastelands. The wilderness/wasteland can take on a broad array of meanings.

What is clear, however, is that God will deliver His people. The Psalmist exclaims that God raises the poor from their affliction. God blesses them indeed.

The Psalmist invokes the imagery of a well-cared for and multiplying flock of sheep (v. 41). This is appropriate as he's already seen God as a shepherd leading and shepherding His people across the wilderness, and even the stormy waters of the sea throughout the Psalm.

IV. PRAISE, PAUSE, AND CONSIDER (PSALM 107:42–43)

Finally, the Psalmist reaches his climactic point. Namely, God delivers on account of His devotion and faithfulness to His Word. The Psalmist concludes by calling us to think and reflect on the mighty acts of God both in Israel's history as well as our own.

Verse 42 says that praise is the right response for the righteous. Indeed, let the redeemed of the Lord say so. In addition, the Psalmist says the wicked will pause, that is cease and shutter from their ways.

When God delivers, God's people praise in triumph, but the enemies of God pause in terror! Whenever we see God reverse our circumstances, we should praise God. Verse 43 suggests that the wise should think closely and purposely look into God's deliverance, because by exploring God's deliverance we more fully come to an understanding of God's covenant love.

THE LESSON APPLIED

God is clearly in the deliverance business. The Psalmist in our lesson encourages Israel to give thanks to God for God's deliverance. In our lesson, God's deliverance is explicitly tied to the faithfulness of God to His people. In short, we are not delivered necessarily because we are good, but because God is good and good to us. In our lives we should thus, give God our best efforts in worship and praise.

God has delivered us all from something and or someone and as a result we should praise God. Right now, as you are reading this in preparation to share God's Word, make it a point to thank God. Reflect on the many ways God has delivered you and thank God. Encourage your class to do likewise. Finally, as delivered people let us strive to live and walk in that deliverance.

LET'S TALK ABOUT IT

Why do you suppose that people so narrowly try to limit the ways in which God can work in a person's life?

Perhaps it is because people love to make universal claims? Maybe people just prefer to function with formulas. The Psalmist lists a barrage of ways in which God can and does deliver. We can be certain and it is to be noted that God can deliver in a multitude of ways and from a mosaic of circumstances. No person can be so downcast that God can not rescue and restore them. Our journeys may not all be the same, but God will deliver.

HOME DAILY DEVOTIONAL READINGS
OCTOBER 18–24, 2021

MONDAY	TUESDAY	WEDNESDAY	THURSDAY	FRIDAY	SATURDAY	SUNDAY
God Has Done Great Things	Joy Fulfilled in Love	God's Joy Is Your Strength	Joy Fulfilled in Christ's Sacrifice	Rejoice in the Lord Always	Fullness of Joy	How Lovely Is God's Dwelling Place
Psalm 126	John 15:9–17	Nehemiah 8:9–12	Philippians 2:1–11	Philippians 4:4–9	Psalm 16	Psalm 84

THE JOY OF WORSHIP

| ADULT TOPIC: | BACKGROUND SCRIPTURE: |
| "OUR HOUSE" | PSALM 84 |

PSALM 84

King James Version

HOW amiable are thy tabernacles, O LORD of hosts!

2 My soul longeth, yea, even fainteth for the courts of the LORD: my heart and my flesh crieth out for the living God.

3 Yea, the sparrow hath found an house, and the swallow a nest for herself, where she may lay her young, even thine altars, O LORD of hosts, my King, and my God.

4 Blessed are they that dwell in thy house: they will be still praising thee. Selah.

5 Blessed is the man whose strength is in thee; in whose heart are the ways of them.

6 Who passing through the valley of Baca make it a well; the rain also filleth the pools.

7 They go from strength to strength, every one of them in Zion appeareth before God.

8 O LORD God of hosts, hear my prayer: give ear, O God of Jacob. Selah.

9 Behold, O God our shield, and look upon the face of thine anointed.

10 For a day in thy courts is better than a thousand. I had rather be a doorkeeper in the house of my God, than to dwell in the tents of wickedness.

11 For the LORD God is a sun and shield: the LORD will give grace and glory: no good thing will he withhold from them that walk uprightly.

12 O LORD of hosts, blessed is the man that trusteth in thee.

New Revised Standard Version

HOW lovely is your dwelling place, O LORD of hosts!

2 My soul longs, indeed it faints for the courts of the Lord; my heart and my flesh sing for joy to the living God.

3 Even the sparrow finds a home, and the swallow a nest for herself, where she may lay her young, at your altars, O LORD of hosts, my King and my God.

4 Happy are those who live in your house, ever singing your praise. Selah

5 Happy are those whose strength is in you, in whose heart are the highways to Zion.

6 As they go through the valley of Baca they make it a place of springs; the early rain also covers it with pools.

7 They go from strength to strength; the God of gods will be seen in Zion.

8 O LORD God of hosts, hear my prayer; give ear, O God of Jacob! Selah

9 Behold our shield, O God; look on the face of your anointed.

10 For a day in your courts is better than a thousand elsewhere. I would rather be a door-keeper in the house of my God than live in the tents of wickedness.

11 For the LORD God is a sun and shield; he bestows favor and honor. No good thing does the LORD withhold from those who walk uprightly.

12 O LORD of hosts, happy is everyone who trusts in you.

MAIN THOUGHT: Blessed are they that dwell in thy house: they will be still praising thee. Selah. (Psalm 84:4, KJV)

LESSON SETTING
Time: Unknown
Place: Unknown

LESSON OUTLINE
I. Desire for the Presence of God (Psalm 84:1–4)
II. Desire for the Person of God (Psalm 84:5–8)
III. Desire for the Participation of God (Psalm 84:9)
IV. Devotional Praise for God's Presence, Person, and Participation (Psalm 84:10–12)

UNIFYING PRINCIPLE
There are times when the pressures of life are a heavy burden to carry. Where can people go to find the pressures of life lifted and then enjoy a period of celebration? The Psalmist recounts a uniquely joyful experience when worshiping in the temple.

INTRODUCTION
In our lesson today we will explore this pearl of a Psalm as it illuminates the Psalmist's longing for God's house.

The Psalmist's longing is not one that we have to work hard to imagine. No! We know these pangs all too well, particularly those of us who have been sidelined the hardest by the social distancing protocols of COVID-19. Having had to make do with virtual worship, we, like the Psalmist, long for (or at least have longed for) the sanctuary too. As we explore this Psalm of longing we will note the Psalmist's desire for the presence of God, the person of God, the participation of God, and conclude with the Psalmist's devotional praise for God's presence, person, and participation in the life of the Psalmist and Israel.

EXPOSITION

I. DESIRE FOR THE PRESENCE OF GOD (PSALM 84:1–4)
The heading of this Psalm grants a few important observations for the diligent student of the Bible. First there is the mention of the word *gittith*, the meaning of this word is unclear. Some scholars maintain it is derived from Gath and refers to a person from that region, others maintain that it is a musical instrument. This commentator sides with the second understanding because of the way Hebrew TANAKH translates this Psalm's heading "for the leader on the gittith." (Jewish Study Bible) This word is also found in the titles of Psalms 8 and 81.

The heading also discloses that this Psalm is a Psalm of the sons of Korah. The sons of Korah have a profound and complicated history. You may recall that Korah led a rebellion against Moses in which he conspired to get 250 community leaders to revolt against Moses while the children of Israel were wandering in the wilderness (see Numbers 16). God dealt severely with Korah and his fellow rebels God killed Korah and his co-rebels, but apparently the sons of Korah remained (Numbers 26:9–11). It is plausible to believe that the sons of Korah were so moved by God's demonstration of power that they recommitted themselves to the worship and praise of God, serving with regard to music in the temple (2 Chronicles 20:19).

In the opening verses of this Psalm the writer openly discuses their longing to be in God's presence. He begins by boasting of the beauty of God's tabernacle, "how amiable" or "how lovely" the Hebrew word used for amiable/lovely is *yedidoth*. This word communicates far more than just aesthetic beauty. It conveys the concept of being "beloved." Coupled with verse 2 "my soul longs…" The Jewish Study Bible posits "There is almost a mystical quality in the intensity of the psalmist's desire to be in God's presence."

The Psalmist in the opening two verses is thus voicing a strong desire to be in the presence of God. Note the Psalmist calls out for God and longs with entirety of their whole existence. The figurative language of poetry is poignant, the Psalmist says essentially their body and soul cry out for God's presence. For the Psalmist the presence of God is like an addiction and they desperately need their fix. This is a disposition we ought to emulate.

It is also important to note that the Psalmist is yearning for the presence of God. The ancient Israelites equated God, God's self, with their place of worship.

For them God was very much present in the tabernacle and later in the temple because God sat enthroned on the Ark of the Covenant. The Psalmist's yearning is a yearning for God's presence and not just a place, because it was God's presence that made the place of worship special and not just a place. The same holds true today. God's presence makes the house of worship beautiful.

Lord of Hosts is one of the many names/titles for God. It is one that elicits images of strength. God is the Lord, the leader of the heavenly forces. This subtle nod to one of God's attributes is more significant when we consider the next verse. The strength and magnificent power of God Almighty (Lord of Hosts) is contrasted to the smallness and frailty of tiny nesting birds, sparrows and swallows. Thus within these opening verses we are introduced to a multidimensional God who can balance incredible beauty with awesome strength, and do both with an attentive carefulness. What an incredible God we serve!

The Psalmist is a bit envious of the birds who are able to literally live in God's presence, or at the least near the altar of God, whereas he, a sojourning traveler, will make his sacrifice and then return home.

Moreover, it states that the birds are able to raise their children in the presence of God, whereas he and his family will have to return home. Here the Psalmist desires not just to abide in the presence of God for his own sake, but also a holy desire for his whole family to abide in the presence of God. Sparrows are typically depicted as worthless or insignificant, while swallows are depicted as restless (*Boice Expositional Commentary*). Therefore it suggests that even the most insignificant and restless of us may find ourselves becoming symbols of delight and inspiration to others when in the presence of God.

Verse four makes plain the Psalmist's preceding argument. Those who are able to dwell in the presence of God are "blessed", literally happy.

The word *Selah* follows. The term *Selah* is most likely a music term. Scholars are not entirely certain of its meaning or etymology, it is used heavily throughout the Psalms and appears typically at major points of separation within a Psalm which is why the Septuagint translates it as "interlude" and many modern thinkers regard it as a musical rest.

II. DESIRE FOR THE PERSON OF GOD (PSALM 84:5–8)

The Psalmist now elaborates on their desire for the person of God. By person of God we mean the understanding of God as a living being, an entity with whom we can love, desire and miss.

The Psalmist opens by stating "Blessed is the man whose strength is in thee". The phrase "strength in thee" can be understood as "finding refuge" or taking confidence in God. Thus, the Psalmist is suggesting that true happiness and blessed bliss come from trusting in God. It is important to note the shift, no longer is the psalmist discussing the presence of God, the Psalmist here is looking to the personable nature of God. The Psalmist posits that God is an entity, one whom we can glean strength from by trusting and placing our confidence. Thus, the Psalmist suggests that those who are in God's (place) presence are blessed (vv.1–4) as are those who make God our place of refuge.

The latter portion of verse five ascribes the same happiness or blessedness to those who have set their heart on the pilgrimage to God's holy house. This line may have served as encouragement to pilgrims whether they were making their ways to God's holy habitation as a ritual or whether they were approaching the Holy land after exile.

"Valley of Baca": "Baca" can be translated as "weeping" as it is in some Bible translations or "balsam tree". The valley ('*emeq*-literally low land) here may have been an arid place on the way to Jerusalem. The exact location of the valley of Baca is unknown, however, it is apparent that it is a distinct place on the way to Jerusalem. Some interpreters hold this place as Rephaim, a place known for its baca trees (2 Sam. 5:22–24). This allows us to understand this specific local as a place of difficulty either a low place, a dry place, or both. This would suggest that on our way to either God's house or a more personal relationship with God we may expect to encounter some difficulties along the way.

However, the Psalmist also reminds us that there is good news even in the valley because they "make it a well; the rain also filleth the pools." The journey to God is a journey of joy where the low dry places can become wells, springs of proverbial joy. This is true of our walk with God, God allows us to find nourishment and celebration in the very things that may have once troubled us. The Psalmist continues to list the benefits of seeking an audience with God. The Psalmist says pilgrims supernaturally go from strength to strength.

This is supernatural indeed. Typically a traveler would go from strength to weakness through fatigue, but not so with those who seek God. God walks with us and thus we go from strength to strength.

Embedded within Black history are our enslaved ancestors who after working all day in the fields would steal away at night and instead of resting, worship God all night. Indeed, they went from strength to strength as the joy of the Lord was their strength (Nehemiah 8:10).

This portion of the Psalm concludes with a prayer, asking for an audience with God—he emphasizes "hear my prayer God". This is the heart of worship to have an audience with God. We can be assured that God indeed hears our prayers (1 Peter 3:12).

III. Desire for the Participation of God (Psalm 84:9)

In this verse the Psalmist references "our shield" and "our anointed." Here the Psalmist is speaking about Israel's king. It is good to note that the Psalmist has already named God as their king (v. 3).

Indeed God was truly the King of Israel, the rulers of Israel were to be regarded as the sons of God. This was a reality, that in time was lost on the monarchy, and it may be a feat lost on us today. God is King. God is supreme ruler of every nation and government. We do well to remember that and make Him King of our lives by removing ourselves from the throne.

The Psalmist prays for God's participation in the life of the King and therefore in the life of their society. This suggests that we as believers should busy ourselves in prayer for our leaders. The Psalmist asks that God be attentive to the king, this is a notable prayer. He is essentially saying Lord, watch the king.

IV. Devotional Praise for God's Presence, Person, and Participation (Psalm 84: 10–12)

The Psalmist concludes this praise-Psalm with deep devotional praise thanking God for God's beautiful amiable presence and dependable personhood and participation in the life of Israel.

Verse 10 is a beautiful passage used regularly by saintly ushers who stand attentively at the doors of our modern sanctuaries. There is great merit for this. The Psalmist here states in a sense that they would much rather stand at the threshold, barely inside the house of worship, than to be all the way in comfortably with the wicked. Imagine that, the writer says "I'd rather be on the outskirts with God than be in the in-crowd seated comfortably with the wicked." Better to be uncomfortable and standing with God than be seated comfortably with the wicked. In the Bible, participating in evil and partnering with wicked sinful people is always a path of least resistance and ease, whereas the path of holiness and godliness seems to constitute and imply some discomfort (Ps. 1; Abraham chose the difficulty of the hill country, whereas Lot took the lush and easy plains of Sodom Genesis 13).

In verse 11, the Psalmist shows devotion to God by listing God as sun and shield. Hence God is light, the source of all things necessary for life, heat, etc. and protection. It is out of the sun that we are given light to grow food to eat, without it, all that is ceases to be alive. In our modern minds we know that all things orbit around the sun, which is true of God.

Indeed all things come of thee and in Him do we have our very being (see, 1 Chronicles 29:14; John 1:4; Acts 17:28). Moreover, the Psalmist also reiterates ultimate protection and sustenance come from the Lord God Almighty. This is further echoed in their praise to God for God's grace and glory. Indeed the Psalmist states that God does not withhold any good thing from His people.

This phrase can also be translated as God's bounty which implies the harvest rains. Again the Psalmist here is making the point that in God lies all that is necessary for life and productivity. The Psalmist concludes with the statement that happiness resides in trusting God.

THE LESSON APPLIED

Life is a journey, one fraught with low moments, dry spells, and an otherwise wide assortment of difficulties. However, the Psalmist reminds us that in God's presence lies the fullness of joy and that God holds pleasure securely in His powerful right hand (Psalm 16:11). We should cultivate the disposition to yearn and deeply desire with all of our being the presence and person of God. We do this by fixing our mind and heart on worship; making it a must-do activity. Remember that God does not stand detached from politics, therefore let us entreat heaven for God's intervention in the political arena. At the least let us pray that God watches and holds accountable our elected officials even if God uses us to answer our own prayers. Let us make it our business to prefer the sometimes-uncomfortable path of sojourning with God more than the easy street of tabernacling with wrong-doers. Finally, by all means let us make it our business to place our trust, our confidence, and our strength in God–this is the only way to be truly happy. "Trust in Him who will not leave you whatsoever years may bring….hold to God's unchanging hand." Let us continually seek God's presence and eagerly return to God's house. We should be convinced there is always a special blessing reserved to make it worth the while to be in God's house!

LET'S TALK ABOUT IT

Why did this turn into a Selah moment in the sanctuary?

Selah is a place to pause and consider, God's abode is a place to pause and consider. The sons of Korah started out in a very bad way, but somewhere along the way they repented and began to sing God's praises. It is highly likely, there is something both reinvigorating and reorienting about being in the amazing presence of God. The Psalmist has a similar experience in Psalm 73. Being in the presence of God should cause us to all pause and consider, especially when we're in the sanctuary of God's House. When we consider Israel's history, we also remember that for them the presence of God was personified and represented by the Ark of the Covenant. The Ark was portable, it moved with them through the wilderness and at other times in their history, this suggests to us that the presence of God can also exist beyond the hallowed walls of the church sanctuary too.

At any rate, when we encounter God's presence we do well to pause and consider. It is this one holy act that may move us from enemy of God as Korah once was to being a friend of God whose acts are recorded in a book of life as the Sons of Korah.

HOME DAILY DEVOTIONAL READINGS
OCTOBER 25–31, 2021

MONDAY	TUESDAY	WEDNESDAY	THURSDAY	FRIDAY	SATURDAY	SUNDAY
A Song of Praise Is Fitting	David's Music Soothes Saul	Paul and Silas Sing in Prison	Praise the Name of the Lord	Psalms, Hymns, and Spiritual Songs	Making Melody to God	Praise God with Musical Instruments
Psalm 147:1–7	1 Samuel 16:14–23	Acts 16:23–26	Psalm 148	Colossians 3:12–17	Psalm 149	Psalm 150

PRAISE GOD WITH MUSIC

ADULT TOPIC: "I JUST WANT TO CELEBRATE"	BACKGROUND SCRIPTURE: PSALM 147; 148; 149; 150

PSALM 149:1–5; 150:1–6

King James Version

PRAISE ye the LORD. Sing unto the LORD a new song, and his praise in the congregation of saints.

2 Let Israel rejoice in him that made him: let the children of Zion be joyful in their King.

3 Let them praise his name in the dance: let them sing praises unto him with the timbrel and harp.

4 For the LORD taketh pleasure in his people: he will beautify the meek with salvation.

5 Let the saints be joyful in glory: let them sing aloud upon their beds.

••• 150:1–6 •••

PRAISE ye the LORD. Praise God in his sanctuary: praise him in the firmament of his power.

2 Praise him for his mighty acts: praise him according to his excellent greatness.

3 Praise him with the sound of the trumpet: praise him with the psaltery and harp.

4 Praise him with the timbrel and dance: praise him with stringed instruments and organs.

5 Praise him upon the loud cymbals: praise him upon the high sounding cymbals.

6 Let every thing that hath breath praise the LORD. Praise ye the LORD.

New Revised Standard Version

PRAISE the LORD! Sing to the Lord a new song, his praise in the assembly of the faithful.

2 Let Israel be glad in its Maker; let the children of Zion rejoice in their King.

3 Let them praise his name with dancing, making melody to him with tambourine and lyre.

4 For the LORD takes pleasure in his people; he adorns the humble with victory.

5 Let the faithful exult in glory; let them sing for joy on their couches.

••• 150:1–6 •••

PRAISE the LORD! Praise God in his sanctuary; praise him in his mighty firmament

2 Praise him for his mighty deeds; praise him according to his surpassing greatness!

3 Praise him with trumpet sound; praise him with lute and harp!

4 Praise him with tambourine and dance; praise him with strings and pipe!

5 Praise him with clanging cymbals; praise him with loud clashing cymbals!

6 Let everything that breathes praise the LORD! Praise the LORD!

MAIN THOUGHT: Let every thing that hath breath praise the Lord. Praise ye the Lord. (Psalm 150:6, KJV)

LESSON SETTING
  Time: Unknown
  Place: Unknown
LESSON OUTLINE
  I. Praise God: Here's How
     (Psalm 149:1–3, 5; 150:3–5)
  II. Praise God: Here's Why
     (Psalm 149:4; 150:2)
  III. Praise God: Here's Where
     (Psalm 149:1; 150:1, 6)

UNIFYING PRINCIPLE
People choose different ways to express their emotions. What are some of the ways that expressions of victory and joy can be shared? Psalms 149 and 150 share great praise for who God is and the joy of praising God with all of who we are.

INTRODUCTION
Today we explore Psalms 149 and Psalms 150, the final two Psalms/songs in Israel's hymn book. These two Psalms agree thematically with Psalms 146–150 which all begin and end with the command "Praise the Lord" (Hallelujah)! Moreover, these psalms are used in daily morning prayer and are sometimes referred to as the *Daily Hallel (P'sukei D'zimrah)*. These psalms when taken together can be seen as a textbook on praising God attending to how to praise God, why we should praise God, where we should praise God and finally who should praise God. It is good news indeed that the Bible points out clearly the path of praise.

EXPOSITION
I. PRAISE GOD: HERE'S HOW
   (PSALM 149:1–3, 5; 150:3–5)
Both Psalms begin with the robust charge to praise God! There is no debate that God should be praised. Moreover, the verbiage of the Psalter is expressive and enthusiastic, the Psalmist here gives us an invitational order to praise God. The word used here in Hebrew is *halal*. *Halal* is typically translated as praise, however it should be noted that when David found himself behind enemy lines and in a bind he feigned madness (1 Samuel 21:13) and the word used there is also *halal*. Which gives us a clue into the nature of this complicated word (command) to praise God (literally *Halal Yah/Yahweh*) is to really make some serious noise, dance, or by some extemporaneous means celebrate the goodness and majesty of God.

In addition to honoring God with a hallelujah, a barrage of other acceptable ways to honor God in praise are listed. While this is a very robust list, it is not an exhaustive list. The Holy Spirit may indeed move on any believer and cause us to emote in ways that transcend this list.

Worship includes singing, and singing a new song. Singing is a part of worship. There is no mention of voice quality, tone, or ability to sing on key. The only qualifier for the biblical notion of singing is having a God-given voice and using it. The Psalmist says sing! Moreover, the Psalmist also suggests that worship entails singing a new song to God. There comes a time in worship in which we may be required to do some new things for God. We as worshipers should not mind updating our songs. The Psalmist says sing a new song to God!

The next requirement for worship is to rejoice—to celebrate (שָׂמַח *sâmach*) which is a word that means to brighten to become gleeful. We can understand this word as an invitation to get glad in God. Thus worship requires a change in our disposition, we should become cheerful and happy in God, about God, and with God. Why? The Psalmist says because God made us! We are also instructed to be joyful before our God our king. The word used for joyful means to spin around, which when taken in concert with rejoicing suggests that worship is not just about a feeling or disposition, it correlates into tangible actions. Worship is work, it is excitement, it is an embodied activity. It is an act of service we perform for God our king who happens to be the audience and judge of our worship.

The Psalmist asserts in verse three that we can also worship God in dance and with instrumental accompaniment. Both song and dance have been a part of many of our preceding lessons about worship.

Dancing seems to flow as the next logical progression in this Psalm. As one moves from singing to embodied expressions of excitement, dance seems next on the list. Worship is thus a whole-body, progressive activity. One should note, there is no prescribed dance (i.e. there is no holy dance) only the declaration that our dance should be aimed at God's amusement in praise. It is interesting and beguiling that many a saint will learn all the newest dance crazes for amusement, but refrain from dancing for God in adoration, only because they have been misled to think God only grants a special dance, the Psalmist is helpful here, he says merely to praise God with our dance.

There is also the mention of musical accompaniment, the Bible depicts the incorporation of musical instruments in worship. The timbrel was a percussion instrument. Archaeologists suggest it may have been the equivalent to our modern tambourine or some other sort off hand held percussion instrument. The lyre was an ancient handheld version of the harp. The Psalms instruct us that the Bible gives credence for the inclusion of drums (percussions) and stringed instruments, which stands to reason that the modern counterparts to those instruments should logically be used in service to God in worship today.

In verse five, the Psalmist further demonstrates how we should praise God. The Psalmist says "Let the faithful exult in glory; let them shout for joy upon their couches" (Jewish Study Bible) The word "saints" (*chasid*) translates well as faithful, hence the JSB's preference in translation. Saints in our modern lexicon is often used to denote any believer or church attender, however, the Psalmist expresses different intention here. The Psalmist is exclaiming that those who are devoted to God, i.e., good, faithful respond to God. Moreover, the Psalmist says they are "joyful" (`alaz), a word which ruminates with the image of a person rejoicing in triumph. Indeed the root of the word paints the picture *of* someone shouting for joy. Those who are faithful to God celebrate God. Moreover, they do this with glory (*kabod*). Here the word suggests honor. The primitive root of the word has to do with weight or weightiness. The term when used here suggests pride. Thus, the Psalmist is suggesting that the faithful cheer on God with pride! They cheer God in the same way a sports fan cheers their team when they win or lose.

The Psalmist concludes his instructions to us in this passage by suggesting that the faithful saints of God cannot contain themselves in worship. He says they "sing aloud on their beds." We have already discussed singing, but this term is nuanced. The word used here is more than singing. It means to be overcome, to cry out, to shout for joy. Hence the Psalmist is suggesting that what we in the Black Church tradition call "shouting" or getting "happy" or "full" is a normative part of worship. Exploration of worship demonstrates that emotions are a huge component. Believers should demonstratively worship God through the movement of our bodies, voices, with great vigor and enthusiasm. Moreover, this kind of carrying on is not just appropriate in the assembly (corporate worship) but that it also should regularly happen privately and at home! Beds here at this verse is actually a type of couch found in ancient abodes. The Psalmists use is poetic and points to the relevancy of religiosity as expressed in worship and praise at home. In essence, the Psalmist says worship is not just reserved for the church building, but it is also appropriate at home as well. Indeed, one ought not have a religion that they cannot feel sometimes.

In verses 3–5 of this Psalm, our lesson gives us more instructions on how faithful believers can worship and praise God.

The Psalmist begins with the mention of praising God on musical instruments. This time a different array of instruments is mentioned: the trumpet (ram's horn), the psaltery (lute, ancient predecessor to the guitar/banjo), the harp (lyre), the timbrel (hand drum) is again mentioned only this time with dance as well, stringed instruments (which can be understood as anything within the stringed family), organs (piped instruments-organs as we know them today were not invented until 3 B.C.), and cymbals (both loud and high sounding).

With regard to the instruments, one notices that in this list the trumpet is mentioned and mentioned first. Theologian Charles Spurgeon suggests there may have been a good reason for it's primacy in the list. "The sound of trumpet is associated with the grandest and most solemn events, such as the giving of the law, the proclamation of Jubilee, the coronation of Jewish kings, and the raging of war." Hence the trumpet blast, or blowing of the ram's horn was in invitation and invocation, an auspicious act indeed.

II. PRAISE GOD: HERE'S WHY (PSALM 149:4; 150:2)

In this section of the lesson we explore the "why" of worship through the lens of the Psalmist. In these passages the Psalmists give rationales for the radical and passionate worship they prescribe. Let's take a look.

Here the Psalmist states "the Lord taketh pleasure in his people" (KJV). Here the Psalmist literally states that God delights in God's people. The word used here is *ratsah*, which means to be pleased with and to accept favorably. It has word connotations that suggest the feelings of delight and relief when a debt is satisfied.

Thus one can think of how it feels when one pays off a debt like a Christmas layaway, a car note, or mortgage; or one can think of how it feels when someone pays you back the money they owe you. In either case the feeling of extreme delight is the feeling the psalmist says God has toward God's people. This alone should be enough to make us want to worship God.

What great news God finds delight in us, imperfections and all.

Moreover, the Psalmist says God "will beautify the meek with salvation" (KJV). Literally, that God will "adorn(s) the lowly with victory" (JSB) or as the CEB puts it "God will beautify the poor with saving help." Each of these translations suggests that because of God's favorable disposition toward us, God will act benevolently on our behalf. Hence, we have a promise attached to praise. What a reason to worship and praise God. The Psalmist suggests we ought to praise God because God is in the business of working on our behalf.

In verse two, present is another reason to worship. The Psalmist says praise God for God's mighty acts and excellent greatness. These robust phrases need little exploration into the Hebrew in order to expound on them, they mean essentially just what they say. God is to be praised for His strength and powerful acts throughout history and in our own personal lives.

Likewise, God is to be praised because God is great and because God is amazing. We know God is amazing because of His powerful and head scratching acts of salvation from the impossible feat of cramming all of the magnitude of His personhood into the finitude of humanity (the Incarnation) to dying on the cross for our salvation and resurrection on the third day—God is to be praised. For parting the Red Sea to parting the modern seas of traffic and commuting cars, God is to be praised! God is great, great enough to love, die and save sinners. God is great, great enough to forgive and extend second chances. God is great and greatly to be praised!

III. PRAISE GOD: HERE'S WHERE (PSALM 149:1; 150:1, 6)

Having now already expressed that God deserves praise, and how to praise God, the lesson now instructs us where (else) this worship behavior should take place. (It has already been discussed in Psalm 149:5 that worship and praise should also occur in the home.)

Here the Psalmist lists that God should be praised literally in the congregation (assembly) of the saints (faithful). This suggests that God should be praised in God's house, this was at one point the tabernacle, then the temple, then synagogues, and now the church. The church should be the headquarters of worship and praise!

Take note, while churches maybe home to a lot of things (foreign and local missions, soup kitchens, tutoring programs, etc.) they must also never fail to be places where the worship of God takes place!

Here the Psalmist expands our understanding of where God can be worshiped. God is to be praised in the church, but also by mentioning the creation term firmament he is suggesting that God is presently being worshiped in the heavens, and that God should be worshiped anywhere under the expanse of the sky. Quite literally, the heavens and earth praise God by their very existence. Thus we can conclude that God should be worshiped any and everywhere on the planet. The Psalmist teaches us that all who have the gift of breath have the responsibility of praising God.

THE LESSON APPLIED

While there are so many ways to praise God mentioned in this lesson, from instrumentation to shouting, singing, and even dancing, we do well to remember that this list although thorough, is not exhaustive. After reading our lesson, which ways to worship resonate with you? Why?

In our lesson, our two psalmists make the collective point that we should use everything within the arsenal of our power and creativity and bend it toward the worship and praise of God. Moreover, we should leave this lesson with a thorough understanding that we are all invited and encouraged to worship and praise God, and as such we should do so heartily.

Thus, when we apply this lesson, we do so through reflection, and ask ourselves are we meeting the high bar for worship set forth by the Bible? Are we truly leaving our all on the altar for God? If we are not then now is the time to begin to formulate a new habit of uninhibited worship-worship befitting God, worship that is a lifestyle, worship that happens in public and in private.

LET'S TALK ABOUT IT

Whereas this is an often quoted Psalm entreating congregants to worship and praise, how often are its directions truly embraced? Do you think it is possible to properly praise God without any kind of emotive demonstration?

"It don't take all of that to praise the Lord!" This is a common phrase in certain circles within the Black church.

There are some who feel that worship should have some reservations and that church should be carried out with tact and decorum. While high liturgy is important, after all the Bible teaches all things should be done "decently and in order" (1 Corinthians 14:40), the Bible also teaches that God should be praised mightily. Liturgy, however, is literally the work of the people. The work of the people is to worship the Lord. So, which is it, controlled or demonstrative worship?

When we look at this lesson, we can easily deduce that it does indeed take all of that. God should be praised in accordance with His greatness and acts in history. Moreover, the Bible says that God delights in our praise. This is all the evidence we need to discern that we should worship with reverence, decency and order, but also passionately. We should not mistake reverence, decency, and order with a lack of passion and burning fire.

Passion comes out regardless as to how deeply it is buried. Hence yes, it does take all of that and more to worship God! Everything that has breath, praise the Lord!

HOME DAILY DEVOTIONAL READINGS
NOVEMBER 1–7, 2021

MONDAY	TUESDAY	WEDNESDAY	THURSDAY	FRIDAY	SATURDAY	SUNDAY
May God's Ways Be Known	The Nations Flock to Mount Zion	Make Disciples of All Nations	Gentiles Seek the Lord	All the Nations Will Glorify God	God's Servants Sealed	Multitudes Praise God
Psalm 67	Isaiah 2:1–5	Matthew 28:16–20	Zechariah 8:18–23	Psalm 86:1–11	Revelation 7:1–8	Revelation 7:9–17

ALL PEOPLE PRAISE GOD

ADULT TOPIC:	BACKGROUND SCRIPTURE:
THE REST OF THE STORY	REVELATION 7:9–17

REVELATION 7:9–17

King James Version

AFTER this I beheld, and, lo, a great multitude, which no man could number, of all nations, and kindreds, and people, and tongues, stood before the throne, and before the Lamb, clothed with white robes, and palms in their hands;

10 And cried with a loud voice, saying, Salvation to our God which sitteth upon the throne, and unto the Lamb.

11 And all the angels stood round about the throne, and about the elders and the four beasts, and fell before the throne on their faces, and worshipped God,

12 Saying, Amen: Blessing, and glory, and wisdom, and thanksgiving, and honour, and power, and might, be unto our God for ever and ever. Amen.

13 And one of the elders answered, saying unto me, What are these which are arrayed in white robes? and whence came they?

14 And I said unto him, Sir, thou knowest. And he said to me, These are they which came out of great tribulation, and have washed their robes, and made them white in the blood of the Lamb.

15 Therefore are they before the throne of God, and serve him day and night in his temple: and he that sitteth on the thronc shall dwell among them.

16 They shall hunger no more, neither thirst any more; neither shall the sun light on them, nor any heat.

New Revised Standard Version

AFTER this I looked, and there was a great multitude that no one could count, from every nation, from all tribes and peoples and languages, standing before the throne and before the Lamb, robed in white, with palm branches in their hands.

10 They cried out in a loud voice, saying, "Salvation belongs to our God who is seated on the throne, and to the Lamb!"

11 And all the angels stood around the throne and around the elders and the four living creatures, and they fell on their faces before the throne and worshiped God,

12 singing, "Amen! Blessing and glory and wisdom and thanksgiving and honor and power and might be to our God forever and ever! Amen."

13 Then one of the elders addressed me, saying, "Who are these, robed in white, and where have they come from?"

14 I said to him, "Sir, you are the one that knows." Then he said to me, "These are they who have come out of the great ordeal; they have washed their robes and made them white in the blood of the Lamb.

15 For this reason they are before the throne of God, and worship him day and night within his temple, and the one who is seated on the throne will shelter them.

16 They will hunger no more, and thirst no more; the sun will not strike them, nor any scorching heat;

MAIN THOUGHT: And I said unto him, Sir, thou knowest. And he said to me, These are they which came out of great tribulation, and have washed their robes, and made them white in the blood of the Lamb. (Revelation 7:14, KJV)

REVELATION 7:9–17

King James Version	*New Revised Standard Version*
17 For the Lamb which is in the midst of the throne shall feed them, and shall lead them unto living fountains of waters: and God shall wipe away all tears from their eyes.	17 for the Lamb at the center of the throne will be their shepherd, and he will guide them to springs of the water of life, and God will wipe away every tear from their eyes."

LESSON SETTING
Time: AD 96
Place: Patmos/Heaven

LESSON OUTLINE
  I. The Great Multitude
     Described (Revelation 7:9)
  II. The Great Multitude in Song
     (Revelation 7:10)
  III. The Angels in Song
     (Revelation 7:11–12)
  IV. The Great Multitude Defined
     (Revelation 7:13–17)

UNIFYING PRINCIPLE
Celebrations that unite people from all over the world are significant and magnificent. How can we celebrate in spite of persecution and a hostile world? The writer of Revelation proclaims that God will preserve believers from every nation, tribe, people group, and language who remain faithful to him despite hardship.

INTRODUCTION
There is a television show called *The Masked Singer*. On this show, a celebrity wears a costume and sings before a panel of judges. The judges evaluate the singer, and at the end of the show try to guess who the singer is. The show concludes with a big reveal, in which the masked singer unmasks and reveals his/her identity. In our lesson today we see an eschatological version of this. We are introduced to a great multitude whose identity remains anonymous (at least initially). Our lesson then observes the incredible song of praise sung by this large choir to the enthroned Creator and their Redeemer, the subsequent praise song from the celestial beings surrounding the throne of God, and then concludes with a huge unmasking, as the identity of the anonymous large, eschatological, mass choir is revealed. The answer may surprise us.

EXPOSITION

I. THE GREAT MULTITUDE DESCRIBED (REVELATION 7:9)
Our lesson literally begins in a manner that is out of this world. Here we find a group of people so numerous that they can not be counted. This should astound now as much as it astounded John's audience.

Humankind has had a knack for counting from the earliest days of our existence. We count, quantify, and categorize everything. Yet with all of our acuity in this manner, John says in heaven, there will be a number so wondrous, so immense that not even the best of human conventions and calculations will be able to quantify.

Moreover, this great number is all-inclusive. It incorporates people from every nation and nationality, from every tribe, and from every language. The implications of this description should not be missed on us today. If we as humans have specialized in counting, then we have surely mastered dividing. We presently divide ourselves in nearly any way imaginable: along racial, ethnic, national, cultural, geographical, linguistic, socio-economical, ideological, and political lines. We live in an era of renewed tribalism. People in the same region may even find themselves divided over hobbies, and sports teams. We as people seem to be able to divide ourselves and to do so with finality! Yet this wondrous crowd is composed of people as unified as they are diverse. This may indeed be one of the greatest miracles to go undetected in the whole canon of Scripture. This infers that only God has the ability to unite the whole human family.

Moreover, this multitude is dressed in all white while brandishing palm branches. The white denotes purity and victory. This group is a victorious group. The branches are the ancient tools of celebration. Hence, we can understand that this is a victory celebration unfolding right before John's eyes, one of immense magnitude.

II. THE GREAT MULTITUDE IN SONG (REVELATION 7:10)

John shows this great multitude opening this section up in song as worshipful expression to God. Moreover, he mentions they sing loudly with a mega voice. Let us explore the components of this end-time song of praise.

Salvation (victory) belongs to our God, this is to say that victory/salvation is a God thing. Saving is God's business it is what God does. God saves us from sin, situations, and even ourselves. We do not earn salvation. It belongs to God and God freely gives salvation to us!

God who sits on the throne, here John says this multitude rejoices in the fact that God is seated on the throne of eternity.

This suggests that God is praise worthy because of God's sovereignty. To be sovereign is to have supreme rule, to be powerful, and finally to possess agency in and of oneself without need for assistance from another. Thus, we get a peak into the reality that it is not the emperor of Rome who really holds power, it is God, the cosmic Creator who is truly all powerful and sovereign. John says in the Scripture, that the large assembly is praising God because He's seated on the throne. God is in charge. Unlike the Roman emperors tormenting the early church, demanding to be worshiped as gods, who came and went, God's reign is eternal. God the Creator of heaven and earth and God never grows weary, there is no searching of His understanding.

God's sovereignty was good news to John's audience as it is to us today. Despite the instability of the world around us we can take great delight in God's sovereignty. John's picture reminds us that the very things that are over our heads are still and will always perpetually be under God's feet. Moreover, the vicissitudes of life that cause us to be up in arms are not enough to disturb God.

The Lamb in verse 10 is clearly Jesus. Here the imagery reminds us that Jesus is indeed the Lamb of God (John 1:29) who takes away the sins of the world. He alone is worthy of worship (Rev. 5) and worthy to open the seal. The imagery of the Lamb is one that speaks to the sacrifice of Christ on the cross as an eternal offering for our sins. It is also important to note the stark contrast between the symbols of Christ the victor and the symbols of Rome. Rome was envisioned as an eagle, a violent hunting bird. Rome like an eagle with outstretched wings was always violent and in search of new people and lands to devour. Christ on the other hand, a Lamb, meek and slain, achieves victory by His conquest of death. Through His outstretched arms on a Roman cross, Jesus conquered the whole of humanity with peace, whereas Rome failed through military arms. To celebrate the Lamb is to celebrate God's conquest of the heart; it is to celebrate Jesus' rule through submission. It is to celebrate a whole new way of being in the world.

III. THE ANGELS IN SONG (REVELATION 7:11–12)

Up to this point, John has been discussing the worship acts of a large victorious multitude of people from all over the world. In these verses, he discloses how the praise of the multitude/ mass choir sparks a reaction from the other members of the heavenly court. This suggests that passionate praise and worship solicits a response of more passionate praise and worship. The past generations understood this well, they would fan the flames of worship and say "catch on saints, catch on church." Real praise begets real praise.

The angels sing their song beginning with "Amen". We end our prayers with "Amen", but these angels begin their praise with it. "Amen" here likely means surely, it is a means of ascribing firm assent/agreement. Perhaps the angels are in strong agreement with the song of the multitude (this is highly plausible), perhaps they are asserting that their own ensuing praise song is also true, or both.

They continue to sing God's praise saying "blessing", *eulogia* (ευλογια), literally good words, in this case words of praise and commendation belong to God. As do "glory", *doxa* (δοζα), a term referring to splendor and brilliance. Strong's notes "the kingly majesty which belongs to God as supreme ruler." The angels also sing God's praises for having wisdom, *sophia* (σοφια), supreme intelligence and understanding, and being worthy of thanksgiving, *eucharistia, (ευχαριστια)*, and honor, time, (τιμε), a word with connotations of value, deference. The angels also sing God's praise for God's power, *dunamis, (δυναμις)*, the word here used is where we derive our word dynamite from. Finally the angels applaud God's might, *ischus*, (ισχυς), a word denoting ability and strength. All of these attributes the angels sing and ascribe to God and moreover that these attributes characterize God for all time.

IV. THE GREAT MULTITUDE DEFINED (REVELATION 7:13–17)

John reports that as soon as the angels completed their song of praise, that he was approached by one of the elders attending the throne with a question about the identity of the white robe clad, palm waving, praise singing, partying multitude. In the ensuing conversation, John discovers that the multitude are denoted as survivors, people who have overcome the great tribulation, they are the saints who have endured martyrdom, kept the faith, and remained vigilant in their Christian witness despite temptation and cultural coercion.

Moreover, the elder further discloses that the multitude are more than survivors, they are also sanctified saints. To be sanctified is to be made holy-free from the stains of sin. These saints are sanctified because they have washed their robes in the blood of the Lamb, Jesus. No wonder these saints have robes so white, they have been purged with the strongest agent known to humankind, the cleansing blood of our Redeemer Jesus.

One should note, that sanctification is not according to humanity's efforts. True, we should aspire to do our best to remain unsullied by the world and unspotted by the wanton desires of the heart, but true holiness, true cleanliness, comes from the hand of God and not our own volition.

Only God can truly remove the stain of sin. They have been cleansed—meaning that while on earth they were sullied, perhaps their reputations were sullied, their faces tear stained, and God has cleansed them! Heaven is a place for people who have gotten their Christian uniforms dirty in service to God. God anticipates our soiled uniforms, apparently because there is already a planned mechanism to wash us clean.

The elder defines the multitude as a sheltered group, noting that God "dwells" with them. The word used here *skēnoō*, (σκενοω) means to shelter. Thus, this group is sheltered by the very sovereign God who resides on the throne of eternity.

This is a marvelous picture, the saints spend their time in the new heaven before the throne of God, praising God in perpetuity and God in turn provides them with shelter. In this world they may not have had a home, a place of belonging, but in eternity they will have shelter/dwelling, in the God of all eternity. The notion of dwelling/shelter points forward to the next

couple of verses that demonstrate God's protection, provision, empathy for those who have stood firm through their tests and trials on behalf of the name of God.

The elder further defines this multitude as people who are shepherded, treated as well cared for sheep by God the divine shepherd. Evidenced by the reality that those robed in white no longer have any need. They are not in need of food or drink. Moreover, God as the ultimate shepherd skillfully navigates them in a way in which they are no longer scorched by the sun or its heat, all the way to refreshing life giving fountains (streams) of living waters. Finally, the elder discloses that the multitude is a soothed assembly, because God wipes the tears from their eyes. When taken together, we come to see this anonymous group clearly, they are a group of survivors, sanctified by Christ, sheltered by God, shepherded by the Great Shepherd, and soothed by the ultimate Comforter.

These terms while reassuring to us, would have had an even greater impact of reassurance on John's original audience, as they often timed faced starvation, isolation, homelessness, tears, torture, and death for their resolute Christian witness in the age of the Roman Empire with its imperial theology.

In a real sense John's pastoral apocalypse was a peek into the future to reassure those suffering in the present that things were certain to get better. This beloved is as timely now as it was then. How fitting, given that we as present-day witnesses are ourselves present in that uncountable mass. It is assurance beyond measure that we should be so encouraged.

THE LESSON APPLIED

Our lesson reminds us that God is deserving of praise eternally! Through the pen of John, we get a glimpse into the eternal celebration of God. A celebration which involves all creatures redeemed and otherwise, heavenly and earthbound. Our lesson begs us to consider the eternal gloriousness of God and God's ever-lasting worthiness. As we peek ahead to a new heaven and a new earth, we must ask ourselves are we now worshiping and praising God as we should? Moreover, this lesson invites us to remember the sovereignty of God and to abstain from the temptation of living in a way that besmirches that.

As John's original audience was encouraged to hold fast to the tenants of their faith, so may we. Let us resolve to trust God and remain steadfast and unmovable always abounding in the work of our Lord knowing that our earnest, back-breaking labor is not in vain (1 Corinthians 15:58). God is redeeming all back to Himself as evidenced by the great multitude. Some of the good news is that people from all nations with various issues and struggles were included in the number. There is yet much hope for us and our inclusion with those who will praise God from everlasting to everlasting. We should follow their lead and wash our robes in the blood of the Lamb.

LET'S TALK ABOUT IT

Can you find vestments of an imperial theology in our present world?

Sure, you can, anytime we lift mere mortals or ideals to a height only rightly occupied by God we are on track to replicating the same sins as the Roman empire. Only Christ, the Lamb is worthy.

Our lesson today unfolds against the backdrop of imperial theology and the oppression that resulted from it. In John's day the emperor of Rome demanded to be worshiped as a god. In some places, it was virtually impossible to thrive and live without assenting to the empire's theology. Imperial theology made Christians walking and breathing targets because believers maintained that Jesus was Lord and the Son of God and not Caesar who carried these titles as well. The divinizing of emperors only predated Jesus' birth by about 40 years. Nonetheless it was ingrained deeply in the Roman way of life.

The empire was political and theological and so was Christianity. The same is true today. Our faith is political. Loyalty to Jesus must manifest itself into our political practice too. We cannot say Jesus is Lord and Master and then not allow His mastery and lordship to manifest in our society. He is Lord of the sanctuary and the Lord of society as well.

HOME DAILY DEVOTIONAL READINGS
NOVEMBER 8–14, 2021

MONDAY	TUESDAY	WEDNESDAY	THURSDAY	FRIDAY	SATURDAY	SUNDAY
Clap Your Hands, All You Peoples	An Everlasting Kingdom	Glory to God Now and Forever	The Lord Is King Forever	God's Faithful Witnesses	The Lord Is Robed in Majesty	A Crescendo of Praise
Psalm 47	Daniel 4:34–37	Jude 20–25	Psalm 10:12–18	Revelation 11:3–10	Psalm 93	Revelation 11:11–19

PRAISE FOR GOD'S ETERNAL REIGN

ADULT TOPIC:	BACKGROUND SCRIPTURE:
WHO'S IN CHARGE HERE?	REVELATION 11

REVELATION 11:15–19

King James Version	*New Revised Standard Version*
AND the seventh angel sounded; and there were great voices in heaven, saying, The kingdoms of this world are become the kingdoms of our Lord, and of his Christ; and he shall reign for ever and ever.	THEN the seventh angel blew his trumpet, and there were loud voices in heaven, saying, "The kingdom of the world has become the kingdom of our Lord and of his Messiah, and he will reign forever and ever."
16 And the four and twenty elders, which sat before God on their seats, fell upon their faces, and worshipped God,	16 Then the twenty-four elders who sit on their thrones before God fell on their faces and worshiped God,
17 Saying, We give thee thanks, O LORD God Almighty, which art, and wast, and art to come; because thou hast taken to thee thy great power, and hast reigned.	17 singing, "We give you thanks, Lord God Almighty, who are and who were, for you have taken your great power and begun to reign.
18 And the nations were angry, and thy wrath is come, and the time of the dead, that they should be judged, and that thou shouldest give reward unto thy servants the prophets, and to the saints, and them that fear thy name, small and great; and shouldest destroy them which destroy the earth.	18 The nations raged, but your wrath has come, and the time for judging the dead, for rewarding your servants, the prophets and saints and all who fear your name, both small and great, and for destroying those who destroy the earth."
19 And the temple of God was opened in heaven, and there was seen in his temple the ark of his testament: and there were lightnings, and voices, and thunderings, and an earthquake, and great hail.	19 Then God's temple in heaven was opened, and the ark of his covenant was seen within his temple; and there were flashes of lightning, rumblings, peals of thunder, an earthquake, and heavy hail.

LESSON SETTING
Time: AD 96
Place: Patmos/Heaven

LESSON OUTLINE
I. The Announcement of The Inauguration Of Christ's Kingdom (Revelation 11:15)

II. The Elders' Adoration Filled Announcement (Revelation 11:16–18)

III. The Heavenly Temple Celebrates Christ's Reign (Revelation 11:19)

MAIN THOUGHT: And the seventh angel sounded; and there were great voices in heaven, saying, The kingdoms of this world are become the kingdoms of our Lord, and of his Christ; and he shall reign for ever and ever. (Revelation 11:15, KJV)

Unifying Principle

Celebrations are ways of culminating a unique event, and creating new ways of being in community. How do people celebrate in a hostile world? Revelation helps us to understand that all of the world is moving toward the just, eternal reign of God.

Introduction

Trumpets make a piercing noise, this has rendered them valuable since their inception to the cause of humankind. People have used trumpets to call troops to war, announce important arrivals, and to otherwise arrest the attention of all who may hear.

It is little wonder that John paints a picture of trumpet blasts in his apocalypse, his original audience would have anticipated something of grand importance would follow. In this lesson we discover the magnitude of the importance of what follows this 7th and final trumpet blast. It should be noted that what follows elicits the praise of heavenly celestial beings and should likewise solicit our response in praise as well. As praise rings throughout heaven, so should it ring here on earth. As we read today we will discover the announcement of the inauguration of Christ's kingdom (a feat certainly befitting the blast of a cosmic trumpet), the enthusiastic dualistic adoration laden response of the heavenly elders, and finally the action packed response of the heavenly temple of God itself.

Exposition

I. The Announcement Of The Inauguration Of Christ's Kingdom (Revelation 11:15)

Our lesson commences with the seventh angel stepping out to play his heavenly fanfare. As we have seen with the previous two angels and their corresponding blasts, there has been the habit of an accompanying woe with the last two performances.

As the reader, we expect a final blast (seven is the number of completion) and a final climactic woe. We are not let down. As the trumpet sounds, John tells us that "great" (loud) voices in heaven sound off.

We are not told who these voices belong to, although our imaginations can scarcely help but run wild. When we take the King James Version translation at face value, great voices, our mind cannot help but run the gamut of great saints like Moses, John the Baptist, Elijah, Hannah, etc., who may constitute this chorus of great voices.

These voices announce the inauguration of Christ's Kingdom, saying together, "The kingdoms of this world are become the kingdoms of our Lord, and of his Christ; and he shall reign for ever and ever."

John depicts a forthcoming day in which all of the activities associated with power will be absolved by the actions and activities of God. There will be no divisive political agendas or anything of the sort, all of the energy spent of maintaining power and status will be absolved into God's kingdom. There will be no separate nations, no separate political parties, only God's reign, only God's Kingdom! Moreover, God's reign will not be like the reign of human sort, whereby empires and kingdoms rise, clash, and fall every so often; no, God's kingdom will be situated eternally. God will reign forever!

One should also note the Christology of this passage. Ownership of this forthcoming kingdom belongs to God (our

Lord) and God's anointed one (the literal meaning of Christ) the Messiah, Jesus of Nazareth. Here we see the pinnacle importance of Christ. Jesus is not just a prophet. Jesus is mightier and more substantial than an angel. He is the Messiah, the reigning monarch of eternity.

II. THE ELDERS' ADORATION FILLED ANNOUNCEMENT (REVELATION 11:16–18)

In this section we move from an anonymous heavenly inaugural announcement to the heavenly elders' adoration clad and worshipful announcement.

The elders are mentioned several times in the book of Revelation (Rev. 4:4; 5:8; 7:11; 11:16; 14:3; and 19:4). In Revelation 4:4, we learn that there are twenty-four elders, and in other verses we are introduced to their position and actions, yet we are not told in any verse in Revelation who these elders are. To be honest, their anonymity is probably only a quagmire to us as a modern audience. It is highly likely that John's original audience had a working understanding of their identity. Moreover, the specific identity of the elders, while a mystery shouldn't impede our reading and understanding of this text, because the identity of the twenty-four elders is not a vital component necessary for thorough interpretation, application, or understanding of the overall themes and meaning of the pastoral apocalyptic work of John's Revelation. Notwithstanding, we may still find ourselves and our students inquiring about their identity. Depending on any number of resources there are a variety of answers. Again it should be noted that the book of Revelation is silent, and thus all interpretations must be taken with a grain of salt. Nonetheless, this commentary understands the number to be symbolic of both Old Testament (12 tribes of Israel) and the New Testament (12 disciples see Matthew 19:28) being represented in heaven. However, we may choose to identify as the elders, their identity is not as important as their function in the book of Revelation. In Revelation, ultimately the elders (along with the other celestials) serve as worship leaders.

As celestial worship leaders, their actions are significant and worth noting, especially because of who they represent. Moreover, even in their anonymity, these elders are clearly high-ranking heavenly officials and thus by nature of their rank and heavenly positioning near the throne are worthy of emulating. Note their actions.

As they hear the heavenly announcement accompanying the seventh trumpet blast, they fall from their thrones to their faces in a posture of worship. This suggests to us, the nature of the response that God, and the Good News of God, especially the Gospel of Jesus Christ rightly warrants.

To begin, notice that the elders fall to their faces immediately. This suggests that worship has an immediacy to it. We should not wait to worship, whenever the good news of God's action in the world occurs or is announced we should in that moment worship. Worship, beloved of God, can not wait. In addition, notice that these elders respond with an embodied response, meaning they move. Their bodies are involved in worship. This suggests that our worship should also likewise involve an embodied response. Yes, our worship is a mindful activity, it is an act that begins in the mind, but it ought not just be relegated to the cognitive domain, worship should be expressed in our bodies as well. Finally, we cannot help but notice their posture. These heavenly nobles are lying face down in a posture of reverence and humility.

We do well to make this our posture before God too. When we hear the Gospel announced we should assume a posture of reverence and a posture of humility. Reverence suggests we give God and the worship of God utmost significance. This is duly noted in our modern era of virtual worship where we worship while cooking or attend to other business. The elders posture calls us onto considering whether we give worship; the presence of God or the gospel requires the same reverence. If we do not bow in body we must at least bow in the heart by being sure to show God the proper reverence warranted our Savior.

To speak of humility, means that we see ourselves rightly as people blessed but also burdened, people who are born in sin and shaped in iniquity who are ourselves in need of forgiveness, grace, and mercy. To assume a humble posture in worship is not to worry about our neighbor, so much as it is to continuously be in pursuit of our own holiness and godliness. It is to say as the saints of old, "it's me Oh Lord standing in the need of prayer."

We do well to also note the actual words the elders utter. They begin by celebrating and thanking God for the preeminent and permeating presence of Christ. Hear their words "which art, and wast, and art to come". Here we note their praise is because of the "is-ness" of Christ. In John's gospel we learn that "in the beginning was the Word" (John 1). This is the permeating preeminence of Christ, namely that there

has never been a time when Christ was not with us. John's prologue reiterates the announcement of adoration levied by the elders. Both purport that Jesus existed even before the foundations of the world were laid. The elders celebrate this reality.

Moreover, they also celebrate that Jesus is now. Interestingly enough, most modern translations do not include the KJV phrase of Jesus as the One to come. We tend to think of this as a natural progression because we think of time in a triune continuum of past, present, and future.

However, many ancient manuscripts do not contain the phrase found in the KJV, instead they refer to Jesus as the One who has been, and the One who is. This is quite acceptable, because in the same way that Jesus has always been, Jesus will always be. There is an eternal "is-ness" with Him.

Jesus is not forthcoming, because He is now, and shall forever be. We are not now or will we ever be waiting His arrival. He is now, was then, and will never cease to be. Just as the elders in John's revelation celebrated the eternal presence of Christ, we can too—particularly when we note the various ways Christ is present with us now.

In Revelation 11:17, the Word reads "because thou hast taken to thee thy great power, and hast reigned" (KJV). Here the elders continue their worshipful announcement, only now in celebration of Christ's power. The elders are rejoicing because Christ is peerless in power. The word used here for take is *lambanō* (λαμβανω), and it is an interesting word. It paints the cognitive image of someone grabbing their own possession to use it as they want. It does not suggest or imply any struggle or violence. In a real sense the elders are saying Jesus grabbed His own power from the presently prevailing powers of the world, in the same way that you and I grabbed our toothbrushes this morning. In the same way that we grabbed our tooth-brush without any struggle, contention, or any doubt that we would achieve our objective is the same way Jesus reached out one of His holy nail scarred hands and reclaimed all of His power. This implies that not only does all power belong to Jesus, but also that no earthly power has the capacity to even claim any co-power with Him. He is peerless in His power and capacity to reign.

Verse 18 reads, "And the nations were angry, and thy wrath is come, and the time of the dead, that they should be judged, and that thou shouldest give reward unto thy servants the prophets, and to the saints, and them that fear thy name, small and great; and shouldest destroy them which destroy the earth" (KJV). Herein we see Christ's final pay out—judgment, the final woe.

The elders recount the disposition of the angry nations, but despite their protest they could not delay or stop God's judgment. The elders say God's "wrath" matriculates nonetheless. In the "wrath" of God, the eternal King issues judgment. The servants of God the ultimate and inevitable King are rewarded. Prophets and saints are named explicitly, probably because of the horrid treatment they received in God's service.

The elders also recount that all who fear God's name, great and small, are also rewarded. The impetus being that in the end, God will look out for all who looked to Him, and looked out for Him doing His bidding while alive. Conversely, there is doom and destruction awaiting all who did the work of destruction while alive.

The word gē (γε) is used here for earth. It is a complex biblical word. On one hand it means land or earth. Thus, we can see God's disposition to take care of the world He created. We should take on a greater ecological concern for our world as stewards on God's behalf. On the other hand, this word is also used to denote the promised land, which is a running symbol for the providential promises of God and the wellbeing of God's people. Thus, we can also responsibly interpret this passage as a promise of impending doom awaiting anyone who worked to destroy the prom-ises of God toward His people.

III. THE HEAVENLY TEMPLE CELEBRATES CHRIST'S REIGN (REVELATION 11:19)

As soon as the elders sing their song of adoration and announcement the very holy city of heaven begins to celebrate! John notes that there are a plethora of supernat-ural phenomenon occurring (lightening, huge hail, earthquakes, even heavenly voices). Truly the heavens are declaring the glorious wondrous nature of God (Psalm 19:1). However, the greatest supernatural accompaniment of this seventh sounding of the trumpet and judgment is that the greatest mystery known to humanity will be solved, namely the location of the Ark of the Covenant. The Ark has been missing since the sack of Jerusalem by Babylon.

For centuries people have speculated as to its whereabouts, some guess Ethiopia, others estimate that due to the activity of the Knights Templar the Ark resides hidden in Europe, there are some fisherman's tales and conspiracy theories that place the Ark in the United States. No one knows. However, on that day, all of the speculation and talk will be over, the Ark will emerge as the new Babylon falls and crumbles at the holy feet of Jesus! John says he saw the Ark restored to its place in the temple. In the Holy of Holies! This paints a final picture of restoration and God's uninhibited lodging with humanity once again. Hallelujah!

THE LESSON APPLIED

God's Kingdom is inevitable! Siblings have to share toys. A brother and sister had a Fisher Price automobile. They were supposed to take turns driving, but the older brother refused to share. When it was his sister's turn, he would allow her to get in the car, and go through the motions of driving, all the while he stood outside the car pushing it and steering it wherever he wanted. He got away with this behavior for a while, until one day their mother caught him. She came up behind him and effortlessly made him release his grip of the car, then she promptly disciplined him and rewarded his sister with candy. That is the image John paints for us in our lesson.

The powers that be may be having their way today, but our divine parent is watching and will soon set the record straight. Jesus will effortlessly take away their power and pay out retribution. The Bible says it and we can be sure of it. However, until that day we should be found waiting and worshiping.

LET'S TALK ABOUT IT

In our lesson there is the constant theme of Jesus' ultimate power. Why is this a recurring theme?

The answer to that lies in an exploration of our lesson's context. John is writing pastorally to encourage his audience who were facing oppression at the hands of earthy ruling agents. Thus, John writes to constantly remind the saints and us that ultimate power resides in Christ alone, and that the powers of this world will be squarely defeated. The best way to do this is by showing that Jesus is supremely more powerful. Unlike worldly powers, Jesus does not have to fight to maintain power; it naturally belongs to Him.

Moreover, John reminds us that Jesus' victory is assured. In fact, it is so assured that John writes it as already having happened. John's encouragement thus functions like a movie preview; he gives us clips of what has already happened to entice us to participate in God's salvation motion picture as it unfolds in our lifetime. Given that in the end we win, let us run on!

HOME DAILY DEVOTIONAL READINGS
NOVEMBER 15–21, 2021

MONDAY	TUESDAY	WEDNESDAY	THURSDAY	FRIDAY	SATURDAY	SUNDAY
A Vision of Praise	Let the Heavens Be Glad	Let All God's Angels Worship Him	King of Kings, Lord of Lords	God Judges the Wicked	The Lord Rejoices over You	The Lord Almighty Reigns
Isaiah 6:1–8	1 Chronicles 16:23–34	Hebrews 1:5–14	Revelation 19:9–16	Revelation 19:17–21	Zephaniah 3:14–20	Revelation 19:1–8

REJOICING IN HEAVEN

ADULT TOPIC:	BACKGROUND SCRIPTURE:
FAMILY RESTORED	REVELATION 19

REVELATION 19:1–8

King James Version

AND after these things I heard a great voice of much people in heaven, saying, Alleluia; Salvation, and glory, and honour, and power, unto the Lord our God:

2 For true and righteous are his judgments: for he hath judged the great whore, which did corrupt the earth with her fornication, and hath avenged the blood of his servants at her hand.

3 And again they said, Alleluia And her smoke rose up for ever and ever.

4 And the four and twenty elders and the four beasts fell down and worshipped God that sat on the throne, saying, Amen; Alleluia.

5 And a voice came out of the throne, saying, Praise our God, all ye his servants, and ye that fear him, both small and great.

6 And I heard as it were the voice of a great multitude, and as the voice of many waters, and as the voice of mighty thunderings, saying, Alleluia: for the Lord God omnipotent reigneth.

7 Let us be glad and rejoice, and give honour to him: for the marriage of the Lamb is come, and his wife hath made herself ready.

8 And to her was granted that she should be arrayed in fine linen, clean and white: for the fine linen is the righteousness of saints.

New Revised Standard Version

AFTER this I heard what seemed to be the loud voice of a great multitude in heaven, saying, "Hallelujah! Salvation and glory and power to our God,

2 for his judgments are true and just; he has judged the great whore who corrupted the earth with her fornication, and he has avenged on her the blood of his servants."

3 Once more they said, "Hallelujah! The smoke goes up from her forever and ever."

4 And the twenty-four elders and the four living creatures fell down and worshiped God who is seated on the throne, saying, "Amen. Hallelujah!"

5 And from the throne came a voice saying, "Praise our God, all you his servants, and all who fear him, small and great."

6 Then I heard what seemed to be the voice of a great multitude, like the sound of many waters and like the sound of mighty thunder-peals, crying out, "Hallelujah! For the Lord our God the Almighty reigns.

7 Let us rejoice and exult and give him the glory, for the marriage of the Lamb has come, and his bride has made herself ready;

8 to her it has been granted to be clothed with fine linen, bright and pure"—for the fine linen is the righteous deeds of the saints.

MAIN THOUGHT: Let us be glad and rejoice, and give honour to him: for the marriage of the Lamb is come, and his wife hath made herself ready. (Revelation 19:7, KJV)

LESSON SETTING
Time: AD 96
Place: Patmos/Heaven

LESSON OUTLINE
I. Hallelujah Victory
(Revelation 19:1–4)
II. A Throne Room Invitation
(Revelation 19:5)
III. Praise: The Only Logical
Response (Revelation 19:6–8)

UNIFYING PRINCIPLE
People want to have victory over the wicked people in their lives and in the world. How will they find victory over the wicked? God has the final judgment of the world, and God is worthy of all praise.

INTRODUCTION
Winning and celebrating seem to go hand in hand. When we win, we celebrate. When our team wins, we celebrate too. In our lived experience, winning and celebration go hand in hand, the same holds true with God. In regards to God, we call this celebration praise. Believers are encouraged to celebrate because God is the perpetual victor in our lives and in the world. God has achieved victory over sin and Satan through the atoning work of Jesus at Calvary and so we always have a reason to celebrate.

In our lesson today, there is a scene shift from the trauma and drama on earth as God finally overturns the evil city of Babylon to the glee of heaven. It is the heavenly fanfare that warrants attention. We will explore several parties' praise each one moving us closer to the very throne of God where we receive a divine invitation to worship. We will also note the reasons for this exciting cosmic worship.

EXPOSITION

I. HALLELUJAH VICTORY (REVELATION 19: 1–4)
Our lesson begins with a change of scenery. As the preceding chapter concludes the inhabitants of earth are mourning the fall of Babylon (Revelation 18:20). The setting shifts from mourning to rejoicing in heaven. The cause for the celebration is victory. The fall/overturning of Babylon is a decisive victory for God and His people. It signifies that all who have kept the faith despite the injunctions of the empire have now been divinely vindicated.

John says he hears what sounds like a huge crowd of people in heaven. We do not know who constitutes this heavenly chorus. Some theologians speculate that this crowd consists of angels, others suggest the crowd is made of people who have been redeemed. From the textual evidence we cannot be certain, however, it is likely that this crowd is made up of people who have borne witness to and experienced the evils of the now fallen Babylon.

John reports that they use the powerful ancient praise word "Hallelujah." This word, while frequent in the Hebrew Bible (Old Testament), does not occur as regularly in the New Testament. Hallelujah, particularly as it appears in Psalms, is a strong and stirring command to praise the Lord. The command was typically tied to remembrance of God's acts of deliverance and was often utilized as a call to worship in the temple. In this instance, it functions in the same way in heaven. The heavenly crowd now rejoices as God has delivered them from the clutches of Babylon, and they are now called to worship in heaven.

This song of worship echoes earlier songs, praising God for salvation and bestowing glory and power on God. The saving work of God should always cause us to pause and respond in praise. Only a strong and absolute God can save.

In verse two, the song of the heavenly chorale continues. The theme of this worship is God's redeeming and righteous vindication. They sing of God's judgments being true and just. It is true because it is based on His own covenant faithfulness and "just" because it is based on His holy character. His judgments are both morally true and legally just (*Baker Exegetical Commentary on the New Testament – Revelation*). Moreover, the praise for God's upstanding judgments as true and just is established in God's holy and righteous dealings with Babylon (the great prostitute). John says she has corrupted the earth by her immorality, *porneia*, (πορνεια).

The KJV translates the word *porneia* as fornication, however the term is a blanket terminology for sexual immorality, thus Babylon has led to the demise of the world because she has lead others down a path that angers and dishonors God (Revelation 17:14:8; 17:2;17:4, 18:3; 18:9). In this instance, John is not necessarily pointing to the sexual practices of Babylon (Rome).

The fact that their behavior is understood in euphemisms not unlike the sexual metaphors used in the Old Testament by various prophetic voices. In short, Babylon has not only corrupted the earth but destroyed it, and thus the saints rejoice as she receives justice for her evil. We too can rejoice that, "God is not mocked: for whatsoever a person soweth, that shall they also reap" (Galatians 6:7).

In verse three, we see the absolute joy in heaven. They praise God by quoting from the vivid imagery of the prophet Isaiah which is taken from the scene describing the fall of Edom (Isaiah 34:10).

The mention of perpetual smoke is the cause for hallelujah. Smoke is war time imagery. We can easily stand alongside John's initial audience and envision the desolation of war and the smoke drifting skyward as a result of fire and debris.

The saints are excited, by this reminder of God's act against Rome. Moreover, this smoke may have an additional meaning, it may also refer to the eternal consequences of sin. At any rate the smoke associated with sinners is a pungent one, which is to be contrasted with the sweet-smelling aroma that accompanies the prayers of the saints (Revelation 8:4). The contrast between the wicked and the righteous is crystal clear.

In verse four, the heavenly praise rally gains additional participants, the elders and heavenly creatures. Moreover, the praise rally has moved more towards God's throne. John reports that the inner circle of elders and creatures surrounding God's throne have joined in praise. The celestial worshipers now exclaim their agreement with a resounding "Amen, Hallelujah!"

First, the elders and celestial creatures (beasts) are symbolic in nature. They stand in as worship leaders in the book of Revelation. They are seemingly derived from a conglomeration of other apocalyptic writings (see Isaiah 6 and Ezekiel 1).

As worship leaders they demonstrate that the Good News of God's activity always warrants a response. Notice that as soon as they hear the good news, they fall from their thrones and assume a posture of worship. In like manner, when we hear of God's victorious actions in our world, we should also worship God.

The Amen affixed here by the heavenly worship leaders is a statement of agreement, they are co-signing to the praises of the multitude in verses 1–3. This suggests they are attesting to the truth of their statements, and that they agree. They do this with praise—Hallelujah.

II. A THRONE ROOM INVITATION (REVELATION 19:5)

In verse five, John tells us that he hears a voice coming from the very throne of God. We do not know if this voice from the throne belongs to God the Creator, Christ the Lamb, or even a celestial attendant in the throne room. Nonetheless, the fact that this invitation is extended from the throne itself is significant. A summons from the throne of heaven should be seen as extremely important.

The voice extends an invitation, technically a command to praise God. This command mirrors the invitations to praise God in Psalms 150:1. The invitation is reserved for all "servants", *doulos* ($\delta o \upsilon \lambda o \varsigma$) literally slaves of God. The terminology of a slave/bondservant makes it clear that this invitation is more or less a command, as servants/slaves of God we understand that worship is an expectation, a part of our job. Moreover, the invitation is also reiterated to all who fear God. To fear God is to show God reverential obedience.

Reverential obedience is a loaded term, on one hand it means reverence and respect, but on the other hand it is the kind of reverence and respect that leads to deference, namely doing what God asks

and expects. It is self-denial and obedience to God. It constitutes true belief and thus love of God. Loving God is to do as God says (John 14:15). The mention of those great and small suggests that all have equal standing in God's eyesight and disbursement of blessings. This is good news, we live in a society that stratifies on the basis of status, but God sees us as equals and extends an invitation to us all regardless of what side of the tracks we may reside.

III. PRAISE: THE ONLY LOGICAL RESPONSE (REVELATION 19:6–8)

After disclosing the invitational command extended from the very throne of heaven, John concludes our lesson with the reasonable response of praise. In the final verses we see a resounding praise from all of the people who serve God and fear God. Bearing in mind that John's writing is pastoral in nature, we can understand his attention to detail in describing this loud and boisterous response is intentional and meant to encourage his audience.

Seeing that John's audience found themselves at odds socially and were castigated and marginalized, John is sure to show us that God has a large and sizable group of people who love Him and fear Him more than the empire. This should put the Bible reader in the mind of God's words to Elijah (1 Kings 19:18) when God encouraged the prophet by reminding him that God has a strong and numerous remnant of people still committed to righteousness. Here John tells us, this is not a strong remnant of 7,000, but a huge crowd, one that emits a sound that can be likened to the sound of Niagara Falls (rushing water) or great thunder. The images here convey not just a large sounding crowd, but also a crowd so vast that they can be heard and felt everywhere. This is a stark contrast from the experience of the early church John served in the present. This suggests that God has the ability to reverse circumstances.

This group praises God and acknowledges the power of God. The phrase in hymnic praise in verse 6 is a response to God's assertion of power. After the fall of Babylon, there is only the reign of God. Thus, the phrase translates roughly that God has begun to reign as King. This is a reoccurring cause for praise throughout the book of Revelation. This should come as no surprise, we as disciples have been taught to pray that God's kingdom would come, a time when things are on earth in the same manner they are in heaven. Now in John's revelation we see this prayer manifest. The natural response to this answered prayer is praise.

In verse seven, this great multitude insists upon rejoicing, celebrating, and giving God the glory deserved only now not for wielding absolute and amazing power, but for the arrival of the wedding day between Christ and the Church. It is good to have a contextual understanding of marriage here as marriage is a custom understood differently across differing cultural backdrops. In ancient Israel marriage was a process. It began with the betrothal period, the waiting period between betrothal and wedding (see Deuteronomy 22:23–24; Matthew 1:18–19) during which time the two families involved would negotiate the terms of the dowry, an amount paid to the bride's family.

Typically, it was only after the dowry was paid in full that the actual wedding took place. The wedding was a grand occasion, accompanied by a period of feasting and merriment (if it could be afforded). It is also worth noting, that even during the betrothal period the bride and groom were thought to be enjoined, remember in the case of our Lord's parents, Joseph thought to privately divorce Mary. This should give us some present encouragement, in that we are now the betrothed of Christ.

He is not putting us away in divorce, but is readying a prepared place for us in heaven (John 14). Given the cultural excursion into marriage, we can now see why they are rejoicing. John is foreseeing a day when the betrothal period has subsided and all that is left is the festivities of the actual marriage feast.

Moreover, in keeping with the metaphor of an ancient wedding, John says that the bride has made herself ready!

One wonders in what way might the bride have readied herself? John responds in an interesting way that is filled with relevant irony. John notes in verse eight that she (the bride) is given wonderful wedding attire. She receives fine linen that is "pure white" (CEB) meaning bright, unspotted, and clean. Here is the irony, the bride prepares herself not through the sole action of her own hand, she is in fact given what she needs to prepare. Her act is the mere reception of what God has provided.

John's depiction of the virtuous bride of the Lamb is in stark contrast to the vagabond ways of Babylon. Although beyond the confines of our printed text, we do well to remember that Babylon, the now fallen foe, was depicted in John's revelation as the great prostitute, renowned for her excessive appearance/dress (Revelation 17:4). She adorns herself in these haughty and gaudy raiment as opposed to the bride of the Lamb, who is given fine linen. Babylon the prostitute is destroyed/brought to ruin whereas the bride of the Lamb is brought into a wedding feast and the welcoming arms of her groom. (*Baker New Testament Commentary, Exposition of the Book of Revelation*).

Finally, it must be noted that the beautiful wedding gown of the Lamb are the acts of righteousness or justice performed by the saints. This should encourage us to be sure to persist in the work of justice because in the end John notes that those acts will be the only eye-catching garb Jesus will behold on that great morning.

THE LESSON APPLIED

In our lesson today, we are afforded one more final opportunity to break from the monotony of our existence to take an inside peek into heaven. There we find praise and worship occurring in unprecedented ways. Praise is not a break from our reality. Nor is it an evasion of our responsibilities, but it reminds us that God is almighty, worthy of praise, and victorious over the evils of our world. Praise does not divorce us from our present realities, if anything it encourages us to work remembering that in the end our works of righteousness and justice will be what Jesus sees on the day of our great cosmological wedding feast.

LET'S TALK ABOUT IT

Why Babylon? Who are they? Why so much happiness at their downfall?

According to the *Dictionary of Biblical Imagery*, "Babylon is one of the dread images of the Bible." There are times when Babylon is used as a proverbial if not literal rod/belt in the hand of God to chastise Israel and other nations (Jer. 21:25), and then there are times as in our lesson where we see Babylon herself being chastised by the hand of God. The biblical origin of Babylon is Nimrod (Gen. 10) and the city is steeped in idolatry, pride, and greed. Babylon is thus the symbol of empire and imperialism. She is the running metaphor for all world systems of domination and subjugation, diabolically opposing God's will for justice and human flourishing.

In Revelation, Babylon is John's way of referring to the Roman Empire. Although Rome like Babylon has since fallen, the spirit of Rome/Babylon lives on through greed, idolatry, and the like. Thus, we like John's original audience stand with anticipation of God's final decisive overthrow of Babylon. We know it is coming and we know it is guaranteed, and as we wait, we wait with worship.

Take courage. Christ is on His way. Ride on King Jesus!

GOOD NEWS FOR ALL

ADULT TOPIC: BACKGROUND SCRIPTURE:
NO DIFFERENCE   ACTS 10:34–47

ACTS 10:34—47

King James Version

THEN Peter opened his mouth, and said, Of a truth I perceive that God is no respecter of persons:

35 But in every nation he that feareth him, and worketh righteousness, is accepted with him.

36 The word which God sent unto the children of Israel, preaching peace by Jesus Christ: (he is Lord of all:)

37 That word, I say, ye know, which was published throughout all Judaea, and began from Galilee, after the baptism which John preached;

38 How God anointed Jesus of Nazareth with the Holy Ghost and with power: who went about doing good, and healing all that were oppressed of the devil; for God was with him.

39 And we are witnesses of all things which he did both in the land of the Jews, and in Jerusalem; whom they slew and hanged on a tree:

40 Him God raised up the third day, and shewed him openly;

41 Not to all the people, but unto witnesses chosen before God, even to us, who did eat and drink with him after he rose from the dead.

42 And he commanded us to preach unto the people, and to testify that it is he which was ordained of God to be the Judge of quick and dead.

43 To him give all the prophets witness, that through his name whosoever believeth in him shall receive remission of sins.

New Revised Standard Version

THEN Peter began to speak to them: "I truly understand that God shows no partiality,

35 but in every nation anyone who fears him and does what is right is acceptable to him.

36 You know the message he sent to the people of Israel, preaching peace by Jesus Christ—he is Lord of all.

37 That message spread throughout Judea, beginning in Galilee after the baptism that John announced:

38 how God anointed Jesus of Nazareth with the Holy Spirit and with power; how he went about doing good and healing all who were oppressed by the devil, for God was with him.

39 We are witnesses to all that he did both in Judea and in Jerusalem. They put him to death by hanging him on a tree;

40 but God raised him on the third day and allowed him to appear,

41 not to all the people but to us who were chosen by God as witnesses, and who ate and drank with him after he rose from the dead.

42 He commanded us to preach to the people and to testify that he is the one ordained by God as judge of the living and the dead.

43 All the prophets testify about him that everyone who believes in him receives forgiveness of sins through his name."

MAIN THOUGHT: Then Peter opened his mouth, and said, Of a truth I perceive that God is no respecter of persons: But in every nation he that feareth him, and worketh righteousness, is accepted with him. (Acts 10:34–35, KJV)

ACTS 10:34–47

King James Version	New Revised Standard Version
44 While Peter yet spake these words, the Holy Ghost fell on all them which heard the word.	44 While Peter was still speaking, the Holy Spirit fell upon all who heard the word.
45 And they of the circumcision which believed were astonished, as many as came with Peter, because that on the Gentiles also was poured out the gift of the Holy Ghost.	45 The circumcised believers who had come with Peter were astounded that the gift of the Holy Spirit had been poured out even on the Gentiles,
46 For they heard them speak with tongues, and magnify God. Then answered Peter,	46 for they heard them speaking in tongues and extolling God. Then Peter said,
47 Can any man forbid water, that these should not be baptized, which have received the Holy Ghost as well as we?	47 "Can anyone withhold the water for baptizing these people who have received the Holy Spirit just as we have?"

LESSON SETTING
Time: Unknown

Place: Caesarea

LESSON OUTLINE

I. **Barriers Are Removed Through Powerful Preaching Not Partisan Preaching (Acts 10:34–43)**

II. **Barriers Are Removed Through the Powerful All-Inclusive Outpouring of God's Spirit (Acts 10:44–47)**

UNIFYING PRINCIPLE

Barriers often keep people from becoming part of particular groups. How are barriers removed? God reveals to Peter that the Gospel of Jesus Christ is for all, and the power of the Holy Spirit is God's gift to everyone who accepts Christ.

INTRODUCTION

Most adults have a working understanding of growing pains, the discomforts associated with growth. This is essentially where we meet the leaders of the young church in our lesson today. They are in the midst of growing pains. From the outset of the church there has been a steady increase in the Jesus movement. Now due to persecution, the disciples and apostles have moved from Jerusalem and ventured into the surrounding areas taking the Jesus movement with them everywhere they settled.

Cornelius, a God-fearer, has just had an encounter with a divine messenger who has instructed him to seek out Peter. In preparation of Peter's encounter with Cornelius, God spoke to Peter in a vision clarifying that in God lies the satisfaction of all (dietary) purity codes. Thus, the stage is now set, for the church to experience radical growth into the previously unchartered waters of the Gentile world. As such the church is becoming an accessible all-inclusive movement. Based on the preceding events, we can infer that this is clearly an important objective for God who sets in motion through Peter and Cornelius a pathway to inclusivity. In our lesson, we will discover the praiseworthy way God breaks down barriers among His people so that we may all be treated as all the same.

EXPOSITION

I. BARRIERS ARE REMOVED THROUGH POWERFUL PREACHING NOT PARTISAN PREACHING (ACTS 10:34–43)

When our lesson begins Peter has just received the background story of why Cornelius and company summoned him. As he hears from Cornelius, he also explains why he came without objection. In addition, Peter is now in front of a modest crowd of onlookers, and it is at this very moment after hearing the story of Cornelius' vision and recanting his own vision that he begins to preach a powerful message about the non-partisan disposition of God. Simply put Peter wants it to be known that God does not play party politics. God is no respecter of persons.

In these verses, Peter lays out the impartial nature of the requirements of God. Perhaps Peter reaches this understanding after pondering the way God appeared to both Cornelius and him. Peter exclaims, that "God is no respecter of persons", *prosopolemptes* (προσωπολημπτης). The Bible word used here is a word that conveys the idea that God "receives faces" or "lifts up the face" that bows down to him seeking acceptance. The point Peter makes is that God makes no distinction in how God reacts to people who seek Him, and that all people have the same potential and accessibility to God regardless of nationality or ethnicity. (Baker Exegetical Commentary on the New Testament , Acts.) Peter furthers this point in verse 35. Here he remarks that the only prerequisites for fellowshiping with our impartial God are to fear Him and to do what's right.

Interestingly enough the CEB translates the term fearing God as worship. This is worth noting, because this quarter's theme centers around worship—moreover, fearing God results in worship. The word worship as it is in English, is derived from the concept of worth. Fear in the Greek, *phobeo*, (φοβεω) means to show reverence for. To hold God with reverence (fear) is to comprehend that God is worthwhile, and worthy, which will result in worship.

Doing right or righteous acts, the other requirement is a long-standing idea communicated throughout the whole counsel of Scripture (Genesis 4:7; Micah 6:8; Ephesians 2:10). These two dispositions render one acceptable. The Greek word used here, *dektos*, (δεκτος) means to find pleasing. Thus, Peter is stating plainly that regardless of one's station, if a person has devout reverence for God and does good works God looks upon them with favor.

In these verses, Peter now explains the role of Christ in removing barriers. Christ is a purveyor of peace. Peter, after discussing the impartiality of God to all people now introduces the Christ card, this is fitting as Jesus is the means of peace for all people. Peter begins by citing the ministry of John the Baptist, whom Jesus sat under and was baptized by. Peter reminds us that John's message was the appetizer to spark our hunger for the feast of peace in Jesus. Jesus is the means of peace in this life, and in the next, because Jesus is the means of making peace with God. Jesus is the means and mediator of peace, to know Jesus is to know peace.

Jesus is the proof of our peace with God. In His incarnation, God united peacefully with humanity. The divine nature of

Jesus coexisted within the frailty of His humanity, meaning Jesus was 100% God and 100% human. This holy union, of holy co-habitation between heaven and earth is the first evidence of God's peace with humanity. In addition, Jesus' ministry as Peter mentions is one of peace. Jesus' ministry put people at peace (v. 38). Moreover, although Jesus succumbed to a violent death on the cross, He was raised in victory on the third morning. We know from the gospels that Jesus did not return for revenge. Instead, He seeks fellowship with His betrayers and earns forgiveness for His assailants (40–41).

Peter makes the bold claim that Jesus is Lord over all (v. 36). Jesus is the means of peace He is the master of peace as well. All people can be at peace because all people have the same Lord, Jesus. Peter is asserting there can not rightly be any jockeying for a higher moral ground based on a special revelation or understanding of the divine. No. Peter reminds us that there is only Jesus and He is Lord over all. This was the message first shared to Israel and now it is making its debut to the nations.

Peter now turns his attention to explore the ways that God has incorporated others in this same glorious work of ministering the gospel of peace. He begins with discussing how he and the other apostles were called to be eye witnesses of Jesus' ministry, life, death and resurrection (v. 39-40). This is as good a place as any to reintroduce the biblical definition of an apostle. Biblically, an apostle was one called to preach Christ who witnessed His resurrection. The origins of this ecclesiological terminology is related to action that these persons were to undertake. Apostles were sent by God with the message of Christ. Modern persons receive the ability to be witnesses through the same means. Grace. It is grace, the unmerited favor, of God that allows us to all be witnesses of what we have seen God do, and how we understand God to have worked in our lives. We too should be walking witnesses of His death and most assuredly of His Resurrection. We should be witnesses, loud, bold, praising witnesses that Jesus lives! We must be witnesses, because God's great grace did not call us to be exclusive recipients, we too like the apostles have been summoned and charged to include others in the reception of God's peace (v. 41–42).

In this portion of his sermon, Peter mentions that the Gospel of Jesus united eye witnesses with the ancient attestants of God, the prophets. In Christ we thus have the removal of the barrier of time and experience. Indeed, the Gospel transcends all barriers. Peter further posits that the prophets all attest that anyone who believes in Jesus receives the forgiveness of their sins. This is the Good News, peace with God by the removal/remission of sin and the imputation of God's righteousness.

The word used for remission/removal here is *aphesis* ($\alpha\varphi\epsilon\sigma\iota\varsigma$); it is a fascinating word. On one hand it means to be let go, and on the other hand it also means to be sent away. It speaks to what God does when we believe in Jesus and receive the forgiveness and peace which God offered therein. God releases our sin, but more than that, God sends it off in orbit beyond our reach, so that even if we want to be bound under its yoke again, it is hoisted far beyond us, beyond our reach.

II. Barriers Are Removed Through the Powerful All-Inclusive Outpouring of God's Spirit (Acts 10:44–47)

As Peter preaches, Luke says the house is visited by another entity, the Holy Ghost. Luke posits that as Peter was preaching the Holy Spirit falls on this intermixed crowd of Gentile God chasers and professing Hebraic Christians, apparently accompanying Peter.

Note that the Holy Spirit falls as the Gospel of Jesus Christ is preached! The Gospel is the vehicle that drives visitation from God, the Holy Spirit. A few things beg our attention. The first is what Peter preaches. We should note Peter preaches Christ, His ministry, death, and resurrection in tangent with the remission of sin.

This is the Gospel of peace. Next, we should note how Peter preaches. Peter preaches in a manner that is convincing and appealing. He preaches like a man who has first been visited by heaven.

One should also note that the Gospel (in our lesson it is preached although it can be conveyed in a number of ways, i.e., sung, acted out, etc.,) is the catalyst for the Holy Spirit's outpouring. Here we see a clear line of departure from the work of the Holy Spirit who cosigns the Gospel as opposed to a work up in emotionalism.

When the Gospel is presented the Holy Spirit is free to pour out and fill us as the Spirit pleases. When the Gospel is preached, and the Holy Spirit is present, praise should be the result.

As the Spirit works, we also take note of the people who receive the Holy Spirit. It is Cornelius and the people he gathers together. They are not of Hebrew origin, or faith. They are God-fearers, but as Peter indicated earlier not even the type of people that Jews would associate with let alone fellowship. Nonetheless God stamps them with approval by filling them with His presence-the Holy Spirit. We know they have the same impartation of the Holy Ghost as the disciples at Pentecost, because Luke is careful to give us the same surrounding details, the saints speak in tongues.

As this holy action unfolds, those who look on do so in absolute and utter bewilderment (v. 45). In their estimation this was an absolute impossibility. They likely assumed that these Gentiles would have been privy participants in all of the tenets of the Law (following the dietary restrictions, feast dates, circumcision) in order to have received the Holy Ghost. However, as Peter preached, God was no respecter of persons. These devout saints met the qualifications of being God-fearing (worshipers) who were engaged in the work of justice in their society and thus when the gospel was declared the Holy Spirit showed up and showed out.

We should not wag our fingers in disbelief or disdain at Peter's travel partners, but rather we should likewise stand in awe and excitement whenever we see God active and working in the lives of others. May we never loose our bright-eyed perplexity of God, especially when the Spirit makes visitation in tangible ways.

In the wake of the Spirit's manifestation and visible work in the lives of Cornelius' associates, the question arises why shouldn't these saints who have received the same gospel and now the same God (The Holy Spirit) as the other disciples and believers be baptized and receive the same baptism (initiation ritual) as everyone else.

Here we see the culmination of our lesson, Cornelius and company are now initiated into the Christian movement. Having received the same gospel and the same divine sign-off through the Spirit, they are now to be included and incorporated into the church. In the same way that there are no longer barriers between God and God's people, when the Spirit falls the barriers between God's people are likewise obliterated. Our story ends without any objections. The lesson being that in Christ we are all the same. God has removed all barriers, and we are all free to worship and praise God with the best of our selves.

THE LESSON APPLIED

We live in a time of tribalism and division. While some maintain that our nation is more divided than ever, it should be noted that while we are the Divided States of America we always have been (remember separate but equal Jim Crow laws). Beyond race, there are a variety of reasons and ways people divide themselves (age, language, income, political ideologies, etc.,) in Christ we have way more that unites us than we could ever have to divide us. We are ultimately united to God in Him, and that makes it possible and plausible to unite with others through Him too. We should strive to celebrate our union in Christ with praise. Make it your business this week to celebrate the peace of God—especially with someone different from you.

LET'S TALK ABOUT IT

Why did Peter and the early believers maintain such an exclusionary disposition?

The answer goes back to their interpretation of Scripture. According to the *Baker New Testament Commentary* "the Jews of Peter's day lived by the doctrine that God had made a covenant with Abraham and his descendants and that they were God's chosen people. They despised the Gentiles because, according to the Jews, God had rejected the Gentiles and had withheld His blessings from them." With this theology and sociological outlook, it was easy to understand why Peter and the disciples traveling with him could not believe that God's Spirit would fall on and fill the Gentiles.

Nonetheless, that is exactly what happens. As we live this lesson out let us make it our business to treat all people as the beloved of God.

Finally, we should all look to praise God as if we are His favorite, because we are. He loves each one of us individually. We are the apple of His eye.

HOME DAILY DEVOTIONAL READINGS
NOVEMBER 29–DECEMBER 5, 2021

MONDAY	TUESDAY	WEDNESDAY	THURSDAY	FRIDAY	SATURDAY	SUNDAY
The Law of Justice	Follow the Path of God's Law	Discern the Good, Acceptable, and Perfect	The Written Law and the Ark of Wood	Jesus Fulfills the Law	Curses upon Disobedience	Obey the Statutes and Ordinances
Deuteronomy 5:6–21	Deuteronomy 5:23–33	Romans 12:1–2, 9–21	Deuteronomy 10:1–11	Matthew 5:17–20	Deuteronomy 27:14–26	Deuteronomy 5:1–3; 10:12–13; 28:1–2

Second Quarter

December

January

February

JUSTICE AND OBEDIENCE TO THE LAW

ADULT TOPIC:	BACKGROUND SCRIPTURE:
THE PROTECTION OF JUSTICE	DEUTERONOMY 5; 10; 27; 28:1–2

DEUTERONOMY 5:1–3; 10:12–13; 27:1–10

King James Version

AND Moses called all Israel, and said unto them, Hear, O Israel, the statutes and judgments which I speak in your ears this day, that ye may learn them, and keep, and do them.

2 The LORD our God made a covenant with us in Horeb.

3 The LORD made not this covenant with our fathers, but with us, even us, who are all of us here alive this day.

• • • Deuteronomy 10:12–13 • • •

AND now, Israel, what doth the LORD thy God require of thee, but to fear the LORD thy God, to walk in all his ways, and to love him, and to serve the LORD thy God with all thy heart and with all thy soul,

13 To keep the commandments of the LORD, and his statutes, which I command thee this day for thy good?

• • • Deuteronomy 27:1–10 • • •

AND Moses with the elders of Israel commanded the people, saying, Keep all the commandments which I command you this day.

2 And it shall be on the day when ye shall pass over Jordan unto the land which the LORD thy God giveth thee, that thou shalt set thee up great stones, and plaister them with plaister:

New Revised Standard Version

MOSES convened all Israel, and said to them: Hear, O Israel, the statutes and ordinances that I am addressing to you today; you shall learn them and observe them diligently.

2 The LORD our God made a covenant with us at Horeb.

3 Not with our ancestors did the LORD make this covenant, but with us, who are all of us here alive today.

• • • Deuteronomy 10:12–13 • • •

SO now, O Israel, what does the LORD your God require of you? Only to fear the LORD your God, to walk in all his ways, to love him, to serve the LORD your God with all your heart and with all your soul,

13 and to keep the commandments of the LORD your God and his decrees that I am commanding you today, for your own well-being.

• • • Deuteronomy 27:1–10 • • •

THEN Moses and the elders of Israel charged all the people as follows: Keep the entire commandment that I am commanding you today.

2 On the day that you cross over the Jordan into the land that the Lord your God is giving you, you shall set up large stones and cover them with plaster.

MAIN THOUGHT: And now, Israel, what doth the LORD thy God require of thee, but to fear the LORD thy God, to walk in all his ways, and to love him, and to serve the LORD thy God with all thy heart and with all thy soul, To keep the commandments of the LORD, and his statutes, which I command thee this day for thy good? (Deuteronomy 10:12–13, KJV)

DEUTERONOMY 5:1–3; 10:12–13; 27:1–10

King James Version	*New Revised Standard Version*
3 And thou shalt write upon them all the words of this law, when thou art passed over, that thou mayest go in unto the land which the LORD thy God giveth thee, a land that floweth with milk and honey; as the LORD God of thy fathers hath promised thee.	3 You shall write on them all the words of this law when you have crossed over, to enter the land that the LORD your God is giving you, a land flowing with milk and honey, as the LORD, the God of your ancestors, promised you.
4 Therefore it shall be when ye be gone over Jordan, that ye shall set up these stones, which I command you this day, in mount Ebal, and thou shalt plaister them with plaister.	4 So when you have crossed over the Jordan, you shall set up these stones, about which I am commanding you today, on Mount Ebal, and you shall cover them with plaster.
5 And there shalt thou build an altar unto the LORD thy God, an altar of stones: thou shalt not lift up any iron tool upon them.	5 And you shall build an altar there to the LORD your God, an altar of stones on which you have not used an iron tool.
6 Thou shalt build the altar of the LORD thy God of whole stones: and thou shalt offer burnt offerings thereon unto the LORD thy God:	6 You must build the altar of the LORD your God of unhewn stones. Then offer up burnt offerings on it to the LORD your God,
7 And thou shalt offer peace offerings, and shalt eat there, and rejoice before the LORD thy God.	7 make sacrifices of well-being, and eat them there, rejoicing before the LORD your God.
8 And thou shalt write upon the stones all the words of this law very plainly.	8 You shall write on the stones all the words of this law very clearly.
9 And Moses and the priests the Levites spake unto all Israel, saying, Take heed, and hearken, O Israel; this day thou art become the people of the LORD thy God.	9 Then Moses and the levitical priests spoke to all Israel, saying: Keep silence and hear, O Israel! This very day you have become the people of the LORD your God.
10 Thou shalt therefore obey the voice of the LORD thy God, and do his commandments and his statutes, which I command thee this day.	10 Therefore obey the LORD your God, observing his commandments and his statutes that I am commanding you today.

LESSON SETTING

Time: 410 BC

Place: Plains of Moab, Mounts Ebal and Gerizim

LESSON OUTLINE

I. **The Assembly of Israel (Deuteronomy 5:1–3)**

II. **A Reminder of the Centrality of the Law (Deuteronomy 10:1–13)**

III. **Spiritual Preparations for Entering Canaan (Deuteronomy 27:1–10)**

UNIFYING PRINCIPLE

People often struggle to do what they know is right. How can people find the strength and motivation to do what is right? Deuteronomy 10 teaches that obedience to God's Law is for our own well-being.

INTRODUCTION

Biblical history attributes the writing of Deuteronomy to Moses, although it has been argued that Moses could not have been the author because he could not have written the details of his death in Chapter 34. It was customary that the book would have had an attached obituary, which was probably authored by Joshua. The book contains addresses that Moses gave during the final months of his life, when the Israelites were camped in the plains of Moab, prior to their entrance into the Promised Land. The title Deuteronomy is translated from the Greek Septuagint and means "second law-giving." There exists a mistranslation of the title, which actually says, "a copy of this law," lifted from chapter 17. The command was that when a new king is inaugurated, he is to "write for himself a copy of this law on a scroll in the presence of the Levitical priests" (Deuteronomy 17:18). The Jewish title, which means "words," comes from the first verse and is typical of the beginning of treaties of this period.

EXPOSITION

I. THE ASSEMBLY OF ISRAEL (DEUTERONOMY 5:1–3)

Moses has assembled Israel to begin the process of ratifying the covenant with a group of people who, primarily, were not part of the Sinai experience. The logistics of addressing the entire nation may make this effort seem unreasonable. The Deuteronomic account is designed for historical posterity. Nonetheless, Moses began his address for the people to "hear" and listen to the list of the ordinances and statues of the law. Moses reminds them that this covenant originated at Horeb, where Moses has a distinct history. Mount Horeb is also known as Mount Sinai (which is prominently named in Exodus) and is where Moses had an encounter with a burning bush (Exodus 3:1), the waters

of Massah and Meribah (17:6), and of course, the incident with the golden calf (33:6). Although Horeb or Sinai is located in the Sinai Peninsula (a great distance from Moab), this mountain will forever be a foundation of Israel's history and serve as a springboard for Israel's future. One of the interesting components of Moses' prologue was the reminder that although the covenant was originally given to those who were present at Sinai, this same covenant would now be issued to *this* generation; therefore, its components needed to be addressed. The ancestors mentioned could have alluded to the patriarchs, Abraham, Isaac, and Jacob; however, it is more probable that it identified the fathers and mothers of the people who were present at Sinai forty years earlier but had subsequently died. Still another rendering of this may be that Yahweh made this agreement not only with *our* parents but also with us, who are gathered here on this occasion. Therefore, it is important that Israel understands the premise of this covenant and the reasons that it becomes the constitution. In the near future, Moses will relent his leadership to Joshua, and a new chapter of Israelite history will begin. This group needed to be reminded of God's laws and power.

II. A REMINDER OF THE CENTRALITY OF THE LAW (DEUTERONOMY 10:1–13)

The Bible records the Ten Commandments twice (Exodus 20:1–17, Deuteronomy 5:6–21). Deuteronomy 5 is the words of Moses, who recounts what God revealed to him on Mount Horeb. Both versions are a part of Israel's story of liberation from Egyptian slavery. Verses 12 and 13 are part of the culmination of

Moses' account, recapping his reception of the Ten Commandments. God instructed Moses to carve two tablets to replace the originals that he destroyed.

Moses was commanded to make an ark of a box that would house the tablets. Moses complied with *Yahweh's* instructions and used tools that allowed him to cut the rock. In neither case would the stones be defiled. The wood chosen to house the commandments was acacia, which was used prominently in the construction of the tabernacle and the Ark of the Covenant (see Exodus 25–27, 30, 35–38). The background of the contents of the ark rests on this tradition; the Exodus account speaks about the ark being overlaid with gold, both inside and out (Exodus 25:10–15). Many believe that the additional items were never placed inside but instead, rested alongside the ark. Moses recalled that the duty of the Levites was to carry the ark and serve as attendants in the worship services. Additionally, Moses explained the justification of the levitical duties and the rationale of not acquiring land as was given to the other tribes. Moses further reminded Israel that he went back to the mountain and stayed forty days and nights, where he was strengthened by the Lord. Moses was given a message that *Yahweh* would not destroy Israel; however, this would be based on Israel's adherence to the commandments and ordinances. Therefore, what else does the Lord require of Israel? Israel was required to display total commitment and dedication to the Lord. The command to adherence was for the protection and good of Israel and Israel's sole option for survival. The future of the people is based in their relationship with Yahweh.

Adherence to the law in itself was not adequate without the love of the Lord as their primary reason for following the law. Israel would fail if they followed the "letter of the law" yet, neglected the "spirit of the law." Israel was to follow the Shema, which commands that they would love the Lord, their God "with all [their] heart, and with all [their] soul, and with all [their] might" (Deuteronomy 6:5). Jesus would later quote the Shema but add that we shall "love the Lord with all [our] strength, all [our] mind, and love [our] neighbor as [ourselves]" (Luke 10:27).

III. SPIRITUAL PREPARATIONS FOR ENTERING CANAAN (DEUTERONOMY 27:1–10)

As Moses and the elders gathered, they charged all of the people for the purpose of reiterating Yahweh's commandments. The laws were designed to provide guidance, order, care, and an overall system that would ensure the protection and destiny of Israel. They were poised to enter into the land of promise. In general, the people did not know what to expect; it is probable that many were still clinging to pagan concepts and worship. Nonetheless, this "rally the troops" call was not as much a "pep rally" as a direct call to action that was extremely important to the future. We will not find any other occasion in Deuteronomy where the elders join Moses in addressing the people (Jewish Bible). This gathering is a covenant renewal ceremony but it is also an indicator that Moses will soon die.

In preparation for crossing into Canaan, the instructions contain aspects of worship that are filled with intricate symbolism. When the day occurs that they will be given permission to cross the Jordan,

Israel is directed to set up a series of large stones, coated with lime. Moses reminds the people that the land is a gift from Yahweh, which is reminiscent of the reoccurring language of the Lord when He reminds Israel that He brought them out of the land of Egypt. The stones were to be coated with lime. The instructions were to coat the stones, similar to the applying of whitewash. These stones, when covered with lime, would highlight any writings or inscriptions that would be added.

The stones were transported from the eastern to the western side of the river for the symbolic ceremony that was to take place. Again, Moses reiterates that they are entering a land *which the Lord gives to you*, a land flowing with "milk and honey," i.e., the land promised to Israel. The milk and honey symbolism described a land of plenty. Moreover, the land was fertile. Israel would exchange twelve stones in the river as a memorial to the crossing. The symbolism would not be lost on both the present and future generations. The stones represented the twelve tribes of Israel, to acknowledge that they had passed through the river and that their future with God was bright. However, there is an issue. The Promised Land was occupied, and Israel would have to fight to occupy it.

Continuing the instructions, the people were to go to Mount Ebal and erect the stones in this chosen place, where they would worship the Lord. The Samaritan Pentateuch reads "Mt. Gerizim," which has been thought of as Joshua's altar. After this, the name of Ebal, the site of the first great altar erected to God, will not again appear in Jewish history. Mount Gerizim, however, will be explicitly mentioned several times;

and God's blessings for the people of Israel are to be placed on Mt. Gerizim (Deut. 11:29), with six tribes appointed to stand on the mount for the blessing. The Samaritans would later build a temple to rival the one in Jerusalem and celebrate Gerizim as the central sacred site for the Samaritan religious community.

The significance of erecting this altar is to commemorate the faithfulness of God, i.e., the gift of the land and the gift of the law that symbolized Israel's mission to bring Canaan under *Yahweh* and His chosen people. Ironically, it was at Shechem that the Lord first "appeared" to Abraham, and there, Abraham built his first altar to the Lord (Gen. 12:6–7). The choice of this location emphasized God's faithfulness to the original Abrahamic promises and hinted that the time for their complete fulfillment might be near; however, Israel must follow the ordinances and statues of the Lord for this to be effective.

Once the altar was completed, they were directed to offer burnt offerings and sacrifices to Yahweh. The people were to offer these sacrifices where only part of the animal was burned on the altar, with the rest eaten by the worshipers. The purpose of the offering was to invoke shalom: peace and fellowship among the people. This was a celebration and a time of worship, which enabled the people to reflect on the blessings of their past and the grace of their future. Included is another reminder of the command to inscribe all of the words of this law on the stones, encompassing both curses and blessings. Constant reminders, such as, "I am the Lord your God which brought you out of the land of Egypt," would probably irritate the contemporary mindset;

however, Israel's culture is based in oral tradition, which is steeped in memorization and the word-of-mouth teaching.

During the celebration or at the conclusion, the announcement was made by Moses and the priests that they have become a people for the Lord. This announcement is a ratification of the covenant. God had blessed Israel and rescued them from a deadly famine and the oppression of Egypt; yet, this was a time for restoration, and the proclamation served as a re-assertion of Israel's connection to the Lord. The objective here is that there is an understanding in the promise of the people that they will obey the laws of the Lord and remain committed to following His commandments and statutes, as written on the stones, proclaimed orally. Israel should now be committed to living as God's Chosen and become the nation that all peoples of the world would emulate. Israel is now poised to become the "evangelistic" arm of God that would serve as a beacon of hope for the salvation of the world. At this juncture, life in the promised land seemed idyllic; however, as previously mentioned, Israel would have to conquer Canaan by force.

THE LESSON APPLIED

Throughout biblical history, great thinkers who were devout in their faithfulness to God realized that they did not possess any material items, obtain any particular status, or have any monopoly on worship styles valuable enough to appease God. Micah presented a rhetorical question, in which he asks God if the manner of sacrifice (worship) was enough to please God, and found that dazzling displays of wealth and public acknowledgment of *Yahweh* were inadequate before God (Micah 6:6–8). Micah realized what many contemporary believers have discovered, God wants us to love Him in a manner that places relationship above any other facet of life. A question for contemporary believers could be, "How deep is your love" for God?

LET'S TALK ABOUT IT

Have many church members lost their faith during COVID-19?

At the time of this writing, the world is in midst of a deadly pandemic from COVID-19. Each day our society is becoming more detached from God. Moreover, many churches are forced to deliver streaming services in an effort to limit physical contact between the membership. Will our society, displaying an obvious lack of belief, trust God as the answer to the ills of this pandemic? Christians must not be dismayed. Because of our covenant through Jesus, this deadly scourge will be eliminated; and we will continue to receive the blessings of our relationship with Him.

HOME DAILY DEVOTIONAL READINGS
DECEMBER 6–12, 2021

MONDAY	TUESDAY	WEDNESDAY	THURSDAY	FRIDAY	SATURDAY	SUNDAY
Death of Saul and Jonathan Mourned	A Lament from a Just Heart	A Cry for Justice	Mercy from the Son of David	David Made King over All Israel	The King Rejoices in God	David Shows Kindness to Saul's Descendant
2 Samuel 1:1–12	2 Samuel 1:17–27	Luke 18:1–8	Matthew 20:29–34	2 Samuel 3:1–5; 5:1–5	Psalm 21	2 Samuel 9:1–7, 9–12

DAVID ADMINISTERS JUSTICE AND KINDNESS

ADULT TOPIC: THE MERCY OF JUSTICE	BACKGROUND SCRIPTURE: 2 SAMUEL 9

2 SAMUEL 9:1–7, 9–12

King James Version

AND David said, Is there yet any that is left of the house of Saul, that I may shew him kindness for Jonathan's sake?

2 And there was of the house of Saul a servant whose name was Ziba. And when they had called him unto David, the king said unto him, Art thou Ziba? And he said, Thy servant is he.

3 And the king said, Is there not yet any of the house of Saul, that I may shew the kindness of God unto him? And Ziba said unto the king, Jonathan hath yet a son, which is lame on his feet.

4 And the king said unto him, Where is he? And Ziba said unto the king, Behold, he is in the house of Machir, the son of Ammiel, in Lodebar.

5 Then king David sent, and fetched him out of the house of Machir, the son of Ammiel, from Lodebar.

6 Now when Mephibosheth, the son of Jonathan, the son of Saul, was come unto David, he fell on his face, and did reverence. And David said, Mephibosheth. And he answered, Behold thy servant!

7 And David said unto him, Fear not: for I will surely shew thee kindness for Jonathan thy father's sake, and will restore thee all the land of Saul thy father; and thou shalt eat bread at my table continually.

• • • • • •

9 Then the king called to Ziba, Saul's servant, and said unto him, I have given unto thy

New Revised Standard Version

DAVID asked, "Is there still anyone left of the house of Saul to whom I may show kindness for Jonathan's sake?"

2 Now there was a servant of the house of Saul whose name was Ziba, and he was summoned to David. The king said to him, "Are you Ziba?" And he said, "At your service!"

3 The king said, "Is there anyone remaining of the house of Saul to whom I may show the kindness of God?" Ziba said to the king, "There remains a son of Jonathan; he is crippled in his feet."

4 The king said to him, "Where is he?" Ziba said to the king, "He is in the house of Machir son of Ammiel, at Lo–debar."

5 Then King David sent and brought him from the house of Machir son of Ammiel, at Lo–debar.

6 Mephibosheth son of Jonathan son of Saul came to David, and fell on his face and did obeisance. David said, "Mephibosheth!" He answered, "I am your servant."

7 David said to him, "Do not be afraid, for I will show you kindness for the sake of your father Jonathan; I will restore to you all the land of your grandfather Saul, and you yourself shall eat at my table always."

• • • • • •

9 Then the king summoned Saul's servant Ziba, and said to him, "All that belonged to

MAIN THOUGHT: And David said, Is there yet any that is left of the house of Saul, that I may shew him kindness for Jonathan's sake? (2 Samuel 9:1, KJV)

2 SAMUEL 9:1–7, 9–12

King James Version	New Revised Standard Version
master's son all that pertained to Saul and to all his house.	Saul and to all his house I have given to your master's grandson.
10 Thou therefore, and thy sons, and thy servants, shall till the land for him, and thou shalt bring in the fruits, that thy master's son may have food to eat: but Mephibosheth thy master's son shall eat bread alway at my table. Now Ziba had fifteen sons and twenty servants.	10 You and your sons and your servants shall till the land for him, and shall bring in the produce, so that your master's grandson may have food to eat; but your master's grandson Mephibosheth shall always eat at my table." Now Ziba had fifteen sons and twenty servants.
11 Then said Ziba unto the king, According to all that my lord the king hath commanded his servant, so shall thy servant do. As for Mephibosheth, said the king, he shall eat at my table, as one of the king's sons.	11 Then Ziba said to the king, "According to all that my lord the king commands his servant, so your servant will do." Mephibosheth ate at David's table, like one of the king's sons.
12 And Mephibosheth had a young son, whose name was Micha. And all that dwelt in the house of Ziba were servants unto Mephibosheth.	12 Mephibosheth had a young son whose name was Mica. And all who lived in Ziba's house became Mephibosheth's servants.

LESSON SETTING
Time: 1003 BC
Place: Jerusalem

LESSON OUTLINE
I. David's Kindness to Mephibosheth (2 Samuel 9:1–7)
II. David Secures Mephibosheth's Future (2 Samuel 9:9–12)

UNIFYING PRINCIPLE
People rely on the kindness and support of others. How can people show radical kindness to one another? King David acted justly, remembered his promise to Jonathan, and was kind to Jonathan's son.

INTRODUCTION
David, true to his covenant with Jonathan (1 Samuel 20:14–16), shows kindness to Jonathan's son Mephibosheth. What is well known is the strength of the relationship between Jonathan and David. From this perspective, it seems as if David should have known about the plight or status of Mephibosheth, as Machir (in another region) was caring for him. David, however, does not forget the pledge he made with Jonathan to provide for his family. Justice comes in a variety of ways, many times that which is just is also kind. Though David did not owe Mephibosheth, he knew that he owed his father. David's kindness was based in his sense of what was right, a member of the former royal family should not be living in obscurity.

EXPOSITION

I. DAVID'S KINDNESS TO MEPHIBOSHETH (2 SAMUEL 9:1–7)
In chapter 8, Samuel reports that David had defeated several countries and tribes, ranging from Philistia to Edom. After chron-

icling the spoils of war, Samuel provides a list of the officers and political positions of David's court and kingdom. The account in chapter 9 shows David asking a question to the members of his court, he asks, "Is there still anyone left of the house of Saul to whom I may show kindness for Jonathan's sake?" The Hebrew term *hesed* indicates loyal love and can be thought of as kindness. The term can also represent a type of obligation that one would display toward another of lesser political or social standing. Hence, David would have obvious standing, as king, above Mephibosheth, who was stripped of any political power that may have been afforded to a member of the royal family.

Mephibosheth was originally named *Meribbaal*, or *Merib-baal,* the latter designation possibly suggesting a relationship of his parent(s) with Baal. The element "baal" was later changed to "bosheth," meaning "shame." He is, nonetheless, known in Samuel as Mephibosheth. Since he was the grandson of the former king (Saul), David could have had Mephibosheth killed, as was customary. However, David spared Mephibosheth's life, who was Jonathan's son, David's friend and ally. The Scriptures provide several scenarios as to why David was compelled to protect him. David was mindful that Jonathan had protected him during his skirmishes with Saul. Prior to David's ascent to the throne of Israel, the House of Saul had been decimated, as Saul committed suicide during the battle at Mount Gilboa, after three of his sons, including Jonathan, were killed (1 Samuel 31). David was distressed by the loss of Jonathan, his friend, and remembered his pledge to take care of his family.

It was logical that Mephibosheth would have been able to live a comfortable life, even after Jonathan died, possibly inheriting monies and land from his father; but that was not the case—Mephibosheth appeared to be in a state of poverty.

David asked if any of Saul's descendants were available, so that David could extend his mercy. Ziba, a servant of Saul, told David that one of Jonathan's sons was still alive but crippled in both feet, since the age of five. His nurse was fleeing from danger during a battle in Jezreel and dropped the child, and he became lame (2 Samuel 4:4). The exact nature of his handicap is not fully revealed, as he could have been completely disabled, or his legs may have been broken and never properly healed. Nonetheless, in a period during which the king was also the general of the army, the child's handicap would disqualify him from ever ascending to the throne. This child was Mephibosheth.

After David asked where the lame son of Jonathan could be found, Ziba declared that he was living under the protection of Machir, son of Ammiel, in Lo-debar, a city located on the east side of the Jordan and south of Lake Gennesaret. There existed a group, including Machir, who remained fiercely loyal to Saul, and harbored Mephibosheth, who was either afraid of David or had no other place of sanctuary.

Machir, who was a wealthy man, had the means to support Mephibosheth and would later become a supporter of David, either because David embraced Jonathan's son or because he promised not to fight against Machir. Nonetheless, David was able to bring Mephibosheth to the court of David and allay any fears that he may have felt. When Mephibosheth arrived, he fell, prostrate, and acknowledged David's sovereignty, declaring that he was the king's servant. It is possible that Mephibosheth may have felt uneasy because kings were known to be deceitful and act in an unsavory manner, especially when wishing to dispose of the enemy. David must have placed Mephibosheth at ease, as it seemed that it was possible that they knew each other. Remember, David was actually an uncle to him. Mephibosheth's submissiveness may have been due to respect; however, it is more likely that he feared that David was plotting to execute him as "Saul's grandson," who could possibly attempt to seize the throne (1 Sam. 20:15).

Sensing Mephibosheth's apprehension, David reassures his nephew, saying, "Do not be afraid." David revealed that he would be kind to Jonathan's son because of his relationship with Jonathan. David then promised to restore all of the land formerly owned by Saul and allow Mephibosheth to regularly "eat at the king's table." Restoring (or, as Omanson and Ellington argue), "giving back" all the lands of Saul suggests that David captured territories that once belonged to the first king of Israel. Had Saul lived (and ostensibly, Jonathan), these lands would have been inherited by Saul's descendants, in this case, Mephibosheth, who had never owned the lands, thereby reducing the terminology of "restoration" (or giving back) to merely an act of "giving." Additionally, the metaphor of "eating at the king's table" simply meant that David would provide for Mephibosheth and his needs.

To further understand David's kindness toward Mephibosheth, an apprecia-tion of the relationship between David and Jonathan is paramount. Jonathan's devotion to David is legendary and well-known. These men were extremely close friends. Even as David served Saul, as a court musician and warrior, David and Jonathan's relationship survived the issues that plagued David and Saul's, the reigning king. Determined to remain committed friends, they made a formidable covenant between them (1 Samuel 18:1–4).

David's relationship with Saul was fractured. David was a legend. He was the youth God used to destroy Goliath and win against the dreaded and menacing Philistines. Saul's jealousy continued because of the opinion that David was more popular with the people than he. Even in victory, David seemed to eclipse Saul. This hatred drove Saul to attempt to kill David, but Jonathan would later intervene and shield David from his father's wrath (1 Sam. 19:1–7; 20:1–34, 41–42).

Saul decided to follow the axiom of "keeping his enemies close" by initially giving his daughter Merab to wed David only to renege and give her to another man. He later gave Michal, who married David, as an instrument of David's destruction. However, Michal loved David, which ruined Saul's plan to use his daughter as a pawn to destroy David. David's marriage to Michal was not fruitful and was fraught with tension and many unpleasantries.

Jonathan could have betrayed David to his father, which would have resulted in David's death; but instead, Jonathan continued to protect David, to such a degree that he renounced his ascension to his father's throne. This is important because it is possible that either (1) Jonathan already knew that God would choose David to succeed Saul; (2) Jonathan was repulsed with his father's behavior toward his brother-in-law, therefore, renouncing his claim; or (3) Jonathan felt that he was not strong enough and did not have the disposition to be king. For whatever reason, Jonathan recognized that David would one day become king—and he would serve an office akin to a Vice President (1 Samuel 23:16–18). Additionally, Jonathan would request protection for himself and his family when David ascended to the throne, thus, the foundation of this lesson (1 Samuel 20:14–15).

II. DAVID SECURES MEPHIBOSHETH'S FUTURE (2 SAMUEL 9:9–12)

David then informed Ziba that all that belonged to Saul was given to Mephibosheth. This statement is misleading because, as king, Saul controlled all of Israel, including the lands and its treasury. These were the items that David had acquired when he ascended to the throne, first in Judah, and then, when he consolidated the entirety of the nation. Therefore, he could not have given Mephibosheth all of the lands formerly controlled by Saul, or else he would have given him the majority, if not all of the kingdom. More than likely, David gave his nephew an estate.

What is surprising is that Ziba and his family would be charged with caring for the land, in the form of cultivation and crop management, that would yield produce to be used to feed Saul's grandson. It is interesting that David referred to Mephibosheth as "the grandson of [Ziba's] master, Saul." This would indicate that David continued to connect anyone who formerly served Saul as someone who was not totally in his favor. However, no one should be concerned for Ziba—he was wealthy, having an estate, with 15 sons and 20 servants. However, he was given charge to maintain and care for the lands given to Mephibosheth, who will live in Jerusalem under the protectorate of David.

Ziba followed David's command, stating that he would obey David's wishes, acknowledging the position of David as king. It is possible that Ziba feared David more so than Mephibosheth, as he continued to be labeled as a servant of the House of Saul. Nonetheless, Ziba knew his lifestyle and position depended on the pleasure of the king. At this point, Mephibosheth's young son Mica is introduced which, for the first time in this narrative, provides information that Mephibosheth has a family. Although the age of the son is not given, David's care would extend to the family of Jonathan's son. Again, Samuel reminds us that Mephibosheth ate at the king's table, as one of the king's sons. This act does not suggest that David gave his nephew a position in his court but that he treated his nephew as part of his family.

David is known to have a heart like God and, in this case, shows his compassion toward Mephibosheth, Jonathan's son. The kindness that David extended is a lesson in both grace and humility; however, it also reveals the commitment, dedication, and love that David had for Jonathan. David kept a promise that was bonded by a covenant the two had made before Jonathan's untimely death. To his credit, David never forgot the pact with his brother-in-law. In turn, the God of Abraham, Isaac, and Jacob never forgot His servant, David.

THE LESSON APPLIED

The objective of this lesson reflects the kindness of David toward someone who should have been considered an enemy. To some observers, David's acts of kindness and mercy could seem effortless because he was the king of Israel and had the available resources that afforded him the ability to be generous and magnanimous. God continues to provide His resources to the faith community today for acts of kindness and blessings by those who would dare to remain in His care. There was a man who had an unusual ankle injury that had plagued him since his childhood. This man walked with a pronounced limp but had a wife and son and managed to work and provide for his family. Additionally, he was well thought of in the community and in his church. No one ever disparaged him or teased his son about the father's disability. Out of curiosity, a boy asked his mother what had happened to this man's leg; and she told him that as a child, he and some friends were playing, and he somehow got his foot caught in a picket fence. When his grandmother saw this, she panicked and pulled his foot through the planks; at which time, his ankle snapped, causing severe ligament damage. He did not get the correct medical attention and was forever to live with the effects of this injury. Nonetheless, his disability never defined him. This man will always be remembered as a stalwart Christian, husband, and father.

LET'S TALK ABOUT IT

Are most churches equipped to the needs of those with disabilities?

In our contemporary society, issues concerning people with disabilities are important. We have grown to acknowledge, accept, and accommodate those who are differently abled. In previous times, persons with disabilities were often shunned and ridiculed, which led families to shield their loved ones in an attempt to protect them from society. Through no fault of their own, in many cases, those who live with disabilities are military personnel (who have suffered debilitating wounds in defense of their country) or victims of an automobile accident or work-related injury. Unfortunately, we find wheelchair-bound victims of gunshot wounds and children with decreased mental capabilities because of parents who abused drugs while the child was in the womb. In biblical history, we find that Jesus was compassionate toward those that were disabled, for which, in many instances, healing and restoration occurred. David was compassionate toward a disabled Mephibosheth because of a promise but also, because he had a heart like God's.

HOME DAILY DEVOTIONAL READINGS
DECEMBER 13–19, 2021

MONDAY	TUESDAY	WEDNESDAY	THURSDAY	FRIDAY	SATURDAY	SUNDAY
God's Holy People Live Justly	Enthroned upon Righteousness and Justice	Be Content; Pursue Righteousness	Do Justice, Love Kindness, Walk Humbly	Seek God's Kingdom and Righteousness	God's King Will Judge with Righteousness	God's Light Has Shined
Leviticus 19:1–2, 11–18	Psalm 89:14–21	1 Timothy 6:6–12	Micah 6:1–8	Matthew 6:25–34	Isaiah 11:1–9	Isaiah 9:1–7

JUSTICE AND RIGHTEOUSNESS REIGN

ADULT TOPIC:	BACKGROUND SCRIPTURE:
THE SOURCE OF JUSTICE	ISAIAH 9:1–7

ISAIAH 9:2-7

King James Version

THE people that walked in darkness have seen a great light: they that dwell in the land of the shadow of death, upon them hath the light shined.

3 Thou hast multiplied the nation, and not increased the joy: they joy before thee according to the joy in harvest, and as men rejoice when they divide the spoil.

4 For thou hast broken the yoke of his burden, and the staff of his shoulder, the rod of his oppressor, as in the day of Midian.

5 For every battle of the warrior is with confused noise, and garments rolled in blood; but this shall be with burning and fuel of fire.

6 For unto us a child is born, unto us a son is given: and the government shall be upon his shoulder: and his name shall be called Wonderful, Counsellor, The mighty God, The everlasting Father, The Prince of Peace.

7 Of the increase of his government and peace there shall be no end, upon the throne of David, and upon his kingdom, to order it, and to establish it with judgment and with justice from henceforth even for ever. The zeal of the LORD of hosts will perform this.

New Revised Standard Version

THE people who walked in darkness have seen a great light; those who lived in a land of deep darkness—on them light has shined.

3 You have multiplied the nation, you have increased its joy; they rejoice before you as with joy at the harvest, as people exult when dividing plunder.

4 For the yoke of their burden, and the bar across their shoulders, the rod of their oppressor, you have broken as on the day of Midian.

5 For all the boots of the tramping warriors and all the garments rolled in blood shall be burned as fuel for the fire.

6 For a child has been born for us, a son given to us; authority rests upon his shoulders; and he is named Wonderful Counselor, Mighty God, Everlasting Father, Prince of Peace.

7 His authority shall grow continually, and there shall be endless peace for the throne of David and his kingdom. He will establish and uphold it with justice and with righteousness from this time onward and forevermore. The zeal of the Lord of hosts will do this.

MAIN THOUGHT: Of the increase of his government and peace there shall be no end, upon the throne of David, and upon his kingdom, to order it, and to establish it with judgment and with justice from henceforth even for ever. The zeal of the LORD of hosts will perform this. (Isaiah 9:7, KJV)

LESSON OUTLINE
 I. **A Promise of Restoration (Isaiah 9:2–3)**
 II. **The Destruction of the Oppressors (Isaiah 9:4–5)**
 III. **A New World Order (Isaiah 9:6–7)**

UNIFYING PRINCIPLE

People suffer injustices and ill treatment. Will there be a time when people can count on being treated fairly? God's kingdom will be one of justice and righteousness.

INTRODUCTION

Isaiah's prophecy of the Messiah is revolutionary for the times during which he lived. Isaiah was born into an influential upper-class family and (although his advice was often ignored) prophesied to the Southern Kingdom of Judah, between 760–673 BC, while advising seven kings! Isaiah constantly warned Judah that if she failed to repent, she would suffer the same consequences that destroyed the Northern Kingdom of Israel. Unfortunately, his words rang true; and in 586, the Babylonians conquered Judah and exiled most of the populace. In this lesson, we see the nation long for the coming of the Messiah, and Isaiah prophesies that God is going to make this occur. Although the Messiah will not come during their lifetimes, He is on the way! An interesting note is that the first verse of chapter nine in the NASB, NKJ, and NIV Bibles (which have 21 verses each) is actually the last verse of chapter eight of the Jewish Bible. Chapter nine of the Jewish Bible starts with verse 2 of the aforementioned bibles, thus, the verses in the chapter number 20.

EXPOSITION

I. A PROMISE OF RESTORATION (ISAIAH 9:2–3)

Isaiah describes a period when there is great oppression in the land. The Assyrians would exert extreme brutality, as Tiglath-pileser III attacked Israel around 733. He installed the puppet ruler Hoshea as king over Israel. This invasion marked the beginning of the end for the Northern Kingdom (2 Kings 15:29). Whereas, the Assyrian capture of the region brought shame and humiliation, the appearance of an ideal Davidic king would usher in an era of change in the Southern Kingdom. Jesus will later live and minister in this region, which encompasses Galilee, and the region will become glorious. Hence, the people of Isaiah's time may walk in darkness; yet, because of the gift of the Messiah, their situation will change. Notice that Isaiah prophesies that it will begin with the appearance of a great light. Darkness, reflecting terror and doom, when contrasted with light, clarity and freshness, allows one who has stumbled to be rescued, given that the light of God triumphs darkness. Scripture is filled with references to darkness and light, such as during the Exodus, when the Lord went before Israel in a pillar of cloud by day, to lead them on their way, and in a pillar of fire by night, to give them light (Exodus 13:21). The great light will outstrip the terror of the dark, as foretold, in that God's people will not be afraid of the terror by night, or of the pestilence that stalks in darkness (Psalm 91:4). The light will also reveal the crimes committed against the innocent, the perpetrators of evil, and the traitors to humanity. Thus, the light will shine on them, not to highlight their personalities or status but to focus on the evil that they have created. In this way, the God of Israel will never cease being a God who is dedicated to their security.

Therefore, those who walk in the light will see the power of God. He will increase the nation. This was a notice that God was the author of this expansion. The enlargement is directed toward human needs more than to territory or physical family growth. This increase happens to be in the happiness that was absent under the yoke of their oppressors and renegade countrymen. God's gift of happiness will bring relief to the people, who have experienced turmoil and strife. Additionally, the light will increase the joy of the people as would be experienced at the birth of a newborn or the culmination of an increased harvest, where the entire countryside is blessed. Isaiah will later speak of the characteristics of these emotions as a time when Jerusalem will become a blessing instead of a burden, writing "be glad and rejoice forever in what I create, for I create Jerusalem for rejoicing and her people for gladness" (Isaiah 65:18). This heightened sense of joy and happiness is a healthy benefit to the people because it can only occur in the absence of war, famine, pestilence, chaos, and oppression. They can now rejoice in the Lord; and since He is in their presence, they can see what He is doing for them. As their joy is realized, the division of the spoils does not reference the division of the spoils of war but focuses on the cultivation of the harvest and the storing of the produce in the barns that the Lord has given.

II. THE DESTRUCTION OF THE OPPRESSORS (ISAIAH 9:4–5)

Continuing to speak about God, Isaiah declares that God will rid the land of the oppressors. In a glimpse of constitutional oaths taken by members of government, the Lord pledges to eradicate Israel's oppressive enemies. The invading forces, the Assyrians, are wreaking havoc on Israel. However, Israel faces intrigue from the inside, from those who have aligned with the enemy. Recall that after a botched anti-Assyrian alliance between Israel and Judah failed to materialize, the vassal king Hosea (the last king of Israel) attempted to create an alliance with Egypt and was subsequently imprisoned by the Assyrians, who laid siege to Samaria, the capital, which ended the Northern Kingdom of Israel, in 722. Despite the strife and warfare, the promise is that Yahweh will "break the yoke of their burden and remove the staff" that is weighing on their shoulders. The symbolism is that the yoke that had been placed on Israel allowed the enemy to guide the nation in a direction away from the Lord, while removing its independence. The staff represents punishment, such as is used to strike an animal or assault a person. Yahweh, through the implementation of the Messiah, will destroy all implements of war. The battle of Midian is referenced to recall God's power upon world events, as occurred when an outnumbered Gideon defeated the Midianites (Judges 7:1–24).

Verse 5 notes, "For every boot of the booted warrior in the battle tumult, and cloak rolled in blood, will be for burning, fuel for fire." This can be better explained as found in the Jewish Bible, "Truly, all the boots put on to stamp with, and all the garments donned in infamy have been fed to the flames, devoured by the fire." The stamping of the boots can be described as the Assyrian soldiers literally stomping their feet on the earth to create a noise of terror. They did this in parades and when forming for battle. The earthshaking drone of the troops marching, stomping their feet, and (also) beating their shields was enough to emit terror in any opposing army. Additionally, the term *stamped* could indicate that they "stamped out" their opposition, under the feet of tyranny.

The garments (battle gear) that this army wore would be symbols of disgrace—those who wore the robes did so in dishonor toward Yahweh—and they were doomed to destruction, as in the flames of a fire. Their garments would be so thoroughly stained in the blood of the battle that it would appear that their clothes had been dipped in blood. The imagery here is that this army would kill many of the Israelite forces, making them seem invincible. Isaiah's prediction is that these men, who were arrayed in the uniforms of the army, were guilty of blood shed. These men would not be spared. God's punishment would be revealed in the burning of the uniforms, i.e., as being used as fuel for the fire, thus, the death of the soldiers. Alternative imagery of this verse could be that the soldiers would lay down their weapons and repent. They will hammer their swords into plowshares and their spears into pruning hooks. Nations will not lift up sword against another and as in the words of the old Negro spiritual, they "ain't gonna' study war no more" (Isaiah 2:4). Nonetheless, this will be the effect of God breaking the yoke that has suffocated Israel.

III. A NEW WORLD ORDER (ISAIAH 9:6–7)

Isaiah reveals that the Messiah will come as a baby who is born as a gift from God, to be a ruler. Luke will describe the child as the Son of the "Most High," to validate His connection to God. Isaiah's prophecy provides an insight into God's gift to a world and people that He unabashedly loves, as "He gave His only begotten Son, that whosoever believes in Him shall not perish, but have everlasting life" (John 3:16). The attributes of everlasting life will usher in a new quality of life, in a new location—not an extension of "this life," where there is an obvious vacuum of justice, righteousness, and peace. The coming of the Messiah will redeem Israel and grant humanity an existence that will eclipse the idyllic experience found in Eden.

J.A. Martin lists five notable highlights about the coming Messiah. (1) He was born as a human child and given as a Son to the covenant people of Israel, as "one of us." The Messiah would not be in the vein of some cosmic deity represented by statues or symbols, who required unwieldy sacrifices that could even be human. The Messiah would be flesh and blood and would know the human experience. He would lead Israel because He would be Israel! (2) The Messiah will not only rule Israel, but His reign will encompass the entire world. The reference to His government being on His shoulders refers to the responsibility that the Messiah will shoulder their needs and concerns by accepting and assuming the mantle of leadership. The Messiah will be a just king that will rule and govern with justice and mercy, steeped in righteousness, of which the leaders of Judah and her enemies were incapable. (3) The Messiah will have four descriptive titles that reflect His character: Wonderful Counselor, Mighty God, Everlasting Father, and Prince of Peace. Isaiah described the Messiah in terms that went far beyond a typical understanding of the term. Being "mighty" ascribed a power to Him to do what no other power or ruler could perform. He would also be known as Everlasting Father. The Son is the second person of the Trinity; He is the essence of God. Jesus will later confirm this by saying, "Believe Me that I am in the Father and the Father is in Me; otherwise believe because of the works themselves" (John 4:11). Lastly, called the Prince of Peace, the Messiah will bring order to a world filled with chaos and deception. This valued shalom is a reflection of God as a destination of refuge from all the ills of society. (4) The Kingdom of the Messiah will be eternal. Although His connection to the throne of David is consistent. Unlike David, whose reign was finite, the Messiah will rule indefinitely, firmly cementing the holy character demanded by the Lord. (5) All of this will be accomplished because of the zeal of the Lord. The coming of the Kingdom will not depend upon Israel, who lacks the power and the integrity to remain faithful to God, but will be the sole responsibility of God, whose sovereign intervention continues to protect His people.

Isaiah reports that there will be no end to the increase of His government. This indicates that the administration of the Kingdom will experience tremendous growth and expansion as the power and influence of the king (Messiah) will rise, causing an escalation in followers who will embrace citizenship in the Kingdom. The Kingdom shall be a kingdom of peace or shalom, which is much sought after in tumultuous times, where warfare, death, and destruction is constant in Israel. The acknowledgement of the throne of David is a connection to the promise that the Lord gave to David, that his seed will forever occupy the throne. Samuel wrote that *Yahweh* would build a royal house for David that would be a line of kings. Although it would originate with David, the dynasty will never end, with the Son of David reigning forever (2 Samuel 7:16). Moreover, Matthew writes that the record of the genealogy of Jesus, the Messiah, the Son of David, reflects the fulfillment of the Davidic Covenant (Matthew 1:1). The Kingdom of the Messiah will highlight justice. The promise of the Kingdom is that righteousness will be coming.

Continuing to compare the Kingdom of the Messiah, Isaiah highlights the concept of the eternal empire. All rulers, from great men to despots, attempt to build the kingdoms and legacies in a manner that these empires will grow in size and populace. Some of the by-products are wealth and power, which increases the desire to keep the royal families in control of the monarchies. Noting that there will be no end to His government, Isaiah is speaking of an eternal reign. There will not be an end to these aforementioned attributes, which create a healthy existence of the common people; and their zeal or passion for the Lord will guarantee Israel's survival.

Isaiah's prophecy will foretell that the child will be born of a virgin who bears a

Son, who will be called Immanuel, meaning "God with us" (Isaiah 7:14). This passage being referred to as the Immanuel prophecy alludes to the fact that the child has already been born in Isaiah's day; however, it actually is a prediction of the future birth of Jesus the Messiah. Luke will later speak of the fulfillment of a virgin named Mary who had found favor with God and would give birth to a Son, having been instructed by the angel Gabriel to name Him Jesus, meaning "the Lord is salvation" (Luke 1:27–31). The names given in Isaiah describe the attributes and platitudes of Yahweh in action.

The Lesson Applied

Throughout history, the Scriptures have influenced musicians of faith to compose marvelous works for worship and the inspiration of believers. Musicians of faith have allowed God to bless them with talent, but God has also allowed the musicians' relationship with Him to serve as a witness to the joy of being one of His children. Musicians who are saved become a conduit in the service of the Lord. Larger than life personalities such as J.S. Bach, Felix Mendelssohn, Anton Bruckner, and Charles Ives represent several classical composers who have set scriptural texts which evolved into masterpieces of music that represent the church and glorify the Lord. One of the all-time favorites, however, is the *Messiah (1742)*, composed by Georg Frederic Handel (1685–1759). While most are familiar with the Hallelujah Chorus, one of the other choruses, *For Unto Us A Child is Born*, is literally the text of Isaiah 9:6. Legend is that Handel composed the oratorio in just 21 days! If this is correct, the light of Jesus must have shone very brightly through him.

Let's Talk About It

Do Believers know and trust the Old Testament prophecies concerning Jesus?

Conduct a personal study on the Old Testament prophecies of Jesus. You might be stunned at the myriad of foresights that served as witness to the coming of the Messiah. There are books, such as Isaiah, that bear witness to God's gift to the world; however, other writings such as the Psalms are also filled with predictions and expectations that served the faithful who anticipated the promised Savior. The people of God realized that the world was spinning out of control and that the only hope for justice, righteousness, peace, and salvation rested in the Messiah. If we observe the events of today, we find ourselves asking God, "Why?" We must continue to trust God that He will deliver us, in our day, and heal our land(s).

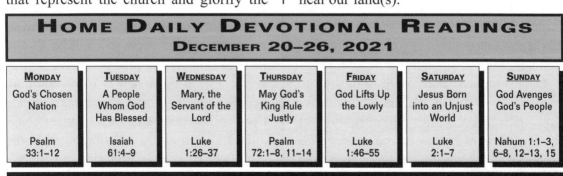

MONDAY	TUESDAY	WEDNESDAY	THURSDAY	FRIDAY	SATURDAY	SUNDAY
God's Chosen Nation	A People Whom God Has Blessed	Mary, the Servant of the Lord	May God's King Rule Justly	God Lifts Up the Lowly	Jesus Born into an Unjust World	God Avenges God's People
Psalm 33:1–12	Isaiah 61:4–9	Luke 1:26–37	Psalm 72:1–8, 11–14	Luke 1:46–55	Luke 2:1–7	Nahum 1:1–3, 6–8, 12–13, 15

JUSTICE FOR GOD'S BELOVED PEOPLE

ADULT TOPIC:	BACKGROUND SCRIPTURE:
THE CONSEQUENCES OF JUSTICE	NAHUM 1

NAHUM 1:1–3, 6–8, 12–13, 15

King James Version	*New Revised Standard Version*
THE burden of Nineveh. The book of the vision of Nahum the Elkoshite.	AN oracle concerning Nineveh. The book of the vision of Nahum of Elkosh.
2 God is jealous, and the LORD revengeth; the LORD revengeth, and is furious; the LORD will take vengeance on his adversaries, and he reserveth wrath for his enemies.	2 A jealous and avenging God is the LORD, the LORD is avenging and wrathful; the LORD takes vengeance on his adversaries and rages against his enemies.
3 The LORD is slow to anger, and great in power, and will not at all acquit the wicked: the LORD hath his way in the whirlwind and in the storm, and the clouds are the dust of his feet.	3 The LORD is slow to anger but great in power, and the LORD will by no means clear the guilty. His way is in whirlwind and storm, and the clouds are the dust of his feet.
• • • • • •	• • • • • •
6 Who can stand before his indignation? and who can abide in the fierceness of his anger? his fury is poured out like fire, and the rocks are thrown down by him.	6 Who can stand before his indignation? Who can endure the heat of his anger? His wrath is poured out like fire, and by him the rocks are broken in pieces.
7 The LORD is good, a strong hold in the day of trouble; and he knoweth them that trust in him.	7 The LORD is good, a stronghold in a day of trouble; he protects those who take refuge in him,
8 But with an overrunning flood he will make an utter end of the place thereof, and darkness shall pursue his enemies.	8 even in a rushing flood. He will make a full end of his adversaries, and will pursue his enemies into darkness.
• • • • • •	• • • • • •
12 Thus saith the LORD; Though they be quiet, and likewise many, yet thus shall they be cut down, when he shall pass through. Though I have afflicted thee, I will afflict thee no more.	12 Thus says the LORD, "Though they are at full strength and many, they will be cut off and pass away. Though I have afflicted you, I will afflict you no more.
13 For now will I break his yoke from off thee, and will burst thy bonds in sunder.	13 And now I will break off his yoke from you and snap the bonds that bind you."
• • • • • •	• • • • • •
15 Behold upon the mountains the feet of him that bringeth good tidings, that publisheth peace! O Judah, keep thy solemn feasts, perform thy vows: for the wicked shall no more pass through thee; he is utterly cut off.	15 Look! On the mountains the feet of one who brings good tidings, who proclaims peace! Celebrate your festivals, O Judah, fulfill your vows, for never again shall the wicked invade you; they are utterly cut off.

MAIN THOUGHT: God is jealous, and the Lord revengeth; the Lord revengeth, and is furious; the Lord will take vengeance on his adversaries, and he reserveth wrath for his enemies. (Nahum 1:2, KJV)

LESSON SETTING

Time: 612 BC
Place: Nineveh

LESSON OUTLINE

I. God's Wrath Toward Nineveh (Nahum 1:1–3)
II. Yahweh, A Refuge of Trust (Nahum 1:6–8)
III. Assyria's Destruction and God's Restoration (Nahum 1:12–13, 15)

UNIFYING PRINCIPLE

People are often discouraged by the injustices they see. How can people hold on to hope that justice will be served? Solomon is known as a king who "executes justice and righteousness" and the prophecy of Nahum is one of the many examples of how God delivers justice.

INTRODUCTION

Little is known of Nahum (whose name means "consolation") except that he came from Elkosh. His message against Nineveh was given to Judah, since the Northern Kingdom, Israel, had already been taken captive. Ninevah will be destroyed! Almost every verse from 1:15—3:19 describes that event, which took place in 612 BC. The date of the composition of the book is another matter. Some scholars argue that the vivid description of the destruction of Ninevah indicates that the book (or a portion of it) must have been written soon after the events. The prophecy of Nahum is an account of what is happening during his day. God's promise to eradicate this enemy is contrasted with the promise that redemption and restoration will occur. Additionally, it serves as a warning for the Southern Kingdom of Judah about the dangers of rebellion against God.

EXPOSITION

I. GOD'S WRATH TOWARD NINEVEH (NAHUM 1:1–3)

The Hebrew term for *oracle* (*maśśā'*) is translated as pronouncement and also, burden, which indicates that the term is not one of joy. In this case, the pronouncement is against the city of Nineveh and actively predicts its doom. This insight given to Nahum is similar to the vision given to Isaiah (1:1), which suggests that the prophet "saw" (2:1), both mentally and spiritually, what God communicated.

Nineveh is to be destroyed. God sent Jonah to preach the impending doom against Nineveh because of the people's wickedness and violence. Nineveh (Assyria) had then, and continued to have, a reputation for brutal atrocities wielded against its captives and its dissenting citizens. However, its most egregious sin was idolatry, as witnessed in temples dedicated to their gods.

Nahum notes that Yahweh is a jealous and avenging God. God's commandments are quite clear: "You shall have no other gods before me." God's people are not to emulate the practice of pagan worship. A connection with Yahweh is all-consuming. He continues by commanding that they "shall not make any idols or likeness of that deity" (Exodus 20:4). Images and idols serve as an invitation to others to belief systems that are hostile to God. Moreover, He says, "I am a jealous God, visiting the iniquity of the fathers upon their children and subsequent generations of those who hate me" (Exodus 20:5). The one who is outside of the cradle of the Lord will hate God! God is very explicit in His laws. Therefore, these terms are resolute and binding. The commandments were initially addressed to Israel but apply to all humanity.

Nahum is explicit that God will punish those who are His enemies. This is evidence that God wants to save Nineveh (Assyria) with the same compassion that He has for Israel. God loves the entire world of which the people of Nineveh are a part. In hindsight, we realize that the Assyrians would not accept God, but *Yahweh* extended His compassion and mercy toward that which they rejected. The Assyrians destroyed the Northern Kingdom of Israel in 722 B.C. Therefore, Assyria became an enemy of their own volition and had to suffer the wrath of God, which would eventually lead to their total destruction. God reserves the right to issue His vengeance and wrath.

Nahum describes that the Lord is slow to anger, which should be interpreted that God has a divine modicum of patience that humans do not possess or understand. It is God's wish that humanity has an opportunity to repent and join Him in a world that ensures a blessed eternal life. For the people of Judah, however, God's slowness to anger is too much of a delay. Israel (and Judah) echoed the calls of Jonah: "Punish your enemies [Assyria] now!" Yet, the Scriptures abound with references to the supreme lovingkindness (*hesed*) of *Yahweh*. It is no secret that God is compassionate toward His people, and His graciousness continues to flourish toward all believers to this day! Moreover, *Yahweh's* embodiment of longsuffering is apparent in His love for Judah. This attribute flows from the Lord and is granted to His people.

The phrase, "And in His great power will not leave the enemy unpunished as in whirlwind and storm" is a description of the manner that these punishments will occur. The imagery here is that God's judgment and power is swift as the wind encompasses every direction.

II. YAHWEH, A REFUGE OF TRUST (NAHUM 1:6–8)

Nahum asks, "Who can stand before His judgment?" This is an affirmation that no mortal can endure or oppose the wrath and power of the Lord. Biblical history is filled with tyrants, agents of evil, and those that would make themselves kings, who attempt to overthrow that which was inaugurated by God. Wickedness and evil caused the forces opposing God to suffer His anger and punishment. In the end, the Assyrians learned that they had no match to combat the power of God.

The second part of Nahum's rhetorical question asks, "Who can endure the burning of His anger?" In this case, the burning of His anger was an annihilating aspect of God, destroying His enemies and their values and philosophies. Second, as in the burning of torches or other materials to provide light, burn could indicate the illumination of both good and evil. Where there is good, God's joy resounds; however, where there is evil, His anger and wrath dominate. It should not be lost that redemption is paramount to God.

Nahum described the strength of God as a power that will break rocks. The imagery here is that rocks will split and crack under intense heat; therefore, His enemies will succumb to the same pressure of God's being "poured out."

Exuberantly, Nahum exclaims that the Lord is good, and He knows those who take refuge in Him! The Lord is also a stronghold or shelter to anyone who would seek His care. Although slanted to highlight a time or "day of trouble," Nahum is describing the act of compassion through redemption. Believers will endure if they take shelter in Him.

Interestingly, *Yahweh* knows who He blesses, those who have found a sanctuary in Him. The verb "know" (*yadah*) reflects a personal connection with someone (or something). In this case, it speaks beyond the intellectual aspects of the term. The sentiment used actually describes God's favor. The value of God knowing His children encompasses an unlimited realm of blessings and protection. The reverse is also valuable, in that our knowing God indicates a shared relationship that complements His desire for all to live with Him.

Nevertheless, the power of God's wrath is compared to an overflowing flood, which no man or army can withstand. An example can be found in the enveloping of the Red Sea, when Pharaoh's army was consumed, in their attempts to kill Israel as they escaped Egypt, during the Exodus (Exodus 15). God's wrath is not constrained by any earthly force or set of circumstances but is unlimited and unrestrained, in that He will pursue His enemies to the ends of the earth. Summarily, Nineveh is the target and the site where retribution will be realized.

III. ASSYRIA'S DESTRUCTION AND GOD'S RESTORATION (NAHUM 1:12–13, 15)

Nahum reassures his people that his message is directly from the Lord, and Yahweh realizes that the enemy is powerful. At its zenith the Assyrian Empire will be destroyed. God acknowledges that He was the one who ultimately afflicted Israel, allowing Assyria to oppress them because of their transgressions. It was because of Israel's perpetual rejection of the covenantal agreements and their disdain for following His laws that *Yahweh* was forced to resort to punishment. If Israel had never turned her back on God, the people would not have had to face exile. Although *Yahweh* was pained to punish Israel, His decision was a result of their actions.

Time is available for *Yahweh* to lift the punishment; however, it will not take effect for many years, yet the affliction will end. In v. 13, *Yahweh* compares Israel to oxen who are overwhelmed by the weight of the yoke, which forces the animals to go in the direction of the farmer. However, *Yahweh* will "break the yoke". When the yoke is removed from impeding them, they will be able to move freely and uninhibited. Interestingly, the action of "tearing off", which can also mean "to pull away," denotes a violent and deliberate act that will separate the animals from the yoke. The term can also mean "to break" to such an extent that the bar and yoke will be yielded irreparable, never to be used again! The promise is that Israel will be separated from the yoke but also that the repentant people will be separated from their fellow countrymen, who are metaphorically a part of the yoke as leaders against God who had exerted matters such as rebellious social pressures that created a poisonous, unholy community. The meaning is not lost on Nahum, as God's promise is that He will liberate and set the people free.

Nahum concludes by paying tribute to *Yahweh,* noting His power and majesty. Judah is commanded and encouraged to worship and celebrate the Lord through their traditional feasts, such as the Feast of Unleavened Bread, the Feast of Harvest or Pentecost, and the Feast of Ingathering or Tabernacles. Israel has reason to rejoice and commend the Lord for His pronouncements on their enemy and the judgment on those who have oppressed them. In language reminiscent of pastors encouraging the slack to pay their tithes, God's command is that Israel pay their vows, which also meant that Israel was to keep their promises, while the enemy was subjecting them to severe persecution. It is easy to plead for God's intervention while the enemy is pressing; however, now that deliverance was at hand, it was time to remember their myriad of promises to serve God and remain faithful in His service. The high places and altars of the Assyrians are now dormant and stagnant; hence, it is time to worship the Lord, who towers above the mountains and sends a message of victory! The Lord brings peace and tranquility to those who are under His care. The defeat of the Assyrians (Nineveh) is complete, and they will never rise again. The danger is that Judah can make the same mistake as the Northern Kingdom and is warned to not follow the example of their kin.

THE LESSON APPLIED

In the account of the aforementioned oracle, the thrust of the lesson may be the defeat of Nineveh (Assyria) and the promise of deliverance that is given to Judah.

However, there is also a "side bar" to the narrative. Believers are blessed to have a Savior that is interested in our lives and provides opportunities to atone and recover from past transgressions. To say that He loves us unconditionally falls short of the manner in which we can describe and realize the depth of God's love for His people. This account provides an example of the omnipotence of God, in that He also loves His enemies to such an extent that Nineveh (Assyria) was given the opportunity to repent! The message is that God's desire is for all people to be saved.

LET'S TALK ABOUT IT

Does God intervene in political and civil matters?

As we have witnessed the scenes centered around the recent elections, both national and statewide, we have listened to the rhetoric and disinformation on display by those who oppose truth and righteousness. One may ask, "Where is God," in all of the disturbances and scenes of hatred that continue to occur. As in the lesson, God has never left His people. The nation continues to face uncertainty; however, the promise of restoration is present. From the pandemic to financial stability, the remnant in America will see the blessings of God!

HOME DAILY DEVOTIONAL READINGS						
DECEMBER 26, 2021–JANUARY 2, 2022						
MONDAY	**TUESDAY**	**WEDNESDAY**	**THURSDAY**	**FRIDAY**	**SATURDAY**	**SUNDAY**
Stephen Prays for Mercy for His Persecutors	Herod's Vengeance	Martyrs Long for Justice	Shine Forth, God of Vengeance!	God's Just Acts	Love One Another	Abel's Blood Cries Out for Vengeance
Acts 7:54–60	Matthew 2:1–8, 16–18	Revelation 6:9–17	Psalm 94:1–10	Psalm 94:11–23	1 John 3:4–13	Genesis 4:1–13

JUSTICE, VENGEANCE, AND MERCY

ADULT TOPIC:	BACKGROUND SCRIPTURE:
UNDESERVED MERCY	GENESIS 4

GENESIS 4:1–13

King James Version	*New Revised Standard Version*
AND Adam knew Eve his wife; and she conceived, and bare Cain, and said, I have gotten a man from the LORD.	NOW the man knew his wife Eve, and she conceived and bore Cain, saying, "I have produced a man with the help of the LORD."
2 And she again bare his brother Abel. And Abel was a keeper of sheep, but Cain was a tiller of the ground.	2 Next she bore his brother Abel. Now Abel was a keeper of sheep, and Cain a tiller of the ground.
3 And in process of time it came to pass, that Cain brought of the fruit of the ground an offering unto the LORD.	3 In the course of time Cain brought to the LORD an offering of the fruit of the ground,
4 And Abel, he also brought of the firstlings of his flock and of the fat thereof. And the LORD had respect unto Abel and to his offering:	4 and Abel for his part brought of the firstlings of his flock, their fat portions. And the LORD had regard for Abel and his offering,
5 But unto Cain and to his offering he had not respect. And Cain was very wroth, and his countenance fell.	5 but for Cain and his offering he had no regard. So Cain was very angry, and his countenance fell.
6 And the LORD said unto Cain, Why art thou wroth? and why is thy countenance fallen?	6 The LORD said to Cain, "Why are you angry, and why has your countenance fallen?
7 If thou doest well, shalt thou not be accepted? and if thou doest not well, sin lieth at the door. And unto thee shall be his desire, and thou shalt rule over him.	7 If you do well, will you not be accepted? And if you do not do well, sin is lurking at the door; its desire is for you, but you must master it."
8 And Cain talked with Abel his brother: and it came to pass, when they were in the field, that Cain rose up against Abel his brother, and slew him.	8 Cain said to his brother Abel, "Let us go out to the field." And when they were in the field, Cain rose up against his brother Abel, and killed him.
9 And the LORD said unto Cain, Where is Abel thy brother? And he said, I know not: Am I my brother's keeper?	9 Then the LORD said to Cain, "Where is your brother Abel?" He said, "I do not know; am I my brother's keeper?"
10 And he said, What hast thou done? the voice of thy brother's blood crieth unto me from the ground.	10 And the LORD said, "What have you done? Listen; your brother's blood is crying out to me from the ground!
11 And now art thou cursed from the earth, which hath opened her mouth to receive thy brother's blood from thy hand;	11 And now you are cursed from the ground, which has opened its mouth to receive your brother's blood from your hand.

MAIN THOUGHT: And he said, What hast thou done? the voice of thy brother's blood crieth unto me from the ground. (Genesis 4:10, KJV)

GENESIS 4:1–13

King James Version

New Revised Standard Version

12　When thou tillest the ground, it shall not henceforth yield unto thee her strength; a fugitive and a vagabond shalt thou be in the earth.

13　And Cain said unto the LORD, My punishment is greater than I can bear.

12　When you till the ground, it will no longer yield to you its strength; you will be a fugitive and a wanderer on the earth."

13　Cain said to the LORD, "My punishment is greater than I can bear!

LESSON SETTING
Time: UNKNOWN
Place: East of Eden

LESSON OUTLINE
I.　**The Offerings of Cain and Abel (Genesis 4:1–7)**
II.　**Results of the First Murder (Genesis 4:8–13)**

UNIFYING PRINCIPLE
Some people become angry when their best efforts don't result in the anticipated outcome. How do people deal with their anger and disappointment? God punished Cain because he allowed his anger to turn to rage and then to murder.

INTRODUCTION
The Scriptures record the story of Adam and Eve living in the idyllic Garden of Eden. After what is known as the "fall," they settled in a region east of Eden, where they raised two of their sons, Cain and Abel, whose account is in Genesis 4. Although we are not provided with full details of the first murder, the response of *Yahweh* can be confusing, in that Cain is not severely punished or executed. However, we are provided with a glimpse of further sibling rivalry, similar to the interpersonal issues with Jacob and Esau, and Joseph and his brothers. Sibling rivalry is a motif throughout Genesis and helps to point us to live in better harmony with those who are most

important to us. This represents the first murder in the entire Bible

EXPOSITION

I. THE OFFERINGS OF CAIN AND ABEL (GENESIS 4:1–7)

Our lesson begins with the account of the first male and female and their union. God created human beings in His image. It seemed that the first couple had it all, and yet they were displaced from Eden because of their disobedience. While they are in Eden, neither the man nor the woman was clothed, according to Genesis 2:25, which states that both the man and his wife were naked and not ashamed! However, after their sin occurred, they had a different definition of the term "naked," which suggests that they were embarrassed before themselves and before God, as they sewed fig leaves for covering. Later, God will clothe both with tunics of animal skins (Genesis 3:21).

This is the first time the couple are noted to have had a physical encounter, but they probably discovered the joy of sex and relationship prior to this account. The man had relations with his wife and knew (*yada*) her, which is a euphemism for sexual relations. There exists a perspective that the verb translated "knew" may have the sense of "had known" in this context. The eleventh century scholar R. Shlomo Yitzhaki, known as Rashi (AD 1040–1105), thinks the conception of Cain occurred in the Garden of Eden before his parents sinned.

When Eve gave birth, she exclaimed that she had given birth to a son with the help of the Lord. Since this was the first birth, Eve did not have any comparison with anyone who had experienced the pain (and joys) of having a child. Although Scripture does not record the finite details of her childbirth, we know that she did not have the comfort or assurance of a mother, female relative, or midwife to assist her. Although she did experience birth pains, she had the Lord to assist her, as Eve's situation is quite unique.

After the birth of her firstborn, in time, Eve became pregnant and gave birth to another son, who they named Abel (*hebel*), meaning "breath" or possibly "vapor," the name, reflective of the brevity or shortness of life (this is easily understood in connection to Abel's short life). In naming this son, Eve may have echoed the understanding of the curse that was placed on her for their disobedience in Eden. God pronounced that He would greatly multiply her pain in childbirth, and in pain, she would bring forth (other) children (Genesis 3:16). Because Eve was created out of Adam's rib, she was not born of a mother; therefore (as aforementioned), her pregnancy and delivery of the first child is unprecedented. The scene immediately accelerates past the sons' childhood and resumes as they have become adults and begun their careers, Cain, a farmer, and Abel, a shepherd. Notice the two occupations, the first voca-

tions, which are represented as simple lifestyles. Later Cain will leave the area and settle in the land of Nod.

When it became time, Cain harvested his crop and brought it to the Lord as an offering. Abel participated in the worship of the Lord by offering the firstborn of the sheep of his flock. Cain's offering from the ground was rejected by God. Cain became very angry because God did not accept his gift in the same manner as Abel's, outright, rejecting Cain's offering. Verse 5 speaks of God not having any regard for his submission, meaning that God was dissatisfied with Cain's gift. The Hebrew term suggests that God did not respect Cain's sacrifice, which can also indicate that the Lord literally refused to gaze upon it or look at it. Cain immediately became angry with the Lord; and his expression (countenance), both physical and spiritual, reflected his displeasure.

The emphasis on Cain's countenance describes his disposition but also his facial expression that revealed the attitude of his heart and his disdain for the situation. Here, God is saying to Cain that if he does well, or will do what is right, it will heal his soul. If not, however, Cain will lose favor with God. The snare of sin was waiting to pounce on Cain, who was angry and out of control. The specter of sin tracking Cain could be thought of as an animal confidently stalking his prey. The writer says that sin was crouching (*rōḇēs*) at his doorstep, with enough power to overcome him. Cain must have had the original temper tantrum because he was so angry that even God could not talk him out of his sin. The snare of sin is powerful and is waiting to trap Cain in its clutches; however, God is offering him a choice and a chance. Cain has the power to fight the lure of this transgression, but it seems that he does not realize that God would strengthen him in his time of weakness. God remonstrates with Cain, arguing that he can overcome this challenge, i.e., the enticement of sin (which will forever be present). He encourages Cain to "master it," not so much to master sin but to control his penchant or liking toward iniquity. Moreover, God's message for Cain is not to allow sin to master him! Herein is an example of the proverbial struggle between good and evil. While Cain becomes angry that his offering is not accepted, God points to the fact that sin is close and Cain's concern should be with its proximity and not the good fortune of his brother. Cain's jealousy portends the sibling relationships of Genesis, Isaac and Ishmael, Leah and Rachel, Jacob and Esau and Joseph and his brothers. God, in this story, is an authority figure who wantonly favors the younger sibling, not unlike the parents in the latter stories or Jacob between Rachel and Leah. In each instance the disfavored individual(s) is given no explanation on why he or she is not preferred and jealousy ensues. Cain kills his brother which does not happen in any of the other relationships, though it is considered at multiple junctures (27:41–45, 37:12–24). It seems that this relationship helps to set the stage for tumultuous sibling relationships in the world of Genesis.

II. RESULTS OF THE FIRST MURDER (GENESIS 4:8–13)

Cain's anger had turned into an uncontrollable rage that actually burned against God; however, since Cain could not lash out against God, he chose the only other person that he felt was the cause of his problems. Nonetheless, Cain lured his brother Abel to a forlorn, isolated place in an unnamed field, which may have belonged to Cain. The Scriptures record that Cain spoke to his brother (v. 8); and while the exact details are omitted, it is probable that the conversation was designed to lead Abel into what would become a "field of blood." Luring his unsuspecting brother into this trap would have been relatively easy. As younger brothers often do, Abel probably idolized Cain, which made this act all the more monstrous and immoral. Since the Scripture does not present evidence to refute this, Cain committed premeditated murder, meaning that he had planned this. It does not seem that the killing was impulsive, which reveals the actual depth of Cain's savage anger but, more importantly, his disdain for God. Remember, prior to this event, no one had committed a homicide, but both brothers would have known how to slay an animal. Cain simply transferred this knowledge to the slaughter of his brother.

Unfortunately, Cain must have forgotten that God sees everything and was present when he committed this dastardly deed. At some point after the crime, God asks Cain, "Where is your brother Abel?" Cain responds by saying, "I do not know." This surely stung Cain, as God emphasized that Abel was his brother, which should have evoked the emotion of a strong bond of brotherly love. This is reminiscent of *Yahweh* asking Adam his whereabouts after the sin, to which Adam admitted that he had hidden himself because he was ashamed and afraid (Genesis 3:9). Cain then lied to God with a flippant answer that seemed to absolve him of any commitment as to where his brother might be. Cain's rhetorical question, "Am I my brother's keeper?" rings bitterly tragic, not only now, but throughout the centuries, as Cain was his brother's keeper! To issue this retort served as a repudiation of Jehovah and everything that was holy.

God responded to Cain's lie by asking him, "What have you done?" Although God knew what had happened, He wanted to hear Cain's defense of this heinous act. This question is reminiscent of God's question to the brothers' parents in the Garden, "Where are you?" (3:9). In both instances God knows the answer but the question serves as a means to demonstrate the shame that is felt by Cain and Adam. Blatant disobedience is absolutely shameful and often produces results that cannot be reversed, like death or removal from utopia, the Garden of Eden.

The phrase "blood crying from the ground" represents Abel's innocent blood, soaking into the earth; while Ryrie argues that God was declaring that "Abel's blood was crying to me for vengeance." While it does not seem to make a difference, in light that Abel was dead, God emphasized the importance of Abel's spilled blood. In the Scriptures, blood is a sign of life, as the term "flesh and blood" refers to the delicate nature of human life, i.e., "For the life of the flesh is in the blood…" (Leviticus 17:11). As a part of the life that was given to Abel, his life force was noticed by its Creator. God takes notice when His creation is harmed, as Jesus declares every one of our hairs is counted (Luke 12:7). The small details God's notices, thus even those things that have greater import, like

life and death, are clearly noted by our Great and Marvelous God.

We are not privy to the details of the scene of the crime, such as whether Cain buried the body or left his brother's corpse for the vultures. However, the observation of this point serves as a reflection of Cain's soul and lack of empathy for his brother, in life, and now in death. If Cain was so unconcerned that he left the body unburied, this would reveal the depth of darkness that had enveloped him.

God then issued His curse upon Cain. What is interesting is that *Yahweh* cursed him from the ground, where Abel's blood was spilled. The importance of this utterance harkens to the earth from which man was created and to where his body will return. The curse is connected to the earth and basically banishes Cain from ever being a successful farmer, as the ground or soil will not produce any crops planted by the hand of Cain, who had killed his brother. Additionally, he is bound to be a "wanderer," who is exiled from his homeland. Cain, however, pleads with God to spare him from such detachment and banishment. Although murder is a capital offense in biblical law (e.g., Exodus 21:12), the Lord yields to Cain's plea and protects him from the fate He had inflicted upon Abel. The irony is pungent: The man who could not extend grace now benefits from God's version. Although it seems as if Cain is "getting away" with murder and justice is not being served, God did not leave Cain "out to dry" because Cain actually belonged to Him (and as it will later be revealed, God protects him). Cain will leave the region and with his wife (most likely his sister), settle in the land of Nod, east of Eden. Together, they will have a child named Enoch and build a city, on which he called the name of the city Enoch, after the name of his son (Genesis 4:16–17). Cain seemed to have a prosperous life after having committed the first murder. While the account points to God's unlimited mercy, it is confusing in the sense that we cannot understand God's ways. Cain's fratricidal actions point to that which is larger than the Law which would come later. There are some things for which no law should have to be written to either stop or encourage. Cain and Abel are the world's first two brothers. They help to point us not only to families' inner workings but what all brothers and sisters ought to seek to avoid. Under God's umbrella of created beings we are all brothers and sisters, there is no law necessary to repute jealousy, envy, and ultimately murder.

THE LESSON APPLIED

While Abel's slaying is horrific, God's protection of Cain seems even more incredible. When Cain pleads to God that his initial punishment is too severe, God places a mark on him, which has been mostly misunderstood. Vengeance upon Cain belonged to the Lord; hence, He placed the sign or symbol on Cain so that it was visible to anyone who came across him. There has been much speculation about the description of the mark,

where it was located, and its very nature. Nonetheless, through the divine power of *Yahweh,* all men who would see the mark knew that Cain was under the protection of the Lord. What God has for Cain is beyond our understanding; nevertheless, we must see this account as a warning against enraged passion but also as a reminder that we belong to the Lord.

LET'S TALK ABOUT IT

Was Cain's murder of Abel the result of accidental rage or premeditation?

The slaying of Abel cannot be considered justifiable, as we are commanded that "we shall not kill" (murder) our fellow human beings. Today's society is inundated with images of young people settling their differences by committing homicides in cities across the country. Law enforcement has discovered that social media, such as Facebook and Twitter, have become platforms of verbal sparring, where flames of dissent are stoked into fatal actions. Prayerfully, those adults that are out of control are steered to anger management sessions, as the world attempts to reign in the pandemic of genocide with which we are all, unfortunately, too familiar. Regrettably, the first murder will be justified by the unsaved, who view it as "it is what it is."

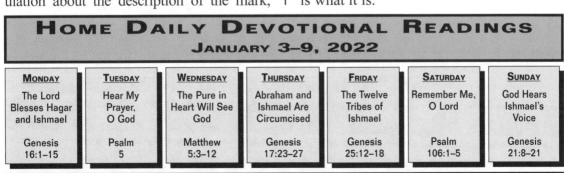

MONDAY	TUESDAY	WEDNESDAY	THURSDAY	FRIDAY	SATURDAY	SUNDAY
The Lord Blesses Hagar and Ishmael	Hear My Prayer, O God	The Pure in Heart Will See God	Abraham and Ishmael Are Circumcised	The Twelve Tribes of Ishmael	Remember Me, O Lord	God Hears Ishmael's Voice
Genesis 16:1–15	Psalm 5	Matthew 5:3–12	Genesis 17:23–27	Genesis 25:12–18	Psalm 106:1–5	Genesis 21:8–21

HAGAR AND ISHMAEL NOT FORGOTTEN

ADULT TOPIC:	BACKGROUND SCRIPTURE:
IMPROBABLE HOPE	GENESIS 21:8–21

GENESIS 21:8–20

King James Version

AND the child grew, and was weaned: and Abraham made a great feast the same day that Isaac was weaned.

9 And Sarah saw the son of Hagar the Egyptian, which she had born unto Abraham, mocking.

10 Wherefore she said unto Abraham, Cast out this bondwoman and her son: for the son of this bondwoman shall not be heir with my son, even with Isaac.

11 And the thing was very grievous in Abraham's sight because of his son.

12 And God said unto Abraham, Let it not be grievous in thy sight because of the lad, and because of thy bondwoman; in all that Sarah hath said unto thee, hearken unto her voice; for in Isaac shall thy seed be called.

13 And also of the son of the bondwoman will I make a nation, because he is thy seed.

14 And Abraham rose up early in the morning, and took bread, and a bottle of water, and gave it unto Hagar, putting it on her shoulder, and the child, and sent her away: and she departed, and wandered in the wilderness of Beersheba.

15 And the water was spent in the bottle, and she cast the child under one of the shrubs.

16 And she went, and sat her down over against him a good way off, as it were a bow shot: for she said, Let me not see the death of

New Revised Standard Version

THE child grew, and was weaned; and Abraham made a great feast on the day that Isaac was weaned.

9 But Sarah saw the son of Hagar the Egyptian, whom she had borne to Abraham, playing with her son Isaac.

10 So she said to Abraham, "Cast out this slave woman with her son; for the son of this slave woman shall not inherit along with my son Isaac."

11 The matter was very distressing to Abraham on account of his son.

12 But God said to Abraham, "Do not be distressed because of the boy and because of your slave woman; whatever Sarah says to you, do as she tells you, for it is through Isaac that offspring shall be named for you.

13 As for the son of the slave woman, I will make a nation of him also, because he is your offspring."

14 So Abraham rose early in the morning, and took bread and a skin of water, and gave it to Hagar, putting it on her shoulder, along with the child, and sent her away. And she departed, and wandered about in the wilderness of Beer–sheba.

15 When the water in the skin was gone, she cast the child under one of the bushes.

16 Then she went and sat down opposite him a good way off, about the distance of a bowshot; for she said, "Do not let me look on

MAIN THOUGHT: And God heard the voice of the lad; and the angel of God called to Hagar out of heaven, and said unto her, What aileth thee, Hagar? fear not; for God hath heard the voice of the lad where he is. Arise, lift up the lad, and hold him in thine hand; for I will make him a great nation. (Genesis 21:17–18, KJV)

GENESIS 21:8–20

King James Version	New Revised Standard Version
the child. And she sat over against him, and lift up her voice, and wept.	the death of the child." And as she sat opposite him, she lifted up her voice and wept.
17 And God heard the voice of the lad; and the angel of God called to Hagar out of heaven, and said unto her, What aileth thee, Hagar? fear not; for God hath heard the voice of the lad where he is.	17 And God heard the voice of the boy; and the angel of God called to Hagar from heaven, and said to her, "What troubles you, Hagar? Do not be afraid; for God has heard the voice of the boy where he is.
18 Arise, lift up the lad, and hold him in thine hand; for I will make him a great nation.	18 Come, lift up the boy and hold him fast with your hand, for I will make a great nation of him."
19 And God opened her eyes, and she saw a well of water; and she went, and filled the bottle with water, and gave the lad drink.	19 Then God opened her eyes and she saw a well of water. She went, and filled the skin with water, and gave the boy a drink.
20 And God was with the lad; and he grew, and dwelt in the wilderness, and became an archer.	20 God was with the boy, and he grew up; he lived in the wilderness, and became an expert with the bow.

LESSON SETTING
Time: 1867 BC
Place: Gerar

LESSON OUTLINE
   I. **Sarah Turns Against Hagar (Genesis 21:8–13)**
   II. **Abraham Banishes Hagar and Ishmael (Genesis 21:14–16)**
   III. **God Rescues Hagar and Ishmael (Genesis 21:17–20)**

UNIFYING PRINCIPLE

People sometimes face situations that feel hopeless. How can people find assurance when their circumstances change? Genesis shows that even though Hagar and Ishmael's circumstances changed, God was still with them.

INTRODUCTION

Our lesson is a primer to the effects of human jealousy. Throughout history, the sin of jealousy has haunted humanity, and Christians are not immune to its clutches. The story of Abraham, Hagar, and Sarah is tragic in that it ripped apart a family. Although Hagar was primarily a slave, she produced a child that was Abraham's only son for 13 years. Sarah may have resented her inability to have a child—her venom, lying dormant during these intervening years—but when God blessed her to conceive, the bitterness surfaced, leading her to rid herself of the older son and his mother. The tragedy is that Sarah's rage provoked her to initiate a "cold–hearted" act akin to manslaughter or, in Abraham's case, patricide. Although the account contains a series of blessings, the apex of the story is that God rescues those who know Him and are not ashamed to call on Him, especially in times of trouble.

I. SARAH TURNS AGAINST HAGAR (GENESIS 21:8–13)

Our account begins at the point where the child, Isaac, was weaned, indicating he was no longer nursing milk from his mother's breast. Isaac, the child of promise, is approximately three years of age, which is customary for the culture.

The birth of Isaac (and the promise) was special for Abraham; and at the end of the weaning period, it was time for a celebration. Remember, Abraham was 100 when the child was born (Genesis 21:5); and following the command of the Lord, Isaac had been circumcised on the eighth day (Genesis 21:4). The ritual of circumcision was a sign of the covenant between Abraham and God, who commanded that, throughout the generations, every male eight days old shall be circumcised (Genesis 17:7–14). Ironically, Abraham and Ishmael, were circumcised together because when God gave this command, Abraham and all of the males in his household underwent the ritual, not to exclude the 99–year–old Abraham and the 13–year–old Ishmael (Genesis 17:23–26). Therefore, in his joy, and in honor of Isaac, Abraham's feast was held to celebrate this particular rite of passage.

All was not well in this fractured family because at some point, Sarah believed that Ishmael was making fun of her or her child. The term used here (*tsaw–khak*) is translated as "mocking" but can also be interpreted as "laughing" or "joking." The Jewish Bible says that Sarah saw Ishmael playing with Isaac and not teasing him; and Brenneman agrees that at the weaning of Isaac, Sarah notices Ishmael laughing and playing with him. The incident, though positive, is interpreted by Sarah as bearing threat to Isaac's inheritance. If the latter is the case, what Sarah witnessed was an older brother playing with his younger sibling, which could have consisted of teasing or physically "roughhousing" him. More than likely, Ishmael loved his baby brother, which makes the upcoming events horrible and casts Sarah in a negative light. Additionally, her response to this scene reveals a serious character flaw of jealousy that had obviously been brewing for years. Her reaction and subsequent decision were unthinkable and unforgiving.

Therefore, Sarah decided to pressure Abraham to banish Ishmael and his mother Hagar. Notice that in verse 10, the actual reason (aside from her jealousy) is revealed when she admits that she does not want Ishmael to share in any part of the inheritance that would be afforded her biological son Isaac. Recall that Ishmael was 13 before Isaac was conceived (Gen. 17:25), and Isaac's weaning had already occurred (Gen. 21:8); therefore, Ishmael is at least 16. At this age, Ishmael should be thought of as a young adult, who would be old enough to have a wife and family and to own land!

Verse 10 reveals that Sarah was determined that the inheritance would not be shared with Ishmael, who was now considered as illegitimate or a "pretender" to Abraham's estate. So, it was because of Ishmael and not Hagar that Abraham was forced to "get rid of" or send them away. As a woman, Sarah could not inherit any of Abraham's wealth, but she loathed the possibility that Ishmael (and his slave mother) could possibly share in the fortune. Sarah's jealousy did not allow her to speak the names of Ishmael or Hagar, reducing them to threatening figures that she simply wanted to disappear (v. 10). Sarah's language of "drive them out" indicates a menacing fury showing that Sarah demanded that Abraham remove them by force, not necessarily by persuasion. Sarah wanted them banished regardless of the means by which it had to be done.

The matter distressed Abraham greatly because of the love he had for his son. Rationally, Abraham's reaction should have been to deny Sarah's demands. The strain must have been intense, although we are not privy to the background struggles that seized the family. It is reasonable to assume that Abraham was not going to acquiesce to Sarah's demands; yet, God sided with Sarah, telling Abraham to listen to her and follow her directions. God's intention was that Abraham focus on the larger picture of the future, from which his descendants through Isaac would emerge. Abraham probably could not see this challenge as part of God's plan; but although he may not have understood, God continued to bless the family. God did not exclude Ishmael, and through him was the promise of another great nation, as God exclaimed, "He is your [Abraham's] descendant." Therefore, both sons were given equal blessings and a future by God; however, Isaac was to be the child of promise.

II. ABRAHAM BANISHES HAGAR AND ISHMAEL (GENESIS 21:14–16)

Following the instructions of the Lord, Abraham got up early in the morning to exile Ishmael and his mother, Hagar. Although the Scriptures speak of "the morning," Reyburn and Frye suggest that this action takes place the morning following the events and speeches in verses 9–13. It is incredible that the provisions Abraham gave to Hagar and his son were meager. We are not privy to the amount of bread that was spared, but the single skin of water would definitely last no more than one day, especially in the wilderness of Beersheba. Hagar and Ishmael were banished to this desert region that would later become a major city in the Negev; however, at this time, it was primarily unsettled, arid, and unforgiving. It seems as if Abraham was not concerned or did not care where they would go or how far they could travel in this desert, although it may be argued that the plain around Beersheba was suitable for winter pasturage and was where some of the patriarchs made their camps. However, notice that Hagar is not given any other provisions, such as clothing or one of Abraham's servants to assist her. Since Hagar was from Egypt, was it possible that Abraham was hoping that she would be able to return to her kin? The biblical record does not reveal Abraham's inner thoughts; however, in his zeal to rid the realigned family of Ishmael and his mother, he places their lives in jeopardy. Was Abraham trying to kill the mother and son, who were still family, or was he aware that God would protect them? If Abraham was not aware of God's plan of protection, he becomes complicit in an act of patricide. When Abraham "gave her the boy," this does not mean that Ishmael was a small child, as has been previously established. This means that Abraham surrendered the boy, as in this culture, the father (not the mother) would have had dominion over their son. Therefore, a better understanding would be that he gave the authority of Ishmael over to his mother.

Invariably, the water was soon consumed, and mother and son realized they were in trouble. Drawing from a mother's instinct for survival and protection of her only son, Hagar directed Ishmael to find shelter under one of the bushes, indicating there was a cluster or thicket of shrubs that were capable of shielding him from the deadly rays of the sun. Hagar must have felt defeated because she sat down within what is described as a distance of a "bowshot," which could indicate that she was some distance from Ishmael because she did not want to witness his death. Hagar sat close to the boy but far enough away, not to see him die. Hagar had given up, realizing that a wicked and uncaring Abraham had sent her into the wilderness, knowing that she and the child would not survive. In her distress, she began to cry out to God to rescue her and Ishmael, which suggests that she was connected to *Yahweh*.

III. GOD RESCUES HAGAR AND ISHMAEL (GENESIS 21:17–20)

There is a transition that occurs from verse 16, which ends with Hagar crying, to verse 17, where Ishmael is also found crying, and God hears, sending an angel to comfort Hagar. God always hears the cries of those with whom He has a relationship. God hears their weeping and an angel appears to ask of Hagar the source of her anguish, i.e., "What is wrong?"

The angel in this scene is not identified; however, the role of these beings is to work for the good of God's people. Although angels, by definition, represent "messengers," such as when Joseph was told to flee to Egypt with the Holy Family (Matthew 2:13), the Scriptures also bear witness to God's dispatching of angels to rescue His people. Examples can be found where angels were sent to liberate a shackled Peter from a dark prison cell (Acts 12:5–11) and to reassure Paul that he would survive a shipwreck (Acts 27:23). In this case, the Lord has dispatched an unnamed angel to comfort and rescue Hagar and Ishmael.

Even though Hagar reached out to God, she may have been afraid of the angel. The record does not detail whether or not the angel appeared to Hagar; but the voice coming from heaven may have been enough to frighten Hagar. Hagar is also reassured that she and her son have found favor with God and will be rescued from a certain death, "…for God has heard the voice of the lad where he is." The language of "where he is" does not speak to the location of the child (under the bush) but of his immediate situation between life and death.

God told Hagar to arise (or get up) and take (or lift up) the child, hold him by the hand, and prepare to move into the next phase of their rescue. Reyburn and Fry also believe the meaning could be "get ready" and "prepare yourself," as in the act of "moving away from this place." If one accepts the concept of Ishmael as a small child, an appropriate term could mean to "pick up" the child; however, when aligned with the probability that Ishmael was an older youth, something equivalent to "help him up" would be better understood. Moreover, there exists a theory that the command to lift the child is not given to Hagar but to the angel. If this is the case, God's intervention is not only personal but physical, as well. That God lifts those who reach out to Him is not unusual, as when the Psalmist composed his gratitude to the Lord for being lifted up from his distress (Psalm 30:1). Likewise, "holding his hand" is an indicator of securing the lad and represents the realization that their future is assured because of the assistance of the Lord! In order for Ishmael to become a great nation, he could not die at this time. God, whose promises are always kept, had guaranteed Abraham that this son would have a great future. Remember that God declared that "as for Ishmael, I have heard you; behold, I will bless him, and will make him fruitful and will multiply him exceedingly. He shall become the father of twelve princes, and I will make him a great nation" (Genesis 17:20).

God then opened Hagar's eyes, meaning that He allowed her to see the larger picture that He had in store. God revealed a well of water. She was able to fill the empty skin and give the child a drink. God was with Ishmael throughout his development and growth; and they lived in the wilderness of Paran, where Ishmael became a hunter.

THE LESSON APPLIED

Family is important but in many cases, the bond is not appreciated until the death angel removes a loved one. Occasionally, family positions are complicated when the family is blended and labels such as "step–children" categorize siblings, in that there may be civil and relational consequences. Strong bonds exist in families who eschew this negative idea of having "half–brothers or sisters." Thankfully, these men and women appreciate the bond of their siblings, while continuing to love the person(s) who are actually their parents. For all of Sarah's efforts to eradicate Hagar and Ishmael, at Abraham's death the two brothers, specifically paired as "sons of Abraham" to the exclusion of their half-brothers, reunited to bury their father (Gen. 25:9).

LET'S TALK ABOUT IT

Who should actually possess Canaan today, the heirs of Isaac or Ishmael?

Islam teaches that Ishmael is the ancestor of Arab tribes and of Muhammad himself. The rivalry has continued throughout history and is witnessed today in the ongoing battle between the Palestinians and Israel. In 1948, Israel was given back much of their original lands by the victors of WWII, France, England, and the United States. The main issue was that the land was occupied by a majority of the descendants of Ishmael who, by the 20th Century, had rejected *Yahweh* and converted to Islam. Not only is there a conflict over who owns the land but there is a battle over religion. Only the return of the Lord will bring this conflict to a conclusion.

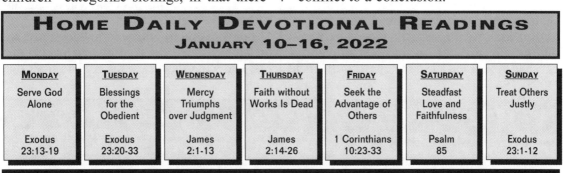

HOME DAILY DEVOTIONAL READINGS
JANUARY 10–16, 2022

MONDAY	TUESDAY	WEDNESDAY	THURSDAY	FRIDAY	SATURDAY	SUNDAY
Serve God Alone	Blessings for the Obedient	Mercy Triumphs over Judgment	Faith without Works Is Dead	Seek the Advantage of Others	Steadfast Love and Faithfulness	Treat Others Justly
Exodus 23:13-19	Exodus 23:20-33	James 2:1-13	James 2:14-26	1 Corinthians 10:23-33	Psalm 85	Exodus 23:1-12

THE LAWS OF JUSTICE AND MERCY

ADULT TOPIC:	BACKGROUND SCRIPTURE:
UNBIASED ACTIONS	EXODUS 23

EXODUS 23:1–12

King James Version

THOU shalt not raise a false report: put not thine hand with the wicked to be an unrighteous witness.

2 Thou shalt not follow a multitude to do evil; neither shalt thou speak in a cause to decline after many to wrest judgment:

3 Neither shalt thou countenance a poor man in his cause.

4 If thou meet thine enemy's ox or his ass going astray, thou shalt surely bring it back to him again.

5 If thou see the ass of him that hateth thee lying under his burden, and wouldest forbear to help him, thou shalt surely help with him.

6 Thou shalt not wrest the judgment of thy poor in his cause.

7 Keep thee far from a false matter; and the innocent and righteous slay thou not: for I will not justify the wicked.

8 And thou shalt take no gift: for the gift blindeth the wise, and perverteth the words of the righteous.

9 Also thou shalt not oppress a stranger: for ye know the heart of a stranger, seeing ye were strangers in the land of Egypt.

10 And six years thou shalt sow thy land, and shalt gather in the fruits thereof:

11 But the seventh year thou shalt let it rest and lie still; that the poor of thy people may eat: and what they leave the beasts of the field

New Revised Standard Version

YOU shall not spread a false report. You shall not join hands with the wicked to act as a malicious witness.

2 You shall not follow a majority in wrongdoing; when you bear witness in a lawsuit, you shall not side with the majority so as to pervert justice;

3 nor shall you be partial to the poor in a lawsuit.

4 When you come upon your enemy's ox or donkey going astray, you shall bring it back.

5 When you see the donkey of one who hates you lying under its burden and you would hold back from setting it free, you must help to set it free.

6 You shall not pervert the justice due to your poor in their lawsuits.

7 Keep far from a false charge, and do not kill the innocent or those in the right, for I will not acquit the guilty.

8 You shall take no bribe, for a bribe blinds the officials, and subverts the cause of those who are in the right.

9 You shall not oppress a resident alien; you know the heart of an alien, for you were aliens in the land of Egypt.

10 For six years you shall sow your land and gather in its yield;

11 but the seventh year you shall let it rest and lie fallow, so that the poor of your people may eat; and what they leave the wild animals may

MAIN THOUGHT: You shall not follow a majority in wrongdoing; when you bear witness in a lawsuit, you shall not side with the majority so as to pervert justice; nor shall you be partial to the poor in a lawsuit. (Exodus 23:2–3, KJV)

Exodus 23:1–12

King James Version	New Revised Standard Version
shall eat. In like manner thou shalt deal with thy vineyard, and with thy oliveyard. 12 Six days thou shalt do thy work, and on the seventh day thou shalt rest: that thine ox and thine ass may rest, and the son of thy handmaid, and the stranger, may be refreshed.	eat. You shall do the same with your vineyard, and with your olive orchard. 12 For six days you shall do your work, but on the seventh day you shall rest, so that your ox and your donkey may have relief, and your home–born slave and the resident alien may be refreshed.

LESSON SETTING
Time: 1462 BC
Place: Sinai

LESSON OUTLINE
I. **Extension of a Commandment (Exodus 23:1–5)**
II. **God's Concern for the People (Exodus 23:6–9)**
III. **Connecting the Sabbath with the Land (Exodus 23:10–12)**

UNIFYING PRINCIPLE
It can be tempting to treat friends with more leniency and enemies with more harshness than they deserve. How can people treat others justly? Exodus demands justice for all people including one's enemies.

INTRODUCTION
Israel has recently been emancipated from Egyptian slavery; and we find that an overwhelmed Moses cannot lend all of his time to governing while remaining the spiritual leader. While under the oppression of Egypt, they were bound to follow the laws of their captors, which, for the slaves, were no laws at all. God realized that these newly freed people did not have a system of governance and needed civil direction guided by their spiritual connection to a just and righteous God. Laws were meant to protect all of society, rich and poor; but because of their prior enslavement, Israel had lost any tradition of municipal guidance or direction. The following Sundry Laws are an extension of the Ten Commandments and part of the laws that were needed to govern the nation in fairness.

I. EXTENSION OF A COMMANDMENT (EXODUS 23:1–5)
The law noted in verse one "not to bear a false report," which is an extension of the ninth commandment: "You shall not bear false witness against your neighbor" (20:16). Failure to follow this commandment would bring undue harm to one's neighbor and could cause irreparable damage to the livelihood of that person's family. Moreover, it is understandable that the next of the Ten Commandments is, "You shall not covet your neighbor's house; you shall not covet your neighbor's wife or his male servant or his female servant or his ox or his donkey or anything that belongs to your neighbor" (20:17). The purpose here is that if a person coveted a neighbor's land or any of his neighbor's possessions, creating a false narrative or accusation could tempt someone to lie in an effort to seize these possessions. Remember, land was given by God to the tribes as they settled in Canaan,

and the promised land was considered sacred. For example, Leviticus records that the land given by God shall not be sold permanently, "for the land is Mine" (Leviticus 25:23).

After the people came to Sinai following the Exodus, Moses was the sole judge for all disputes (18:16), that is, until Jethro, his father–in–law convinced him to delegate some of his responsibilities. In order to settle a dispute, the law would later declare, "A single witness shall not rise up against a man on account of any iniquity or any sin which he has committed; on the evidence of two or three witnesses a matter shall be confirmed" (Leviticus 19:15). Human disputes were destined to occur; however, the Lord understood the frailty and weakness of the human spirit, which can cause the "telling of a lie" by one or more conspirators in order to gain an advantage.

Continuing the decree, one was not to follow the masses or any charismatic leader in the pursuit of evil. Again, history is littered with accounts of despots who have been able to sway a multitude of innocent people, while leading their minions astray. Following the leadership of the wicked is an affront to God, as such persons would be involved in idolatry and pagan worship. Additionally, the danger for the gullible is that following evil leaders does not absolve one from guilt. *Yahweh* did not want anyone to be persuaded to try to gain favor with the powerful, influential, or wealthy, who could convince the common person to literally "sell his/her soul" to the advantage of the influencers. The thrust of this edict is that a man should be honorable and independent, able to resist the temptation to side with a mob (and a suffocating "mob mentality"), from which truth becomes largely invisible. When this occurs, the innocent suffer and are persecuted, and the law becomes something of an afterthought. Moreover, one should not side against the poor in a dispute because of the persuasion of wealthy and influential plotters. In most cases, because of the lack of wealth, social status, or influence, the poor had no advocate to serve as a "buffer" between lawlessness and justice. If anything, those who are God's chosen should be willing to stand for the poor or oppressed.

The next edict centered around the animals that belonged to a neighbor. If you meet your neighbor's beast, specifically, oxen and donkeys, the just man would immediately return the animal to his rightful owners. Notice that, in verse 3, the emphasis on returning a lost animal to a friend or neighbor is on the animals that belonged to one's enemies. For a lack of concern, or because of a sense of enmity, one could be tempted to keep the animal of an enemy, as gaining an advantage. However, continuing the law of righteousness, which focuses on fairness to all (especially the enemy), was paramount, as it is easier to hate the adversary and favor the friend. This manner of favoritism was frowned upon by God. Authentic ownership was sanctioned by God, in that one of the most precious commodities outside of land ownership was animals. Animals were the basic foundation of agrarian life, as beasts of burden and animals that provided milk, cheese, and meat for consumption. One could easily sell the lost animal or, if it was a sheep or goat, could kill it and eat the meat. Animals do not know to which field and family they belong. An animal, such as a beast of burden, a donkey or ox, was wealth to a farmer; so, by taking the wandering animal, one would be committing robbery against his neighbor. Here, the concept of theft is real! Stealing in this manner would be no different than going into the neighbor's field to steal the animal.

Continuing with a focus on the rights or concerns for animals, God commanded, "If you see the donkey of one who hates you lying helpless under its load, you shall refrain from leaving it to him, you shall surely release it with him" (v. 5). Again, notice the emphasis on the animal of the enemy! Talmudic sages hold that this commandment is meant to benefit the animal, as well as its owner, citing it as the basis of the obligation to prevent animals from suffering. The fact that the remedy given was for two people to assist in righting the animal was also a sign that community was important to the future and prosperity. This edict will be reinforced later, as commanded that "you shall not see your countryman's donkey, or his ox fallen down on the way and pay no attention to them; you shall certainly help him to raise them up" (Deuteronomy 22:4). The concept was that one had to assist others facing difficulty or an economic loss. By helping the animal to its feet was to release its burden, which coincides with the Lord lifting the burdens in the lives of believers.

II. GOD'S CONCERN FOR THE PEOPLE (EXODUS 23:6–9)

The command in verse 6 is that one should not subvert justice in the case of a brother in need of assistance. In this case, "brother" is not relegated to one of a biological nature but serves as a reflection that all men are brothers. Again, because of the possibility of bribery or social favoritism, the concept here is that one should not ignore the truth in the matter of a dispute that may harm his neighbor. One of the pitfalls of corruption is that the family bond of the idea that "blood is thicker than water" serves as a powerful inducement to unite over an issue, regardless of where the truth may lie. The needy could be one who does not have a large or connected family and thus, not have the protection of a large clan. Additionally, this message serves as an example for the magistrates or judges in that they are not to be given to bribes or subvert justice (*mishpat*). Obviously, corruption extended to those who were supposedly given to honestly serving the integrity of the people; but unethical officials had the reputation of "looking the other way" when it served their interests. The poor and marginalized did not have this type of influence.

Again, this edict is an indictment against the greed of unsavory officials who would accept tainted witness in order to serve their interests. This is considered a "step up" to another level of accountability, as the law shifts from the ordinary person to the magistrates, judges, and officials. These men were given power to rule justly and serve the welfare of the people. Officers of the land were supposedly beyond reproach, as they are to resist falsely charging anyone, which could result in a lengthy imprisonment or severe punishment. Many of these charges could bring prosecution, to which the results would be a death sentence. Since there was no method of atoning a fraudulent sentence, God states that He will not acquit the guilty of their transgressions. Always on the side of righteousness, however; God will punish those who are guilty. In the concept of an "eye for an eye," the wrath of God will fall on those who subvert justice; and He will serve notice on the witness who perjures himself to convict the innocent.

Continuing, verse 8 is definitely directed toward the officials and judges: God declares that "you shall not take a bribe, for a bribe blinds the clear-sighted and subverts the cause of the just." The fact that "the bribe blinds the clear-sighted" means that those with money have the power to corrupt people who would normally be upstanding citizens beyond reproach, i.e., the clear-sighted. As Moses relinquished some of his authority to regional judges, these men probably came from each of the tribes. These leaders were to judge the people fairly, conforming to the righteous standards set forth in the Word of God. Additionally, God had given them a heavenly pattern for their actions toward each other. If their actions did not conform to this pattern, those actions were to be changed or punished; and any nonconformity to the pattern of justice was a perversion. Moreover, they were not to show partiality, as the judges were to treat each person as though they had no prior knowledge of him or her. Accepting a bribe was obviously wrong because it twists the ability of judges to act in fairness toward the parties in the litigation; and the warning here is that bribes are not to be accepted, nor offered! Therefore, it was absolutely essential that the standard set forth in the Law be followed precisely. Their lives and prosperity (Deuteronomy 16:20) depended upon their establishing impartial justice in the promised land.

Verse 9 signals a change in direction, as the law moves from the officials and citizens of the land to the care of the stranger or the alien. God loves all of humanity and in many cases, the stranger or alien would be a refugee or a wanderer that did not have any wealth or means of support. God will command that "when you reap the harvest of your land, you shall not reap to the very corners of your field, nor shall you gather the gleanings of your harvest, nor shall you glean your vineyard, nor shall you gather the fallen fruit of your vineyard; you shall leave them for the needy and for the stranger. I am the LORD your God" (Leviticus 19:9–10). God wanted the nation to remember the treatment they had received while in Egypt. While enslaved, Israel was severely oppressed by sadistic taskmasters. Israel was to treat others in a manner that was akin to God's love and blessings for the dispossessed. Since Israel was God's chosen, Israel should not have had an issue with following this commandment.

III. CONNECTING THE SABBATH WITH THE LAND (EXODUS 23:10–12)

Verses 10–11 move to God's concern for the land, which is necessary to sustain His people. Traditionally, wise agriculturalists learned about crop rotation and alternating fields to preserve the soil and allow the land to rest. As with the allowance for gleaning, the needy will continue to have access to produce that would serve as life-sustaining substance. Moreover, the harvest would yield such an abundance that even the domestic animals and wild beasts would be able to eat freely of the fields. This command extended to all of their lands, i.e., vineyards and olive groves, where the produce could be considered excessive.

Concluding this set of laws, God gives

credence to the pattern of *Yahweh's* timetable of creation. Work is only allowed for six days, but on the seventh day, all (including their animals) were to rest. "By the seventh day, God completed His work which He had done, and He rested on the seventh day from all His work which He had done. Then God blessed the seventh day and sanctified it, because in it He rested from all His work which God had created and made" (Genesis 1:2–3). As He had commanded with His concern for protecting the land, God's edict is directed to protect the person who worked the land and the animals. The day of rest represents the Sabbath Law, "to keep [the Sabbath] holy." Although the seventh day of rest would be a day of refreshing, the people are not to simply take the day off but to sanctify this special day for the worship of God. This edict is a reinforcement of the fourth commandment, which emphasizes keeping the seventh day as a holy day, reserved for the concentration on their relationship with the Lord. God will not compete with any type of work or other activities on the seventh day; therefore, God is to be the singular focus of the people.

THE LESSON APPLIED

Notice that the ninth commandment is given in the purity of righteousness; however, God also issued it as a warning because human character has the nature of corruption. Biblical language warns against "bearing false witness," which means "telling a lie." The lack of adhering to this law creates a scenario to which other problems are connected, such as taking bribes, being part of a conspiracy, following an unjust crowd for the sake of popularity, or even stretching the truth. Remember, once someone tells a lie to justify his or her actions, additional lies must be created to support and continue the excuses. God wants His people to be fair and honest, which is a reflection of His nature.

LET'S TALK ABOUT IT

Are the civil laws of society adequate in their concern for the marginalized?

In our contemporary society, laws and ordinances are "on the books" in an attempt to guide society and establish civil order. However, are these laws fair to all? Many would argue that the laws of the United States are slanted to protect the interests of the wealthy and people of means; whereas, another segment of the population refute this by saying there are more than enough allowances that provide social services, such as EBT cards and subsidized housing. God, however, has concern for all, protecting the prosperous and also shielding the poor. It is our job to follow His directives and follow His plan.

HOME DAILY DEVOTIONAL READINGS						
JANUARY 17 –23, 2022						
MONDAY	**TUESDAY**	**WEDNESDAY**	**THURSDAY**	**FRIDAY**	**SATURDAY**	**SUNDAY**
True and False Witnesses	Addressing Church Conflicts	The Duty to Forgive	Moses' Court of Appeal	Speak Truth and Act on It	God Is an Impartial Judge	Appoint Leaders to Administer Justice
Deuteronomy 19:15-21	Matthew 18:15-20	Matthew 18:21-35	Exodus 18:13-26	Ephesians 4:25-32	Deuteronomy 10:14-22	Deuteronomy 16:18-20; 17:8-13

JUSTICE, JUDGES, AND PRIESTS

ADULT TOPIC: BACKGROUND SCRIPTURE:
INCORRUPTIBLE LEADERS   DEUTERONOMY 16:18–20; 17:8–13; 19:15–21

DEUTERONOMY 16:18–20; 17:8–13

King James Version

JUDGES and officers shalt thou make thee in all thy gates, which the LORD thy God giveth thee, throughout thy tribes: and they shall judge the people with just judgment.

19 Thou shalt not wrest judgment; thou shalt not respect persons, neither take a gift: for a gift doth blind the eyes of the wise, and pervert the words of the righteous.

20 That which is altogether just shalt thou follow, that thou mayest live, and inherit the land which the LORD thy God giveth thee.

• • • Deuteronomy 17:8–13 • • •

8 If there arise a matter too hard for thee in judgment, between blood and blood, between plea and plea, and between stroke and stroke, being matters of controversy within thy gates: then shalt thou arise, and get thee up into the place which the LORD thy God shall choose;

9 And thou shalt come unto the priests the Levites, and unto the judge that shall be in those days, and enquire; and they shall shew thee the sentence of judgment:

10 And thou shalt do according to the sentence, which they of that place which the Lord shall choose shall shew thee; and thou shalt observe to do according to all that they inform thee:

11 According to the sentence of the law which they shall teach thee, and according to the judgment which they shall tell thee, thou shalt

New Revised Standard Version

YOU shall appoint judges and officials throughout your tribes, in all your towns that the LORD your God is giving you, and they shall render just decisions for the people.

19 You must not distort justice; you must not show partiality; and you must not accept bribes, for a bribe blinds the eyes of the wise and subverts the cause of those who are in the right.

20 Justice, and only justice, you shall pursue, so that you may live and occupy the land that the LORD your God is giving you.

• • • Deuteronomy 17:8–13 • • •

8 If a judicial decision is too difficult for you to make between one kind of bloodshed and another, one kind of legal right and another, or one kind of assault and another—any such matters of dispute in your towns—then you shall immediately go up to the place that the LORD your God will choose,

9 where you shall consult with the levitical priests and the judge who is in office in those days; they shall announce to you the decision in the case.

10 Carry out exactly the decision that they announce to you from the place that the Lord will choose, diligently observing everything they instruct you.

11 You must carry out fully the law that they interpret for you or the ruling that they announce to you; do not turn aside from the

---

MAIN THOUGHT: You shall appoint judges and officials throughout your tribes, in all your towns that the LORD your God is giving you, and they shall render just decisions for the people. (Deuteronomy 16:18, KJV)

DEUTERONOMY 16:18–20; 17:8–13

King James Version

do: thou shalt not decline from the sentence which they shall shew thee, to the right hand, nor to the left.

12 And the man that will do presumptuously, and will not hearken unto the priest that standeth to minister there before the LORD thy God, or unto the judge, even that man shall die: and thou shalt put away the evil from Israel.

13 And all the people shall hear, and fear, and do no more presumptuously.

New Revised Standard Version

decision that they announce to you, either to the right or to the left.

12 As for anyone who presumes to disobey the priest appointed to minister there to the LORD your God, or the judge, that person shall die. So you shall purge the evil from Israel.

13 All the people will hear and be afraid, and will not act presumptuously again.

LESSON SETTING
Time: 1423 BC
Place: Sinai

LESSON OUTLINE
I. Appointing Judges and Their Responsibilities (Deuteronomy 16:18–20)
II. Guidance for Settling Difficult Cases (Deuteronomy 17:8–13)

UNIFYING PRINCIPLE
People sometimes distort justice. What actions can we take to prevent manipulations of justice? In Deuteronomy, judges, officials, and priests work together to administer justice for God's people.

INTRODUCTION
Israel is preparing to move into the newly settled promised land and is having to adjust to the conflicts that arise between neighbors, adversaries, and competing businessmen. Moses is dead by the time Israel moves into Canaan; but many of the laws listed in these chapters are extensions of what was given in Exodus. The manner by which these laws are listed make it appear that they have not entered the land of promise; however, we cannot look at this section chronologically because

Deuteronomy means "second–law–giving" or "a copy of this law." Moses' death is recorded in Deuteronomy 34, but we are not privy to the actual details of the death of this great prophet. Justice and righteousness are central themes and are required for Israel. In this lesson, we find that God insists on the virtue of incorruptible leaders, while also demanding fealty (loyalty) from His people.

I. APPOINTING JUDGES AND THEIR RESPONSIBILITIES (DEUTERONOMY 16:18–20)
God has provided a continuing section of laws that conclude Chapter 16, which begins by commanding the observation of the Feasts or Passover, Weeks, and Booths. There is a reminder to remain obedient to the edicts of the Lord. Additionally, there exists a reminder that will remain a constant theme in the life of Israel, which is to remember the horrific period of Egyptian slavery and who was responsible for their deliverance. These laws provide the manner by which officials are to be selected, as God allowed the people to appoint judges from their ranks. When Israel returned to Sinai after the Exodus, Moses was forced

to relinquish his role as judge because the responsibility to serve the judicial and spiritual needs of the people was overwhelming.

As he stepped away from this segment of duty, Moses appointed the first group of judges. He allowed the elders of each tribe to be candidates and then appointed them as heads (judges) and officers for the tribes. He charged the judges, saying, "Hear the cases between the people and judge righteously between them" (1:13–16). Although it is not clear what methods would be used to vet these persons, it remains probable that the prospective individuals were natives of their tribes and regions. The fact that they were appointed does not provoke images of an election. In this case, it is more likely that the tribal elders were given the responsibility of making the judicial selections. Judges were responsible for impartially administering justice, especially during disputes; however, they were also to protect the marginalized and poor, serving as a buffer against the enemies, while preserving peace in the land. The officers probably served as assistants to the judges and in other administrative roles within the courts. These officials could also serve as scribes, (lawyers), bailiffs, or court reporters. The courts were not located in buildings but were positioned at the gates of the city; and in the case of a city having more than one gate, the courts were set up at the main gate. The outdoor setting allowed the people to witness court proceedings in an open and unobstructed manner, which provided a sense of fairness. Nonetheless, while these judges and officers were responsible to serve the people, they were ultimately accountable to the Lord. Remember, this is God's system of justice and administration;

and if they are to survive, the commitment from those in positions of leadership must remain faithful to the Lord.

Moreover, these appointed judges and officials were warned against using their positions for financial or political gain. One of the more prevailing temptations addressed is bribery, which is an easy trap, as it can be accomplished in secret places between only two persons. Bribery is one of the "sleaziest" forms of corruption and is supported by lies. Innocent people would not know that the trial was "stacked against them" because of the clandestine operation. God curses the judge who accepts a bribe, which is a subversion of justice (27:25). The command that they shall not judge unfairly is an admonition to the judges, sometimes called a "Mirror for the Magistrates," quotes Exodus 23:6, "You shall not pervert the justice due to your needy brother in his dispute, for bribes blind the eyes of the discerning [of the wise]." God is the standard. He does not ask from us what He does not commit to, "For the LORD your God is the God of gods and the Lord of lords, the great, the mighty, and the awesome God who does not show partiality nor take a bribe" (10:17).

Again, reverting to the resonant theme of justice, God demands that the people must follow justice and only pursue the justice that would allow *Yahweh* to bless the land that they had been allowed to possess. Canaan was occupied by pagan inhabitants. Additionally, if the people wanted to receive justice, they must make justice a part of the national fabric. Then, in their pursuit for integrity, the people would be embraced by the Lord and righteously follow His Law. There is an emphasis on the land "which the Lord is giving you" (verse 20). This truism was necessary as many would become pompous and go astray.

II. GUIDANCE FOR SETTLING DIFFICULT CASES (DEUTERONOMY 17:8–13)

If the people were to live in the land of promise, with prosperity and blessings, they would have to be guided by the justice and righteousness of the Lord. *Yahweh* realized that through the weakness of human nature, there would be issues that must be addressed. There would be cases that presented challenges that would be too difficult to decide in a normal fashion. Even in our contemporary society, there are complex court cases; and with a system that is riddled with compromises and plea bargains, we consistently need God's intervention. In this instance, there will be situations that are too baffling for [one] to decide, cases that go beyond that which is possible for human knowledge to resolve. One example is the controversy between homicide and manslaughter, for which the analysis of evidence, the discernment of accuracy, and the truthfulness of witnesses becomes a challenge. Judges need to be able to distinguish between premeditated and unintentional offenses. For example, the homicide committed by Cain against his brother Abel could have been argued as manslaughter instead of murder, if it could have been proven that Cain acted from impulse rather than having planned the offense. If this case were to be presented in a court of law, it would have been very difficult to adjudicate. Clearly, an act of assault, which could be a bodily attack or an attack on a property, would be even more difficult to settle because of the need to determine the validity of the evidence and witnesses. Lawsuits of this era usually concerned land disputes, which may have involved money. However, punitive damages could be awarded for such acts as when a man violates a young girl, and he has to pay the girl's father fifty shekels of silver and take the girl as his wife (Deuteronomy 22:29). If the case is too difficult for the judges of the respective towns or tribes, the case was to move to another place chosen by the Lord. Regardless of the situation or the complexities of the cases, wisdom and total trust in God is needed

The location to where the move was to occur was not as important as that of the added (new) persons who would hear the case. The case would be presented to the Levitical priest (or judge) who was in office or serving during the period of the dispute, although the system of their rotation is not clear. Nonetheless, they were to present the evidence and all of the procedures that were part of the trial formerly held at the city gate. Functioning as an appeals court, the Levitical priests would adjudicate the case and make a final ruling. Remember, these priests were the descendants of Aaron and were not provided tribal lands but were scattered throughout the land to serve the spiritual needs of the Nation. The sanctuary, most likely the tabernacle, was where the case would be heard. Any rebellion against the tribunal was considered "contempt of court" and a capital offense. This made the rule of justice paramount in the land and helped prevent anarchy.

Continuing, the people were instructed to follow the rulings made by the Levitical judges that had taken the case. The sanctuary was holy; therefore, the rulings were to be based on holiness, regardless of how they were decided. The loser of the case (especially) had to be gracious, even in defeat, and know that the Lord was able to bless him because his spirit was pure. The Levites were also given instructions as to their responsibility to fairly judge the case. Moreover, their obligation went beyond the cases themselves, as they were to minister to all parties concerned in the dispute. Since *Yahweh* is a God of reconciliation, the judgment was not designed to alienate the plaintiff or the respondent. The party that lost the case, as well as the victor, were commanded to learn from the experience, or from the concepts that the ruling would teach them (v. 10).

Then, as now, the verdict commanded it imperative that all parties follow the terms of the edict. This was a necessary component. They are to remember that this change of venue and move to an appellate court is sanctioned by the Lord because, in this place, a proper verdict is issued by priests of His choosing. Therefore, all must do exactly as stated in the provisions of the ruling. Moreover, there exists a warning that the parties should not turn from the decisions; as they must not "turn from the right or the left," meaning there must not be any alterations or changes.

Another warning is issued to the person who acts presumptuously or arrogantly toward the decisions of the rulings of a case. Although this may seem as if it is designated toward the loser of a case, the person displaying conceit, in theory, could be the winner of such disputes. Nonetheless, an appalling attitude in either situation will not be tolerated. As an example, following the Exodus, some of Israel rebelled against God, for they did not trust in Him, even after all He had done (Deuteronomy 1:32). Even after He spoke to them, they would not listen but rebelled acting presumptuously and fled into the hill country (Deuteronomy 1:43). This act of disobedience was an insult to God; and in this edict, He refuses to tolerate rebellion and disrespect. Therefore, all parties had to listen to and follow the rulings of the priests, who served as appellate judges because they were agents of the Lord. Remember, God provided the conditions of both the lower and higher courts; and in this situation, the right to have a difficult case heard is designed by God to dispense justice and impartiality. That which may be lost by the opposing forces involved in the dispute is that it is actually Yahweh who is providing integrity and justness. There exists, however, severe consequences for failure to obey the courts and ostensibly, the Lord. The edict is that the man that fails to listen and obey shall die! Although there is no description of how the offenders will be put to death, facing a death sentence in any manner would be frightening. Concluding the commandments, God assures that by the death of those who refuse to honor the priests who are charged with these cases, they are rejecting the counsel and wisdom of *Yahweh*. The death of the guilty would serve as an agent of the purging of evil, especially, since the issue of bribery had been a focus in reflecting the treachery that could destroy the fabric of society. Disobedience in any form is dangerous and was equally warned, as a notice to both parties. This segment of the Law serves as a deterrent to those who would be tempted to flaunt the edicts of the Lord. The objective is to remove all vestiges of iniquity from the newly settled promised land that would tarnish the people or land.

In conclusion, the people would understand the seriousness of disobedience to a loving God, who set up the parameters of justice and protection for their future. The people would realize that only when their justice was intertwined with God's justice would they fear or respect the edicts of the Lord. *Yahweh* knew that the people needed to have a somewhat visible example that would frighten them against disobedience. An illustration can be found when "Israel saw the great power which the LORD had used against the Egyptians, [and] the people feared the LORD, and they believed in the LORD and in His servant Moses" (Exodus 14:31). The people were to fear the Lord and follow the judgments of the Levitical priests, who were God's servants. The result of the edict is that the offenders will be destroyed and "cut off" from the love and eternal grace of the Lord.

THE LESSON APPLIED

We live in a society of a litigious people who sue for almost anything. Believers are discouraged from becoming a part of this way of life. Some lawsuits are justified, such as was the historic decision in the *Brown v. Board of Education* case. For accident victims and people who are being misused, the courts are sometimes the only source of relief. However, unnecessary or frivolous litigations should not become a part of the believer's makeup. Paul asks, "When you have a case against your neighbor, dare you go to the den of the unrighteous and not go before the saints?" (1 Corinthians 6:1). Paul said this because he believed that the courts and its officials had become corrupt, driven by greed and political aspirations. Christians are directed to avoid lawsuits.

LET'S TALK ABOUT IT

Are the civil laws of society adequate in their concern for the marginalized?

How would authentic civil and criminal justice function in our contemporary society, if always administered justly? Is that even probable? Again, looking at what Paul faced in his day, we are provided with a possible solution in that, since courts have implications over the matters of life, should not the judges who are in positions of authority be Christians or believers that are aligned with the Church? Ideally, Christian judges would not be motivated by money or positions of power. While this seems improbable, Christians are reminded to accept the authority of the church and follow the civil laws of the state. While each (the church and the state) is independent of one another, they both should be held accountable to the standards of the Lord.

HOME DAILY DEVOTIONAL READINGS JANUARY 24–30, 2022						
MONDAY	**TUESDAY**	**WEDNESDAY**	**THURSDAY**	**FRIDAY**	**SATURDAY**	**SUNDAY**
God Executes Justice for the Poor	Remembering Our Marginalized Ancestors	Woe to Those Who Mistreat Workers	Justice for the Weak and Orphaned	Jesus' Compassion for the Helpless	Do Not Oppress the Alien	Justice for the Poor
Psalm 140	Deuteronomy 26:1-11	James 5:1-11	Psalm 82	Matthew 9:27-38	Leviticus 19:32-37	Deuteronomy 24:10-21

JUSTICE AND THE MARGINALIZED

ADULT TOPIC: COUNTERCULTURAL COMPASSION	BACKGROUND SCRIPTURE: DEUTERONOMY 24:10-21

DEUTERONOMY 24:10–21

King James Version

WHEN thou dost lend thy brother any thing, thou shalt not go into his house to fetch his pledge.

11 Thou shalt stand abroad, and the man to whom thou dost lend shall bring out the pledge abroad unto thee.

12 And if the man be poor, thou shalt not sleep with his pledge:

13 In any case thou shalt deliver him the pledge again when the sun goeth down, that he may sleep in his own raiment, and bless thee: and it shall be righteousness unto thee before the LORD thy God.

14 Thou shalt not oppress an hired servant that is poor and needy, whether he be of thy brethren, or of thy strangers that are in thy land within thy gates:

15 At his day thou shalt give him his hire, neither shall the sun go down upon it; for he is poor, and setteth his heart upon it: lest he cry against thee unto the LORD, and it be sin unto thee.

16 The fathers shall not be put to death for the children, neither shall the children be put to death for the fathers: every man shall be put to death for his own sin.

17 Thou shalt not pervert the judgment of the stranger, nor of the fatherless; nor take a widow's raiment to pledge:

18 But thou shalt remember that thou wast a bondman in Egypt, and the LORD thy God redeemed thee thence: therefore I command thee to do this thing.

19 When thou cuttest down thine harvest in thy field, and hast forgot a sheaf in the field, thou shalt not go again to fetch it: it shall be for the stranger, for the fatherless, and for the widow:

New Revised Standard Version

WHEN you make your neighbor a loan of any kind, you shall not go into the house to take the pledge.

11 You shall wait outside, while the person to whom you are making the loan brings the pledge out to you.

12 If the person is poor, you shall not sleep in the garment given you as the pledge.

13 You shall give the pledge back by sunset, so that your neighbor may sleep in the cloak and bless you; and it will be to your credit before the LORD your God.

14 You shall not withhold the wages of poor and needy laborers, whether other Israelites or aliens who reside in your land in one of your towns.

15 You shall pay them their wages daily before sunset, because they are poor and their livelihood depends on them; otherwise they might cry to the Lord against you, and you would incur guilt.

16 Parents shall not be put to death for their children, nor shall children be put to death for their parents; only for their own crimes may persons be put to death.

17 You shall not deprive a resident alien or an orphan of justice; you shall not take a widow's garment in pledge.

18 Remember that you were a slave in Egypt and the LORD your God redeemed you from there; therefore I command you to do this.

19 When you reap your harvest in your field and forget a sheaf in the field, you shall not go back to get it; it shall be left for the alien, the orphan, and the widow, so that the LORD your God may bless

MAIN THOUGHT: Remember that you were a slave in Egypt and the LORD your God redeemed you from there; therefore I command you to do this. (Deuteronomy 24:18, KJV)

DEUTERONOMY 24:10–21

King James Version	New Revised Standard Version
that the LORD thy God may bless thee in all the work of thine hands. 20 When thou beatest thine olive tree, thou shalt not go over the boughs again: it shall be for the stranger, for the fatherless, and for the widow. 21 When thou gatherest the grapes of thy vineyard, thou shalt not glean it afterward: it shall be for the stranger, for the fatherless, and for the widow.	you in all your undertakings. 20 When you beat your olive trees, do not strip what is left; it shall be for the alien, the orphan, and the widow. 21 When you gather the grapes of your vineyard, do not glean what is left; it shall be for the alien, the orphan, and the widow.

LESSON SETTING
Time: 1423 BC
Place: Sinai

LESSON OUTLINE
I. Laws Concerning the Pledge
   (Deuteronomy 24:10–13)
II. Laws Concerning Wages of the Poor
   (Deuteronomy 24:14–17)
III. Laws Concerning the Bounty
   (Deuteronomy 24:18–21)

UNIFYING PRINCIPLE
Some people are poor and marginalized. How can their dignity and worth be respected? Deuteronomy demands justice for all who are poor or marginalized.

INTRODUCTION
In this lesson, there is a focus on laws that are designed to ensure proper and humane treatment of those that are economically challenged and relegated to living on the fringes of society. The plight of the poor is very real, as Jesus would later state quoting Deuteronomy 15:11, "For you always have the poor with you; but you do not always have me" (Matthew 26:11). Nonetheless, these laws are designed to protect the indigent from exploitation and Israel from committing the sin of not being their "brother's keeper." These edicts regulate the provisions of borrowing and the practice of lending, defining the pledge and the responsibility of the financier. Additionally, the widow and the orphan are spotlighted, and the manner by which all of society can assist them in their plight for survival. What must not be lost is that God is also invested in the persons with means, as He does not want this group to lose their dignity.

I. LAWS CONCERNING THE PLEDGE (DEUTERONOMY 24:10–13)
A "would be" lender's behavior is addressed in vv. 10–11. In this case, the pledge serves as collateral. It is the guarantee that the borrower will repay the debt. God demanded that the dignity of each person be observed. Israel's economic system may have been a partial bartering system, by which goods and commodities were traded between parties. For example, a person might trade a basket of grain for an equal basket of figs, or trade two goats for one sheep. Money or currency was recognized as early during the time of Abraham (Genesis 24:35). However, Israel's form of currency is relegated to pieces of silver and gold. These chunks made of precious metals were probably unformed and were valued according to their weight, such as

shekels, half–shekels, and quarter–shekels. However, these were undeniably not coins, which are pieces of metal bearing a stamp that are issued by a governing body. The use of coined money is first mentioned in a connection to Persian coinage, the *daric* or *drachma* (Ezra 2:69; Nehemiah 7:70), and the *'adarkon* (Ezra 8:27).

Nonetheless, people without enough goods or money and would have to resort to "borrowing" from one who did have these items, to be repaid at an agreed–upon time. The idea of being able to loan money or commodities presented an opportunity for the "haves" to exploit the "have nots," by inaugurating the practice of "loan sharking" and interest abuse! The lenders assumed a position of superiority over the borrower and would take undue liberties, such as going into the borrower's house to personally determine what was to be used as collateral. The lenders would actually take what they wanted, while not necessarily allowing the borrower any decision over the surety. Moreover, the lenders could change the original agreement as to the items that were used for collateral, if they felt the borrower would not be able to pay. In essence, if they saw an item that they personally coveted, they could properly seize it, even if its value was far greater than the original value of the loan.

Yahweh charged Moses to demand that the dignity of the borrower be preserved. Loans based upon the agreed security of a pledge were permitted; however, charging interest to their own countrymen was not. These provisions were designed to prevent the creditor from abusing his legitimate rights, or enforcing them, arbitrarily or vexatiously, with malice.

Verse 12 commands that if the borrower is a poor man, the lender shall not sleep with his pledge. Although this edict may shock the sensibilities, it is easily misunderstood. The verb, *shakab*, can be translated as "sleep," "lie down," and "rest." Verse 13 brings clarity to the Law, stating that "when the sun goes down you shall surely return the pledge to him, that he may sleep in his cloak." This edict is an expansion of the original concept of Exodus 22:26–27, which states, "If you ever take your neighbor's cloak as a pledge, you are to return it to him before the sun sets, for that is his only covering; it is his cloak for his body. What else shall he sleep in?" Remember, the borrower may sleep in a tent or out in the elements, and his cloak or mantle would be the only item that would shield him from the chill of the cold nights of the region. The borrower could be so poor that all he could offer as a pledge was this garment off his back. As an act of mercy the lender was to return the garment prior to each nightfall, regardless of the time period of the loan, in order that the borrower would not be cold through the night. "You shall not sleep with it" means that the lender shall not use it for his needs. By acting in this manner, the lender would act in love toward his neighbor, as he loved himself. Additionally, the Lord would smile upon this act of righteousness and the graciousness of the lender would be blessed!

II. Laws Concerning Wages of the Poor (Deuteronomy 24:14–17)

The focus moves to the oppression of the domestic worker (Deuteronomy 24:14). The concern is not only for Israelites but is also applied to alien residents. Servants would fit the category of the poor and needy and would be vulnerable to exploitation by those of means.

In this section, a definition or distinction between slaves and servants is important, as these two designations can be confusing. Slave ownership was an integral part of biblical life; but unlike modern slavery, ancient slavery was not based on race. Most of these people, however, were day workers. They worked for wages that were to be paid at the end of each day. Unfortunately, paying them fair wages did not happen at times. The clause in v. 15, "sets his heart on it" means that he needed the money he worked for in order to feed and take care of his family. Wealthy employers were warned not to try to take advantage of this worker by suborning, withholding, or "cheating" the person of his/her wages. God would punish the employer for his sins.

These laws reflect God's surveillance concerning servanthood or slavery. We are given a bird's eye view of ancient debt–bondage manumission, which means that a slave will be freed after serving the period of his/her time. Traditionally the set period of time was seven years based on biblical precedent. For example, "If your kinsman, a Hebrew man or woman, is sold to you, then he shall serve you six years, but in the seventh year you shall set him free." Additionally, when the man (or woman) was released from his obligations, he was not to be sent away "empty handed," meaning that he was to be given provisions for his journey (Deuteronomy 15:12–13).

Here, the narrative shifts to the edicts of personal responsibility, as "fathers shall not be put to death for the actions of their sons, nor shall sons be executed for the crimes of their fathers" (Deuteronomy 24:16). Restricting punishment of the responsible individual, this law applies specifically to civil and criminal law, as responsibility for a crime is to be confined to the criminal; his family are not to suffer with him. This clarification is necessary as family units consisted of "tight" clans that would support the movement and opinion of the family, especially when espoused by the head (father) of such a clan or tribe. In some ancient societies, children, especially sons, would be punished in acts of retribution to satisfy the victor's lust for revenge; however, the Lord forbade such a practice, as "each was to die for his own sin." Nevertheless, a father could be the cause of his son's (children's) death, if the father rebelled against God, and the rest of his house were part of the revolt. If this was the case, no one in the family would be spared from their offenses against God.

Verse 17 observes that justice must not be perverted or corrupted in the case of an alien or an orphan. Recalling the edicts of previous declarations, this law serves as a continuation that shows God's protection of the oppressed. Notice the similarities between the alien and the orphan, as traditionally, both find many of the same forces aligned against them. The alien or foreigner is in the land probably to make a living and would be dispossessed and poor. This person would be seeking work at the mercy of an employer that could choose to be mean and cruel. Likewise, the orphan, who may not have inherited the wealth of a prosperous father, is also powerless and (dependent upon his/her age) could be totally unprotected. If the orphan came from a poor family, that child could be categorized as a "street urchin," who lived by begging or "hustling" for survival. Both the alien and the orphan were without a family in a culture that valued the tribe. Neither the foreigner nor the waif would be connected to anyone and thus, not have the protection of the family structure. Additionally, the law covers the protection afforded to the widow, who, traditionally, was probably poor because in this culture, widows could not inherit the property of their deceased husbands. Numbers 27:8–11 rules that a man's daughters are to inherit his ancestral property in the event that he dies without sons. This law does not grant women a general right to inherit or own land but seeks to preserve a man's name by protecting his lineage from extinction and maintaining its connection to his ancestral inheritance. Furthermore, if the father of the family lacks brothers, the inheritance may pass to the nearest relative in the family (not the widow), "and he shall possess it" (Numbers 17:11). We know partially how this functioned because of the witness of Ruth and Boaz, who functioned as her kinsman-redeemer (Ruth 4:1–10) Moreover, as in the case of the borrower, one cannot take the widow's garment to serve as a pledge. In this culture, bartering with a woman was not popular; nonetheless, she was to be afforded protection by her countrymen and by the Lord.

III. LAWS CONCERNING THE BOUNTY (DEUTERONOMY 24:18–21)

God, however, did not want the people of Israel to forget their position nor their emotional state when they were enslaved languishing in Egypt. Throughout Israelite history, *Yahweh* would have to constantly remind the arrogant that it was because of His intervention that they had been rescued from the horrors of Egyptian oppression. The Scriptures are littered with such reminders of His power to provide intervention and liberation. "We were slaves to Pharaoh in Egypt, and the LORD brought us from Egypt with a mighty hand" (Deuteronomy 6:21), who destroyed the Egyptians as He "brought the [Red] sea upon them [the Egyptian army] which you saw with your own eyes" (Joshua 24:7). He "[revealed] Himself as Savior when they were in Egyptian bondage to Pharaoh's house" (1 Samuel 2:27). This forced servitude not only strained Israel's relationship with God but also induced the people to align themselves with the pagan gods of Egypt. Additionally, God's constant reference to their bondage went beyond the mistreatment of His people, who had no rights or protection – especially for the widows and orphans – as their existence in Egypt was a death sentence. As God's chosen people, Yahweh's redemption of Israel served to position them as a model for all of humanity to emulate, thus bringing all of the world to Him. Hence, the newly emancipated Israel was to "do better;" because of their experiences, the people "knew better."

Yahweh continues to "look out" for the widow and orphan, as He did with the alien, by extending the commands to allow "gleaning," or having access to the "overflow" of Israel's bounty. A previous command was, "When you reap the harvest of your land, you shall not reap to the very corners of your field, nor shall you gather the gleanings of your harvest, nor shall you glean your vineyard, nor shall you gather the fallen fruit of your vineyard; you shall leave them for the needy and for the stranger" (Leviticus 19:9–10). However, in this case, when harvesting the sheaves, if one was forgotten, it was to be left for the widows and orphans, as Ruth would benefit from this law (Ruth 2:3). When the olive trees were harvested, the limbs were struck with poles to knock down the fruit to be collected when it fell to the ground. The edict was to only "hit the limbs once," so as to leave some of the fruit on the limbs of the trees. When picking grapes from the vines, the reaper was to go over it only once, thus leaving grapes on the vines. All of this was directed toward the care of the widows and the orphans, which reveals the gift of the "land of plenty," blessed by the Lord.

THE LESSON APPLIED

As Israel evolved into a prosperous nation, the separation between the "haves" and the "have nots" expanded. This left a caste system, similar to the high, middle, and lower classes we have today. In many cases (as is today), members of the "lower classes" did not have access to the credit that was afforded the upper classes, which left the poor open to exploitation by those in financial power. This allowed for many abuses, such as erroneous wages, inhumane agreements that allowed lenders to force women and young girls (children) into slavery, and the forcing of the poor into that which was an abomination to an ever–loving God. These laws sought to prohibit what could be categorized as social and economic oppression. Yahweh, however, saw the greed of many humans as a pathway to rejecting the care of their brothers and the Nation, and would remand those indicted for eventually rejecting Him – again!

LET'S TALK ABOUT IT

Are the current lending systems favorable to most believers of color?

In the African American experience, sharecropping was a system that extended chattel slavery far beyond the constitutional amendments that forbade the practice. In effect, the Emancipation Proclamation, the 13th Amendment, and many Jim Crow laws and the social acceptance that African Americans were inferior promoted the blatant swindles that occurred during this period of time in which sharecropping was common. Whereas, most African Americans no longer have to deal with sharecropping there are other oppressive techniques that are used to economically depress our communities. Currently, our wages do not equal that of our white counterparts and the average Black household has about five percent the wealth of the average white household. Sharecropping is no longer in practice but we still have much to overcome to experience equitable economic practices in this our land of promise and freedom, oppression and pain.

HOME DAILY DEVOTIONAL READINGS
JANUARY 31–FEBRUARY 6, 2022

MONDAY	TUESDAY	WEDNESDAY	THURSDAY	FRIDAY	SATURDAY	SUNDAY
David's Sin with Bathsheba	David Murders Bathsheba's Husband	Walk in the Light	Create in Me a Clean Heart	Redemption through Repentance	Christ, the Sacrifice for Our Sins	Nathan Tells a Pointed Parable
2 Samuel 11:1-13	2 Samuel 11:14-27	1 John 1:5-10	Psalm 51:1-14	Psalm 32	1 John 2:1-11	2 Samuel 12:1-9, 13-15

NATHAN CONDEMNS DAVID

<table>
<tr><td>ADULT TOPIC:
SPEAKING TRUTH TO POWER</td><td>BACKGROUND SCRIPTURE:
2 SAMUEL 12</td></tr>
</table>

2 SAMUEL 12:1–9, 13–15

King James Version	New Revised Standard Version
AND the LORD sent Nathan unto David. And he came unto him, and said unto him, There were two men in one city; the one rich, and the other poor.	AND the LORD sent Nathan to David. He came to him, and said to him, 'There were two men in a certain city, one rich and the other poor.
2 The rich man had exceeding many flocks and herds:	2 The rich man had very many flocks and herds;
3 But the poor man had nothing, save one little ewe lamb, which he had bought and nourished up: and it grew up together with him, and with his children; it did eat of his own meat, and drank of his own cup, and lay in his bosom, and was unto him as a daughter.	3 but the poor man had nothing but one little ewe lamb, which he had bought. He brought it up, and it grew up with him and with his children; it used to eat of his meagre fare, and drink from his cup, and lie in his bosom, and it was like a daughter to him.
4 And there came a traveller unto the rich man, and he spared to take of his own flock and of his own herd, to dress for the wayfaring man that was come unto him; but took the poor man's lamb, and dressed it for the man that was come to him.	4 Now there came a traveller to the rich man, and he was loath to take one of his own flock or herd to prepare for the wayfarer who had come to him, but he took the poor man's lamb, and prepared that for the guest who had come to him.'
5 And David's anger was greatly kindled against the man; and he said to Nathan, As the LORD liveth, the man that hath done this thing shall surely die:	5 Then David's anger was greatly kindled against the man. He said to Nathan, 'As the LORD lives, the man who has done this deserves to die;
6 And he shall restore the lamb fourfold, because he did this thing, and because he had no pity.	6 he shall restore the lamb fourfold, because he did this thing, and because he had no pity.'
7 And Nathan said to David, Thou art the man. Thus saith the LORD God of Israel, I anointed thee king over Israel, and I delivered thee out of the hand of Saul;	7 Nathan said to David, 'You are the man! Thus says the LORD, the God of Israel: I anointed you king over Israel, and I rescued you from the hand of Saul;
8 And I gave thee thy master's house, and thy master's wives into thy bosom, and gave thee the house of Israel and of Judah; and if that	8 I gave you your master's house, and your master's wives into your bosom, and gave you the house of Israel and of Judah; and if that

MAIN THOUGHT: Nathan said to David, "You are the man!"
(2 Samuel 12:7, NRSV)

2 SAMUEL 12:1–9, 13–15

King James Version	*New Revised Standard Version*
had been too little, I would moreover have given unto thee such and such things.	had been too little, I would have added as much more.
9 Wherefore hast thou despised the command-ment of the LORD, to do evil in his sight? thou hast killed Uriah the Hittite with the sword, and hast taken his wife to be thy wife, and hast slain him with the sword of the children of Ammon.	9 Why have you despised the word of the Lord, to do what is evil in his sight? You have struck down Uriah the Hittite with the sword, and have taken his wife to be your wife, and have killed him with the sword of the Ammonites.
• • • • • •	• • • • • •
13 And David said unto Nathan, I have sinned against the LORD. And Nathan said unto David, The LORD also hath put away thy sin; thou shalt not die.	13 David said to Nathan, 'I have sinned against the LORD.' Nathan said to David, 'Now the LORD has put away your sin; you shall not die.
14 Howbeit, because by this deed thou hast given great occasion to the enemies of the LORD to blaspheme, the child also that is born unto thee shall surely die.	14 Nevertheless, because by this deed you have utterly scorned the LORD, the child that is born to you shall die.'
15 And Nathan departed unto his house. And the LORD struck the child that Uriah's wife bare unto David, and it was very sick.	15 Then Nathan went to his house. The LORD struck the child that Uriah's wife bore to David, and it became very ill.

LESSON SETTING
Time: 1005 BC
Place: Jerusalem

LESSON OUTLINE
**I. Nathan's Parable
(2 Samuel 12:1–4)**
**II. David Condemns Himself
(2 Samuel 12:5–9)**
**III. God Punishes David
(2 Samuel 12:13–15)**

UNIFYING PRINCIPLE
People often see acts of injustice being committed. How are we called to respond when we witness unjust acts? Nathan sought God's guidance and received wisdom for how to address David's sin.

INTRODUCTION
David had an affair with Uriah's wife, one of David's warriors that served in his army, who was away and in the midst of a battle. As a result of this union she became pregnant. Knowing that Uriah was not the father, David devised a plan to hide their dalliance. David arranged for Uriah to return to his home on leave to "sleep with" his wife, as a cover for the pregnancy, thus shifting the fatherhood to Uriah. Because of Uriah's unfettered loyalty as a soldier, he refused; thus, David set him up to be killed in a battle with the Ammonites. After a proper period of mourning, David then took Bathsheba, Uriah's widow, as his wife. God was not pleased, and this began a curse against the House of David. Nathan the prophet is chosen to confront the king. Prophets clearly confront kings, rulers, and the powers of their day with the word of God when necessary.

I. NATHAN'S PARABLE
(2 SAMUEL 12:1–4)

After witnessing the injustice that David had committed, God sent the prophet Nathan to confront the king about his horrid indiscretion. Nathan first appears in connection with the arrangements David made for the building of the temple (2 Samuel 7:2–3). Nathan was very close to David and was disappointed with how he had managed this situation. David, who had been anointed as the future king by Samuel, trusted and believed in the prophets of the Lord; therefore, he would listen to Nathan and respect his counsel. Nathan could have feared confronting the king. Kings could condemn their advisors (as well as their enemies) who pointed out their sins, face execution or be subject to banishment from the court and the country.

Nathan presented a parable to bring attention to an injustice between two men that were polar opposites in wealth and social standing. Although this story is exhibited as an allegory, Nathan presented the case as if it had recently occurred and justice needed to be served. Crafting his approach, Nathan wove an account of a wealthy person that had taken advantage of a poor man, who was a just and righteous person.

Wealth could be measured in terms of animal holdings, thus, the emphasis in verse 2 is centered around the many flocks and herds that were owned by the rich man and not the amount of money he possessed. This is because the contrasting comparison occurs between the many animals of the wealthy and the singular animal owned by the poor man. The poor man owned what we might call a house pet, a domesticated animal described as an ewe lamb. The definition of this ewe lamb (*kibśâ*) is that it is a female offspring of sheep that was considered ceremonially clean, representing the fact that the animal was pure and could be used as a sacrifice to the Lord. However, it seems that the lamb was actually purchased for the enjoyment of the poor man's family (especially his children), so much so, that the lamb was "like a daughter" to him, i.e., it was a pet, around which there should be no negative overtones. His children were obviously fond of the animal, as they enjoyed feeding and caring for the lamb. Several items should be observed: (1) The poor man owned the animal; (2) it was the only one the man owned; (3) the family had hand–fed the creature; and (4) it slept in the living quarters with the family. Each of these observances portrays the intense feelings and attachment the family had to this lamb. Both men lived in the same city, but the rich man viewed the poor man (and his possessions) as expendable.

Nathan inserts the addition of a traveler who came to stay with the rich man; and in the hospitality of their culture, the rich man had a sumptuous dinner prepared for his guest. We are not privy to the man's identity or the reason why he visited; but for the purpose of the story, it is not important. In an act of extreme greed, the wealthy man overlooked the many animals that were part of his flocks and decided that he would seize the only animal from the house of the poor man. We are not aware as to how the rich man acquired the animal; it may have strayed while outside its perimeter, which according to the law, obligated its return, unharmed (Exodus 23:4). No matter, the rich man captured the docile lamb and slaughtered it for the dinner at his house!

II. DAVID CONDEMNS HIMSELF (2 SAMUEL 12:5–9)

Upon hearing this parable, David was furious and determined that the offender deserved to die. It was unjust that a rich man who had plenty of lambs would steal the only lamb from a poor man, who was attached to the animal and probably could not have afforded to purchase another. Additionally, since the lamb was a family pet, replacing the animal would never satisfy the personal affection and bond felt by the family, especially his children.

As if Nathan was presenting the case from the perspective of the dishonored man, David demanded restitution for the lamb, fourfold. This would be in accordance with the Mosaic Law, which states, "If a man steals an ox or a sheep and slaughters it or sells it, he shall pay five oxen for the ox and four sheep for the sheep" (Exodus 22:1). This represents retribution and restitution by compensating for the loss and returning the same kind of animals.

At this juncture, Nathan had David and moved to cement the moral of this narrative by declaring, "You are the rich man in this story." When Nathan said to David, "You are the man," it is not to be taken as a comment of praise, as in the language of our contemporary society. Nathan cleverly recited this story, and not once had David suspected that he was the guilty party. Moreover, David now understood that Nathan knew of Uriah's death and the subsequent theft of his wife. David was probably crushed, for several reasons: one, that he had slept with the wife of one of his subordinates; two, that he had impregnated her; and three, that he had Uriah murdered as a "cover up." Because of his relationship with Nathan and God, David knew he was in trouble. To make sure that David understood that this message was not of Nathan, he declared, "Thus says the Lord".

David was anointed king of Israel to be a just and righteous king, not given to corruption. Saul had fallen out of favor with *Yahweh,* partly because of his insecurities, cowardice, and moral decay, which, as a result, created a buffer between the first king and God. When David was anointed king, his position had been consecrated, which made David the representative of *Yahweh;* but his sin degraded his position, in the eyes of the people and Yahweh Himself! Spence–Jones states that rank and authority are given to men that they may lead others to do right; it is a fearful misuse of these entities when they give prestige to sin. As the second king of Israel, David was extremely blessed and, although the Nation continued to be embroiled in wars, God gave David anything he wanted, including more wives and concubines, if he desired. Recall that on several occasions, God had delivered David from the murderous hand of Saul; still yet, *Yahweh* had to remind David (just as He had Israel, repeatedly) that it was Him who brought them out of Egypt. The repetition of the phrase, "It is I," is not an accidental edit of the translation but Samuel's method of revealing the emphasis on God being God!

Continuing, God lists some of the items that David received, such as the control of "[his] master's house." This indicates that David was given the palace and the royal household – the entire kingdom of Saul. David was in possession of Saul's family; and although Saul only had one wife, Ahinoam (1 Samuel 14:50), he probably had an entourage of concubines. "Your master's wives" defined the wives given over to David's care and bed. He had a plethora of intimate female companions, David did not have to succumb to the greed that tempted him to seduce another man's wife. David had license to choose among any of the women of his kingdom; but not satisfied with these blessings, he lusted after a married woman and had her husband killed to accomplish his clandestine deed. In addition to the fact that David could have had more wives if he desired, God reminded David that he would have been given additional lands, if he desired! God's blessings over David were not limited; if only he had trusted God and not resorted to his own lust.

David had been ungrateful and unfaithful to the Lord, who had given him all of the desires of his heart. David was charged for despising the word of the Lord, as God sees everything. In pursuing the affair with Bathsheba, David violated at least four of the Ten Commandments (coveting, murder, lying, and adultery). As king, he thought himself above the Law and therefore, displayed a contemptuous arrogance toward the very God who had blessed him, as found in the New Jerusalem Bible. Most translators note that this is actually *Yahweh* speaking and is better understood as His stating, "You have despised My word," or asking, "Why have you despised Me?"

III. GOD PUNISHES DAVID (2 SAMUEL 12:13–15)

The conversation shifts as David says to Nathan, "I have sinned against the LORD," to which Nathan replies, "The LORD also has taken away your sin; you shall not die" (v. 13). David's confession notes that he realized that during his coupling with Bathsheba, he was separated from the Lord, both in mind and spirit, as he could not have seduced the woman if he had been of the attitude and presence of the Lord. David's confession that he had "sinned against the Lord" was pure in contrast to that uttered by Saul, "…that I should sin against Jehovah" (1 Samuel 12:33), as Saul only sought to appease Samuel. David, who has a heart after God, would later compose a psalm as a contrite sinner's prayer for pardon, describing the prayer when Nathan came to him after he had gone into Bathsheba (Psalm 51). God favors David and shields him from his sin by keeping him alive; however, the sin will not go unpunished. David will be punished. The Jewish Bible uses the term "remitted," meaning that punishment for his indiscretion will be transferred to the young child, who was to surely die. This edict would align with a God who keeps lovingkindness for thousands and forgives iniquity, transgression, and sin; yet, He will by no means leave the guilty unpunished, "visiting the iniquity of fathers on the children and on the grandchildren to the third and fourth generations" (Exodus 34:7). God's judgment on David may seem to contradict the law that "fathers shall not be put to death for their sons, nor shall sons be put to death for their fathers; everyone shall be put to death for his own sin" (Deuteronomy 24:16). Whereas, the unborn child was not guilty of the sin but was a byproduct of the sin and, thus, would only live for seven days. David's sexual relationship with Bathsheba was supposed to be a secret; but (ironically) Nathan assured David that the decree that brought about Uriah's death (and Bathsheba's subsequent pregnancy) was brought to light, resulting in the Hebrew understanding that thou hast made the enemies of Jehovah to despise – that is, to despise Jehovah's government, the theocracy over which David was the visible head and earthly representative. The death of the adulterous offspring of David and Bathsheba proved that God's righteous rule could reach and punish the king himself and would thus, vindicate His justice from their reproach. Nathan was finished with his condemnation of David's actions, and the prophecy that was given against David had come from the Lord. Nathan, without fear of retaliation from the king's rebuke, then returned to his house unscathed by David, who realized that he was responsible for his own sin. Nathan's role was to help demonstrate that no one is above God's Law, not even a lustful king. In this way, Nathan shows the importance of prophets who are mouthpieces for God. A prophet can ill-afford to be a soothsayer but must be filled with righteousness and a love for the truth.

THE LESSON APPLIED

As king of Israel, David seemed to have it all, but one lapse in judgment resulted in a stern punishment for both Bathsheba and him. One may wonder, perhaps, why David was not punished with death, as he had so sternly advocated for the guilty (rich) man.

Both adultery and murder were sufficient cause for the execution of even a king (Ex. 21:12; Lev. 20:10). David's sin was heinous, but the grace of God was more than sufficient to forgive and restore him, as Nathan could testify. And yet, though David could be restored to fellowship with his God, the impact of his sin remained and would continue to work its sorrow in the Nation as well as in the king's life.

LET'S TALK ABOUT IT

What are some of the traits and characteristics of a good leader?

Leaders should be just in their dealings, wise in their decision-making, and people of good moral character, with a willingness to serve with integrity. They are also responsible to God for the type of leadership they provide. God has set up governmental authorities to administer wise and prudent leadership. In the book of Kings, God asks Solomon what is it that he desired most. To his credit, Solomon requested wisdom to rule the people. Good leaders recognize the value of seeking God's guidance. The one essential characteristic good leaders utilize is to seek God's will as a personal and leadership priority. Jesus promised that if we seek God first all other things He will grant unto us.

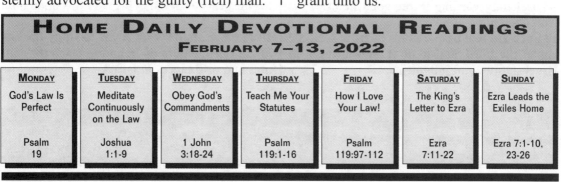

HOME DAILY DEVOTIONAL READINGS
FEBRUARY 7–13, 2022

MONDAY	TUESDAY	WEDNESDAY	THURSDAY	FRIDAY	SATURDAY	SUNDAY
God's Law Is Perfect	Meditate Continuously on the Law	Obey God's Commandments	Teach Me Your Statutes	How I Love Your Law!	The King's Letter to Ezra	Ezra Leads the Exiles Home
Psalm 19	Joshua 1:1-9	1 John 3:18-24	Psalm 119:1-16	Psalm 119:97-112	Ezra 7:11-22	Ezra 7:1-10, 23-26

EZRA SEEKS GOD'S LAW

ADULT TOPIC:
RESTORING LAW AND ORDER

BACKGROUND SCRIPTURE:
EZRA 7:1–26

EZRA 7:1–10, 23–26

King James Version

Now after these things, in the reign of Artaxerxes king of Persia, Ezra the son of Seraiah, the son of Azariah, the son of Hilkiah,

2 The son of Shallum, the son of Zadok, the son of Ahitub,

3 The son of Amariah, the son of Azariah, the son of Meraioth,

4 The son of Zerahiah, the son of Uzzi, the son of Bukki,

5 The son of Abishua, the son of Phinehas, the son of Eleazar, the son of Aaron the chief priest:

6 This Ezra went up from Babylon; and he was a ready scribe in the law of Moses, which the Lord God of Israel had given: and the king granted him all his request, according to the hand of the Lord his God upon him.

7 And there went up some of the children of Israel, and of the priests, and the Levites, and the singers, and the porters, and the Nethinims, unto Jerusalem, in the seventh year of Artaxerxes the king.

8 And he came to Jerusalem in the fifth month, which was in the seventh year of the king.

9 For upon the first day of the first month began he to go up from Babylon, and on the first day of the fifth month came he to Jerusalem, according to the good hand of his God upon him.

10 For Ezra had prepared his heart to seek the law of the Lord, and to do it, and to teach in Israel statutes and judgments.

New Revised Standard Version

After this, in the reign of King Artaxerxes of Persia, Ezra son of Seraiah, son of Azariah, son of Hilkiah,

2 son of Shallum, son of Zadok, son of Ahitub,

3 son of Amariah, son of Azariah, son of Meraioth,

4 son of Zerahiah, son of Uzzi, son of Bukki,

5 son of Abishua, son of Phinehas, son of Eleazar, son of the chief priest Aaron—

6 this Ezra went up from Babylonia. He was a scribe skilled in the law of Moses that the Lord the God of Israel had given; and the king granted him all that he asked, for the hand of the Lord his God was upon him.

7 Some of the people of Israel, and some of the priests and Levites, the singers and gatekeepers, and the temple servants also went up to Jerusalem, in the seventh year of King Artaxerxes.

8 They came to Jerusalem in the fifth month, which was in the seventh year of the king.

9 On the first day of the first month the journey up from Babylon was begun, and on the first day of the fifth month he came to Jerusalem, for the gracious hand of his God was upon him.

10 For Ezra had set his heart to study the law of the Lord, and to do it, and to teach the statutes and ordinances in Israel.

MAIN THOUGHT: For Ezra had set his heart to study the law of the LORD, and to do it, and to teach the statutes and ordinances in Israel. (Ezra 7:10, KJV).

Ezra 7:1–10, 23–26

King James Version	*New Revised Standard Version*
••••••	••••••
23 Whatsoever is commanded by the God of heaven, let it be diligently done for the house of the God of heaven: for why should there be wrath against the realm of the king and his sons?	23 Whatever is commanded by the God of heaven, let it be done with zeal for the house of the God of heaven, or wrath will come upon the realm of the king and his heirs.
24 Also we certify you, that touching any of the priests and Levites, singers, porters, Nethinims, or ministers of this house of God, it shall not be lawful to impose toll, tribute, or custom, upon them.	24 We also notify you that it shall not be lawful to impose tribute, custom, or toll on any of the priests, the Levites, the singers, the doorkeepers, the temple servants, or other servants of this house of God.
25 And thou, Ezra, after the wisdom of thy God, that is in thine hand, set magistrates and judges, which may judge all the people that are beyond the river, all such as know the laws of thy God; and teach ye them that know them not.	25 'And you, Ezra, according to the God-given wisdom you possess, appoint magistrates and judges who may judge all the people in the province Beyond the River who know the laws of your God; and you shall teach those who do not know them.
26 And whosoever will not do the law of thy God, and the law of the king, let judgment be executed speedily upon him, whether it be unto death, or to banishment, or to confiscation of goods, or to imprisonment.	26 All who will not obey the law of your God and the law of the king, let judgement be strictly executed on them, whether for death or for banishment or for confiscation of their goods or for imprisonment.'

LESSON SETTING
Time: 458 BC
Place: Babylon to Jerusalem

LESSON OUTLINE
I. The Genealogy of Ezra
   (Ezra 7:1–5)
II. Ezra Travels from Babylon to
    Jerusalem (Ezra 7:6–10)
III. Ezra Is Granted Authority
     (Ezra 7:23–26)

UNIFYING PRINCIPLE
People sometimes face situations in which they fear others will oppose their efforts. What motivates people to behave benevolently toward others? God's hand was on Ezra, and he was able to return to Jerusalem in an effort to restore respect for God's Law.

INTRODUCTION
Israel is being allowed to return from captivity after the Babylonians were defeated by the Persians. Several of their kings, Cyrus and Darius, issued decrees enforced by Artaxerxes to allow their return to Jerusalem, and their rebuilding of the temple, which was completed on the third day of the month of Adar (February–March), in the sixth year of the reign of Darius. This eponymous book is named for its principle character. Ezra is a priest who is a descendant of Aaron and is recognized by Artaxerxes to lead Israel in its resettlement. This account is about God's intervention in human affairs and His consistent love for His people.

I. THE GENEALOGY OF EZRA (EZRA 7:1–5)

This section begins with a genealogy of Ezra that validates his authority. Ezra's family tree presented here (vv. 1–5) is important to connect him to Aaron, his ancestor. As head of the clan of Levitical priests, the sons of Aaron would continue their role as holy clerics. The names listed here do not represent a complete lineage, as some are omitted. Ezra is probably a shortened form of Azariah, meaning "the LORD has helped." Ezra is listed as the son of Seraiah which cannot be taken literally. Seraiah is listed as the father of Jehozadak (1 Chronicles 6:14). Seraiah lived before the Exile and was captured when "the captain of the guard took Seraiah the chief priest and Zephaniah the second priest, with three other officers of the temple" (2 Kings 25:18), who were summarily executed by the Babylonians after the fall of Jerusalem. Although many Hebrew names are similar, the expression that is translated "son of" does not necessarily refer to an actual son but indicates that Ezra was simply one of Seraiah's descendants. It is important to understand the emphasis of the connection to Ezra's lineage because it establishes his authentic priestly credentials.

The opening phrase of verse 1 refers to the events recorded in Chapter 6 and consisted of an interval of probably 57 to 58 years. These events most likely began with Darius, the king of Persia, who installed the original decree by Cyrus that emancipated the Jews and allowed the Exiles to return to Jerusalem to begin the rebuilding of their temple.

II. EZRA TRAVELS FROM BABYLON TO JERUSALEM (EZRA 7:6–10)

Ezra was highly favored by God when he left Babylon for Jerusalem in 458 B.C. The language that "he went up" invokes the imagery of his "going up" or ascending to the holy city of Jerusalem, which was located on Mount Zion. Jerusalem was topographically situated or elevated higher than all that surrounded it, which is why one always ascended old Jerusalem. As previously mentioned, Ezra was skilled in his ability to serve both the people and the Lord. Ezra was well–versed in his knowledge of the Law of Moses. Although Ezra was not alive during the original giving of the Law, he represents the "remnant" of those dedicated to *Yahweh* who embraced the Torah and passed it down through successive generations. Even in exile, these priests continued to love the Lord and trust that deliverance would be forthcoming. Ezra is described as a "scribe". These are not the scribes mentioned in the New Testament. His scribal profession may give some indication on how he was able to gain an audience with and favor with the emperor. As someone who could read and write, Ezra would have been a part of the elite of society given that fewer than five percent of people could read or write at this point in history.

Whereas Ezra assumes the principal position of instructor of the people in the teaching of the Law, it is important to establish his reliability as a scribe and an authority of the Torah. Ezra was highly respected by the king, who granted him all he requested because the hand of the Lord his God was upon him. The Persian king also favored Ezra because sending the Exiles back to Canaan was financially profitable for Persia. Israel would continue to be subservient to Persia. Resettling the land with former Exiles that were intelligent, industrious, and self–sufficient would give the Persians an expanded tax base and happier constituency. A happier constituency is important because it means less resistance and fewer ideological and violent revolts. The Persian imperial policy is one that would be adopted and adapted by Alexander the Great and eventually the Romans. People tend to make better servants when they are happy and at home than when they are in constant fear.

Ezra was not alone in his journey to Jerusalem, since the accompanying troupe included some of the sons of Israel, priests, Levites, singers, gatekeepers, and temple servants. The list of these categories suggests that proper worship was foremost in the mind of Ezra. They would be prepared when they reached Jerusalem. They would be able to worship God during their journey. Although we are not privy to the total of these categories, it is not an accident or literary device to highlight these groups. While the priests' and Levites' duties are obvious, notice that singers are present (music was a staple of temple worship), as are gate or doorkeepers (who would function as ushers in the present–day church). However, listed also are temple servants (similarly called Nethinim). Mentioned only in Ezra and Nehemiah, modern translations of Nethinim are "temple servants" or "temple slaves."

With his contingent reached, Ezra left Babylon on the first day of the first month (Nisan 1st) and arrived in Jerusalem in the fifth month (Ab), which corresponds to the modern–day July–August. The journey covered 900 miles and lasted four months, in 458 B.C., which was the seventh year of the Persian king. Nisan is only used in biblical texts after the Babylonian Exile, as it was earlier known as Abib; after the Exile, the Israelites adopted the Babylonian name for the month. Ezra is probably remembering the importance of the first month because, beginning on the fourteenth day, Israel was commanded to eat unleavened bread (Exodus 12:18); and the reference to the Exodus itself occurred in the first month of the year. If this was Ezra's mindset, the return of the Babylonian Exiles is implicitly connected to the Israelites' original journey to the promised land, after their enslavement and years of wandering in the desert.

Ezra's heart is set to study the Law of the Lord. In Hebrew culture (as in the imagery of the Bible), the heart is the center of spiritual activity and human life. As the Scriptures testify, the heart is the "home of personal life" and may be used to describe the attributes of a person, such as one who may have a "discerning heart" (1 Kings 3:12), a "pure heart" (Psalm 24:4), or a "good heart" (Luke 8:15). Unfortunately, one may also have a heart that is wicked (Genesis 8:21) or hardened, such as was displayed by the Egyptian Pharaoh (Exodus 14:8). This form of a degenerate heart reveals a rogue spirit that is separated from the will of God. The state of Ezra's heart exceeds his intellectual desire to please God; whereas, in this case, the heart could be interchanged with the "soul," meaning that Ezra's soul desires to please the Lord.

Ezra is determined to study the Law, meaning that he is resolute in his efforts to become skilled in all facets of the Torah. As a priest and professional scribe, Ezra realized that many of Israel's problems came from disregarding God's commandments. As with a constitutional scholar of today, Ezra realized that adherence to the Law brought order and a stabilized society.

In his practice of the Law, Ezra decided that his knowledge thereof would not be used as a platform for self–aggrandizement but to bring about justice and protection for the people. The language in this passage is highly influenced by Deuteronomy 4:14, where, "The Lord commanded me [Moses] at that time to teach you [Israel] statutes and judgments, that you might perform them in the land where you are going over to possess it." Here, Ezra is envisioned as a lawgiver like Moses, who will provide the people with the Law, along with its "correct" interpretation. Ezra is prepared for the task of interpreting, explaining, and applying the ancient law to a new context in which Israel is ruled. If Israel was to survive this new set of opportunities to become the "Great Nation" that was promised to Abraham and the other patriarchs, the Torah could not be relegated to the "words on a page" of some dusty set of scrolls. Instead, it must be a living document that captures the heart and soul of the people, while affirming the supremacy of *Yahweh* as God.

III. Ezra is Granted Authority (Ezra 7:23–26)

In preparation for their release from exile, Artaxerxes listed certain freedoms the people were to have as he gave them permission to go to Jerusalem (v. 13). The Exiles were allowed to take silver and gold with them and could "get more" in Babylon (vv. 15–16, 20). They could offer sacrifices on the altar at the temple (v. 17) and were also granted the freedom to make their own decisions (v. 18). Interestingly, they were given back their utensils of worship for the temple (vv. 19–20). Apparently not all of them had been carried back

with Zerubbabel (1:7–11). They could have whatever else they needed for the temple, up to a certain limit (7:21–22). As previously mentioned, there existed some benefits for Artaxerxes. Artaxerxes was an astute and calculating king who (through this) was actually preparing for any future uprising he may have to face. It was beneficial and efficient for Persia not to have to fight with other countries or to have to prepare for an insurrection within its borders. In return for granting these privileges, the king would receive some benefits from the expedition. Sensing Ezra's zeal to not only return to Jerusalem but to be held responsible for his people, the king invoked Ezra's God, to provide Ezra with motivation and a sense of duty. Additionally, Ezra was responsible for administering justice to all the people of the area, that is, to all who knew the laws of his God.

Ezra was also given the authority to set up a government (a puppet régime that remained subservient to Persia), with the necessary judges, magistrates, and officials who would serve as the "peacekeeping society" of the newly settled province. It is not an accident that verses 25–26 are dominated with references to the "wisdom of your God" and the "law[s] of your God" because the Persian king is playing into Ezra's devotion to his relationship with *Yahweh*. Remember, Artaxerxes is a pagan king who sees himself as a semi–deity but worships a pantheon of gods. Israel should be considered a province within the Persian Empire, not a nation or a sovereign state. There is clear evidence that the Persian Empire was highly organized with provincial leaders to collect taxes, adjudicate cases, protect the citizenry, and enforce imperial policy.

Ezra would not abuse his authority because he is too interested in the justice of a righteous God, who was delivering Israel to a sense of freedom. The confidence of the king reveals the measure of respect that Ezra commanded. Therefore, as in the departure from Egypt during the Exodus, Ezra was allowed to lead a contingent home. Because of his relationship with the Persian king, Ezra could have taken credit for the emancipation; but instead, he praised the Lord for these blessings and realized his favor would bring honor to the Lord.

THE LESSON APPLIED

This account of Ezra serves as a lesson that God remains faithful to those who are connected to Him, regardless of their situation. The notion that Artaxerxes is seeking to compartmentalize his subjects while stabilizing his kingdom may, in fact, be accurate; however, God intervenes in human affairs when it affects the lives and existence of His people. Although the Persians had a different disposition than that of the Assyrians or the Babylonians (as the former were bloodthirsty oppressors of the people and lands that they conquered, and the latter wished to clone their captives into neo–Babylonians), Israel was indeed subject to Persia. *Yahweh,* however, continues to bless Israel, through even the actions and directives of their oppressors. Although Israel may not have been apprised of God's overall plan, there looms on the horizon a series of blessings that will permanently redeem Israel unto the Kingdom of the Lord.

LET'S TALK ABOUT IT

To whom does Ezra owe his allegiance, Artaxerxes or God?

The person of Ezra must not be mistakenly portrayed as some "Stepin' Fetchit" character who was a pawn in the hands of King Artaxerxes or Persia, and a "sell–out" to Israel. The fact that Ezra was granted authority to be the most powerful official in Jerusalem was based on Ezra's integrity. We must remember that it is actually *Yahweh* who controls the destinies of both Ezra and the Persian king. Almost as a "second Moses," Ezra faced challenges to his leadership, but *Yahweh* remained with him. Pseudo leaders will emerge to believe that Israel would fare better under their direction; however, these individuals would not have the hand of God for guidance and direction. In Ezra, the Lord had His man! Authentically called leaders of God must constantly trust God above all else because they represent Him!

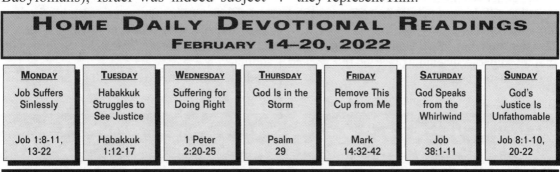

HOME DAILY DEVOTIONAL READINGS						
FEBRUARY 14–20, 2022						
MONDAY	**TUESDAY**	**WEDNESDAY**	**THURSDAY**	**FRIDAY**	**SATURDAY**	**SUNDAY**
Job Suffers Sinlessly	Habakkuk Struggles to See Justice	Suffering for Doing Right	God Is in the Storm	Remove This Cup from Me	God Speaks from the Whirlwind	God's Justice Is Unfathomable
Job 1:8-11, 13-22	Habakkuk 1:12-17	1 Peter 2:20-25	Psalm 29	Mark 14:32-42	Job 38:1-11	Job 8:1-10, 20-22

BILDAD MISUNDERSTANDS GOD'S JUSTICE

ADULT TOPIC: ENDURING FALSE CHARGES	BACKGROUND SCRIPTURE: JOB 8

JOB 8:1–10, 20–22

King James Version

THEN answered Bildad the Shuhite, and said,

2 How long wilt thou speak these things? and how long shall the words of thy mouth be like a strong wind?

3 Doth God pervert judgment? or doth the Almighty pervert justice?

4 If thy children have sinned against him, and he have cast them away for their transgression;

5 If thou wouldest seek unto God betimes, and make thy supplication to the Almighty;

6 If thou wert pure and upright; surely now he would awake for thee, and make the habitation of thy righteousness prosperous.

7 Though thy beginning was small, yet thy latter end should greatly increase.

8 For enquire, I pray thee, of the former age, and prepare thyself to the search of their fathers:

9 (For we are but of yesterday, and know nothing, because our days upon earth are a shadow:)

10 Shall not they teach thee, and tell thee, and utter words out of their heart?

• • • • • •

20 Behold, God will not cast away a perfect man, neither will he help the evil doers:

21 Till he fill thy mouth with laughing, and thy lips with rejoicing.

22 They that hate thee shall be clothed with shame; and the dwelling place of the wicked shall come to nought.

New Revised Standard Version

THEN Bildad the Shuhite answered:

2 'How long will you say these things, and the words of your mouth be a great wind?

3 Does God pervert justice? Or does the Almighty pervert the right?

4 If your children sinned against him,
  he delivered them into the power of their transgression.

5 If you will seek God and make supplication to the Almighty,

6 if you are pure and upright, surely then he will rouse himself for you and restore to you your rightful place.

7 Though your beginning was small, your latter days will be very great.

8 'For inquire now of bygone generations,
  and consider what their ancestors have found;

9 for we are but of yesterday, and we know nothing, for our days on earth are but a shadow.

10 Will they not teach you and tell you
  and utter words out of their understanding?

• • • • • •

20 'See, God will not reject a blameless person,
  nor take the hand of evildoers.

21 He will yet fill your mouth with laughter,
  and your lips with shouts of joy.

22 Those who hate you will be clothed with shame,
  and the tent of the wicked will be no more.'

MAIN THOUGHT: Then Bildad the Shuhite answered: "How long will you say these things, and the words of your mouth be a great wind?" (Job 8:1–2, KJV)

LESSON SETTING
Time: UNKNOWN
Place: Uz

LESSON OUTLINE
I. Bildad Supports God's Justice
   (Job 8:1–6)
II. Bildad's Reflection on Life
   (Job 8:7–10)
III. Bildad's Conclusion: Job WIll
   Be Restored
   (Job 8:20–22)

UNIFYING PRINCIPLE
People tend to rationalize why bad things happen. How do people respond when they are faced with tragedy—natural disasters, birth defects, atrocious crimes, etc.? Job remained faithful to God after several tragic events in his life, even while his friends questioned God's justice and Job's innocence.

INTRODUCTION
Job was a model for God, an upright and righteous man; however, Satan believed that Job was faithful to God only because of His protection and blessings. Satan challenged God by saying that Job would curse God if His hand or hedge was removed from insulating Job. Satan was allowed to afflict Job, with the restriction that he could affect Job's body and possessions but could not touch his life (Job 2:6). Job faced a series of calamities. "Now when Job's three friends heard of all this adversity that had come upon him, they came each one from his own place, Eliphaz the Temanite, Bildad the Shuhite and Zophar the Naamathite; and they made an appointment together to come to sympathize with him and comfort him" (Job 2:11). Job's friends come and sit with him and challenge his innocence.

I. BILDAD SUPPORTS GOD'S JUSTICE (JOB 8:1–6)
Job seems to believe that his life is futile; and in his complaint, he accuses God of treating him unfairly. Job asks why God has made him "His mark"? Job says that "He [God] has set me up as His target, surrounded by a flurry of God's arrows," i.e., "His arrows surround me" (Job 16:13). He also declares that the arrows actually find their mark: "For the arrows of the Almighty are within me" (Job 6:4)! Job does not understand why God has selected him for punishment, as it seems that Job has now become a burden for God. Job asserts that God does not have to be worried because Job will soon be dead, and God will no longer be able to harass him because the land of the dead is Job's only place of freedom.

Bildad answers Job's complaints, asking him, "How long will you say these things," possibly indicating that Job has been complaining for some time against God, with "words coming from his mouth as a mighty wind." The NASB translates the term as "mighty wind;" whereas, the words are "blustering wind" in the NIV. The Hebrew term blustering (kăb-bîr) means great, strong, or powerful. In this case, Bildad sarcastically deems Job as being rash, incorrect, and wrong, using words that are "full of hot air" and destructive, like the windstorm that killed his 10 children (1:19). Bildad begs Job to seek God's help, for Yahweh is just and righteous; but it seems that although Job knows this, despair and pain have defeated him and crushed his spirit. Job's reaction is not unlike believers that become depressed when facing obstacles that Satan attempts to use to influence a lack of trust in God.

At this juncture, Job has not yet accused the Deity of jettisoning the principle of just retribution, but Bildad chastens Job nonetheless. Continuing to press Job, Bildad presents him with two rhetorical questions that are designed to allow Job a moment to think about his response. First, "Does God pervert justice?" Second, "Does God pervert what is right, or does God suborn righteousness?" Job realizes that God is a just God, but he may be confusing justice with judgment. Spence-Jones notes that "justice" is not altogether the same thing as "judgment." Judgment is the act, and justice, the principle that underlies or ought to underlie the act. It is, of course, impossible for God to pervert either, echoing, "Shall not the Judge of all the earth do right?" (Genesis 18:25). Job is in a "woe is me" state and has accused God of purposely punishing him for a perceived sin. Job even asks God, "Have I sinned, and what have I done to You, the One who carefully watches all men?" Job is a man of faith who has previously praised God. Job feels that he is innocent; but even if he is guilty, he believes that God has targeted him, and it would be beneficial for all that God simply leaves him alone because he is soon to die (Job 7:20–21).

Job is in a state of severe depression because of what he perceives as God's injustice towards him. In a series of despairing messages, Job is told of the loss of his loved ones and wealth, without any notice or reason. On a day that probably began as normal, Job's perception of being a target seems to be quite accurate. While his sons and daughters were having dinner in their oldest brother's house, their oxen were plowing, and the donkeys were feeding beside them. When the following sequence of tribulations took place: (1) The marauding Sabeans killed Job's servants, and the first messenger alone escaped to relay the story (v. 15). (2) While the first messenger was speaking, a second came in and said that fire from heaven had fallen and burned up Job's servants, and he alone had escaped to relay the message (v. 16). (3) While the second messenger was speaking, a third came in and said that the Chaldeans raided the camel herd, stealing them, and killing additional servants; and he alone had escaped (v. 17). (4) While he was speaking, the fourth messenger came and told Job that his house had collapsed, killing his sons and daughters; and he alone had escaped (v. 18–19). Job's spirit was crushed wondering why God had allowed this to happen. Bildad observes that if Job's sons had transgressed against God, their punishment was just and therefore, an act of justice. Bildad attributes the death of Job's children not to Job, but to his children (v. 4). Nonetheless, while not addressing the actual offense, Bildad places the reason for their deaths on their sin, not that God had exhibited some such "bloodlust" and indifference toward Job and his family. After Job is told about the loss of his children, he proceeds into a state of mourning, tearing his robes, shaving his head, and probably donning sackcloth and ashes. Incredibly, Job worships God, declaring, "Naked I came from my mother's womb, and naked I shall return there. The Lord gave and the LORD has taken away, but blessed be the name of the Lord." At this time, even after all of his loss, Job did not sin, nor did he blame God (Job 1:20–22).

Bildad shifts from questioning Job and

offers his advice. His conditional phrase, "If you would seek God and implore the compassion of the Almighty" (v. 4), is an effort to convince Job to plead for God's mercy. Bildad assures Job that if he remains pure and upright, God will "rouse" (*'ûr*) Himself for Job's restoration, which will include his lands and properties. This verb seems to refute the idea that the God who keeps Job "will not slumber, and He who keeps Israel will neither slumber or sleep" (Psalm 121:3–4). Still, Job remains steadfast in the sense that God has not left him, even though the "target" on him remains.

II. BILDAD'S REFLECTION ON LIFE (JOB 8:7–10)

Bildad reminds Job that his beginning was insignificant or small. Unfortunately, we do not have any references to Job's parents or where he was born. When Job appears in biblical history, he is already an honorable adult, who is firmly established. Although he was wealthy, Bildad probably meant that Job's life was meaningless and inconsequential, as far as his legacy was concerned. Almost in a sense of prophecy, Bildad accurately stated, "Yet your end will increase greatly" (Job 8:7). Although Bildad may have been speaking of the restoration of Job's wealth, this suggests that he was declaring that Job's life would later have a deeper meaning that would extend beyond riches and land. In an imagery of Job's relationship to God, this test would serve as a standard of how to remain faithful to *Yahweh,* even during times of tribulation. Therefore, Job should find comfort in the eternal care of the Lord.

Bildad urges Job to inquire how past generations witnessed the blessings of God during their times of trouble. Remember,

Job lived before the Exodus and possibly before the Flood; therefore, inquiring of past generations suggests that Job may have looked to a patriarch, such as Abraham. Additionally, there existed traditions of how wise men of past generations would have responded to issues, both physical and spiritual. Bildad implies that the records of these remote times have been, in some way or other, preserved, either in writings or by oral tradition. Writing was certainly known in Egypt and Babylonia from a time anterior to Abraham, and to the Hittites at a date not very much later. Additionally, even Moses imparted the wisdom of the learned from previous generations saying, "Ask now concerning the former days which were before you, since the day that God created man on the earth, and inquire from one end of the heavens to the other" (Deuteronomy 4:32).

Bildad tells Job that we are only here ("of yesterday") for a short time, and through our lifetimes, our knowledge is limited. Our days on earth are as a shadow, which must have light to bring its reflection, as when the light disappears, the shadow also disappears. This imagery suggests that while we are alive, we are constantly in the phase of disappearing, as shadow is used in Old Testament poetry as a symbol of the briefness of life. Recall that the concept of a shadow is also compared with the term vapor, such as in the words of James, "You are just a vapor that appears for a little while and then vanishes away" (James 4:14). The metaphors here are intended to induce Job to understand the brevity of life and the importance of living a just and righteous existence. Job will later agree with this assessment saying, "Man, who is born of woman, is short-lived and full of turmoil and like a flower he comes forth and withers, he also flees like a shadow and does not remain" (Job 14:1–2).

Referring to the aforementioned past generations who could bear witness to God's righteousness and justice, Bildad asks, "Will they not teach and tell you?" The idea here is that the sages of the past were heavily invested in the children of the future; and their words, both written and oral, would be forever conducive to their survival. There may seem to be a discrepancy in verse 10 that says, "… bring forth words from their minds?" (NASB), and "… utter words from their heart?" (NKJV); yet, the term *lēḇ* can be translated as both mind and heart. In this context, the elders would speak wisdom from their minds, the center of intellect, or allow the heart to declare the sought-after knowledge, as the heart is the "seat of wisdom." Recall the focus on the heart in the second part of the Shema that states, "You shall love the Lord your God with all your heart and with all your soul and with all your might" (Deuteronomy 6:5) which connect the two centers of intellect and emotion.

III. BILDAD'S CONCLUSION: JOB WILL BE RESTORED (JOB 8:20–22)

Bildad concludes his speech by telling Job that God will not reject a man of integrity, meaning that God measures each person by his dedication to humanity and his faithfulness to Him. A man of integrity is an upright man who is reliable in all matters. The NKJV records that God will not cast away the blameless (v. 20), suggesting that those who are innocent of wrongdoing are protected by the Lord. This is not to suggest that the aforementioned man (the man of integrity) has been acquitted of a crime, either social or spiritual, because that man would have initially been accused of the crime, needing an advocate to step in to steer him through the legal system. Instead, in this imagery, Bildad infers that the man of integrity (who is blameless) has not been linked to an offense but is pure and righteous. In contrast, God will not support those who are evil and commit acts of immorality against humanity and against God. According to Bildad, if Job were blameless (v. 6), he would not be treated this way by God. For God to allow the wicked to prosper would infer the impossible: that God was sinful Himself. God cannot lie, and He cannot sin!

And yet, He (God) will "fill the righteous man's mouth will laughter," meaning that God will bring joy to the life of the just man who remains faithful to Him. This will cause the man who is rewarded by God to shout for joy and also witness the goodness of the Lord. Biblical history is filled with references to the joy expressed by those that God has delivered; and the term "shouting" can also mean singing. Recall Moses' sister, Miriam the prophetess, who took the timbrel in her hand; and all the women went out after her with timbrels and with dancing, while exhorting the group to "sing to the Lord, for He is highly exalted" (Exodus 15:20-21). Practically, all of God's deliverances are followed by acts of worship, signaling that "He is worthy to be praised" (Psalm 18:3). Consequently, God will condemn the wicked; and their houses and attitudes will not trouble Job any longer. The imagery of the tent is contrasted as in the tent of the righteous to that of the evildoers, of whom we are reminded, "I would rather be a doorkeeper in the house of my God than dwell in the tents of wickedness" (Psalm 84:10). At the end of any issue, God will fight Job's battles, protect him, and restore his life: "For those who hate you and become your enemies will become enemies of the Lord, ultimately, they will fear [respect] you and fear the Lord." Job had not complained of enemies, but this is reminiscent of what Job could have said, "Let those be ashamed and humiliated altogether who rejoice at my distress; Let those be clothed with shame and dishonor who magnify themselves over me" (Psalm 35:26). Although Job had asserted that he would soon "be no more" (7:8, 21), Bildad maintains that the wicked perish before their time, not the righteous, among whom Job is counted. Hence, Job will be restored!

THE LESSON APPLIED

Job lived in the land of Uz, which is traditionally thought of as being located between Edom (west) and Syria (east). Other traditions place Uz between Idumea and Arabia. The evidence for supporting the Edom/Syria region comes from God moving Abram (Abraham) and his family from the land of Ur, which is located in the region of Chaldea (Chaldeans), or that which is Babylonia. This evidence supports Job's locale here, in that the raiding party that robbed the estate, taking camels and killing his servants, were Chaldeans. The evidence that supports the Idumea/Arabia region notes that because of the association of Saba and Dedan among the sons of Keturah, and the account of a raid on the oxen and asses of Job by a group of Sabeans (Job 1:15), some scholars are led to posit the presence of Sabeans in north Arabia.

LET'S TALK ABOUT IT

Do believers feel that suffering is a result of individual or corporate sin?

When people suffer, the thought remains that the cause is that the person committed an egregious sin that God refuses to redeem during a designated period. Unfortunately, what is not usually considered is that people suffer because of the events and decisions by others in the circle of the afflicted. An example is found in the senseless accidental shootings of young children during drug conflicts or domestic disputes. Recently, a young three-year-old child was tragically gunned down by a so-called family friend who was angered because of such a botched deal. Yet, it is unfair to label the distraught family as a collective group of "sinners." We have all sinned and fallen short of the Glory of God; however, there are the innocent who will be protected in both life and death by the grace of the Lord.

HOME DAILY DEVOTIONAL READINGS
FEBRUARY 21–27, 2022

MONDAY	TUESDAY	WEDNESDAY	THURSDAY	FRIDAY	SATURDAY	SUNDAY
Abraham Pleads for Justice	Trust in God's Coming Justice	The Lord Loves Justice	Righteousness, Peace, and Joy	Jesus Demonstrates God's Justice	Job Cries Out for a Redeemer	Job's Fortunes Are Restored
Genesis 18:20-33	Psalm 37:1-11	Psalm 37:21-28, 34-40	Romans 14:13-23	Matthew 12:1-13	Job 19:23-29	Job 42:1-11

SERVING A JUST GOD

ADULT TOPIC:	BACKGROUND SCRIPTURE:
HOPE FOR JUSTICE	JOB 42

JOB 42:1–6, 10–17

King James Version

THEN Job answered the LORD, and said,

2 I know that thou canst do every thing, and that no thought can be withholden from thee.

3 Who is he that hideth counsel without knowledge? therefore have I uttered that I understood not; things too wonderful for me, which I knew not.

4 Hear, I beseech thee, and I will speak: I will demand of thee, and declare thou unto me.

5 I have heard of thee by the hearing of the ear: but now mine eye seeth thee.

6 Wherefore I abhor myself, and repent in dust and ashes.

• • • • • •

10 And the LORD turned the captivity of Job, when he prayed for his friends: also the Lord gave Job twice as much as he had before.

11 Then came there unto him all his brethren, and all his sisters, and all they that had been of his acquaintance before, and did eat bread with him in his house: and they bemoaned him, and comforted him over all the evil that the LORD had brought upon him: every man also gave him a piece of money, and every one an earring of gold.

12 So the LORD blessed the latter end of Job more than his beginning: for he had fourteen thousand sheep, and six thousand camels, and a thousand yoke of oxen, and a thousand she asses.

13 He had also seven sons and three daughters.

14 And he called the name of the first, Jemima; and the name of the second, Kezia; and the name of the third, Kerenhappuch.

New Revised Standard Version

THEN Job answered the LORD:

2 'I know that you can do all things,
 and that no purpose of yours can be thwarted.

3 "Who is this that hides counsel without knowledge?" Therefore I have uttered what I did not understand, things too wonderful for me, which I did not know.

4 "Hear, and I will speak; I will question you, and you declare to me."

5 I had heard of you by the hearing of the ear,
 but now my eye sees you;

6 therefore I despise myself,
 and repent in dust and ashes.'

• • • • • •

10 And the LORD restored the fortunes of Job when he had prayed for his friends; and the Lord gave Job twice as much as he had before.

11 Then there came to him all his brothers and sisters and all who had known him before, and they ate bread with him in his house; they showed him sympathy and comforted him for all the evil that the LORD had brought upon him; and each of them gave him a piece of money and a gold ring.

12 The LORD blessed the latter days of Job more than his beginning; and he had fourteen thousand sheep, six thousand camels, a thousand yoke of oxen, and a thousand donkeys.

13 He also had seven sons and three daughters.

14 He named the first Jemimah, the second Keziah, and the third Keren-happuch.

MAIN THOUGHT: "Therefore I have uttered what I did not understand, things too wonderful for me, which I did not know." (Job 42:3, KJV)

JOB 42:1–6, 10–17

King James Version	New Revised Standard Version
15 And in all the land were no women found so fair as the daughters of Job: and their father gave them inheritance among their brethren. 16 After this lived Job an hundred and forty years, and saw his sons, and his sons' sons, even four generations. 17 So Job died, being old and full of days.	15 In all the land there were no women so beautiful as Job's daughters; and their father gave them an inheritance along with their brothers. 16 After this Job lived for one hundred and forty years, and saw his children, and his children's children, four generations. 17 And Job died, old and full of days.

LESSON SETTING
Time: UNKNOWN
Place: Uz

LESSON OUTLINE
I. Job's Discourse with God
   (Job 42:1–6)
II. God Restores Job
   (Job 42:10–17)

UNIFYING PRINCIPLE
Even the most downcast people can still have hope. How does our hope keep us focused on what is important? Job had a frank, heart–to–heart conversation with God, and God blessed Job's faithfulness.

INTRODUCTION
The continuation of the account of Job records that he reconciled his differences with the Lord. Through a series of dialogues with *Yahweh,* Job realizes that listening to God's instruction brings him closer to God. He also realizes that God can do all things and is actually invested in his well–being, especially his future. Much has been made of Job's misfortunes, but this section focuses on his repentance, restoration, and the subsequent fullness of his blessings. Job will live to be a very old man, so, these events occur over a period of many years. The book is mostly Hebrew poetry but does evolve into prose (narrative).

I. JOB'S DISCOURSE WITH GOD (JOB 42:1–6)
Previously, God has spoken about His power shown in creatures (Job 40:15–24; 41). He focuses on two creatures, the Behemoth (Job 40:15) and the Leviathan (Job 41:1). God tells Job to look at the Behemoth, which is a large and powerful beast (40:15), and the Leviathan (41:1), a dragon, reptile, serpent–like creature of the sea. The identification of these ancient creatures is difficult to compare, as they take on mythological proportions that are frightening to humans. God then poses this rhetorical question, "Can you [Job] draw out [of the water] the Leviathan with a fishhook," meaning that the Leviathan is too powerful to be caught with a normal fish tool. Of course, the answer is that it would be impossible, and much of Chapter 41 is filled with similar questions. These statements are designed to reveal God's power over all of Creation. Moreover, the reverse answer is that it is possible for God, who has the power to catch the Leviathan with a fishhook, or to "press down his tongue with a cord" (Job 41:1). God compares the Leviathan's power with that of man, saying, "No one is so fierce that he dares to arouse him;" not even the bravest of warriors will provoke this dangerous and

powerful beast. Consequently, if humans are afraid of these creatures, "Who then is he that can stand before Me [God]?" (Job 41:10). God declares that He created the Behemoth, just as He made Job, confirming that no man has authority over God.

Previously, Job had replied to God when asked who is a "faultfinder" that can contend with the Almighty, or if there is one who can criticize God. Now, in his second reply, Job acknowledges that God can do all things. Job's response acknowledged his insignificance and inability to provide an adequate answer, but he does not acknowledge God's dominion or his own sin of pride (Job 40:1–4). Job understands that the message of the powerful Behemoth and the Leviathan was presented to reveal his own inadequacy. The phrase, "No purpose of His can be thwarted or withheld from you," reflects Job's understanding that God knows and sees all events, both physical and spiritual. Whatever God desires for humanity will occur, although humans may not understand His actions. Therefore, if it is God's purpose that Job's life takes on these unusual directions, that purpose has a deeper meaning. Job repents of his pride and rebellion and finds contentment in the knowledge that he has God's fellowship. If we know God, we do not need to know why He allows us to experience what we do. He is not only in control of the universe and all its facets but also, our lives; and He loves us. Though His ways are sometimes beyond our comprehension, we should not criticize Him for His dealings with us or with others. God is always in control of all things, even when He appears not to be.

Job asks, "Who can hide His counsel or guidance without knowledge?" The Jewish Bible infers that without knowledge is translated as "who causes to know." However, this verse is actually better understood as God's saying, "Job, who are you to question my counsel without the knowledge of My wisdom," or "Who are you to question My wisdom?" Job was told to "Stand and consider the wonders of God" (Job 37:14), i.e., things that were too wonderful, which he could not realize or comprehend.

Job recalls that prior to his misfortune, he was blessed. Job was prominent in the society of Uz; and yet, he lost everything and could not restore himself. Elihu had previously criticized Job for speaking without knowledge, with "words lacking wisdom" (Job 34:35). Job realizes that he had not understood that God was actually in control of his life and fortune. In his poverty and loss, Job did not understand why God had made him a target. Although Job did not curse God, he believed that "perhaps [his] sons [had] sinned and cursed God in their hearts" (Job 1:5); but he had nonetheless blamed God for not protecting him from these series of calamities. However, Job now discarded his complaints about God's inability to rule the world with justice.

Job presents a new perspective as he accepts that he cannot continue to challenge God. Job admits that he had not been able to meet any of God's previous rhetorical questions. He begs God to listen to his pleas, i.e., his request, "Please let me [or allow me to] speak," which signals Job's willingness to repent from the criticism of Elihu and his erroneous assessments. Previously, *Yahweh* had commanded Job, "Pay attention, listen to me, keep silent and let me speak. Then if you have anything to say, answer me, if not, listen to me; keep silent and I will teach you wisdom" (Job 33:31–33). Job embraces God's invitation to express himself by repeating, "I will ask or question you and you shall answer me" (Job 40:7). Obviously, Job had heard about all that God had done, in Creation and in human care, by those who had passed down the accounts of His greatness and majesty. Now, Job declares, "I now know you from a personal perspective." Additionally, Job may have been reminded that he heard God in the thunder of His voice (Job 37:5) and received an answer from God in a whirlwind (Job 38:1). Job had heard God, but now, he is allowed to see God. This statement may not indicate that Job physically saw the Lord, or it could mean that Job saw God as a theophany, i.e., a form whereby God appears as a visible manifestation. As with Moses and the burning bush, Job is one of the fortunate to be able to "see" God.

At this juncture, Job finally repents by retracting or rejecting his previous thoughts and statements towards God. The NKJV records Job declaring, "I will abhor myself," meaning that Job is repulsed by his lack of understanding and judgment of God. This is a much stronger assessment than the language he used when he earlier described himself as insignificant (Job 40:3–5), where Job was humbled but not yet remorseful. Ashamed and humiliated, Job is determined to show his repentance in dust and ashes. Here, Job echoes the language of Abraham in Genesis 18:27, "I am but dust and ashes." Recall that Job was found sitting on a pile of ashes (Job 2:8) and when his friends saw this, they sprinkled dust on their heads (Job 2:12). This could be taken to indicate that Job donned himself in ashes and sackcloth, after having torn his robes,

which was the traditional sign of mourning. This sign is ascribed as a reaction of men; however, as a sign of humiliation, after Tamar was raped by Amnon, she tore her long–sleeved garment and put ashes on her head (2 Samuel 13:18). There, as here, dust and ashes express a person's lowly state.

II. GOD RESTORES JOB (JOB 42:10–17)

The next section changes from Hebrew poetry and is written in prose, or a narrative form. The scene shifts to God blessing Job by restoring his fortunes: "The Lord restored the fortunes of Job when he prayed for his friends" (Job 42:10). *Yahweh* was angry with Job's friends (Bildad, Zophar, and especially, Eliphaz) who conspired to convince Job that his tragedies were a result of his sins against God. God has an issue with these friends because they said things about God that were not true. Job, however, is correct in what he is saying about God. In some languages, the contrast between Job's speaking of the truth and what his friends said may have been expressed in the following way: "Because you, [his friends], have lied in what you have said about Me, only my servant Job has told the truth." In a sign of God's restoration, Job's fortunes were increased twofold; however, this does not explicitly include his healing. Some see the restoration as evidence of God's justice; others understand it as starting over at the end of the test.

Job has a gathering of people who have come to celebrate his good fortune. Verse 11 notes that these were his sisters and brothers; however, this does not necessarily indicate that they are his biological siblings. Job's wife is not mentioned but is present by implication, when there are "more children" in verse 13. While it is possible, it probably suggests that this is a circle of friends from the community. One of the issues here is that this group is gathered to celebrate, but where were they when Job was struggling? Unlike the three friends, Bildad, Zophar, and Eliphaz, who were part of the original dialogue, Job referred to another group when he stated, "He has removed my brothers far from me, and my acquaintances are completely estranged from me, my relatives have failed, and my intimate friends have forgotten me" (Job 19:13). It seems that they were Job's acquaintances before his problems occurred but had abandoned him during his struggles. Ironically, they came to his house (which indicates that Job's house remained standing after his son's house was destroyed) and were having a dinner, much like his sons and daughters were having when they were killed. As was customary in the culture, especially after a crisis, they gave him gifts of money and gold rings, indicating that these friends were also wealthy. Here, we find that they were doing what friends do, as they consoled Job and comforted him for his extensive trials. But now, it seems as if all is forgiven, as they had gathered to welcome Job back into their "society."

However, it is the Lord who blesses Job immeasurably, as He provides Job more than what he had previously, and his wealth (livestock) is doubled. Additionally, Job is blessed with another ten children, to compensate for the ones he lost (note that the number of children is not doubled). Interestingly, the renowned Rabbi and Jewish leader Nahmanides, also known as Moses Ben Naham (1194–1270), cannot believe that God would have allowed for the death of Job's original children, so he explains that the ten restored children are the original ones, secreted away by Satan along with the cattle and servants, to execute the test. Nonetheless, Job has seven sons and three daughters to replace those that were lost.

Interestingly, the names (and the meanings of the names) of Job's daughters— Jemimah or "Dove;" Keziah or "Cassia;" and *Keren-happuch* or "Horn of kohl [mascara]"—are provided to support the statement, "In all the land, no women were found so 'fair' as Job's daughters" (v. 15), to describe their beauty. Note: The New Jerusalem Bible says, "His first daughter he called Turtledove, and the second Cassia, and the third Mascara," whereas, another version translates it, "The first he named Turtledove, the second had the name Cinnamon Bloom, and the third Eyeshadow." The naming of the daughters, and not the sons, recalls the episode of Zelophehad's daughters, who complained to God in Numbers 27:1–11, which established that daughters may inherit from their father when there are no sons. Job wants his daughters to be protected and financially secure; and as desirable women. Their status would be considered part of his overall wealth. The sons were not omitted from their inheritance and would be considered the normal succession of birthright, as this law does not grant women a general right to inherit or own land but seeks to preserve a man's name by protecting his lineage from extinction, and by maintaining its connection to his ancestral inheritance. The Jewish Bible says that Job gave them estates, i.e., houses and land.

After God's restoration, Job lived another

140 years and, through four generations, was able to see the lives of his sons and grandsons. Job's lifespan mirrors those of the elders. According to Jewish tradition, his "latter years" (140) were exactly twice the number of his former ones (70). Therefore, if we estimate Job being 70 when his torment occurred (half of 140), when the 140 years are added to the 70, we arrive at 210 years. According to the *Septuagint* (the Greek translation of the Hebrew Bible), however, "Job lived after the affliction 170 years, and all the years he lived were actually 240 years." Aligned with the elders, the LXX adds that Job is actually known as Jobab (Gen. 36:32–33), placing him in the fraternity of the patriarchs. Nevertheless, Job dies a contented and comfortable man, who was "full of days," meaning that he died a very old man. Job becomes a "hero of the faith" and a great figure in the history of Israel, not because of his contributions but because of his faithfulness to God and how he survived during his ordeal.

The Lesson Applied

The Book of Job may be the oldest book of the Old Testament, composed before Genesis, because Job is older than Moses, who is credited with writing the Pentateuch (Genesis through Deuteronomy). Scholars debate the origin of the book and its actual writer, as some believe it was written during the time of David and Solomon, while others believe it may have been written by Elihu (Job's friend), Moses, Isaiah, or Job himself. The placement of the book in our modern Bible is in the Wisdom Literature section (Job–Song of Solomon), following the Histories (Joshua–Esther), and before the Prophets (Isaiah–Malachi). Set in patriarchal times, the book is an account of Job's reactions to the suffering that took place without the benefit of revelation.

Let's Talk About It

Do believers actually trust God for deliverance in the time of their troubles?

The story of Job and his suffering brings believers to ask the age–old question, "Why do the good suffer?" This is theodicy, the vindication of divine goodness and providence in view of the existence of evil. Theodicy is an answer to resolving the problem of evil; and while human suffering seems to be unfair, the resolution of the theodicy question is realized in the intervention and vindication of God. While there is a pious belief that Christians are to understand the necessity of being humble before God, realistically, the pain of "going through it" leaves a bitterness in the psyche of believers that can only ask, "Why" or "What have I done to deserve this?" We do not know why the innocent suffer along with the wicked.

THIRD QUARTER

March

April

May

BABYLONIAN CAPTIVITY ENDS

EZRA 1:1–8, 11; 2:64–70

King James Version

NOW in the first year of Cyrus king of Persia, that the word of the LORD by the mouth of Jeremiah might be fulfilled, the LORD stirred up the spirit of Cyrus king of Persia, that he made a proclamation throughout all his kingdom, and put it also in writing, saying,

2 Thus saith Cyrus king of Persia, The LORD God of heaven hath given me all the kingdoms of the earth; and he hath charged me to build him an house at Jerusalem, which is in Judah.

3 Who is there among you of all his people? his God be with him, and let him go up to Jerusalem, which is in Judah, and build the house of the LORD God of Israel, (he is the God,) which is in Jerusalem.

4 And whosoever remaineth in any place where he sojourneth, let the men of his place help him with silver, and with gold, and with goods, and with beasts, beside the freewill offering for the house of God that is in Jerusalem.

5 Then rose up the chief of the fathers of Judah and Benjamin, and the priests, and the Levites, with all them whose spirit God had raised, to go up to build the house of the LORD which is in Jerusalem.

6 And all they that were about them strengthened their hands with vessels of silver, with gold, with goods, and with beasts, and with precious things, beside all that was willingly offered.

7 Also Cyrus the king brought forth the vessels of the house of the LORD, which Nebuchadnezzar

New Revised Standard Version

IN the first year of King Cyrus of Persia, in order that the word of the Lord by the mouth of Jeremiah might be accomplished, the LORD stirred up the spirit of King Cyrus of Persia so that he sent a herald throughout all his kingdom, and also in a written edict declared:

2 'Thus says King Cyrus of Persia: The LORD, the God of heaven, has given me all the kingdoms of the earth, and he has charged me to build him a house at Jerusalem in Judah.

3 Any of those among you who are of his people—may their God be with them!—are now permitted to go up to Jerusalem in Judah, and rebuild the house of the LORD, the God of Israel—he is the God who is in Jerusalem;

4 and let all survivors, in whatever place they reside, be assisted by the people of their place with silver and gold, with goods and with animals, besides freewill-offerings for the house of God in Jerusalem.'

5 The heads of the families of Judah and Benjamin, and the priests and the Levites—everyone whose spirit God had stirred—got ready to go up and rebuild the house of the LORD in Jerusalem.

6 All their neighbours aided them with silver vessels, with gold, with goods, with animals, and with valuable gifts, besides all that was freely offered.

7 King Cyrus himself brought out the vessels of the house of the LORD that Nebuchadnezzar

MAIN THOUGHT: As soon as they came to the house of the LORD in Jerusalem, some of the heads of families made freewill offerings for the house of God, to erect it on its site. (Ezra 2:68, KJV)

EZRA 1:1–8, 11; 2:64–70

King James Version	New Revised Standard Version
had brought forth out of Jerusalem, and had put them in the house of his gods; 8 Even those did Cyrus king of Persia bring forth by the hand of Mithredath the treasurer, and numbered them unto Sheshbazzar, the prince of Judah. • • • • • • 11 All the vessels of gold and of silver were five thousand and four hundred. All these did Sheshbazzar bring up with them of the captivity that were brought up from Babylon unto Jerusalem. • • • 2:64-70 • • • 64 The whole congregation together was forty and two thousand three hundred and three-score, 65 Beside their servants and their maids, of whom there were seven thousand three hundred thirty and seven: and there were among them two hundred singing men and singing women. 66 Their horses were seven hundred thirty and six; their mules, two hundred forty and five; 67 Their camels, four hundred thirty and five; their asses, six thousand seven hundred and twenty. 68 And some of the chief of the fathers, when they came to the house of the LORD which is at Jerusalem, offered freely for the house of God to set it up in his place: 69 They gave after their ability unto the treasure of the work threescore and one thousand drams of gold, and five thousand pound of silver, and one hundred priests' garments. 70 So the priests, and the Levites, and some of the people, and the singers, and the porters, and the Nethinims, dwelt in their cities, and all Israel in their cities.	had carried away from Jerusalem and placed in the house of his gods. 8 King Cyrus of Persia had them released into the charge of Mithredath the treasurer, who counted them out to Sheshbazzar the prince of Judah. • • • • • • 11 the total of the gold and silver vessels was five thousand four hundred. All these Sheshbazzar brought up, when the exiles were brought up from Babylonia to Jerusalem. • • • 2:64-70 • • • 64 The whole assembly together was forty-two thousand three hundred and sixty, 65 besides their male and female servants, of whom there were seven thousand three hundred and thirty-seven; and they had two hundred male and female singers. 66 They had seven hundred and thirty-six horses, two hundred and forty-five mules, 67 four hundred and thirty-five camels, and six thousand seven hundred and twenty donkeys. 68 As soon as they came to the house of the LORD in Jerusalem, some of the heads of families made freewill-offerings for the house of God, to erect it on its site. 69 According to their resources they gave to the building fund sixty-one thousand darics of gold, five thousand minas of silver, and one hundred priestly robes. 70 The priests, the Levites, and some of the people lived in Jerusalem and its vicinity; and the singers, the gatekeepers, and the temple servants lived in their towns, and all Israel in their towns.

LESSON SETTING
Time: Mid Fifth Century BC
Place: The Providence of Judah

LESSON OUTLINE

I. The Proclamation of Cyrus (Ezra 1:1–4)
II. Responses to the Proclamation (Ezra 1:5–8; 11)
III. The Conclusion of the List (Ezra 2:64–70)

UNIFYING PRINCIPLE

Sometimes people focus on their adverse situations rather than seeking guidance. Why do we act and speak according to our situations rather than seeking liberation from them? Ezra shows us that when we recognize and confess our failings, God is ready to listen and support us, even in unexpected ways.

INTRODUCTION

Ezra—Nehemiah's book is set after the Babylonians destroyed Jerusalem and its Temple and took many of its people into exile. This book picks up about 50 years later and tells some Israelites' return to Jerusalem and what happens when they rebuild their cities and their lives there. Today's lesson primarily focuses on three key leaders who led the rebuilding effort.

What drives the story are the decrees of two Persian kings, Cyrus and Artaxerxes. What counts as restoration is the fulfillment of their demands. Over the next three weeks, we will focus on the book's design and Zerubbabel's efforts.

In today's lesson, King Cyrus authorizes the Jews in exile in Babylonia to return to the land to rebuild the Temple; the returning exiles carry with them treasures earlier plundered from the Temple. The authors say this fulfills the prophet Jeremiah's promise to the exiles that they would one day return to Jerusalem. According to the prophet Jeremiah, "This whole country will become a desolate wasteland, and these nations will serve the king of Babylon seventy years" (Jeremiah 25:11).

Now, this fulfillment should trigger our hopes in the many other prophetic promises that exile was not the end of the story. We have hoped for a future messianic king from David's line (Isaiah 11; Hosea 3).

We have hoped for a rebuilt temple where God's presence will dwell with His people (Ezekiel 40–48, Zechariah 2). We have hoped for God's kingdom to come over all the nations offering His blessing, just like He promises Abraham (Isaiah 2, Zechariah 8). So, with all of these hopes in mind, we will dive into our story and read the story of Zerubbabel. His name means "planted" or "in Babylon." He represents the generation born in Babylonian captivity where he leads a wave of Israelites returning to Jerusalem. The name Ezra in Hebrew means *Ezrah*, which means "the Lord help me." It is a fitting name for Ezra because he asks for the Lord's help in prayer. He gives his testimony in the book, namely that the Lord has helped him return from Babylonian captivity to Jerusalem.

EXPOSITION

I. THE PROCLAMATION OF CYRUS (EZRA 1:1–4)

The story begins "in the first year of King Cyrus of Persia." This is the first year Cyrus had authority over Babylon and Judah. Cyrus ruled only a small region of the Median Empire (in modern Iran) until 550 B.C. He took control of the enormous empire, later known as the Persian Empire. Under his effective leadership, the empire expanded in all directions.

Cyrus waited for several years before moving against Babylon. In 539 B.C., life in Babylon was terrible. The king of Babylon was so intensely disliked that when Cyrus entered the city to capture it, no one opposed him. From that point onward, the Persian Empire included all of what we know as Syria, Israel, and Iran. Although Cyrus worshiped the local gods there, he sought suitable religious options for the people under his reign. Cyrus sought to reestablish religions devastated by Babylon. He highly regarded sacred cities such as Jerusalem, which Cyrus does not mention by name.

Notice the three claims describing what Cyrus has done: First, he returned religious images stolen by the Babylonians to their rightful places. Second, he rebuilt temples for those images. Finally, he resettled the displaced peoples in their homelands.

Why would Cyrus choose such an enlightened and magnanimous course? He likely sought to gain divine favor by restoring indigenous religions and people. He may have done so to gain popular support for his regime. It is interesting to note what he writes about his respect for the gods: "May all the gods whom I have resettled in their sacred cities ask daily Bel and Nebo for a long life for me and may they recommend me to Marduk, my lord" (Edict of Cyrus).

Curiously, this strategy seems to have worked with the God of Israel, or at least from Cyrus' point of view. Isaiah 45 proclaims God commanded him and states that God also stirred the spirit of the Jews, Levites, and Benjamites to return to Jerusalem to build the Temple, confirming His sovereignty over the whole affair (Isaiah 45:2,11–13, KJV). Ezra announces that "the Lord" of Israel, "stirred up the spirit of Cyrus king of Persia." This fulfills God's prophecy, which verse one attributes to "Jeremiah."

Although, unlike Isaiah, he did not identify Cyrus by name, Jeremiah did prophesy the downfall of Babylon and Judah's restoration (Jeremiah 25:11–12; Jeremiah 29:10). Ezra 1:2-4 provides a Hebrew translation of the proclamation Cyrus issued by the Lord's inspiration. In this brief statement, Cyrus, who claimed to be king of the whole earth (v.2), ordered the Temple's rebuilding in Jerusalem and allowed displaced Judeans to return there (v.3). Moreover, he encouraged Jews who did not return to offer financial support to those who did (v.4). These aspects of the decree in (Ezra 1:2–4) make it seem almost as if Cyrus was an admirer, if not closeted practitioner, of the Jewish faith. From the Cyrus Cylinder, however, we know that he recognized every regional God.

Verse three, therefore, should be translated a bit differently than the NKJV: "who is among you of all his {not "His"} people? /may his God {not "God"} be with him, and let him go up to Jerusalem, which is in Judah, and build the house of the God of Israel, he is the God who is in Jerusalem {not "(He is God"), which is in Jerusalem"}." The Cylinder shows that Cyrus was a polytheist who recognized regional gods and their limited authority.

Unlike Ezra—Nehemiah, he did not affirm the ultimate sovereignty of the one true God, the Lord of Abraham, Isaac, and Jacob. Nevertheless, this one God did choose us, and worked through Cyrus, to accomplish His purposes. Through Cyrus, the Persian "messiah" (Isaiah 45:1), God began to restore Judah.

II. RESPONSES TO THE PROCLAMATION (EZRA 1:5–8,11)

"Everyone whose heart God has moved" indicates leaders of small groups of people. Israel's nation had been divided into tribes, tribes into families, and families in "the father's house." Judah and Benjamin are the two tribes of the Southern Kingdom from which Nebuchadnezzar took exiles back to Babylon. The decree of Cyrus, therefore, applies primarily to persons from these tribes. "(T)he priests and the Levites" deserve specific mention because not only are they the religious leaders of Israel, but they rebuilt a temple that could not function appropriately without priestly and Levitical personnel.

The NKJV of 1:5 misses the original Hebrew manuscript's nuance by translating: "with all those whose spirits God has moved." All of those who returned from Babylon to Jerusalem, both laypeople and leaders, were people motivated by God.

The Hebrew expression "whose spirits God had moved" uses the same verb found in 1:1 (NRSV): "everyone whose heart God had moved." Both verses depict God alone as the author of restoration, as the One who stirred Cyrus to proclaim liberation and who stirred up the people to embrace their new freedom.

Note in verse six that "all their neighbors," the returning people "assisted them with articles of silver and gold." All here includes not only the Jews who chose to stay in Babylon but the Gentiles as well.

The expression "articles of silver and gold" echoes Exodus 12:35–36. Jewish tradition explained, accepting silver and gold offerings would remind the people of God's precious blessing. The Psalmist refers to the symbol in Psalm 105:36-37.

By mentioning "silver and gold" in verse six and repeating the phrase in verse 11, the author reminds his Jewish readers of Egypt's first Exodus. Babylon's departure represented a second Exodus, another time when God delivered God's people from foreign oppression. The phrase "in addition to all the freewill offerings" (v.6) is a technical phrase that refers to freewill offering for the Temple (Ezra 1:4). If someone wanted to thank God for something unusual, that person would make a unique offering out of his or her own free will.

Cyrus went a step further (v.7) in his support for Jewish restoration. He brought "out the articles belonging to the temple of the Lord, which Nebuchadnezzar had carried away from Jerusalem and had placed in the temple of his god" (Ezra 1:7; see also 2 Chronicles 36:18). Ezra-Nehemiah names "Mithredath" as the treasurer who turned the sacred implements over to "Sheshbazzar the prince of Judah" (v.8).

The text does not record the mystery of who Sheshbazzar was or how he related to Zerubbabel. All we know for certain is that Sheshbazzar was a leader of Judah (Ezra 1:8). He had some initial role in the rebuilding process. However, soon, he appears to have turned all or part of the assignment over to Zerubbabel.

III. The Conclusion of the List (Ezra 2:64–70)

A total of 42,360 also appears in Nehemiah 7:66. Unfortunately, it does not sum up the list's actual numbers (Ezra=29,818; Nehemiah=31,089). Although commentators have proposed many solutions to this dilemma, in all likelihood, it reflects the awkward Hebrew numbering system along with possible copying inconsistencies. It may also mean that women were included in the total but not in the constituent numbers indicated above.

Verses 68–69 mention unique gifts for

the rebuilding effort. The people gave freely, "according to their ability" (v.69), and they also gave generously, as the large totals testify. The chapter ends with the resettlement of those who came up from Babylon to Judah in their respective towns and cities (v.70).

THE LESSON APPLIED

Christians have a distinct way of speaking the right language. We use words and phrases that have unique meaning to us. Knowing and using these bits of language helps us to feel included. We can walk into churches throughout the country and be asked, "Are you born again?" An affirmative response will provoke a responsive recognition and an enthusiastic embrace.

But have you ever taken a non-Christian friend to a Christian fellowship group, only to realize that your friend does not have the slightest idea what anyone is talking about? How sad that the very ones who need to know the Lord may be put off by our exclusionary words and mannerisms that communicate, inadvertently: "You do not belong here, but we do." People are not likely to return to places where they do not feel they belong.

It is time for Christians to become sensitive to the way our language tends to excludes people, especially women. We comfortably refer to all Christians as "sons" of God or "brothers" in Christ because our subculture uses male nouns to refer humankind as men. Many segments of our society no longer hear such phrases without offense. Those who refuse to embrace inclusion may risk losing the very people who most need to hear the Gospel.

LET'S TALK ABOUT IT

Who's in charge here?

Ezra 1 answers this question simply and repeatedly: God is in charge. This passage vividly illustrates God's sovereignty over His people—indeed, over all people, and all of human history.

As we take the fullness of God's sovereignty seriously, our ways of thinking and acting will change. We will begin to see our "secular" jobs as "spiritual" turf, where God's standards still apply. We will also think differently about national affairs. Today, too many Christians limited God's interest to prayer in schools, abortion, family values, and sexual orientation. Undoubtedly, these issues stand under God's sovereignty and within His care, but so do such cries against hunger, poverty, racism, healthcare, and education.

Embracing God's sovereignty will move us to consider whether we pray for the world only from the perspective of our personal needs and agendas.

HOME DAILY DEVOTIONAL READINGS
MARCH 7–13, 2022

MONDAY	TUESDAY	WEDNESDAY	THURSDAY	FRIDAY	SATURDAY	SUNDAY
Rebuilding the Temple and Praising God	Jews Discouraged from Rebuilding	Worship in the Heavenly Sanctuary	Bowing in Thanksgiving	The Time to Rebuild Has Come	The Temple's Foundation Laid	God Provides through King Darius
Ezra 3:8-13	Ezra 4:1-5	Revelation 5	Psalm 138	Haggai 1	Haggai 2:1-9, 15-19	Ezra 6:1-12

FREEDOM TO WORSHIP

EZRA 6:1–12

King James Version

THEN Darius the king made a decree, and search was made in the house of the rolls, where the treasures were laid up in Babylon.

2 And there was found at Achmetha, in the palace that is in the province of the Medes, a roll, and therein was a record thus written:

3 In the first year of Cyrus the king the same Cyrus the king made a decree concerning the house of God at Jerusalem, Let the house be builded, the place where they offered sacrifices, and let the foundations thereof be strongly laid; the height thereof threescore cubits, and the breadth thereof threescore cubits;

4 With three rows of great stones, and a row of new timber: and let the expenses be given out of the king's house:

5 And also let the golden and silver vessels of the house of God, which Nebuchadnezzar took forth out of the temple which is at Jerusalem, and brought unto Babylon, be restored, and brought again unto the temple which is at Jerusalem, every one to his place, and place them in the house of God.

6 Now therefore, Tatnai, governor beyond the river, Shetharboznai, and your companions the Apharsachites, which are beyond the river, be ye far from thence:

7 Let the work of this house of God alone; let the governor of the Jews and the elders of the Jews build this house of God in his place.

8 Moreover I make a decree what ye shall do to the elders of these Jews for the building of this house of God: that of the king's goods,

New Revised Standard Version

THEN King Darius made a decree, and they searched the archives where the documents were stored in Babylon.

2 But it was in Ecbatana, the capital in the province of Media, that a scroll was found on which this was written: 'A record.

3 In the first year of his reign, King Cyrus issued a decree: Concerning the house of God at Jerusalem, let the house be rebuilt, the place where sacrifices are offered and burnt-offerings are brought;its height shall be sixty cubits and its width sixty cubits,

4 with three courses of hewn stones and one course of timber; let the cost be paid from the royal treasury.

5 Moreover, let the gold and silver vessels of the house of God, which Nebuchadnezzar took out of the temple in Jerusalem and brought to Babylon, be restored and brought back to the temple in Jerusalem, each to its place; you shall put them in the house of God.'

6 'Now you, Tattenai, governor of the province Beyond the River, Shethar-bozenai, and you, their associates, the envoys in the province Beyond the River, keep away;

7 let the work on this house of God alone; let the governor of the Jews and the elders of the Jews rebuild this house of God on its site.

8 Moreover, I make a decree regarding what you shall do for these elders of the Jews for the rebuilding of this house of God: the cost is

MAIN THOUGHT: "May the God who has established his name there overthrow any king or people that shall put forth a hand to alter this, or to destroy this house of God in Jerusalem." (Ezra 6:12, KJV)

EZRA 6:1–12

King James Version	New Revised Standard Version
even of the tribute beyond the river, forthwith expenses be given unto these men, that they be not hindered.	to be paid to these people, in full and without delay, from the royal revenue, the tribute of the province Beyond the River.
9 And that which they have need of, both young bullocks, and rams, and lambs, for the burnt offerings of the God of heaven, wheat, salt, wine, and oil, according to the appointment of the priests which are at Jerusalem, let it be given them day by day without fail:	9 Whatever is needed—young bulls, rams, or sheep for burnt-offerings to the God of heaven, wheat, salt, wine, or oil, as the priests in Jerusalem require—let that be given to them day by day without fail,
10 That they may offer sacrifices of sweet savours unto the God of heaven, and pray for the life of the king, and of his sons.	10 so that they may offer pleasing sacrifices to the God of heaven, and pray for the life of the king and his children.
11 Also I have made a decree, that whosoever shall alter this word, let timber be pulled down from his house, and being set up, let him be hanged thereon; and let his house be made a dunghill for this.	11 Furthermore, I decree that if anyone alters this edict, a beam shall be pulled out of the house of the perpetrator, who then shall be impaled on it. The house shall be made a dunghill.
12 And the God that hath caused his name to dwell there destroy all kings and people, that shall put to their hand to alter and to destroy this house of God which is at Jerusalem. I Darius have made a decree; let it be done with speed.	12 May the God who has established his name there overthrow any king or people that shall put forth a hand to alter this, or to destroy this house of God in Jerusalem. I, Darius, make a decree; let it be done with all diligence.'

LESSON SETTING
Time: Mid Fifth Century BC
Place: The Providence of Judah

LESSON OUTLINE
I. The Archival Search
   (Ezra 6:1–2)
II. The Memorandum
   (Ezra 6:3–5)
III. Darius' Reply
   (Ezra 6:6–12)

UNIFYING PRINCIPLE
Sometimes people focus on their adverse situations rather than seeking guidance. Why do we act and speak according to our situations rather than seeking liberation from them? Ezra shows us that when we recognize and confess our failings, God is ready to listen and support us, even in unexpected ways.

INTRODUCTION
Ezra—Nehemiah's book is set after the Babylonians destroyed Jerusalem, the Temple, and took many of the Holy City's inhabitants into exile. The book(s) picks up about fifty years later. It tells the story of some of the returning Israelites to Jerusalem, and what happens when they rebuild their cities and their lives there. Over the next three weeks, we will focus on the book's discussion of Zerubbabel's efforts.

The books of Ezra and Nehemiah are narratives of the restoration of the Jewish people to their homeland. The royal decrees of two Persian kings, Cyrus and Artaxerxes are what drive the action in this story. The fulfillment of their royal demands counts as restoration. In Ezra 1, Cyrus commands the Jews to return to their land and resume temple worship; in accord with that, Ezra 1–6 narrates the return and the rebuilding of the temple.

In chapter six, Ezra brings the first part of Ezra's book to a glorious conclusion with the completion of the new Temple and the celebration of Passover. In verses 6–12, after discovering the good wishes that Cyrus has for Judah's exiles, Darius assists in bringing these good wishes to fruition. After receiving the letter from Tattenai and Shethar-bonznai,

Darius orders the search of the archives, first in Babylonia and then in Ecbatana. When the search located Cyrus' decree, with its command that the Temple in Jerusalem must be rebuilt with the cost of construction paid from the royal treasury, Darius upholds this decree. He adds that a portion of the tribute of the province from beyond the river must go to pay for the rebuilding of this house of God. He further rules that the province must also pay the daily cost of providing whatever is needed for Israel's cultic sacrifices. We are told that Darius does this because he wants to propitiate the God of heaven.

Also, Ezra underscores the contribution of the prophetic ministries of both Haggai and Zechariah, the son of Iddo. The latter was active around the same time as Darius' decree. The Lord's activity through the prophets brings the fruition of God's activity in Cyrus and Darius' hearts so that the elders of the Jews built and prospered (Exodus 34:6).

In addition to clarifying those critical physical components of Israel's salvation history, Ezra's book also records the preparation for the eschatological restoration of Israel. Bede emphasizes this through a mystical interpretation of the Temple's dedication in Adar citing that the Temple "was begun at the beginning of the seventh month because it is with the grace of the Holy Spirit leading us that we complete it. But it was completed in the 12th month in order to signify the perfection that is contained in this number." Bede has in view Christ's body, the Church, as the fulfillment of the Temple, since twelve is "the number of apostles, in whose faith and teaching the church is completed."

EXPOSITION
I. THE ARCHIVAL SEARCH (EZRA 6:1–2)

In verse one, Tattenai instructed Darius in his letter, "Let a search be made in the royal archives of Babylon" (Ezra 5:17). That was where he expected to find Cyrus' memorandum since the Jerusalem Jews had returned from Babylonian regions. So, a search was first done in the archives stored in the treasury at Babylon. Darius' scribes found no records in Babylon, so they searched next in Ecbatana's citadel in the province of Media. A scroll was found, and the Chronicler excerpted from it.

In verse two, it is more likely that "Babylon" refers to the city, not the region. The city was an administrative center where records usually were kept for the area, including Judea. A better translation of verse two, then, would begin with "but" (as in the NRSV) since the narrator highlights the contrast between where the document was expected to be found and where it is found. However, no indication is given of the circumstances under which the school is found. However, passive verbs of this kind often are used in the Bible to highlight God's activity behind the scenes. These two verses narrate the pivotal events by which God ensures that the Temple's rebuilding goes forward.

II. THE MEMORANDUM (EZRA 6:3–5)

In the first year of King Cyrus, the king issued a decree concerning God's temple in Jerusalem. This dates the memorandum to 539 B.C., the first year in which Cyrus was king of Babylonian lands. He had been recognized as the king of Media and Persia several years before that.

Especially noting that the Temple was to be built as a place to present sacrifices, the decrees further specified the Temple's dimensions: ninety feet high and ninety feet wide, with three courses of large stones and one of the timbers. In all probability, the Temple's size replicated that of Solomon's, as did the location. They were detailing the measurements and the number of stones and timbers, set limits on the measurements, and the number of courses of stones and timbers sets limits on what the Jews were allowed to do in the Temple's rebuilding process.

The Persian government needed to define the scope of the repairs carefully since the financing was to be paid by the royal treasury. To promote goodwill among subjected peoples, imperial funding was given for various cultic centers and temples throughout the empire. However, even though Cyrus had committed royal funds for the construction of the Temple, the resources would have come from revenue collected throughout the Trans-Euphrates' satrapy.

Cyrus also specified within the decree that the gold and silver articles of God's house are to be returned to the Temple in Jerusalem. By ordering the return of the Temple articles Nebuchadnezzar had confiscated, Cyrus acknowledges the continuity between the two structures. Unlike the temple built by expatriate Jews in Egypt, Jerusalem's building was honored as the legitimate house of God where the Temple treasures and articles belonged.

III. DARIUS' REPLY (EZRA 6:6–12)

In Ezra 6:6–7, Darius gave instructions to Tattenai, the governor, Shethar-Bozenai, the secretary, and all the other officials involved in the original inquiry. "Stay away from here. Do not interfere with the work on the Temple of God." He did not mean that the officials of the region must never enter Jerusalem. The king wanted his ministers to understand that nothing must hinder the temple's completion. However, the actual work and supervision of the project remained with the governor of the Jews and the Jewish elders.

In Ezra 6:8–10, Darius further endorsed the original decree by extending financial and material support to the project. He added his pronouncement, specifying what Tattenai and the others were to do for these elders of the Jews in the construction of this house of God. Temple-related expenses were to be fully paid out of the royal treasury, from the revenues of Trans-Euphrates. As satrap over the territory that included Judea, Tattenai was responsible for paying construction expenses from his region's income. These officials should ensure that work on the Temple would not stop because of financial needs.

Darius next provided a list of supplies

necessary for the daily sacrifices. Taenia and his men were to supply the Jews with young bulls, rams, and male lambs for burnt offerings to the God of heaven.

They were also to supply wheat, salt, wine, and oil as requested by the priests in Jerusalem. All these were elements of the daily sacrifices, and Darius commanded a fresh resupply of these items daily. The king's interest in the daily sacrifices was to enable the Jews to pray for the well being of both the king and his sons. The Persian kings viewed the gods within their realm as tribal deities, and thus that it was in their best interest to win the favor of all the various gods.

In Ezra 6:11–12, Darius concluded his decree with stern warnings: if anyone changes the edict, a beam is to be pulled from his house, and he is to be lifted and impaled on it. This seems harsh and incongruous with the degree of the crime. However, the edict of the king was inviolate: "in accordance with the laws of the Medes and Persians, which cannot be repealed" (Daniel 6:8). To disregard such an edict was a major offense.

May God, who has caused His name to dwell here, points to Jewish influence in the substance and wording of the decree. The phrase was used before the time of the Temple, when the Israelites stood on the threshold of entering the promised land (Deuteronomy 12:11). The Persian king assumed God would protect his parochial interests and overthrow any king or people who might destroy this temple in Jerusalem.

LESSON APPLIED

These days churches are in as much the same position as Judah in BC 521. There is a story told about church leaders attempting to go with plans to build a sanctuary, but despite their good intentions, the project stalled for several reasons. Some parishioners wondered, "Will we try to build again?" Others wondered, "Is now not the time to build?" Yet others urged, "Let us build right now."

Throughout the building process, in situations like these, the leaders have to complete a thorough case study of the situation. They have to consider all aspects of their building plans. However, more important, they have to pray and wait upon the Lord. Waiting on the Lord is important, because God has the last say. The story goes that even when the elders on the board would not restart the ambitious building plan, God moved in their hearts. Without any arm-twisting, the elders voted three weeks later to go ahead with the project.

Why has this happened now? The answer has to do in part with their leaders. They had people like Haggai and Zechariah who had spoken prophetically of God's call. They also had people like Zerubbabel and Jeshua who expressed God's call-in tangible ways. They moved ahead with confidence, not in themselves but in God, who alone enabled them to be the church He had called them to be.

LET'S TALK ABOUT IT

Why is the investigation in Ezra 5–6 different than Ezra 4?

In Ezra 4, the Persian king finds the "incriminating evidence" the officials want him to find. He stops the rebuilding activity in Jerusalem. However, in Ezra 6, the Persian king finds the vindicating evidence that God wants him to find. He directs the

Temple building to continue. The Temple is guaranteed restoration to function as it did previously in the relationship between God and Israel. God forward, the post-exilic community can be confident that God desires this relationship to be restored and that he will actively work to make it so. He is more than a match for any group of scheming government officials.

At a more detailed level, Darius' favorable response is portrayed as the result of his political agenda, the actions of the Persian officials, and the diligent work being done by the Judeans. The actions of the officials and the king are out of the Judeans' hands. The actions of the officials and the kings are out of the Judeans' control. However, they do their part by throwing themselves wholeheartedly into the work. For this part, God weaves the officials' and the king's actions and desires into a set of circumstances that gives success to the Judeans' work. God's people can invest confidently in the work God has called them to in the world, knowing that he can take care of what they cannot in order to make their work for him a success.

After 16 years of procrastination and delay, finally, the Jews began to rebuild God's Temple again. What enabled them to start again?

This question is not merely academic but related to our personal lives, for we all find ourselves like the Jews at times: worn out, preoccupied, and unwilling to do what God has called us to do. Perhaps we wander from intimacy with the Lord, and prayer rarely proceeds from our mouths, not to mention from our hearts.

The work on rebuilding the Temple had stopped for 16 years due to opposition from the land's people. Then, under the ministries of the prophets Haggai and Zechariah, the work resumed. However, they barely got started again when Tattenai, the governor of the province that included Israel, confronted the Jews with whether they had proper permission to rebuild the temple. They told him about Cyrus' decree. However, because God's eye was upon them, Tattenai permitted them to continue construction until word got back from the current king, Darius.

How do we begin to rebuild again after devastation?

Restoration begins with God, who is sovereign over all things and who inspires successful new beginnings. God called Haggai and Zechariah into prophetic service, and they called God's people to obedience. God did not rebuild the temple Himself; rather, He raised and used people who would respond to His imitative. Thus, God's people should look to God to initiate a new beginning, and then respond to His call in obedience to His sovereignty.

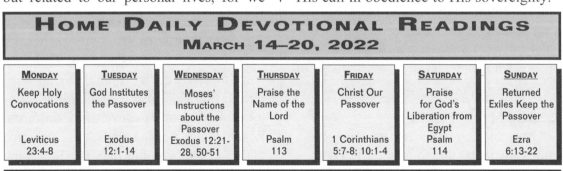

HOME DAILY DEVOTIONAL READINGS
MARCH 14–20, 2022

MONDAY	TUESDAY	WEDNESDAY	THURSDAY	FRIDAY	SATURDAY	SUNDAY
Keep Holy Convocations	God Institutes the Passover	Moses' Instructions about the Passover	Praise the Name of the Lord	Christ Our Passover	Praise for God's Liberation from Egypt	Returned Exiles Keep the Passover
Leviticus 23:4-8	Exodus 12:1-14	Exodus 12:21-28, 50-51	Psalm 113	1 Corinthians 5:7-8; 10:1-4	Psalm 114	Ezra 6:13-22

CELEBRATE PASSOVER LIBERATION

ADULT TOPIC:	BACKGROUND SCRIPTURE:
THE CELEBRATION OF COMPLETION	EZRA 6:13–22; LEVITICUS 23:4–8

EZRA 6:13–22

King James Version

THEN Tatnai, governor on this side the river, Shetharboznai, and their companions, according to that which Darius the king had sent, so they did speedily.

14 And the elders of the Jews builded, and they prospered through the prophesying of Haggai the prophet and Zechariah the son of Iddo. And they builded, and finished it, according to the commandment of the God of Israel, and according to the commandment of Cyrus, and Darius, and Artaxerxes king of Persia.

15 And this house was finished on the third day of the month Adar, which was in the sixth year of the reign of Darius the king.

16 And the children of Israel, the priests, and the Levites, and the rest of the children of the captivity, kept the dedication of this house of God with joy.

17 And offered at the dedication of this house of God an hundred bullocks, two hundred rams, four hundred lambs; and for a sin offering for all Israel, twelve he goats, according to the number of the tribes of Israel.

18 And they set the priests in their divisions, and the Levites in their courses, for the service of God, which is at Jerusalem; as it is written in the book of Moses.

19 And the children of the captivity kept the passover upon the fourteenth day of the first month.

20 For the priests and the Levites were purified together, all of them were pure, and killed the

New Revised Standard Version

THEN, according to the word sent by King Darius, Tattenai, the governor of the province Beyond the River, Shethar-bozenai, and their associates did with all diligence what King Darius had ordered.

14 So the elders of the Jews built and prospered, through the prophesying of the prophet Haggai and Zechariah son of Iddo. They finished their building by command of the God of Israel and by decree of Cyrus, Darius, and King Artaxerxes of Persia;

15 and this house was finished on the third day of the month of Adar, in the sixth year of the reign of King Darius.

16 The people of Israel, the priests and the Levites, and the rest of the returned exiles, celebrated the dedication of this house of God with joy.

17 They offered at the dedication of this house of God one hundred bulls, two hundred rams, four hundred lambs, and as a sin-offering for all Israel twelve male goats, according to the number of the tribes of Israel.

18 Then they set the priests in their divisions and the Levites in their courses for the service of God at Jerusalem, as it is written in the book of Moses.

19 On the fourteenth day of the first month the returned exiles kept the passover.

20 For both the priests and the Levites had purified themselves; all of them were clean.

MAIN THOUGHT: The people of Israel, the priests and the Levites, and the rest of the returned exiles, celebrated the dedication of this house of God with joy. (Ezra 6:16, KJV)

EZRA 6:13–22

King James Version	New Revised Standard Version
passover for all the children of the captivity, and for their brethren the priests, and for themselves.	So they killed the passover lamb for all the returned exiles, for their fellow-priests, and for themselves.
21 And the children of Israel, which were come again out of captivity, and all such as had separated themselves unto them from the filthiness of the heathen of the land, to seek the LORD God of Israel, did eat,	21 It was eaten by the people of Israel who had returned from exile, and also by all who had joined them and separated themselves from the pollutions of the nations of the land to worship the LORD, the God of Israel.
22 And kept the feast of unleavened bread seven days with joy: for the LORD had made them joyful, and turned the heart of the king of Assyria unto them, to strengthen their hands in the work of the house of God, the God of Israel.	22 With joy they celebrated the festival of unleavened bread for seven days; for the LORD had made them joyful, and had turned the heart of the king of Assyria to them, so that he aided them in the work on the house of God, the God of Israel.

LESSON SETTING
Time: Mid Fifth Century BC
Place: The Providence of Judah

LESSON OUTLINE
I. Finishing the Temple
   (Ezra 6:13–15)
II. Dedicating the Temple
   (Ezra 6:16–18)
III. Celebrating Passover
   (Ezra 6:19–22)

UNIFYING PRINCIPLE
Celebrations provide opportunities for persons to rejoice after a difficult task. How can we celebrate and show thanksgiving to the person who made the victory possible? After the Temple was completed, the Israelites celebrated God by sharing the Passover.

INTRODUCTION
Ezra—Nehemiah's book is set after the Babylonians destroyed Jerusalem, the Temple therein, and took many of its people into exile. This book (The Hebrews who produced the Old Testament often considered Ezrah and Nehemiah as one

continuous work) picks up about 50 years later and tells the return of some of the Israelites and what happens to them as they rebuild their cities and their lives there.

The book primarily focuses on three key leaders who led the rebuilding effort. What drives the story are the decrees of two Persian kings, Cyrus and Artaxerxes. What counts as restoration is the fulfillment of their demands. Over the next three weeks, we will focus on the book's design on Zerubbabel's efforts.

In Ezra 1, Cyrus commands that the Jews return to their motherland and resume their cultic worship; in accord with that, Ezra 1–6 narrates the return and the rebuilding of the Temple.

In verses 13–22, the Jewish elders were able to get the Temple built, and it was completed in the month of Afar, on the third day when King Darius ruled. The people of Israel, the Levites, the priests, and other exiles, celebrated the temple's dedication with joy. For the dedication, they gave 100 bulls, 400 lambs, and 200 rams. They also gave 12 male goats, one for every tribe of Israel, to atone for all of Israel's sins.

On the 14th day of the first month, all exiles observed the Passover. The Levites and priests purified themselves so they could be ceremonially clean. The Levites butchered the Passover lamb for all exiles, their relatives, the priests, and themselves.

The Israelites that had come back from the exile along with all that had separated themselves from their Gentile neighbors celebrated for seven days with joyfulness during Festival of Unleavened Bread because the Lord had given them joy when He changed Assyria's attitude so they could rebuild the Temple.

EXPOSITION

I. FINISHING THE TEMPLE (EZRA 6:13–15)

Tattenai, Shethar-Bozenai, and the other regional officials appropriated funds, administered the supply of animals, and other important resources (wine, grain, oil, and salt); while coordinating with the Jewish leaders for the delivery and implementation of these resources. These men performed their duties with diligence. The Jews built and prospered under the preaching and teaching of the prophets Haggai and Zechariah.

The Temple was eventually completed according to the God's command and the decrees of Cyrus, Darius, and Artaxerxes, kings of Persia. Once again, divine providence and the will of man intersected. Revelation permits a glimpse of the cosmic dimensions of what appears as chance, fate, or political maneuvering. God "changes times and seasons; God sets up kings and deposes them" (Daniel 2:21).

One problematic element does occur in this sentence, the inclusion of Artaxerxes. Artaxerxes reigned well after the completion of the Temple. Most likely, the writer simply looks at this occasion to pay tribute to the Persian kings who positively affected Temple worship, remembering the suppositive position that Artaxerxes later assumed when he sent Ezra to Jerusalem.

The temple was built in the sixth year of King Darius's reign, March 515 B.C. 72 years after the demolition of Solomon's Temple (Jeremiah 25:11; Jeremiah 29:10). Ezra chapters 1 and 6 reproduce Cyrus and Darius's commands, but not those of God and Artaxerxes. We know that God's command to complete the Temple came through the prophecies of Haggai and Zechariah. Though these are not reproduced in Ezra-Nehemiah, they appear in Haggai and Zechariah (Ezra 5:1–2). God is mentioned on the list because God is sovereign even over the great kings of Persia.

Including Artaxerxes in this group of leaders seems strange because in Ezra 4:17–22, a letter from Artaxerxes appears because it is thematically relevant, although it is chronologically out of place (Ezra 4:6–23). However, the letter from Artaxerxes to Ezra does not support the Jewish rebuilding effort of the wall; he will later support Jewish restoration (Ezra 7; Nehemiah 2), but the reader of Ezra-Nehemiah is not given that information yet. Undoubtedly then, the inclusion of Artaxerxes in 6:14 demonstrates, once again, the tendency of the editor to favor thematic relevancy over theological order as opposed to a chronological presentation of events (Ezra 4;6:23).

II. Dedicating the Temple (Ezra 6:16–18)

Then the people of Israel—the priests, the Levites, and the rest of the exiles—celebrated. The last stone was laid, and the people gathered to dedicate the new building. The writer only viewed the returning exiles as constituting the true Israel.

Yet intermingled with the joyous celebrations are elements of disappointment. For one thing, what may seem to us an excessive number of offerings pales in comparison with what had been sacrificed during the dedication of the original Temple. On that occasion, King Solomon and the people "were sacrificing sheep and oxen that could not be counted or numbered for multitude" (2 Chronicles 7:1–2). By comparison what is described in Ezra 6 is only a meager amount of sacrifices to commemorate this remarkable celebration.

Then, as a sin offering for all Israel, 12 male goats, one for each of Israel's tribes, was rightly a part of the celebration and was appropriately sacrificed in the new Temple. The exiles stood as representatives of the nation as the altar was purified for the atonement for their sins.

Although only members of the tribes of Benjamin, Judah, and Levi were present, they sacrificed on behalf of all tribes, thereby associating the Temple once again with Solomon's reign, its corresponding symbolism of a unified Israel, and the Temple's religious jurisdiction over a unified state. Completing the dedication was the installation of the priests and Levites according to the book of Moses. Yet, it certainly must have been a sad reminder to the people of their failure before God. In this line of thought, it is also significant that the sin offering consisted of "twelve male goats, according to the number of the tribes of Israel" (v.17). Yet, at the time of the offering, only two tribes remained intact: Judah and Benjamin.

In verse 18, the leaders re-established the "divisions" of the priests and Levites who labored in the Temple. In other words, they made sure that the Temple, now rebuilt, immediately began to function correctly.

III. Celebrating Passover (Ezra 6:19–22)

In keeping with Moses's original Passover, the people gathered on the fourteenth day of the first month. Passover was what set the Jewish calendar; it signaled the beginning of a new year. It represented new life since the Israelites were recused from Egyptian slavery and passed over by God's judgment. Passover symbolized God's salvation (Exodus 12:1–14).

With the second Temple completed, the priests and Levites purified themselves and were all ceremonially clean. At this point, the historical model appears to come from King Josiah's reinstitution of the Law and Covenant (2 Chronicles 35:1–19). In the writings of Moses, each family was to prepare and offer a sacrifice. However, as the nation became more organized and centralized, the priests and Levites inherited this responsibility. We see this in our text.

When Judah and Israel disintegrated politically, and the Jews were scattered, religious observances and attitudes changed. Stripped of national leadership and cut off from the temple, the religious practice lost its cohesion. When the exiles returned to Jerusalem, the Jews, lacking political institutions, turned again to the Temple and its hierarchy and ceremonial standards as their communal identity source. During this time, worship, ceremonial cleanness, and ecclesiastical governance grew in importance. Without a king or kingdom, Israel emerged as a predominantly religious community.

For seven days (v.22), they rejoiced in celebration of the Feast of Unleavened Bread. This festival immediately followed Passover. Whereas, Passover spoke mainly of God's mercy in the way that God's judgment passed over Israel, the Feast of Unleavened Bread reminded the people of God's deliverance. It was to continue as a lasting ordinance marking the day God brought the Jews out of Egypt (Exodus 12:17–20). When the exiles gathered in Jerusalem, they observed the feast with joy because God had changed the king of Assyria's attitude so that he assisted them in their work on the house of God.

Calling Darius king of Assyria appears odd, but it may merely designate him as a foreign ruler. Because each new empire assimilated the last, the Persian kings were viewed as rulers of Babylon and, because Babylon absorbed Assyria, as rulers of Assyria.

The proposal of the Temple's reconstruction in Ezra 1 began with God moving the heart of a pagan king; the Temple was completed with God exercising sovereignty over the world's dominant ruler of the time. From start to finish, God ruled, faithfully and divinely implementing God's own purposes.

LESSON APPLIED

True faith gets noticed; a community of faith draws attention. Consequently, there will come times when the Church will encounter the "giant" of government, but despite whatever the government's position may be, so long as the Church pursues God's kingdom objectives, persisting in the holy habits of religious life and working to offer grace to society through Jesus Christ the Church will prevail.

Every human institution and each political system has been damaged by fallen human nature. Even so, circumstances do arise in which the faith community can work amicably with the government. Great mutual benefit results when such cooperation occurs. The onus falls on us to pray for our government "and all those in power that we may live peaceful and quiet lives in all godliness and holiness. This is good, and pleases God our Savior, who wants all men to be saved and to come to a knowledge of the truth" (1 Timothy 2:2–4).

When we are faced with trials and tribulations, we are to use all methods, legal and ethical, to contest our case, and trust that God will bring about the structuring of his kingdom through the just degree of the kings of our land. "The heart of the king belongs to the Lord" (Proverbs 21:1); God "turns it wherever (H)e will."

Therefore it is incumbent upon us to pray, work, and trust in God's sovereignty. And when, we see God answer our prayers, we should rejoice!

LET'S TALK ABOUT IT

How would the government regard Judea and Jerusalem? What policies would they enforce or ignore? What special interests might they pursue?

Every time the imperial Colossus Persia stretched into a new territory, or era following a new king's ascension, a sense of uncertainty probably settled upon Judea.

For this reason the Jews kept a low profile since their return to Judea. From time to time, there was activity around the Temple, but it was inconsequential. However, when the powerful and moving prophetic messages ignited the people's will to complete the Temple things changed.

The saints of Judea launched into a flurry of activity. So much so that it caught the attention of the government. After an inspection by the regional authorities, the Jewish community waited to see how the government would respond to their construction project. They waited to see if the giants would shift the effort, or if government intervention would roll over and crush their efforts.

The theme of exclusivity, which first arose in the careful investigation of lineage in chapter two and formed the basis of the community's refusal of the assistance offered in Ezra 4:1, is furthered in the application of the term "Israel" to the "returned exiles" (Ezra 6:16). Who understood themselves as the purified remnant of Israel of old, and could they truly lay claim to the designation of being the people of God?

As Ezra's book progresses, this theme of exclusivity will grow increasingly intense, especially in the marriage reforms that will occupy so much of both Ezra and Nehemiah's writing. Despite this, a clear note of tolerance and outreach is sounded in the inclusion of "all who had joined them and separated themselves from the pollutions of the nations of the land to worship the Lord, the God of Israel" (v. 21), that is those Israelites who had not experienced exile for whatever reason but who had literally thrown out the old leaven of their lives and now pledged themselves to the faith. Likewise, in Hezekiah's great feasts of Passover and Unleavened Bread following his renewal of the Temple, in the celebration (2 Chronicles 30:1), allowance was made for those who were willing to conform to the ideas of purity and worship in Jerusalem.

What were the three declarations of what God had done to inspire their joyful praise?

The first declaration is that God is the source of their joy: "the Lord had made them joyful" (verse 22). The second is that God is the source of their success. God overcame the opposition to the project by directly influencing the present administration, as He had Cyrus in chapter one.

Finally, the saints declare that God is the source of their strength which allowed them to complete the reconstruction of the Temple: He aided them (literally: "[H]e strengthened their hands") in their completion of the Temple.

HOME DAILY DEVOTIONAL READINGS
MARCH 21–27, 2022

MONDAY	TUESDAY	WEDNESDAY	THURSDAY	FRIDAY	SATURDAY	SUNDAY
Remember God's Blessings	Hear and Act	Humble Yourselves and Resist the Adversary	Bless the Lord, O My Soul	God's Love Is Everlasting	Remember Christ and Endure	Keep the Lord's Commandments
Deuteronomy 8:12-20	James 1:19-27	1 Peter 5:5-9	Psalm 103:1-10	Psalm 103:11-22	2 Timothy 2:8-13	Deuteronomy 8:1-11

LEST WE FORGET

ADULT TOPIC:	BACKGROUND SCRIPTURE:
THE RESOLVE TO REMEMBER	DEUTERONOMY 8

DEUTERONOMY 8:1–11

King James Version

ALL the commandments which I command thee this day shall ye observe to do, that ye may live, and multiply, and go in and possess the land which the LORD sware unto your fathers.

2 And thou shalt remember all the way which the LORD thy God led thee these forty years in the wilderness, to humble thee, and to prove thee, to know what was in thine heart, whether thou wouldest keep his commandments, or no.
3 And he humbled thee, and suffered thee to hunger, and fed thee with manna, which thou knewest not, neither did thy fathers know; that he might make thee know that man doth not live by bread only, but by every word that proceedeth out of the mouth of the LORD doth man live.
4 Thy raiment waxed not old upon thee, neither did thy foot swell, these forty years.
5 Thou shalt also consider in thine heart, that, as a man chasteneth his son, so the LORD thy God chasteneth thee.
6 Therefore thou shalt keep the commandments of the LORD thy God, to walk in his ways, and to fear him.
7 For the LORD thy God bringeth thee into a good land, a land of brooks of water, of fountains and depths that spring out of valleys and hills;
8 A land of wheat, and barley, and vines, and fig trees, and pomegranates; a land of oil olive, and honey;
9 A land wherein thou shalt eat bread without

New Revised Standard Version

THIS entire commandment that I command you today you must diligently observe, so that you may live and increase, and go in and occupy the land that the LORD promised on oath to your ancestors.
2 Remember the long way that the LORD your God has led you these forty years in the wilderness, in order to humble you, testing you to know what was in your heart, whether or not you would keep his commandments.
3 He humbled you by letting you hunger, then by feeding you with manna, with which neither you nor your ancestors were acquainted, in order to make you understand that one does not live by bread alone, but by every word that comes from the mouth of the LORD.

4 The clothes on your back did not wear out and your feet did not swell these forty years.
5 Know then in your heart that as a parent disciplines a child so the LORD your God disciplines you.
6 Therefore keep the commandments of the LORD your God, by walking in his ways and by fearing him.
7 For the LORD your God is bringing you into a good land, a land with flowing streams, with springs and underground waters welling up in valleys and hills,
8 a land of wheat and barley, of vines and fig trees and pomegranates, a land of olive trees and honey,
9 a land where you may eat bread without scar-

MAIN THOUGHT: Take care that you do not forget the LORD your God, by failing to keep his commandments, his ordinances, and his statutes, which I am commanding you today. (Deuteronomy 8:11, KJV)

DEUTERONOMY 8:1–11

King James Version	*New Revised Standard Version*
scarceness, thou shalt not lack any thing in it; a land whose stones are iron, and out of whose hills thou mayest dig brass.	city, where you will lack nothing, a land whose stones are iron and from whose hills you may mine copper.
10 When thou hast eaten and art full, then thou shalt bless the LORD thy God for the good land which he hath given thee.	10 You shall eat your fill and bless the LORD your God for the good land that he has given you.
11 Beware that thou forget not the LORD thy God, in not keeping his commandments, and his judgments, and his statutes, which I command thee this day:	11 Take care that you do not forget the LORD your God, by failing to keep his commandments, his ordinances, and his statutes, which I am commanding you today.

LESSON SETTING

Time: During the Persian Period (539–332 BC)

Place: Near the Jordan River

LESSON OUTLINE

I. The Impact of Hindsight (Deuteronomy 8:1–5)

II. The Implication of Foresight (Deuteronomy 8:6–10)

III. The Importance of Insight (Deuteronomy 8:11)

UNIFYING PRINCIPLE

Humility can be thought of as a weakness in today's society. Why do people forget the road they traveled in life and who helped them in their accomplishments? Deuteronomy extols humility as liberating and explains its purpose.

INTRODUCTION

Deuteronomy 8–11 recalls the Exodus and wilderness experience of the Israelites. Up to this point little has been said in Deuteronomy (save for the ill-fated attempt to take the land from Kadesh-Barnea in Deuteronomy 1) about the promised people's sojourn to the Promised Land. We must otherwise go to Exodus and Numbers to find out what happened along the wilderness trek. However, Moses' words in Deuteronomy 8 impress upon Israel the need to learn an important lesson from their past, namely their experience of God's care and discipline in the wilderness period. These experiences of God's care, (when they were unable to help themselves) and discipline were designed to teach them humility through remembrance. The remembrance of those experiences should have kept them from the experience of sinful, self reliant, God ignoring pride in their own achievements when they entered into Canaan.

Thus, Moses wanted his people to "remember" their wilderness experience. "Remembering" is a common theme throughout Deuteronomy. Thirteen times in this book, Moses asks the people to "remember." Usually, they are reminded of their deliverance from Egypt, with an emphasis on their wilderness journey and the valuable lessons contained therein.

The context for deciding whether to trust and obey is specific to each "Israelite." Israel's wilderness generation faced the decision while on the boundary between a hand-to-mouth nomadic life in the wilderness and a more secure, settled life in Canaan. The context for the decision required by the writer of Deuteronomy is quite different. This "Israel" lives much later in a situation of prosperity.

EXPOSITION

I. THE IMPACT OF HINDSIGHT (DEUTERONOMY 8:1–5)

Israel could genuinely hope to live if they would follow every command that Moses was issuing on God's behalf. Life without God at the center is a slow form of death; so, Moses urged Israel to take God's commands seriously. If Israel responded adequately, the nation would live and increase in numbers and possess the land that God had promised to Abraham, Isaac, and Jacob.

If the nation needed any encouragement to follow the Lord, they had only to remember how the Lord led them for the past 40 years. That leading had been focused on two purposes. First, God had sought to humble them. It may appear odd to think of a nation full of slaves requiring to be humbled, but they needed precisely that. Pride is native to the human heart, and it knows no socioeconomic or ethnic boundaries. Pride was the first sin, and it forms the wellspring for all others. Solomon observed, "there are six things the Lord hates, seven that are detestable to him: haughty eyes" (Proverbs 6:16–17).

Second, God, in His leading of Israel, had determined to test them in order to know what was in their heart, whether obedience to God's commands was their intent or not. The older generation had failed on all accounts and were sentenced to roam until they died. The conquest of Canaan would show what was in the hearts of the younger generation, but they too would have to have their devotion tested.

Moses' hearers had themselves been humbled, of course, though they were teenagers at the time when Israel sinned at Kadesh Barnea, they had, learned the critical lesson that humanity does not live by bread alone. This generation learned to lean on God by having received manna. The word manna is derived from the Hebrew word *man* (meaning "what is it"). God miraculously provided this food to teach His people total dependence on Him (Exodus 16:1–30; Numbers 11:4–9). Manna represented the Word of God, which is even more essential to life, sustenance, and well-being than food. Jesus reiterated this as a rebuttal to Satan (Matthew 4:4; Luke 4:4) in the wilderness when He was faced with temptation. Spiritual needs are as profound as physical needs, and they must be satisfied. Spiritual longing can only be met by every word that comes from the mouth of the Lord. Here we find an explicit reference to divinely created longings that exist universally in the human heart. God made humanity with a spiritual nature that can find satisfaction in nothing less than the Creator.

Moses recalls how God's provision for Israel went further than providing their food. He miraculously provided their clothing and for their health as well. Their clothes did not wear out, during the four decades that Israel wandered in the wilderness.

All of God's disciplinary actions were paternal. He dealt with Israel as a parent disciplines their child. The differences between punishment and discipline have to do with both the intent behind the actions and the affections which motivated them. People are sometimes penalized to enact retribution for their past actions. God however, disciplines as a means to teach, and always in the best interest of those whom He disciplines.

II. The Implication of Foresight (Deuteronomy 8:6–10)

Moses described the life God desires from His chosen people in terms of three categories. The first category is behavioral: they were to recognize the commands He gave in what they did. The second category is habitual and goes deeper than remembering God's commands consistently. Israel was to walk in God's ways whether a particular commandment addressed their behavior or not. Lastly, the third category is motivational. Israel was to respect God at all times. They were to possess a nature of reverence and fear that would motivate them to remain faithful to God. They were to abstain from any activity that they knew or understood to be unacceptable before God.

Such ethical care is not merely based on what God may do to them for violating their covenant with God. Morality should be based on the recognition of God's generosity and faithfulness. In the case of Israel, their behavior was to be motivated by gratitude for Israel's good standing and favor with God. After all, they were receiving a good land that could provide for them. Israel's new land would contain plenty of water sources, mineral wealth as well as natural fertility. Its rocks contained iron and copper (which combined with tin produces bronze) that could be used for weapons and household implements.

A land filled with such resources was designed to have a spiritual impact when it was received. When Israel had eaten and was satisfied, they were directed to praise the Lord for the good land.

God uses both positive reinforcement and painful adversity to achieve His purposes with His people. As a wise parent, God understands how to apply these elements precisely to accomplish His divine purpose. Moreover, God's Word is always productive (Isaiah 55:11).

III. The importance of Insight (Deuteronomy 8:11)

Prosperity brings with it as many spiritual hazards as adversity. Although Israel was about to transition from a nation of homeless ex-slaves to a settled people, they would face many dangers. In particular, they would need to be careful and not forget the Lord. Each day they could hardly deny their need for God's favor and protection. Later, when their enemies were vanquished, and life was less tense, they would find themselves lulled into a false sense of independence. That might lead to a pattern of failing to observe his commands, laws, and decrees.

Lesson Applied

While Moses' speech in Deuteronomy 8 is directed to the generation of Israelites who are poised to leave the wilderness and enter the Promised Land, the writer of Deuteronomy is addressing Israelites who have been in the land for centuries.

For both audiences, the message had to do with God's providential care and the importance of Israel not forgetting about it. Moses reminds his listeners that when Israel was hungry in the wilderness, the

Lord provided manna for physical sustenance. Nevertheless, there was more to the experience than getting enough calories to survive. God was teaching that "people do not live on bread alone. No, they live based on "whatever the Lord says" (Deuteronomy 8:3). Physical nourishment is essential, but life in its fullness requires something more.

Our lives have a spiritual dimension; our spirits need to connect with the Spirit. Lots of people in 21st century America are seeking some form of connection, but not always in the right place of connectivity with God.

LET'S TALK ABOUT IT

What does it mean that man shall not live by bread alone?

The meaning of "man shall not live by bread alone" is best grasped in the context of Israel's desert wandering experience. After years of them living as wilderness sojourners, the people prepared to settle down in their won land. God sent the Israelites instruction through Moses in the opening chapters of the book of Deuteronomy.

In the first six chapters of Deuteronomy, Moses reminded God's people of all the things He had done to provide for them in the past. Then he began to give notice to the Israelites of potential dangers in their future. As a reminder in this chapter, God focused on prosperity as a serious threat that could lull them into a feeling of self-satisfaction. Israel was never to fail to remember the 40 years of God's protection and provision in the wilderness.

In Israel's wilderness experience, God had humbled them by letting them go hungry, but He provided them with manna to teach them to depend on Him their daily provision. Manna symbolized God's divine involvement in sustaining life. If they tried to provide food for themselves by hoarding manna for the next day, the food was always spoiled. Each and every day, the people had to be provided with food by *Yahweh*.

Through these wilderness tests, the people of Israel came to grasp that their survival was contingent on God's contribution alone. Moreover, their survival was contingent on obedience to every word that came out of the mouth of God. Their entire existence depended on obeying every single one of God's commands and remembering their covenant with God.

What is the characterization of the land?

This land will be a land of super abundance. This expected land is the fulfillment of a dream for Israel. More than that, it is the reinstatement of the bygone glory from onset of Eden.

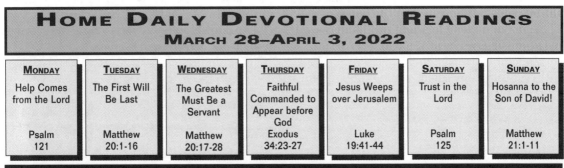

MONDAY	TUESDAY	WEDNESDAY	THURSDAY	FRIDAY	SATURDAY	SUNDAY
Help Comes from the Lord	The First Will Be Last	The Greatest Must Be a Servant	Faithful Commanded to Appear before God	Jesus Weeps over Jerusalem	Trust in the Lord	Hosanna to the Son of David!
Psalm 121	Matthew 20:1-16	Matthew 20:17-28	Exodus 34:23-27	Luke 19:41-44	Psalm 125	Matthew 21:1-11

TRIUMPHAL ENTRY INTO JERUSALEM

ADULT TOPIC:	BACKGROUND SCRIPTURE:
A Leader with Humility	Matthew 21:1–11

MATTHEW 21:1–11

King James Version

AND when they drew nigh unto Jerusalem, and were come to Bethphage, unto the mount of Olives, then sent Jesus two disciples,

2 Saying unto them, Go into the village over against you, and straightway ye shall find an ass tied, and a colt with her: loose them, and bring them unto me.

3 And if any man say ought unto you, ye shall say, The Lord hath need of them; and straightway he will send them.

4 All this was done, that it might be fulfilled which was spoken by the prophet, saying,

5 Tell ye the daughter of Sion, Behold, thy King cometh unto thee, meek, and sitting upon an ass, and a colt the foal of an ass.

6 And the disciples went, and did as Jesus commanded them,

7 And brought the ass, and the colt, and put on them their clothes, and they set him thereon.

8 And a very great multitude spread their garments in the way; others cut down branches from the trees, and strawed them in the way.

9 And the multitudes that went before, and that followed, cried, saying, Hosanna to the son of David: Blessed is he that cometh in the name of the Lord; Hosanna in the highest.

10 And when he was come into Jerusalem, all the city was moved, saying, Who is this?

11 And the multitude said, This is Jesus the prophet of Nazareth of Galilee.

New Revised Standard Version

WHEN they had come near Jerusalem and had reached Bethphage, at the Mount of Olives, Jesus sent two disciples,

2 saying to them, 'Go into the village ahead of you, and immediately you will find a donkey tied, and a colt with her; untie them and bring them to me.

3 If anyone says anything to you, just say this, "The Lord needs them." And he will send them immediately.'

4 This took place to fulfil what had been spoken through the prophet, saying,

5 'Tell the daughter of Zion, Look, your king is coming to you, humble, and mounted on a donkey, and on a colt, the foal of a donkey.'

6 The disciples went and did as Jesus had directed them;

7 they brought the donkey and the colt, and put their cloaks on them, and he sat on them. 8 A very large crowd spread their cloaks on the road, and others cut branches from the trees and spread them on the road.

9 The crowds that went ahead of him and that followed were shouting, 'Hosanna to the Son of David! Blessed is the one who comes in the name of the Lord! Hosanna in the highest heaven!'

10 When he entered Jerusalem, the whole city was in turmoil, asking, 'Who is this?'

11 The crowds were saying, 'This is the prophet Jesus from Nazareth in Galilee.'

MAIN THOUGHT: "Tell the daughter of Zion, Look, your king is coming to you, humble, and mounted on a donkey, and on a colt, the foal of a donkey." (Matthew 21:5, KJV

LESSON SETTING
 Time: Between BC 4–AD 33
Place: Jerusalem

LESSON OUTLINE
 I. The Preparation for the
    Triumphal Entry
    (Matthew 21:1–5)
 II. The Triumphal Entry
    (Matthew 21:6–9)
 III. The Coming One
    (Matthew 21:10–13)

UNIFYING PRINCIPLE

People long for leaders who can liberate them from tyranny and be worthy of their praise. What does humility teach us about leadership? Matthew describes Jesus' humility, and the crowds blessing Him.

INTRODUCTION

Matthew's Gospel introduces us to Jesus in several ways. Matthew traces Jesus' ancestry paternally back to David, introduces Jesus symbolically as a new Moses, and as Immanuel meaning "God is with us." The rest of Matthew's Gospel can be summed up as follows: Jesus announced and taught about God's Kingdom (Matthew 4–7), Jesus brought the Kingdom in to day-to-day life (Matthew 8–10). Jesus was accepted by many and rejected by others, especially the Pharisee's "religious rulers." Finally, Matthew 14–20 explores the big expectations people have about the Messiah.

As Matthew explores messianic expectations, the action picks up. In these chapters we observe how Jesus heals the sick, and feeds the masses—these miracles link Jesus to Moses. As a result there is great excitement about Jesus, but not among the religious leaders. Their images of a Messiah are built on passages like Psalm 2 and Daniel 2, which depict a Messiah who delivers Israel from pagan oppressors. From their perspective, Jesus is a false teacher making blasphemous claims, hence they increase their opposition to Jesus hatching a plan to kill Him. In response, Jesus withdraws to teach His faithful disciples.

In Matthew 21, the Gospel writer presents Jesus as the Messiah, leading a nonviolent revolutionary Kingdom of heaven, against every sin that hindered people from entering the Kingdom. This sets the stage, because in Matthew 21–23, we note the clash between Jesus' Kingdom and the kingdom of Rome, which is safeguarded by Israel's religious leaders. Jesus comes to Jerusalem riding on a donkey, and the crowds are hailing Him as the Messiah. The Triumphal Entry, as it is called, occurred on Sunday of Passion Week. All four Gospels record this occasion and its significance.

EXPOSITION

I. THE PREPARATION FOR THE TRIUMPHAL ENTRY (MATTHEW 21:1–5)

Jesus and the disciples have almost completed their long journey from Galilee's region in the north to Jerusalem. They have now traveled the last leg from Jericho to the town of Bethphage on the Mount of Olives, not far from Jerusalem's gates.

Jesus and His disciples were traveling from Galilee toward Jerusalem. He has informed them repeatedly that in Jerusalem, He will suffer "at the hands of the elders, the chief priests, and the teachers of the law and that he must be killed and on the third day be raised to life" (Matthew 16:21; 17:22; 20:18–19, NIV). As Jesus rides in the direction of the gates, a large crowd followed Him, in time He is joined by more people coming out of Jerusalem, who have overheard He is arriving. They put their outer clothing and branches on the roadway in front of Him as symbols of submission and triumph.

They also shouted out lines from Psalm 118 that are intended for the promised deliverer. Amongst the celebration it is apparent that many people do not know who Jesus is. Some respond by saying that He is a prophet from Nazareth of Galilee.

Before coming into Jerusalem, Jesus directs two of His disciples to go into a village where they find a donkey and its colt tied up. Jesus has decided to ride the colt into Jerusalem to fulfill a prophecy about the Messiah intentionally. Zechariah predicted the King would come humble and riding a donkey (Zechariah 9:9). The symbolism of this is too straightforward to miss. Donkeys are not original work animals or appropriate for war. Triumphant leaders of that era would parade on their chariot horses, much as today's generals might ride on into a city on the back of a tank or armored car. Riding a donkey is more likely a modern person sitting in a pickup truck. In the future, Christ will come in might and power (Revelation 19:11–16), but here His arrival suggests His role as a sacrificial Savior.

Jesus selects two disciples to go into a nearby village and bring Him an animal to ride into the city (Matthew 21:2). Upon entering the village, they immediately find a donkey tied up along with a young colt.

They are to bring the animals to Jesus saying, "The Lord needs them" to anyone inquiring about their endeavor. It has been suggested that the donkeys' owner might have been one of the people who saw Jesus raise Lazarus (John 11:44–45; 12:12–13) and had already been asked to provide the animals.

Before this moment in verse 4, Jesus has been reserved about making His identity as Messiah widely known (Matthew 16:20; Mark 8:30). In his Gospel, John points out that this is because He knows the time is not yet right for that news (John 2:4; 7–8). Case and point people misunderstood Him and His ministry (John 6:15). However, now it is time for Christ to claim His title (Matthew 21:9) openly.

In verse 5, Matthew is referencing two Old Testament Scriptures that convey similar messages. The first line of the verse comes from Isaiah 62:11, with the rest of the verse coming from Zechariah 9:9. He shows how Jesus' entrance into Jerusalem on the donkey and colt is a fulfillment of these prophecies (Matthew 21:1–4). Both verses are directed at the "daughter of Zion," which is a common Old Testament name for the city of Jerusalem (2 Samuel 5:7; 1 King 8:1). Note that Matthew does not quote Zechariah's middle lines that the King is coming "righteous and having salvation," but that is exactly what Jesus is doing. These words from Zechariah point forward to the arrival of the Messiah in Jerusalem.

II. THE TRIUMPHAL ENTRY (MATTHEW 21:6–9)

The previous chapter ended with Jesus and His followers near, (about a 15 mile walk) Jerusalem on a Roman occupied road that ascended about 3,000 feet above sea level. The road was likely crowded with people coming to Jerusalem for the Passover and those who were following Jesus.

The disciples do as Jesus asked, apparently without questioning Him. This is noteworthy because they have often shown that they do not always fully understand Jesus' words or His mission. However, the disciples have been obedient followers of the Lord, ready and willing to leave everything behind to follow Him (Matthew 19:27). Most English translations for verse 7 read a bit awkwardly. The disciples brought the two animals and "put on them their cloaks, and he sat on them."

The second "them" means the cloaks, not the donkey. Jesus did not sit on both the donkey and the colt at the same time. He sat on the colt to fulfill Zachariah's words. The disciples put their outer cloaks over the animal so Jesus—and the animal—would be more comfortable.

This is the moment churches celebrate on Palm Sunday: The Lord Jesus' arrival into Jerusalem at the beginning of Holy Week or Passion Week. Jesus has been warning His followers that He is going to Jerusalem to be apprehended, nailed to a cross, and then be raised from the dead on the third day (Matthew 17:22–23).

When Jesus and the crowd finally reach the city, however, Jesus enters to cheers in Jerusalem and receives the honor from the people. Matthew has mentioned that there was a large crowd following Jesus as He was passing through Jericho on His way toward Jerusalem (Matthew 20:29).

Now the crowd, perhaps along with the followers who know Jesus to be the healing, miracle-working "prophet" (Matthew 21:11) spread their outer garments on the road before Him as He rides into town. They also throw palm branches in front of His path along the way. This is a profound act of honor and acclamation.

The crowd shouts words from Psalm 118:25–26. The word "Hosanna" literally means "save," as used in Psalm 118, but it came to be a cry of praise for the One who has come to deliver and save. The crowds call Jesus "Son of David," a name for the promised King (Matthew 1:1). They also shouted out, "Blessed is he who comes in the name of the Lord! And Hosanna in the highest!"

Some scholars point out that verse 9 was likely a greeting exchanged during the Passover season. However, in this case, the words "Hosanna" are directed at Jesus, specifically. The following verse allows us to see that the whole city was excited because of Jesus' arrival. Some people want to know why the crowd is crying out to Him. Basically, they want to know who Jesus is. Others in the crowd described Him as the prophet of Nazareth. Still, others believed Him to be the Messiah at this moment. However, they give up hope later in this chapter when Jesus was arrested, as their expectation of Him as Messiah was to take the throne of Israel and overthrow the occupying Roman force (John 18:4–12).

III. THE COMING ONE (MATTHEW 21:10–13)

Those who did not know Jesus desired to know who He was and why His arrival was the center and cause for so much attention and revelry. These people like so many in Jerusalem were waiting for a

Messiah to come and to reign as King over them. They desperately wanted God to show Himself through a savior who would overthrow the Romans and return Israel to her former days of glory. They did not realize that was not what the Messiah had come to do at this time (Zechariah 9:9).

The reality that Messiah was predicted to come riding on a donkey should have been an important clue about the nature of the Messiah, because donkeys are not war-like animals. For these saints of old who misunderstand Jesus' impending work in Jerusalem, they, like us, will have to wait. It will not be until Christ's second coming (Revelation 19:11–16) that He will fulfill the role of Conqueror.

Those who did not know His identity, asked Jesus who He was. Some of Jesus' followers answered, recounting Him as a prophet from Nazareth in Galilee. They could not yet fully grasp that Jesus was the Son of God, the Savior who would die for their sin. Instead, this group only pictured Him as a mighty prophet like those in the Old Testament who did great miracles and delivered messages from God.

Jesus later enters the temple in Jerusalem, where He drives out those, who were gambling in His father's house. He overthrows the tables where the money was being exchanged. This appears to be a second, separate incident from the one recorded in John's Gospel (John 2:13–22).

Jesus' anger is not about business or money itself, but the crass way these men are profiting from the people's spiritual needs (Matthew 21:12–13). Devout believers coming to make sacrifices from out of town were required to purchase animals for sacrifice and pay their annual tax.

This tax could not be paid with foreign money, there were several currencies in use in and around Israel at the time. This is why "money changers" were necessary, they provided the service of trading out other currencies into acceptable temple currency. This service required some kind of temple bank to set the exchange rates between currencies. It was all necessary.

Thus, Jesus' anger may have been directed at either of two issues. Perhaps it is possible that Jesus objected to this market's placement inside the temple grounds, which were intended to be a holy place exclusively devoted to prayer and the worship of God. Or, perhaps, the money changers were overcharging those who came to worship. They were taking advantage of vulnerable-traveling people.

These people who journeyed to that special place had no other options for buying animals, including pigeons, or changing their money for temple currency. These money changers worked the temple like a business, buying low and selling high, perhaps depending on the supply and demand of resources.

In this case, Jesus does not render a sermon about dishonesty or fraudulent conduct. Instead, He acts, pointing onward to the coming judgment of God. Jesus swiftly and surgically removed the cancerous money changers from the temple. He overturns tables and chairs. He is forceful enough to cause a disruption sending those there for business out into the streets (Mark 11:15–18). Jesus quotes Old Testament Scripture. He references Isaiah 56:7 to say, "My house will be called a house of prayer." Jesus may be applying Isaiah's quote of the Lord to Himself, describing the temple as His house. One of the purposes of God's house is to be a place for people to gather and pray to the Lord, including people from "all the nations" (Mark 11:17).

LESSON APPLIED

The signal is given to the colt owner "the Lord needs it" with the operative word being "it". The word "it" here requires us to ask ourselves how available have we made everything we own for the Lord's use? In this passage, Jesus exercises a right of usage that had been in some way established previously. This is to say that when we acknowledge Jesus as Lord, we are also acknowledging His rightful claim over our lives, our possessions, our plans, and our futures.

We are never more than stewards, our belief in Jesus makes that role of mere stewards all the more cemented. Discipleship means we learn to release unhesitatingly anything God claims. If "the Lord need it," whatever it may be, becomes His to use. Like the colt owners, we may experience a temporary loss of usage or access (a lost job, separation of friends, a possession needed by someone else), or it may mean permanent loss (to rust, thieves, destruction, death). However, we are ultimately experiencing God's choice to deprive us of something that was never truly ours to

begin with. Our surrender to the Lordship of Christ is literally us saying to God, "all that I am and have is yours, Lord!" Notwithstanding the truth that we may very well feel intense loss when God takes us at our word and removes something from us with only the reminder that, "The Lord needs it."

LET'S TALK ABOUT IT

Why did Jesus choose to ride in Jerusalem on a donkey if, in fact, He is the promised King?

It was prophesied in the book of Zechariah chapter 9 that there would be a King that would come to them, gentle and riding on a donkey, on a colt, the foal of a donkey. He was fulfilling prophecy.

If Jesus were coming as a military king in war armor to make war with Rome, He would have ridden in on a horse and carried weapons in His hands. However, Jesus did not come to kill but to save. He is not rich, He is poor. He is not proud, He is meek. He is not riding a great war chariot outfitted with a menacing war horse, He is riding a borrowed donkey.

He came into this world as an offering of peace. He is indeed a King, even the King of Kings, but in this dispensation Christ's Kingdom is not of this world. We must take our King for who He is, not who we want Him to be.

HOME DAILY DEVOTIONAL READINGS
APRIL 4–10, 2022

MONDAY	TUESDAY	WEDNESDAY	THURSDAY	FRIDAY	SATURDAY	SUNDAY
God Is Gracious, Righteous, and Merciful Psalm 116:1-15	Keep the Festival Where God Chooses Deuteronomy 16:1-8, 15-17	Jesus Anointed and Betrayed Matthew 26:1-2, 6-16	Jesus Institutes the Lord's Supper 1 Corinthians 11:23-26	Love One Another John 13:31-35	God's Steadfast Love Endures Forever Psalm 118:1-9	Jesus Shares Passover with His Disciples Matthew 26:17-30

THE PASSOVER WITH THE DISCIPLES

ADULT TOPIC: THE UNFORGETTABLE LEADER	BACKGROUND SCRIPTURE: MATTHEW 26:17–30

MATTHEW 26:17–30

King James Version

NOW the first day of the feast of unleavened bread the disciples came to Jesus, saying unto him, Where wilt thou that we prepare for thee to eat the passover?

18 And he said, Go into the city to such a man, and say unto him, The Master saith, My time is at hand; I will keep the passover at thy house with my disciples.

19 And the disciples did as Jesus had appointed them; and they made ready the passover.

20 Now when the even was come, he sat down with the twelve.

21 And as they did eat, he said, Verily I say unto you, that one of you shall betray me.

22 And they were exceeding sorrowful, and began every one of them to say unto him, Lord, is it I?

23 And he answered and said, He that dippeth his hand with me in the dish, the same shall betray me.

24 The Son of man goeth as it is written of him: but woe unto that man by whom the Son of man is betrayed! it had been good for that man if he had not been born.

25 Then Judas, which betrayed him, answered and said, Master, is it I? He said unto him, Thou hast said.

26 And as they were eating, Jesus took bread, and blessed it, and brake it, and gave it to the disciples, and said, Take, eat; this is my body.

27 And he took the cup, and gave thanks, and

New Revised Standard Version

ON the first day of Unleavened Bread the disciples came to Jesus, saying, 'Where do you want us to make the preparations for you to eat the Passover?'

18 He said, 'Go into the city to a certain man, and say to him, "The Teacher says, My time is near; I will keep the Passover at your house with my disciples."'

19 So the disciples did as Jesus had directed them, and they prepared the Passover meal.

20 When it was evening, he took his place with the twelve;

21 and while they were eating, he said, 'Truly I tell you, one of you will betray me.'

22 And they became greatly distressed and began to say to him one after another, 'Surely not I, Lord?'

23 He answered, 'The one who has dipped his hand into the bowl with me will betray me.

24 The Son of Man goes as it is written of him, but woe to that one by whom the Son of Man is betrayed! It would have been better for that one not to have been born.'

25 Judas, who betrayed him, said, 'Surely not I, Rabbi?' He replied, 'You have said so.'

26 While they were eating, Jesus took a loaf of bread, and after blessing it he broke it, gave it to the disciples, and said, 'Take, eat; this is my body.'

27 Then he took a cup, and after giving thanks

MAIN THOUGHT: "I tell you, I will never again drink of this fruit of the vine until that day when I drink it new with you in my Father's kingdom." (Matthew 26:29, KJV)

MATTHEW 26:17–30

King James Version	New Revised Standard Version
gave it to them, saying, Drink ye all of it;	he gave it to them, saying, 'Drink from it, all of you;
28 For this is my blood of the new testament, which is shed for many for the remission of sins.	28 for this is my blood of the covenant, which is poured out for many for the forgiveness of sins.
29 But I say unto you, I will not drink henceforth of this fruit of the vine, until that day when I drink it new with you in my Father's kingdom.	29 I tell you, I will never again drink of this fruit of the vine until that day when I drink it new with you in my Father's kingdom.'
30 And when they had sung an hymn, they went out into the mount of Olives.	30 When they had sung the hymn, they went out to the Mount of Olives.

LESSON SETTING
Time: AD 30
Place: Jerusalem

LESSON OUTLINE
I. Preparation for the Passover
   (Matthew 26:17–19)
II. Prediction of Betrayal During
   the Meal (Matthew 26:20–25)
II. Institution of the Lord's Supper
   (Matthew 26:26–30)

UNIFYING PRINCIPLE
People need reminders of times of liberation in history. How do people deal with the burdens of daily life? In celebrating the Passover with His disciples, Jesus reminded them of the freedom He gave from fear and want.

INTRODUCTION
For Matthew this Passover meal is both a beginning and an end.

It was the last supper, Jesus' last meal with His disciples before His arrest, trials, and crucifixion. However, it was also the first supper, the inauguration of the continued remembrance of Jesus by his new community. In fulfillment of Old Testament pattern and prediction, Jesus was (as it were) bringing from His treasure things new and old (Matthew 13:52). In this light, the Lord's Supper is not the Passover, but it is associated with the Passover. In the future, when they render the Lord's Supper as the disciples eat the bread and drink the wine, they will remember that Jesus did indeed shed His blood for them for the forgiveness of their sins.

Moreover, they will remember His promise to share the table with them in the future Kingdom. As Paul puts it, every time they eat the bread and drink the cup, they will be announcing the Lord's death until He comes (1 Corinthians 11:25).

The Lord's Supper is divinely ordained to remind Jesus' followers of what He has done and what He will do. Their present existence is framed by Jesus' past coming (action) to redeem them and by his future coming to reign over the earth. These truths are powerfully impressed into His people's hearts whenever they participate at the Lord's Table in faith. The ordinance of the Lord's Supper is neither an impotent memorial—an empty ritual—nor is it an automatic source for saving grace. No, not at all! However, when it is received in faith, the ordinance of the Lord's Supper dynamically strengthens the people of God, because it proclaims the central truth of the Gospel of Jesus; Christ has died, Christ has risen, and Christ will come again. The early Christians observed the Lord's Supper in the context of a regular worship fellowship as a meal or "love feast" (Acts 2:42; 20:7–12; 1 Corinthians 11:20–22; Jude 1:12) as it came to be called.

EXPOSITION

I. PREPARATION FOR THE PASSOVER (MATTHEW 26:17–19)

The Passover meal was instituted and observed as a God appointed memorial for all of Israel. During the Passover meal (a Seder) Israel remembers their liberation and deliverance from Egypt, this miraculous liberating event was at the center of God's redemptive work in the Old Testament. In our lesson text here, Jesus now cultivates a new memorial meal to serve as a new orienting center of God's redemption. Only this redemption will not just belong to one sole ethnic group or ancestry, it will be a global event.

Naturally, such a momentous occasion warrants to be remembered by a new and unique ceremonial meal.

In verse 17, the first day of the Feast of the Unleavened Bread brings up complicated issues of chronology. Said simply, we are left to debate the precise timing of these events and their precise calendar chronology. The main complicating issue is that Matthew, Mark, and Luke all present this meal Jesus will have with His disciples as the Passover meal. This is a meal that was generally eaten with lamb that was sacrificed on Passover day with great pomp and circumstance during a grand ceremony at the Temple in Jerusalem. Nevertheless, John seems to declare that the Last Supper took place before the Passover (John 13:1) and that Jesus was crucified on the Passover (John 18:28).

Adam Clarke suggests another solution for our consideration, he posits that "It is common opinion that our Lord ate the Passover some hours before the Jews ate it: for the Jews, according to custom, ate theirs at the end the 14th day, but Christ ate His the preceding even, which was the beginning of the same sixth day, or Friday; the Jews begin their day at sunsetting, we at midnight. Thus, Christ ate the Passover on the same day with the Jews, but not on the same hour."

The uncomplicated solution is that Jesus, knowing that He would no longer be alive before the regular time for the meal, intentionally held the last meal in secret one day early. Luke 22:15–16 indicated that Jesus strongly desired for such a meal to be had with His disciples before His death. It also suggests their awareness that their time to be spent with Him was drawing short.

II. PREDICTION OF BETRAYAL DURING THE MEAL (MATTHEW 26:20–25)

In verse 20, the Jewish day began in the evening at sundown. According to the Jewish calendar, Jesus ate the Passover meal with His disciples and was killed on the same day. In our text, we note that there seems to be no roasted lamb at the Last Supper, however, it would be incorrect to say that there was no Passover lamb at this last supper! The reason being, Jesus Himself was the Passover Lamb. Paul would later allude to Christ, as our Passover Lamb sacrificed for us (1 Corinthians 5:7).

Amid their Passover meal, (v.21) Jesus made an astonishing announcement. He informed His disciples that one of their own, one of the Twelve—one who had lived, heard, and learned from Jesus for three years—would betray Him.

We are so well acquainted with this story, that when we read this story, it is very easy to fail to recognize its weight and magnitude. It is easy to lose appreciation for how awful and dreadful it must have clearly been for one of Jesus' own to betray Him. The thought of betrayal has the most dreadful thought to bring up at a feast. However, this betrayal would lead to the sacrifice of the true Paschal Lamb.

In verse 23, Jesus made His announcement as a blanket statement, not to specifically point out a particular disciple. We make this assumption because they all dipped their bread with Him. Jesus' dialog here is not hostile, He does not crudely castigate the betrayer as many of us would have likely (perhaps rightly) done. Instead, He identified the betrayer as a friend, one who ate at the same table with Him. This kind act of benevolence fulfilled the prophecy penned in Psalm 41:9, "Even my close friend, someone I trusted, one who shared my bread, has turned against me."

It was noble for the 11 other disciples (v.25) to ask the question, "Lord, is it I?" Nevertheless, it lacked the same integrity for Judas to ask, we the reader know that he has already arranged for the arrest for Jesus. It should also be noted that it was a beautiful trait in the disciples' character that they did not suspect one another.

However, almost incredulously, every one of them inquired as the form of the question implied, surely Lord, you do not mean me?

It is fair to assume that Jesus disclosed the betrayal of Judas with love in His eyes, and that in this discussion Jesus demonstrated to Judas that He loved him, even knowing his deceitful action.

III. INSTITUTION OF THE LORD'S SUPPER (MATTHEW 26:26–30)

In verse 26, Jesus did not give the customary explanation of the meaning of each of the foods. He reinterpreted them in Himself. The focus was no longer on Israel's suffering in Egypt but the sin-bearing suffering of Jesus on their behalf.

This is how we recall what Jesus did for us on the cross. As we eat the bread, we should remember how Jesus was broken, pierced, and beaten with stripes for our sins. As we drink the cup, we should remember that His blood, His life was poured out on Calvary for us.

This is how we fellowship with Jesus. Because His redemption has restored our relationship between God and us. We can now sit down to have communion with God and enjoy each other's company through the intervention of Jesus.

In verse 28, remarkably Jesus publicly announced the institution of a new covenant known as the Lord's Supper. No mere person could ever institute or organize a new covenant between God and humanity, but Jesus is God incarnate. He has the power to establish a New Covenant, one established with blood, even as the old covenant was established with blood (Exodus 24:8).

The New Covenant involves an inner transformation that purifies us from all sin. "For I will forgive their iniquity, and their sin, I will remember no more" (Jeremiah 31:34). This transformation puts God's Word and will in us "I will put My law in their minds and write it on their hearts" (Jeremiah 31:33). This covenant is all about a new, close relationship with God "I will be their God, and they shall be My people" (Jeremiah 31:33).

Another way of saying that the blood of Jesus validated the New Covenant is to say that the blood of Jesus made the new covenant able to be done. His bloody death also made this new covenant sure and reliable.

In other words, the blood of Jesus is confirmed with the life of God Himself. Thus, because of what Jesus did on Calvary's cross on Friday evening, we have a new covenant connection with God.

Unfortunately, many followers of Jesus live as if it never happened—as if there is no inner transformation through proper cleansing from sin. Far too many believers live below the high call of God's Word and will for our lives. Sadly, far too many professed believers still live as if there is no new and close relationship with God available freely for our enjoyment. Jesus' blood was shed for many to be saved.

Christ's blood was not shed for the small number of apostles alone. There were but eleven of them who partook of the covenant symbolized by the cup, and yet the Savior does not say, "This is my blood which is shed for the favored eleven." No! Jesus says, "This is my blood which is shed for many."

In verse 30, nobody thinks of Jesus singing, but He did. He raised His voice in adoration and worship to God the Father. In a way, we can only wonder what His voice sounded like. Maybe Jesus had a stunning and captivating voice. However, we do know for sure that He sang out with more than His voice, and He lifted His whole heart in praise. This causes us to remember that God wants to be praised with singing. God delights in our praise. Moreover, if Jesus could praise audibly, then surely we can, too.

LESSON APPLIED

Nearly every one of the Gospels mention Jesus eating, and they mention that He gave thanks (Matthew 14:19; 15:36; Luke 22:19). This is the case when He fed the multitudes with only a handful of food to start with, and it is the case here again at His last supper. Imagine that, and then let it really sink in to your spirit.

Even knowing full well that He was about to die. Jesus gave thanks for the sustenance of life. Just think He gave thanks for nutrition that would never build His divine muscles nor strengthen His flesh and bones. Yet this food was still worthy of the Savior's gratitude. Beloved, this simple act has profound implications for us today. A truly grateful heart for life's basics is a heart at peace with its Creator.

Even when chaos and danger swirl around us, gratitude is the correct attitude. Even when we are about to go into a garden and desperately plead with God to change His plan, as Jesus was about to do, gratitude is appropriate. Can we like Jesus, bless God even in the face of betrayal? Regardless of what may be going on in our lives, these facts are always clear: a generous Giver has given us life, and His providence surrounds us daily. If we do not think so, we have not opened our eyes.

Child of God, you will take your next breath only if God provides it. You will eat your next meal only if God gives it. You will see your next sunset, cherish your closest loved one, drink in a beautiful landscape, and feel the coolness of the breeze only if God lets you.

Although human hearts take His goodness for granted, God remains good. He often lavishes His blessings on those who will never see them, yet He lavishes anyway. Look at yourself and thank Him for life. Most of all, look at Jesus and thank Him for the body and the blood for which He gave over to torture so that we can be forgiven and gain eternal life.

Consider that "Gratitude makes even a temporal blessing a taste of heaven."– William Romaine

LET'S TALK ABOUT IT

Why would one of Jesus' disciples, Judas, to be particular, want to betray Him?

The Bible does not really disclose Judas' motives aside from getting money. Following Jesus didn't exactly reap financial dividends. Matthew alone has the exact amount of money Judas accepted to betray Jesus, thirty pieces of silver, the price paid for a slave (Exodus 21:32). This fulfilled Zachariah 11:12–13 and Jeremiah 18:1–4; 19:1–13; 32:6–15.

Yet, other scholars suppose that Judas betrayed Jesus because Jesus failed to meet his expectations as Messiah. In truth, we do not really know why Judas conspired against Jesus. We are left only to our own best gleaning and inference making.

The truth of the matter is that Judas' rationale is not important at all. What really matters is that Jesus was crucified for the salvation of the world. This reality illuminates a glorious truth, namely that when we belong to God—as Jesus did and as we do know, God can take the worst that people may do to us, and allow it to ultimately work for us! God is more than able to re-work life's worst into His best. God takes the wrinkles of wrong and irons them into the right of His will.

What kind of hymn would the Jews have sung at a Passover Feast? Why do you think these hymns would have been chosen to sing at this time?

During the Passover the Jews would sing the Hallel, which means "praise God." The Hallel consisted of Psalms 113–118 and the Great Hallel, Psalm 136.

HOME DAILY DEVOTIONAL READINGS
APRIL 11–17, 2022

MONDAY	TUESDAY	WEDNESDAY	THURSDAY	FRIDAY	SATURDAY	SUNDAY
John Proclaims the Lamb of God	Jesus Prays in Gethsemane	Jesus Is Arrested	Jesus Is Crucified	Why Have You Forsaken Me?	God Is My Strength and Might	Jesus Is Risen!
John 1:29-36	Matthew 26:36-46	Matthew 26:47-56	Matthew 27:35-43, 45-50	Psalm 22:1-9, 14-19	Psalm 118:14-17, 19-29	Matthew 28:1-10

THE PASCHAL LAMB LIVES!

ADULT TOPIC:	BACKGROUND SCRIPTURE:
THE ETERNAL HOPE	MATTHEW 27; 28:1–10

MATTHEW 28:1–10

King James Version

IN the end of the sabbath, as it began to dawn toward the first day of the week, came Mary Magdalene and the other Mary to see the sepulchre.

2 And, behold, there was a great earthquake: for the angel of the Lord descended from heaven, and came and rolled back the stone from the door, and sat upon it.

3 His countenance was like lightning, and his raiment white as snow:

4 And for fear of him the keepers did shake, and became as dead men.

5 And the angel answered and said unto the women, Fear not ye: for I know that ye seek Jesus, which was crucified.

6 He is not here: for he is risen, as he said. Come, see the place where the Lord lay.

7 And go quickly, and tell his disciples that he is risen from the dead; and, behold, he goeth before you into Galilee; there shall ye see him: lo, I have told you.

8 And they departed quickly from the sepulchre with fear and great joy; and did run to bring his disciples word.

9 And as they went to tell his disciples, behold, Jesus met them, saying, All hail. And they came and held him by the feet, and worshipped him.

10 Then said Jesus unto them, Be not afraid: go tell my brethren that they go into Galilee, and there shall they see me.

New Revised Standard Version

AFTER the sabbath, as the first day of the week was dawning, Mary Magdalene and the other Mary went to see the tomb.

2 And suddenly there was a great earthquake; for an angel of the Lord, descending from heaven, came and rolled back the stone and sat on it.

3 His appearance was like lightning, and his clothing white as snow.

4 For fear of him the guards shook and became like dead men.

5 But the angel said to the women, 'Do not be afraid; I know that you are looking for Jesus who was crucified.

6 He is not here; for he has been raised, as he said. Come, see the place where he lay.

7 Then go quickly and tell his disciples, "He has been raised from the dead,and indeed he is going ahead of you to Galilee; there you will see him." This is my message for you.'

8 So they left the tomb quickly with fear and great joy, and ran to tell his disciples.

9 Suddenly Jesus met them and said, 'Greetings!' And they came to him, took hold of his feet, and worshipped him.

10 Then Jesus said to them, 'Do not be afraid; go and tell my brothers to go to Galilee; there they will see me.'

MAIN THOUGHT: Jesus said to them, "Do not be afraid; go and tell my brothers to go to Galilee; there they will see me." (Matthew 28:10, KJV)

LESSON SETTING
Time: AD 30
Place: Jerusalem

LESSON OUTLINE
I. The Descent of the Angel to the Empty Tomb
(Matthew 28:1–4)
II. The Commissioning of the Women
(Matthew 28:5–7)
III. The Appearance of Jesus to the Women
(Matthew 28:8–10)

UNIFYING PRINCIPLE
The world is full of sadness and despair. How can we find hope amid our anguish? In Matthew, Jesus allays our fears and gives us the courage to face the future.

INTRODUCTION
Easter Sunday is usually celebrated with Easter eggs, the Easter bunny, and special Easter recitals, but last year Easter was celebrated in a new and unprecedented way for many churches. Easter in 2020 was the first ever widespread virtual Easter for many churches across the world. Everyone should thank God for modern technology.

This year also reinforced and reminded many of us that the Church is not relegated solely to a physical location or a building. The Church, the *ekklesia*, is about people.

The Church has been alive and well throughout many innovations and technological breakthroughs for over 2,000 years. God has established the Church as an entity that He delights in and engages with whether we gather remotely, in homes, in cathedrals, or without a building at all—by the rivers of Babylon, as the Psalmist says (Psalm 137). Saints,

God has carried His Church through epidemics, pandemics, World Wars, the Great Depression, recessions, etc., and He will bring us through this present crisis today. "Through many danger toils and snares, we have already come; Tis grace that brought us safe thus far and grace will lead us home!"

As a reminder, Death, Hell, and the tomb itself could not and did not stop the first Easter, much the same way that COVID–19 did not and could not stop the Church in 2020! Nonetheless, two years later, we certainly are not immune to emotions that come with a pandemic.

Yet we are not at all dismayed, because we have a faith that anchors our souls. As you may well be experiencing a flood of emotions reflecting upon that time in history, take courage, many of these same sensations were felt on the first Easter.

After the Sabbath, at daybreak on the first day of the week, Mary Magdalene and the other Mary went to see the tomb (Matthew 28:1). These women watched Jesus suffer. They watched Him die and be buried. We read about many women as witnesses of all of the events in Matthew 27:55. This is something to consider as we remember the gruesome events of loneliness and isolation many people were subjected too during the COVID pandemic's earliest days.

Recall that some of the saddest stories during the whole pandemic were accounts of people dying in hospitals all alone. Family members were not allowed to visit. They died separated from loved ones. There were funerals with no visitations and graveside services with only ten chairs, each one socially distanced six feet apart. The Bible reminds us that Jesus was "a man of sorrows", literally one who was familiar with deep sorrow (Isaiah 53:3).

This teaches us that Jesus understands our pain, and knows well how to relate to the human condition. In fact, the shortest verse in the Bible is "Jesus wept" (John 11:35). It happened at the graveside service of Lazarus. Jesus wept over his death. God made us with the ability to weep. It is part of the grief, mourning, and loss process. Our profound emotionality and grief in the face of death convey our love. First Thessalonians 4:13–18 causes us to remember that we do not "grieve as those who have no hope" because Jesus died and rose again, we will see our loved ones (if they are in Christ) again and together we will be with Christ forever.

In Matthew 28:2–4, we read of an aggressive earthquake and an angel that came and rolled the stone way. In verse 5, the angel told the women present in the tomb, "do not be afraid." This is one of the profound lessons of Easter. The lesson is: do not be afraid of living and do not be afraid of dying. What news! We do not have to live in fear. The women were filled with joy when the angel told them that Jesus was risen (Matthew 28:6–8). Both women were afraid, but the women were also filled with joy.

Lastly, the women encounter Jesus (Matthew 28:8–9). What an incredible turn of events, the story holds that they were shocked and astonished. The first Easter was nothing like they were anticipating. Initially they thought Jesus was dead, and all of their hope was gone. They initially went out to pay their last respects to someone dead. However, surprise, the tomb was empty and Jesus made Himself known to them!

EXPOSITION

I. THE DESCENT OF THE ANGEL TO THE EMPTY TOMB (MATTHEW 28:1–4)

Matthew follows Mark's account (Mark 16:1–8), though he omits a few details and adds a few others. The principal difference is that Matthew has emphasized the role of the angelic figure.

Matthew's account begins, "Mary Magdalene and the other Mary went to see the tomb" (Matthew 28:1). Mark mentions, "Mary Magdalene, and Mary, the mother of James, and Salome" (Mark 16:1). Matthew says the women "went to see the tomb." In Mark's account, the women visit the tomb to perfume Jesus' body and then mourn for Him (Mark 16:1–3). The Jewish custom was to mourn at the graveside (often time this meant within the tomb itself) for seven days. The passage of time and the proximity made it necessary to perfume the decomposing corpse. However, Matthew has no interest in the women's plans to anoint the body or in their concern about who would be on hand to assist them in rolling aside the stone. His concern is to call our attention to the dramatic appearance of the angel.

Matthew continues, "And suddenly there was a great earthquake" (Matthew 28:2). This earthquake may have inspired the scribal gloss in Matthew 27:51–53, in which an earthquake occurs and tombs are opened. As Matthew's text stands, we have an earthquake Friday afternoon, when Jesus died, then another one early Sunday morning, when Jesus rose from the dead. The first earthquake opened the tombs of some saints, but they did not venture forth until the second earthquake at the Resurrection of Jesus Himself.

The cause of this earthquake was the action of the "angel of the Lord" who rolled back the stone and sat on it."

Whereas, in Mark, we are only told that the women saw "a young man, dressed in a white robe, sitting on the right side" (Mark 16:5), Matthew speaks explicitly of an angel whose appearance was "as lightning, and his clothing were as white as snow." One may wonder if this angel is none other than Michael, who in Daniel 12:1–2 is associated with the dead's resurrection. In this passage, we are told that the righteous will "shine like the brightness of the sky" and be "like the stars forever" (Daniel 12:3). However, the reference to "clothing white as snow" may also allude to Daniel 7:9, where it is said of God that "his clothing was white as snow" and the hair of his head like pure wool" (Daniel 7:9). There will be additional allusions to Daniel 7 in Matthew's conclusion, where the risen Jesus commissions His disciples.

The mention of the "angel of the Lord" aptly explains how the women found the stone rolled away (Mark 16:4). The epithet "angel of the Lord" is commonplace in the Old Testament, occurring dozens of times. Matthew's description of the angel, ("young man" in Mark 16:5) in this manner links the Resurrection of Jesus with significant events in Israel's sacred history. The expression signifying that this angel has "descended from heaven" also alludes to Jesus' Resurrection, just as the angel of the Lord came down from heaven to roll back the stone, so will the risen Jesus ascend up into to Heaven.

Mark says nothing about guards at the tomb, but Matthew does and comments noting their sheer fear, "for fear of him the guards shook and became like dead men" (Matthew 28:4).

II. THE COMMISSIONING OF THE WOMEN (MATTHEW 28:5–7)

Matthew then recounts the appearance of the angel to the women: "But the angel said to the women, 'Do not be afraid" (Matthew 28:5). The women's tradition as the first to learn of the Resurrection of Jesus serves an essential apologetic purpose, though perhaps not from the perspective of late antiquity. Indeed, in no invented tradition would women play such an important role. Whether the early church liked it or not, women came to the tomb first. In the first century, both in Jewish and Greco–Roman society, women were not viewed favorably as witnesses or spokespersons. Despite both Jewish and pagan views of women as witnesses and public speakers, the angel explains Jesus' absence from the tomb to the women.

The tomb, naturally, is where the women expected to find Jesus. He is not in the tomb because "he has been raised"; that is, His corpse had not been removed and placed somewhere else (as the women may have imagined). The angels add, "as he said," to remind the women that Jesus foretold His own resurrection "on the third day" (Matthew 16:21; 17:22–23; 20:17–19). The women are invited to look inside the dimly lit tomb to see for themselves that the body of Jesus is, in fact, no longer present. The women are then commissioned to take the Good News of the Resurrection to the disciples of Jesus, assuring them that they will see Him in Galilee.

III. THE APPEARANCE OF JESUS TO THE WOMEN (MATTHEW 28:8–10)

Matthew has rewritten Mark 16:8 "so they went out and fled from the tomb, for terror and amazement had seized them; and they said nothing to anyone, for they were afraid," which is how our earliest copies of the Gospel of Mark conclude. Later (discovered) copies of Mark include an extended ending (verses 9–20), though usually with scribal marking or other notation indicating the likelihood that this portion of the narrative was a later addition. It may well be that Mark's Gospel originally concluded much like the Matthew 28, verse 8. Then again, we know the women eventually did share the Good News of Easter, so whether the concluding verses of Mark are a later addition or not is an inconsequential notation in the grand scheme of salvation. Nonetheless, in Matthew's telling of Easter morning the crucial difference in his narrative is found in Matthew 28:9-10.

In Matthew's account of the women's response to the words of the angel he writes: "So they left the tomb quickly with fear and great joy and ran to tell his disciples" (Matthew 28:8). In comparison to Mark 16:8, we are told that the women were afraid and spoke to no one. As mentioned, Mark's narrative eventually continued beyond Mark 16:8, reporting that the women recovered and obeyed the angel's directive. In any case, Matthew has made it clear that they did so initially.

When the women see Jesus, Matthew reports "And they came to him, took hold of his feet, and worshiped him" (v.9). This is related somehow to John 20:17, where Jesus tells Mary, "Do not hold on to me," though we are not explicitly told that Mary held Jesus' feet.

Several suggestions have been made as to the significance of the women taking hold of the feet of Jesus. Perhaps it was done out of joy, or an act of obedience or worship, or perhaps it was a demonstration of submission. Early patristic interpreters and a number of later commentators believe the purpose was to show that the risen Jesus was truly physical and that He was not a ghost. This is the position taken by this commentator. We see this concern in Luke 24:36–43, where the risen Jesus eats food in the disciples' presence and invites the disciples to handle Him. The same point is made in John 20:24–29, where the risen Jesus invites a skeptical Thomas to examine His hands and side.

Matthew has defended the proclamation of the Resurrection of Jesus by showing that the body of Jesus was not stolen by His disciples (Matt 27:62–66; 28:11–15) and that the post-Easter Jesus that the women and disciples encountered possessed a tangible physical body. Jesus instructs the women, "Do not be afraid; go and tell my brothers to go to Galilee; there they will see me" (v.10). Whereas, in Mark 16:6–7, the young man/angel of the Lord instructs the women to go and report to the disciples, here in Matt 28:10, the risen Jesus Himself repeats these instructions.

As we shall see in Matthew 28:16–20, the report has reached the disciples, and they do as they are instructed.

LESSON APPLIED

When we are faced with a God-given assignment, it is usually with terror and great joy that we run to embark on it. How frequently has a stirring inside of you led to a significant change in your life? Think about it: new jobs, new relationships, major moves, transitional life experiences, none of these things come without dueling feelings of both dismay and great joy. This great joy serves a purpose.

Without the hope attached to joy, the significant changes of life would be nearly impossible to make. Why would we make any change if there were no benefit to be gained from it? Joy is the best benefit we can hope for. Joy is why we do it. Fear can also serve a purpose. Fear heightens our awareness so that we can be sharper and more focused as we navigate the difficult decisions and obstacles that are inevitable with significant life changes. Fear also makes us alert to pitfalls and mistakes we might desire to avoid.

Everything worth doing starts with fear and great joy. The women at the tomb were blessed with the first vision of a risen Christ; a vision that would change all things for everyone, forever. For a brief moment, they embrace within them the fear and joy that would explode out into the world and last forever. For a moment, they reached past their fears and grabbed hold to an Easter experience. In that moment undoubtedly they held in full even if they did not understand in full, the embodiment of fullness—Christ. In holding Him, He utterly changed their world, because that's what happens when we reach past fear to grab hold of Jesus, our postures and countenances are forever raised.

May the God of Resurrection, fill our grieving, doubting hearts with the light of new life. May God continue to send us forth with joy to proclaim God's Good News to all who we may encounter for the sake of Jesus, our Risen Savior.

LET'S TALK ABOUT IT

Who believed and who did not believe that Jesus rose from the dead?

The women believe and are filled with joy and fear. The disciples did not believe initially, perhaps their own cultural biases prevent them from believing the women's report, nonetheless, later they come to believe. The guards believe what they see but are afraid. Finally, the religious leaders never believe. They use treachery to arrest Jesus and try Him, defamation to charge Him, and finally bribery to silence the truth about Him.

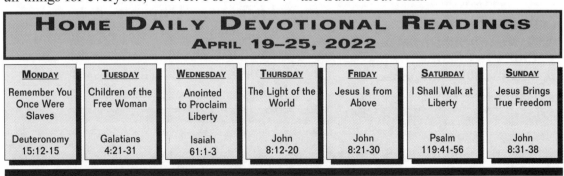

HOME DAILY DEVOTIONAL READINGS
APRIL 19–25, 2022

MONDAY	TUESDAY	WEDNESDAY	THURSDAY	FRIDAY	SATURDAY	SUNDAY
Remember You Once Were Slaves	Children of the Free Woman	Anointed to Proclaim Liberty	The Light of the World	Jesus Is from Above	I Shall Walk at Liberty	Jesus Brings True Freedom
Deuteronomy 15:12-15	Galatians 4:21-31	Isaiah 61:1-3	John 8:12-20	John 8:21-30	Psalm 119:41-56	John 8:31-38

FREEDOM IN CHRIST JESUS

ADULT TOPIC: BACKGROUND SCRIPTURE:
EXPERIENCING LIBERATION   JOHN 8:31–38

JOHN 8:31–38

King James Version

THEN said Jesus to those Jews which believed on him, If ye continue in my word, then are ye my disciples indeed;

32 And ye shall know the truth, and the truth shall make you free.

33 They answered him, We be Abraham's seed, and were never in bondage to any man: how sayest thou, Ye shall be made free?

34 Jesus answered them, Verily, verily, I say unto you, Whosoever committeth sin is the servant of sin.

35 And the servant abideth not in the house for ever: but the Son abideth ever.

36 If the Son therefore shall make you free, ye shall be free indeed.

37 I know that ye are Abraham's seed; but ye seek to kill me, because my word hath no place in you.

38 I speak that which I have seen with my Father: and ye do that which ye have seen with your father.

New Revised Standard Version

THEN Jesus said to the Jews who had believed in him, 'If you continue in my word, you are truly my disciples;

32 and you will know the truth, and the truth will make you free.'

33 They answered him, 'We are descendants of Abraham and have never been slaves to anyone. What do you mean by saying, "You will be made free"?'

34 Jesus answered them, 'Very truly, I tell you, everyone who commits sin is a slave to sin.

35 The slave does not have a permanent place in the household; the son has a place there for ever.

36 So if the Son makes you free, you will be free indeed.

37 I know that you are descendants of Abraham; yet you look for an opportunity to kill me, because there is no place in you for my word.

38 I declare what I have seen in the Father's presence; as for you, you should do what you have heard from the Father.

LESSON SETTING
Time: AD 90 and AD 100
Place: Jerusalem

LESSON OUTLINE
I. A Wonderful Promise
  (John 8:31–32)
II. A Shocking Response
  (John 8:33)
III. A Serious Warning
  (John 8:34–38)

UNIFYING PRINCIPLE
Bad habits and vices bind many people. How can one experience deliverance? Jesus is the Truth that sets us free and enables us to be His disciples.

MAIN THOUGHT: "So if the Son makes you free, you will be free indeed." (John 8:36, KJV)

INTRODUCTION

The debates in the preceding chapter continues into the eighth. The focus remains on the identity of Jesus, and the question remains, "Who is Jesus, really?" Thus, a majestic series of "I Am'" statements adorn this chapter in response. Near the beginning, we hear Jesus say, "I Am the Light of the World" (John 8:12); in the middle He says, "Unless you come to believe that I Am, you will die in your sins" (John 8:24); later, "When you have hoisted the Son of Man, you will know that I Am" (John 8:24); then again, "When you have hoisted the Son of Man, you will know that I am" (John 8:28). And climatically, at the end He says, "Amen, amen, I want to tell you something very important: Before Abraham was, I Am" (John 8:58). Thus, in this eighth chapter, Jesus defines His divine person before a misunderstanding world.

Jesus' "I Am" statements also help us to discern the main divisions in our chapter. The woman taken in adultery story (7:53–8:11) introduces the chapter and immediately precedes the first "I Am" statement. This story was placed in our canon relatively late (as explained in the "Historical interpretation" below). However, it presents, pictorially and dramatically, the heart or grace in our two chapters' mysterious (and sometimes even seemingly harsh) "I Am" statements. Jesus' accrediting confrontation gives us Jesus' first explicit self-disclosure. "I am the light of the world" (John 8:12–20) which shows us how Jesus' luminous presence is brought convincingly into the world. In the middle of the chapter, Jesus' life or death confrontation, "Unless you believe that I Am, you will die in your sins," introduces us to the heaven or hell consequences of taking or of not taking Jesus seriously. It shows the urgency of accepting Jesus. Most briefly, and I think most personally of all, in Jesus' homemaking confrontation (John 8:31–36). Jesus describes the liberating truth and freedom that He promises to give His real disciples.

EXPOSITION

I. A WONDERFUL PROMISE (JOHN 8:31–32)

In this passage, Jesus' opponents explicitly state no less than twice that they are descendants of Abraham (John 8:33) and that Abraham is their father (John 8:39). It is not clear from this passage the exact identity of Jesus' opponents; however, contextually we know that Jesus is in the Temple. In addition, in verse 30, we read that "many put their faith in him."

In verse 31, Jesus apparently addresses His remarks to these Temple worshipers and religious leaders who John notes had placed their belief in Him, and perhaps even others who were in ear shot. Perhaps those who believe are Jewish God fearers, who believe in Jesus to some degree or another, but refuse to relinquish their firm grip in salvation through the Law. Or, perhaps they are individuals who cannot accept Jesus' claim to be the Son of God (John 2:23–24). They may be people who believe, but are under the social pressure to follow tradition waiver, we do not know. Whoever they are, Jesus tells them that if they stand by His teaching, they will be His disciples and they will know the truth (John 8:31–32); that is, they should also fully accept His message, namely, His claim to be the Son of God.

A dialogue between Jesus and the religious leaders about becoming free as a consequence of being a disciple of Jesus and knowing the truth follows subsequently in verse 32.

When Jesus tells the Jews that the truth will set them free (John 8:32), they become angry and indignant. They fail to grasp what Jesus means by freedom. They reply by saying that they are descendants of Abraham and have never been enslaved by anyone (John 8:33). According to John, this is undoubtedly one of the many well-known instances of misunderstanding Jesus' words found throughout the Gospel. In this Gospel, misunderstandings like this function as a literary device for John to explain his ideas about Jesus Christ and his readers' message. The device follows an established pattern: first Jesus makes a statement, it is then misunderstood by His hearers, after which it is restated and explained by Jesus (John 3; John 4). In this case, Jesus starts telling the Jews that the truth will set them free (John 8:32). Next, the reaction of the Jews makes clear their misunderstanding about the term "freedom" as used by Jesus (John 8:33). Finally, Jesus repeats and explains His statement by saying that they are sinners, and therefore slaves who are definitely in need of being set free, namely by "the Son" (John 8:34,36).

II. A SHOCKING RESPONSE (JOHN 8:33)

As to the reaction of the Jews in John 8:33, the author of John introduces a well-known Jewish tradition, according to which their famous ancestor—Abraham and Joseph in particular, as well as the other sons of Jacob were regarded as "noble" persons. And since "nobility and "freedom" were thought to be closely connected, these famous ancestors were not only regarded as "noble" but also as "free" people in every respect. In verse 33, the Jews first state that they are the descendants of their free and noble ancestor Abraham. They feel that they are also free men, meaning that there is no need for them to be set free as Jesus suggested.

Being proud to be descendants of Abraham and, therefore free, Jesus' interlocutors continue by explicitly stating that they have never been slaves of anyone (v.33). Many scholars think that this response conveys that they have never been mentally enslaved by others. In the eyes of the author of the Gospel, mental or internal freedom-spiritual independence means little compared to the kind of freedom of which Jesus is speaking. But his interpretation seems to be rather forced and far-fetched—at least to me. These scholars resort to such an interpretation because they realize that the Israelites endured real slavery in Egypt and later in Babylon. Which, according to them, makes it unlikely that the Jews might have understood Jesus' words about freedom in a literal, political-social sense.

But most importantly, these scholars do not seem to sufficiently realize that it is the author of the Gospel who has put these words into the mouths of Jesus' interlocutors. It also seems to be much more plausible than the Jews (as portrayed by the author of the Gospel). Indeed, Jesus' words about freedom are to be understood in a literal, political-social sense. They are convinced that any other nation has never enslaved them. Of course, historical facts refute their sentiments. However, the author of the Gospel has them simply forget the less glorious pages in their history and allows them to boast of their freedom.

Similarly, Jesus' interlocutors state no one has ever subjugated them. As Abraham's descendants, they have been free from time immemorial. By this reaction, they show that they have entirely misunderstood Jesus. He is not speaking of freedom in a literal, political-social sense, but in a religious-ethical sense.

III. A SERIOUS WARNING (JOHN 8:34–38)

In verses 34 and 36, he explains his words of verse 32 by saying that they are slaves; they are slaves to sin because they are sinners. Only the Son (that is, Jesus Himself) can set them free (again, in a religious-ethical sense). Although Jesus knows that it is indisputable that the Jews are the descendants of Abraham in the physical sense (John 8:37), their origin has nothing to do with their present status; on the contrary, whereas Abraham was a free man, Jesus' misunderstanding objectors were slaves.

The basic meaning of John 8:35 seems to be clear to the reader. According to John, elsewhere in the Gospel, we find the contrasts slave/master and slave/friend. Here, however, it is the contrast between slave and son, undoubtedly because it is a household position at stake. Slaves do not always stay with the same master in the same household. They can be sent away, sold, and do not generally have any share in the family's heritage.

But in contrast to slaves, sons will remain within the family and ultimately receive their share of the heritage. The term "household" used in this verse is also the common word for "family," which included all people living in the same house; not only family members but also the slaves were considered part of the household. Finally, the expression "abides to the age" means to stay forever, to stay for as long as one lives. It is an Old Testament idiom and is found a few times in the Johannine writing. The terminology used in John 8:35 clarifies that Jesus is presenting a contrast between a slave and a son. In this sense, a slave cannot claim to be a permanent part of someone's household, whereas the son will be a member of the family for as long as he lives.

In John 8:31–34, 36, Jesus (as the author of the Gospel portrays Him) rejects the claim of the Jewish leaders that they are free people. Instead, Jesus calls them sinners and slaves. The only way to become free is to accept the message of Jesus as the truth and believe in Jesus as the Son of God. In the dialogue between Jesus and the religious leaders, John introduces a motif that has come to symbolize conclusion in Hellenistic writings. This writing was used to demonstrate that being "free" or being "a slave", in the moral sense of the terms, has nothing to do with one's birth or the status of one's ancestors. Even if someone's ancestors were free in the sense of being politically or socially free, it is only proper conduct that makes a person truly free.

In the case of the Jews, as portrayed in John 8. There is no similarity of conduct between Abraham and the interlocutors of Jesus. Since Abraham's descendants refuse to accept Jesus' message and are even planning to kill the Son of God; they are slaves to sin (John 8:37–41).

LESSON APPLIED

Whether you are a person who professes absolute belief in Jesus today, or whether you are an unbeliever, (a fake believer-thinking you believe when you do not) these words of Jesus are meant for you.

There is so much to be grasped here in John 8:31. In this verse, there are real and unreal disciples. There are authentic and inauthentic disciples. There is discipleship that is solely outward, and discipleship that goes down to the source—the root.

The world is not divided into a two-party system of disciples of Jesus and non-disciples. The truth is, it is divided into three groups: non-disciples, unreal disciples, and real disciples. Real disciples are people who are not make-believe following Jesus, nor are they people that say they follow Him and have only a surface level connection with Him. People who truly follow Jesus are "authentic disciples" they are "true Christians" or "real believers." Jesus is not saying that "true Christian" is a second stage in the Christian life, one is not first a believer, and then later, attains the status of disciple.

One of today's most fundamental convictions is that Jesus is known, mainly through His Word as a real, living, and precious person. And the only reason I say "mainly," and not "only," is that in the fellowship of obedience and suffering from day today, our knowledge of Jesus goes deeper and deeper but always through His Word. But if you want to see the face of Jesus and most clearly, most surely, you must look at Him through His Word.

LET'S TALK ABOUT IT

What does Jesus urge the Jews who believed in Him to do? What will they experience if they heed His counsel?

Jesus talks of the need to remain in His Word. Remaining in the Word is regularly and consistently making the teachings of the Bible your: spiritual scope to perceive the ways of God, your moral rudder that steers your life, and your divine anchor that joins you to Christ. Jesus proclaims that as we remain in His Word, we shall "know the truth." As we remain in Christ's Word, we become acquainted with the truth of God, we become united to the truth of God, and transformed by it. Jesus further declares that the truth shall make us free. As we mature in the likeness of Christ (i.e., using His Word, believing, and obediently responding to His Word), we will grow out of the bondage and corruption of sin.

What does the statement "the truth will set you free" mean?

"The truth will set you free" is often said in academic spaces that want to encourage academic freedom and the capability of learning without restrictions or limitations. Many educational institutions have this statement conspicuously inscribed on a sign near the entrance of a building. But "the truth will set you free" did not begin in an academic setting; Jesus said it in John 8:32. In context, Jesus' statement has nothing to do with classroom learning. John 8:32 conveys a higher form of knowledge than the ability to be well educated in a classroom.

Jesus had just concluded a speech at the temple where He delineated differences between Himself and His listeners. "You are from below; I am from above. You are of this world; I am not of this world. I told you that you would die in your sins; if you do not believe that I am he, he will indeed die in your sins" (John 8:23–24).

The outcome of Jesus' message was that "even as he spoke, many believed in him" (verse 30). Then, in verse 31, Jesus began to speak just to those who had believed.

True discipleship is more than intellectual assent. Those who are "true" followers of Christ will "hold to" His Word. That means they will not only accept His teachings as truth, but they will also obey His teachings. Action is evidence of faith (James 2:17). True discipleship of Jesus implies understanding that Jesus speaks the truth about God and the Scriptures.

The truth Jesus' disciples receive brings with it freedom. Jesus continues, "And the truth will set you free" (John 8:32). At that particular time in history, the Jews were controlled under the regulations of the Roman government. Even though Rome gave them an outstanding amount of autonomy, they were intensely aware of the Roman presence surrounding them in the form of soldiers, governors, and empirically appointed kings. When Jesus said, "the truth would set you free," He was not talking about political freedom (though the following verse indicates that's how the Jews took it).

Jesus provides the best commentary for his statement in verse 34. The freedom Jesus offers is spiritual freedom from the bondage of sin—that is, release from the lifestyle of habitual lawlessness.

How did they react regarding Jesus' offer of freedom, and was their statement true? (John 8:33)

The Jews were completely resentful when Jesus provided them "freedom." His offer of freedom conveyed that they were somehow not now free—which they refuted. They responded that they had not been in slavery and consequently had no need for the freedom Jesus provided. They felt that their genealogy alone protected their right connection with God.

A cursory reading of the Bible tells us that the Jewish leaders' response was not true at all! At various times in their history, they had been subdued by enemy nations around them. Many of the Jews' ancestors had been slaves in Egypt, Assyria, and Babylon. Furthermore, at that very time, they were under the control of the Roman Empire. But because this was not the kind of slavery Jesus had in mind, He chose not to address these historical facts to them.

Jesus was speaking of spiritual slavery rather than physical slavery. Similarly, anyone who does not believe Jesus' words today is no different than the religious leaders in Jesus' day, they are guilty of being in spiritual bondage.

HOME DAILY DEVOTIONAL READINGS
APRIL 25–MAY 1, 2022

MONDAY	TUESDAY	WEDNESDAY	THURSDAY	FRIDAY	SATURDAY	SUNDAY
Out of the Depths I Cry	Go and Sin No More	God's Righteousness Disclosed in Christ	The Justified Have Peace with God	God's Free Gift Brings Justification	Seek the Lord and Repent	Baptized into Christ's Death
Psalm 130	John 7:53–8:11	Romans 3:19-31	Romans 5:1-11	Romans 5:12-21	Isaiah 55:6-13	Romans 6:1-14

FREEDOM FROM SIN

ROMANS 6:1–14

King James Version

WHAT shall we say then? Shall we continue in sin, that grace may abound?

2 God forbid. How shall we, that are dead to sin, live any longer therein?

3 Know ye not, that so many of us as were baptized into Jesus Christ were baptized into his death?

4 Therefore we are buried with him by baptism into death: that like as Christ was raised up from the dead by the glory of the Father, even so we also should walk in newness of life.

5 For if we have been planted together in the likeness of his death, we shall be also in the likeness of his resurrection:

6 Knowing this, that our old man is crucified with him, that the body of sin might be destroyed, that henceforth we should not serve sin.

7 For he that is dead is freed from sin.

8 Now if we be dead with Christ, we believe that we shall also live with him:

9 Knowing that Christ being raised from the dead dieth no more; death hath no more dominion over him.

10 For in that he died, he died unto sin once: but in that he liveth, he liveth unto God.

11 Likewise reckon ye also yourselves to be dead indeed unto sin, but alive unto God through Jesus Christ our Lord.

12 Let not sin therefore reign in your mortal body, that ye should obey it in the lusts thereof.

New Revised Standard Version

WHAT then are we to say? Should we continue in sin in order that grace may abound?

2 By no means! How can we who died to sin go on living in it?

3 Do you not know that all of us who have been baptized into Christ Jesus were baptized into his death?

4 Therefore we have been buried with him by baptism into death, so that, just as Christ was raised from the dead by the glory of the Father, so we too might walk in newness of life.

5 For if we have been united with him in a death like his, we will certainly be united with him in a resurrection like his.

6 We know that our old self was crucified with him so that the body of sin might be destroyed, and we might no longer be enslaved to sin.

7 For whoever has died is freed from sin.

8 But if we have died with Christ, we believe that we will also live with him.

9 We know that Christ, being raised from the dead, will never die again; death no longer has dominion over him.

10 The death he died, he died to sin, once for all; but the life he lives, he lives to God.

11 So you also must consider yourselves dead to sin and alive to God in Christ Jesus.

12 Therefore, do not let sin exercise dominion in your mortal bodies, to make you obey their passions.

MAIN THOUGHT: For if we have been united with him in a death like his, we will certainly be united with him in a resurrection like his. (Romans 6:5, KJV)

ROMANS 6:1–14

King James Version	*New Revised Standard Version*
13 Neither yield ye your members as instruments of unrighteousness unto sin: but yield yourselves unto God, as those that are alive from the dead, and your members as instruments of righteousness unto God.	13 No longer present your members to sin as instruments of wickedness, but present yourselves to God as those who have been brought from death to life, and present your members to God as instruments of righteousness.
14 For sin shall not have dominion over you: for ye are not under the law, but under grace.	14 For sin will have no dominion over you, since you are not under law but under grace.

LESSON SETTING
Time: AD 57
Place: Corinth or Kenchreai (rendered as Cenchrea in the King James Version)

LESSON OUTLINE
I. We Died to Sin
(Romans 6:1–2)
II. We Were Buried into Christ's Death
(Romans 6:3–8)
III. We Should not Let Sin Reign
(Romans 6:9–14)

UNIFYING PRINCIPLE

In life, we are always struggling to do what is morally right. How can we overcome temptations? Through Jesus' death and Resurrection, we become dead to sin and instruments of righteousness.

INTRODUCTION

Paul begins this chapter by describing the Gospel's miraculous power—namely that it sets people free from sin's control. It is not that Christians do not or cannot sin anymore, but that we are free to make our own choice; we have the freedom to choose to do right, or contrarily we have the freedom to choose to do what is wrong. This great, Christ-bought freedom, thus brings with it great responsibility. Believers must utilize every God-given opportunity as a chance to make the right choice to live toward the high call of replacing immoral thoughts and actions with moral ones. A failure to realize and maximize on this wonderful opportunity and freedom is a strong indicator that one may still be living a life that is still enslaved to sin. Despite our failures to make the better choices in the past, believers must remember that we have the ability and power to choose what is right. Making the choice to serve God with our freedom is making the choice to reap the rewards of God: blessings untold, abundant joy, and eternal life.

EXPOSITION

I. WE DIED TO SIN (ROMANS 6:1–2)

Paul apparently anticipated that his statement in Romans 5:20, "Where sin increased, grace increased all the more" (NIV), would be misinterpreted by some to suggest that they ought to "sin more in order to experience more grace." In fact, the apostle cites this erroneous reasoning in verse one, before debunking it almost seemingly with his next breath.

Jesus paid the sin debt with His life so we could be forgiven for our sins. The availability of God's compassion must not become an excuse for careless living and moral laxity. Just like the people in Corinth, we live in a world marked by increasing moral laxity. Being surrounded by temptations and examples of sinful behavior will increase the tendency to justify sin. Our freedom in Christ should not be used as an excuse to sin, nor should our life of obedience to Christ degenerate into legalism. Instead, we should resist sin, and increase our appreciation of God's grace.

In verse 2, Paul denies the possibility of positivity resulting from believers persisting in sin outright. The concept that someone would claim to believe the Gospel while planning to continue in sin is preposterous to Paul. He knew people would think that way, and he also knew that such thinking would be wrong.

The Gospel's point was not just to gain forgiveness for sin, but more so to gain freedom from sin and sin's tyranny in our lives.

To make his response clear, Paul introduces a new concept. He claims poignantly that in Christ, believers die with regard to sin. Up until this point, Paul has written about the accomplishments of Christ's death, but now here he begins to teach that because of Christ's death for our sins, those who believe in Him have participated in His death. In Paul's theological understanding, Christ's believers are dead to sin.

II. We Were Buried into Christ's Death (Romans 6:3–8)

Baptism is a foundational initiation ritual into the Christian faith. It is a sterling symbol, a panoramic picture of a deep and abiding spiritual truth. For Paul baptism is twofold, on one hand saints are baptized into Christ, and on the other hand we are also baptized into His death. Meaning, we are joined with Him. As Christ died, we died to our old, immoral lifestyle, and a new life has thus begun. Paul's argument is that Christians were buried absolutely for a short period of time in the water. In addition, baptism also symbolized, anticipated, and even replicated Paul's whole hearted assurance of a future bodily resurrection.

After all Paul asserts that "as Christ was raised from the dead… we too may live a new life." Paul's ideology is a wonderful tool in the spiritual tool box of the believer, because if we think of our old selves, our old sinful lives, as dead and buried, then we have a powerful reason to resist sin. We can intentionally choose to treat the old nature's desires and temptations as if they were dead. Then we can proceed to enjoy our wonderful new life with Jesus (Galatians 3:27; Colossians 3:1–4).

Paul wants to convince believers that sin is no longer a desirable or necessary lifestyle. We do not have to run at sin's every whim and beckon, we are no longer slaves to sin. We are free. To sin is to choose to sin. Therefore, it is high time to stop living in sin and start living in Christ (2 Corinthians 5:17; Galatians 2:20; Ephesians 4:22; Colossians 3:9).

Verse 5, our baptism painlessly acts out the union that Christ painfully made real. In this verse, the phrase "like this", or "likeness," implies a willing submission or conformity to God's plan. God planned that believers would also die in Christ's death, thus dying to sin and our wanton rebellion against God. Dying to sin is an overall process. When we accept Christ as our Lord and Savior and die to our old nature, we begin a life of regularly dying to the enticements of the world and living to please the One to whom we belong. In the same way that Christ was resurrected, believers also will be resurrected from death to eternal life with God. What people do with Christ now, will significantly influence what happens to them later. The sobering corollary to this equation is that those who have not died with Christ in the now, will not have the ability to live with Him later.

As a result in verse 6, believers need no longer be slaves of sin. History records instances where slaves who were set free continued to live as if they were slaves, despite their manumission. Perhaps because they could not accept that they were actually free, or maybe they were so conditioned to slavery that they could not imagine freedom. Likewise, until we accept our emancipation through Christ, we will remain slaves. However, once we have accepted God's gracious gift of emancipation, we will be able to engage fully in a new birth, one bent toward obedience as opposed to spiritual rebellion and revelry. At one point in our existence we were indeed subjects of sin, and therefore subject to do the bidding of sin, but now we have been set free by Christ.

Yet, before we can start to live freely and embrace the freedom found in Christ, we must first decide to live surrendered to Christ. This is a great seemingly oxymoronic truth. In essence, our freedom is both procured by Christ and found only in living for Him. While it is true that we are identified with Christ in His death, yet it is also true that we continue to live in this world. Believers are in a transition period, suspended between our death to sin's power (yet still being tempted by sin), and our sharing of Christ's Resurrection.

We live in this tension beginning at the moment of our conversion and continuing into the first day of eternity, at Christ's return. This is all because we died with Him, thus both the present and the future are sure—guaranteed; we will also live with Him.

For Paul, the Resurrection had immediate by-products. It was not just a guarantee of eternal life in the future. His conversion teaching included the firm idea that new life in Christ (this side of physical death) is the beginning of resurrected living. This truth is evident when Paul says, "Since then, you have been raised with Christ, set your hearts on things above, where Christ is seated at the right hand of God" (Colossians 3:1). Getting accustomed to this new life requires that believers "put the death… whatever belongs to their earthly nature" (Colossians 3:5). The new life has exchanged the old life; old habits and patterns must also be exchanged for new habits and patterns. We are quite literally new creations (2 Corinthians 5:17).

III. WE SHOULD NOT LET SIN REIGN (ROMANS 6:9–14)

If we have been united with Christ (and we have) then it stands to reason that since we are in Him what is true for Him can be and also will be true for us. This association starts in our minds by an act of mental reckoning or accounting. Indeed, the Greek word for to count (*logizesthe*) means "to consider, reckon, declare." We can consider ourselves dead to sin. In other words, just as a corpse cannot respond to temptations or enticements, neither can we respond to them. Nevertheless, we are alive to God because we have been given new life and a new lifestyle, and we have been given the sure promise of eternal life (Ephesians 2:5; Colossians 2:13).

While we are living in our bodies, there will always be the possibility that some deeds will be sinful, used as a tool to distort our relationship with God or others, because our bodies are mortal, (decaying and dying) (Romans 6:12) and subject to sin. Yet although we are subject to sin, we should not yield to sinful desires and temptations—again we are not subjects/slaves to sin. Paul tells believers, "Offer yourselves to God and Offer the parts of your body to him as instruments of righteousness." We have a choice. God has given us new life; thus, our bodies are to be given to Him to promote righteousness. We are to reject sin, and instead be wholly committed to living for the Living God. We make these choices moment by moment. Later, Paul will return to this thought by saying, "Therefore, I urge you, brothers, in view of God's mercy, to offer your bodies as living sacrifices, holy and pleasing to God, this is your spiritual act of worship" (Romans 12:1).

Sin cannot and will not ever again reign over us and enslave us because we are not under the Law but grace. If we were still under the Law, then sin would have the free range to be our master. By itself, the Law constructs both the proof and the pinpoint accurate recognition of sin, but it cannot direct nor prompt a person to do what is right.

Believers who are under grace can overcome sin. It is only by living in that great and amazing grace from God that we can defeat the power of sin in our lives.

Paul does not make grace our master, in opposition to sin; our new master is God. When we govern our lives under the Law alone, sin is our lord.

However, when we live under grace, our master is God. As an effective motivator, we find grace (that gives us God's love, mercy, and acceptance) to be much more powerful than the Law (that brings fear, guilt, and judgment). This is because grace allows room for failure and growth, while the Law alone on the other hand, accepts nothing short of perfection.

LESSON APPLIED

In the Old Testament, God disciplined people for their sin and disobedience. God sent consequences for sin. However, Jesus' crucifixion and Resurrection cleared the debt and consequences of sin for those who become Christ's followers.

Jesus changes the way we view sin. Paul explores this reality in our lesson today by raising the rhetorical question "(s)hall we continue in sin that grace may abound?" Before responding emphatically "certainly not" (Romans 6:1).

For believers who have accepted Christ's atoning work at Calvary, Paul announces that God no longer punishes us for our sin because of Christ's sacrifice. Good news, God has already forgiven your sins on the cross. However, we should be mindful that the "fallout" from our sin and disobedience often, can sometimes be much worse than if God still administered the consequences. Consider the sin of adultery for example, it will have long-lasting effects on your life and the lives of others. Even if you think no one knows about your illicit affair, and that you may have you gotten away with it, that sin will impact your relationship with your spouse, children, and other family members (on both sides).

It will also impact the other individual in the affair. Moreover, it will also take its toll on your emotions, just knowing that you have been adulterous, betraying the trust and affections of your spouse will weigh on you. In addition, knowing that you've broken the holy tripartite covenant arrangement you, your spouse, and God will wreck havoc on your emotions and your conscience as the Holy Spirit convicts you.

Every sin has its consequences on you and others. When you are faced with the temptation to choose to sin, remember that God is, and that God is present with you. In those trying moments ask God to help you, knowing that God is well able to give you victory over sin, and the ample rewards of a mind at peace and a heart full of joy. We are free, so let us choose to operate in our freedom in a way that will offer us a blessed and full life.

LET'S TALK ABOUT IT

How did we die to sin?

In the lawful sense, we died in the sight of God's judgment. In the transformational sense, believing in Christ is dying to sin. In the baptismal sense, that burial suggests we have died with Christ. In the ethical sense, sinful desires may be present at the moment, but they are seriously wounded.

In the resurrection sense, we interchange our sinful life for Christ's Resurrection life. Paul spoke of this death as a fact, and concluded that believers could no longer live in sin, nor be enslaved to sin.

Living in sin describes a lifestyle of habitual sinful practices. It is a life where sin reigns. Death is the currency of that kingdom. The subjects are slaves, and their future is hopeless. Why would anyone, given their freedom, want to remain in such a place, living such a life?

Dying to sin describes the most frequent way a slave gained freedom (by dying). Our baptism—death to sin released us from the bondage of sin. This release is but one glorious aspect of the salvation that God has given us through Christ. Should the idea of dying to sin seem extreme to us, it should be noted and considered that since the Fall, the problem of sin has been so deeply rooted in us that radical action was required to eliminate it. Thank God for His intervention: "For he has rescued us from the dominion of darkness and brought us into the kingdom of the Son he loves" (Colossians 1:13). Unless we consider ourselves dead to sin, our transgressions will continue to influence us. They will haunt us with feelings of guilt and shame which destroy our ability to over them. We are only victorious through Christ.

HOME DAILY DEVOTIONAL READINGS						
MAY 2–8, 2022						
MONDAY	TUESDAY	WEDNESDAY	THURSDAY	FRIDAY	SATURDAY	SUNDAY
No Longer Slaves of Sin	God Bestows the Spirit	We Have Died to the Law	An Inner Struggle to Obey	No Condemnation for Heirs with Christ	Receive the Holy Spirit	All Things Work Together for Good
Romans 6:15-23	Ezekiel 36:25-30	Romans 7:1-13	Romans 7:14-25	Romans 8:1-4, 10-17	John 20:19-23	Romans 8:18-30

FREEDOM FOR THE FUTURE

ADULT TOPIC: BACKGROUND SCRIPTURE:
HOPE FOR THE FUTURE   ROMANS 8:18–30

ROMANS 8:18–30

King James Version

FOR I reckon that the sufferings of this present time are not worthy to be compared with the glory which shall be revealed in us.

19 For the earnest expectation of the creature waiteth for the manifestation of the sons of God.

20 For the creature was made subject to vanity, not willingly, but by reason of him who hath subjected the same in hope,

21 Because the creature itself also shall be delivered from the bondage of corruption into the glorious liberty of the children of God.

22 For we know that the whole creation groaneth and travaileth in pain together until now.

23 And not only they, but ourselves also, which have the firstfruits of the Spirit, even we ourselves groan within ourselves, waiting for the adoption, to wit, the redemption of our body.

24 For we are saved by hope: but hope that is seen is not hope: for what a man seeth, why doth he yet hope for?

25 But if we hope for that we see not, then do we with patience wait for it.

26 Likewise the Spirit also helpeth our infirmities: for we know not what we should pray for as we ought: but the Spirit itself maketh intercession for us with groanings which cannot be uttered.

27 And he that searcheth the hearts knoweth what is the mind of the Spirit, because he maketh intercession for the saints according to the will of God.

New Revised Standard Version

I CONSIDER that the sufferings of this present time are not worth comparing with the glory about to be revealed to us.

19 For the creation waits with eager longing for the revealing of the children of God;

20 for the creation was subjected to futility, not of its own will but by the will of the one who subjected it, in hope

21 that the creation itself will be set free from its bondage to decay and will obtain the freedom of the glory of the children of God.

22 We know that the whole creation has been groaning in labour pains until now;

23 and not only the creation, but we ourselves, who have the first fruits of the Spirit, groan inwardly while we wait for adoption, the redemption of our bodies.

24 For in hope we were saved. Now hope that is seen is not hope. For who hopes for what is seen?

25 But if we hope for what we do not see, we wait for it with patience.

26 Likewise the Spirit helps us in our weakness; for we do not know how to pray as we ought, but that very Spirit intercedes with sighs too deep for words.

27 And God,who searches the heart, knows what is the mind of the Spirit, because the Spirit intercedes for the saints according to the will of God.

MAIN THOUGHT: I consider that the sufferings of this present time are not worth comparing with the glory about to be revealed to us. (Romans 8:18, KJV)

ROMANS 8:18–30

King James Version

28 And we know that all things work together for good to them that love God, to them who are the called according to his purpose.

29 For whom he did foreknow, he also did predestinate to be conformed to the image of his Son, that he might be the firstborn among many brethren.

30 Moreover whom he did predestinate, them he also called: and whom he called, them he also justified: and whom he justified, them he also glorified.

New Revised Standard Version

28 We know that all things work together for good for those who love God, who are called according to his purpose.

29 For those whom he foreknew he also predestined to be conformed to the image of his Son, in order that he might be the firstborn within a large family.

30 And those whom he predestined he also called; and those whom he called he also justified; and those whom he justified he also glorified.

LESSON SETTING

Time: AD 57

Place: Corinth or Kenchreai (rendered as Cenchrea in the King James Version)

LESSON OUTLINE

I. The Glory That Will Be Revealed (Romans 8:18–25)

II. The Help of the Holy Spirit (Romans 8:26–27)

III. The Fact That All Things Work Together for Good (Romans 8:28–30)

UNIFYING PRINCIPLE

Living in the world, we sometimes suffer because of evildoers. Where can one find inspiration and hope for the future? God promises to bring good out of our suffering and give us a blessed future.

INTRODUCTION

In the first seven chapters of Romans, God's Holy Spirit is mentioned only once, however, in chapter 8, Paul alludes to the Spirit 20 times. Paul skillfully calls our attention to the Holy Spirit, who: frees us from death and sin, enables us to fulfill God's Law, changes our nature, gives us the ability to overcome the desires of our unredeemed flesh, confirms our adoption as God's children, and guarantees our eternal glory. In short, there can be no success or progress in the Christian life apart from utter dependence on their Person of the third member of the Holly Trinity the Holy Spirit.

Paul closes the chapter with profound teaching about the believer's absolute security. Not only are we saved by the blood of Christ and indwelt by the Spirit, but we also are safe in the Father's love.

The God who is in control of all things, has graciously saved us from sin and death, and has begun the process of transformation in us. This God will never let us go.

The Holy Spirit is the Divine Person who acts to sustain, create, and preserve the spiritual life of believers who place their confidence in Jesus Christ. The Holy Spirit is the third Person of the Trinity, equal in every manner to God the Father and God the Son. The Holy Spirit communicates with us, teaches, guides, comforts, and chastises us. The Holy Spirit is the Spirit of Jesus the Comforter and the

Advocate for believers. Ever since the day of Pentecost, the Holy Spirit has indwelt all believers, illuminating our understanding and application of God's Word. He fills us, seals us, intercedes on our behalf, comforts, cautions, sanctifies, and enables us to resist sin and serve God.

EXPOSITION

I. THE GLORY THAT WILL BE REVEALED (ROMANS 8:18–25)

In verse 17, Paul states that believers will share in Christ's suffering. He completes that thought with verse 18, concluding that the sufferings we now face are entirely shaded by the glory that awaits those who trust in Christ.

The existent suffering is non-permanent, while the future glory is eternal. Suffering is part of the series of sharing in Christ's death; it will culminate in sharing His glory. His glory is revealed in us when we suddenly become what God has intended us to be. God will allow us to share in the glory that belonged to Christ alone. We will share with Christ in the glory of son-ship. On that day, we will fully reflect God's image.

Human beings and the remaining creation presently face hardship, and both will be acknowledged in the future. When Adam sinned, God judged all of creation: "Cursed is the ground because of you" (Genesis 3:17). Since then, the world has experienced decay and pollution, mainly because people have forgotten or ignored their responsibilities as stewards of the earth. Diseases, deformities, and suffering always remind us that all is not right with us or with the world. When people treat nature with care, the environment displays a remarkable willingness to cooperate. All creation looks onward to its liberation from the effects of the Fall.

The divulging of the Sons of God will occur at the second coming of Christ when He returns for His people. We will share in His glory (Romans 8:18) and receive our complete redemption (Romans 8:23).

The entire world is looking forward to the conclusion of God's plan. People are the largest group of holdouts in anticipating at that time. It is humbling to realize that we humans are the last to respond as creatures developing an eager expectation for Christ's return.

The expectation is that the creation itself will be liberated from its bondage; the word used for hope indicated anticipating a future event. Eventually, this frustration will end, and creation will be brought into the glorious freedom of the children of God, freedom from sin, evil decay, and death.

Revelation 22 narrates the future removal of the curse from the earth. The whole creation was groaning in labor pains until now. Paul pictures the fallen earth in pain similar to the discomfort of childbirth. He believes that the current pain will end at the birth of the new earth. Thus this groaning is not impatient but "eager" (Romans 8:23). It is not the denoting of hopelessness, but the sound of total concentration on a hopeful conclusion. It is not the despairing cry of the hopeless but the eager longing of the hopeful.

Before the glory is revealed, there is a groaning time, creation moans and hopes for its freedom and transformation into the new heaven and new earth. We groan, longing for our release from the cycle of sin and decay (Romans 8:23). We long for the full redemption of our bodies in the Resurrection. In this process, we are not alone, for the Holy Spirit cries with us, expressing our unutterable longing for God. Nevertheless, until the time of our release and redemption, we must cry, wait, and hope.

If we hope for what we do not have; we must wait for it patiently. Our redemption is both present and future. It is present because the moment we believe in Jesus Christ as Savior, we are saved (Romans 3:21–26; 5:1–11; 6:1–11, 22–23); our new life (eternal life) begins. However, at the same time, we are not entirely given all the benefits and blessings of deliverance that will be ours when Christ's new kingdom is wholly established. While we can be hopeful about our salvation, we still look ahead with expectation and trust toward that full change of body and identity what lies beyond this life.

Anticipating for things "patiently" is a quality that must be developed in us (Romans 5:3–4; James 1:3–4; 5:11). Patience is the Spirit's fruit we must carry in our lives. It includes fortitude, endurance, and the ability to bear up under pressure to attain our desired goal.

II. THE HELP OF THE HOLY SPIRIT (ROMANS 8:26–27)

Similarly, our "hope" gives us fortitude; the Holy Spirit helps us in our distress. At times, our frailty is so intense that we do not even know what we should pray for, nor how we should pray. At those times, the Spirit voices our prayers for us. He intercedes by appealing to God Himself, the only one who can help us.

We may not know the correct words to say, but the Holy Spirit does. His groanings to God become effective intercession on our behalf.

The companionship of the Spirit in prayer is one of the themes of this chapter. The Spirit literally "joins in to help" us, expressing what we cannot fully express for ourselves. The Father knows all hearts, and He knows what the Spirit is saying (Romans 8:26). God can look deep past our inarticulate groanings to understand the needs we face and our hidden feelings.

Even when we do not know the right words to pray, the Holy Spirit prays with us, always in harmony with God's own will. With God helping us pray, we do not need to be afraid to come before Him.

III. THE FACT THAT ALL THINGS WORK TOGETHER FOR GOOD (ROMANS 8:28–30)

Because the Spirit's efforts to advocate on our behalf are conveyed in full accordance with God's will, everything that takes place in this life is directed toward that goal. While the things that happen to us may not be "good," God will cause everything to work together for the ultimate good of His children—namely our maturity. The point is, God works all things for good, not "all things work out."

Suffering will nevertheless bring pain, loss, and sorrow; sin will bring shame. However, under God's control, the eventual outcome will be for our good.

God works behind the scenes, ensuring that good will result for those who love Him. This is true even in the midst of mistakes and tragedies. At times, this will happen rapidly, often enough to help us trust the principle. Nevertheless, there will also be occurrences whose outcomes for good we will not know until eternity. Our ultimate future is to be like Christ. God's blueprint is more than just a request; God summons us with a purpose in mind: we are to be like Christ and share in His glory.

Believers are people who God knew in advance. God's foreknowledge refers to His intimate knowledge of us and our relationship with Him based on His choosing us. God selects believers to reach a particular goal: to become like His Son. When all believers are conformed to Christ's likeness, the resurrected Christ will be the firstborn of a new race of humans, who are purified from sin. Because we are God's children, we are Christ's brothers and sisters.

God's foreknowledge does not imply that all our decisions are predetermined. Since God is not finite by time as we are, He "sees" past, present, and future simultaneously. Parents occasionally "know" how their children will behave before the fact. We do not conclude from these parents' foreknowledge that they made their children act that way.

Insofar as we can understand it, God's foreknowledge means that God knows who will accept the offer of salvation. The predestination plan begins when we trust Christ and comes to its conclusion when we become fully like Him. Receiving an airline ticket to Nashville means we have been predestined to arrive in Nashville.

To explain foreknowledge and predestination in any way that implies that every action and choice we make has been not only known but even predetermined seems to contradict those Scriptures that declare that our choices are real, that they matter, and that there are consequences to the choices we make. What is apparent is that God's purpose for human beings was not an afterthought; it was settled before the world's foundation. Humankind is to serve and honor God. If we have trusted Christ as Savior, we can rejoice that God has always known us. God's love is eternal. His wisdom and power are supreme. He will guide and protect us until we one day stand in His presence.

God's plan for the salvation of those who believe in Christ has three steps: chosen, called, and glorified. When we are finally conformed to the image of Christ, we will share His glory.

LESSON APPLIED

Is it easy or challenging to be patient and wait something out with a smile? Usually, when we do not get the things we want, we become grumpy and complain about the things we do not have. But one of the nine Fruit of the Holy Spirit, is patience.

Let us say there is a very high slide in the park, and all you want to do is go down that slide. After asking mom or dad: "Can I please go down the slide?" They kindly say: "No sweetie, not today." This is not what you wanted to hear, and you start to get annoyed and angry, complaining, asking again and again. They do not want to allow you to go down the slide because it is just too high and blistering hot after a sunny day. They know that you are not ready for such a high slide at this moment, and it will burn your skin.

Nevertheless, when the time's right-after waiting—the experience to go down the slide will be amazing and a blessing for you. Our mothers and fathers love us so much, and they will always want to protect us. Jesus loves us even more than our parents ever could, and He always wants to protect us, even against our own requests and our own heart's desires to keep us safe.

Whenever you have to wait for an extended period of time, or struggle with a complicated problem, remember to pray and ask the Holy Spirit to help you stay calm, not getting annoyed or angry, but instead waiting patiently. Moreover, if you do not get it right the first time and you grow inpatient, do not give up. Pray and try again!

The Holy Spirit is patiently helping you! He knows the exact time when our request will be a blessing to us. So wait patiently and trust the Lord for His right and perfect time.

LET'S TALK ABOUT IT

What does it mean that there is no condemnation in Christ?

"No condemnation" can be explained in courtroom language. To have "no condemnation" declared is to be found innocent of the accusation, to have no sentence inflicted, and to have a "not guilty" verdict rendered. By the grace of God, followers of Jesus Christ will not come face to face with the condemnation of God. "We have passed from death to life" (1 John 3:14).

The Bible instructs us that every human being will be brought before the judgment throne of God for a final and resolute judgment (2 Corinthians 5:10), and Christ will be the judge (John 5:27). We are all inherently under the condemnation of God: "Whoever does not believe stands condemned already" (John 3:18). Nevertheless, Christians will not be found guilty on Judgment Day (John 3:19; Matthew 25:33–34).

However, the "no condemnation" is more than just an acquittal on Judgment Day, because followers of Christ are in Him, we have the joy of being regarded as justified. Paul reassures us that we need not fear condemnation because we can come to God as our loving, forgiving Father (Romans 8:15–16). Christians who live in regret and guilt over past failures are needlessly condemning themselves. Fear can be deadening, "but perfect love drives out fear" (1 John 4:18). As Christians, we must comprehend that our justification is discovered in Christ alone—in His completed work on the cross (Romans 3:28).

Believers can find solace and confidence that we have been adopted into God's family, we have been made heirs of God and joint—heirs with Christ (Romans 8:17). Nothing can detach us from the love of God in Christ (Romans 8:39).

HOME DAILY DEVOTIONAL READINGS
MAY 9–15, 2022

MONDAY	TUESDAY	WEDNESDAY	THURSDAY	FRIDAY	SATURDAY	SUNDAY
Receiving the Spirit through Faith	Abraham's Blessing Comes through Christ	God's Power Grants Life and Godliness	A Faithful and Just People	A Wise and Faithful Builder	Walk Blameless before God	No Longer Subject to the Law
Galatians 3:1-5	Galatians 3:6-17	2 Peter 1:2-4	Hosea 2:16-23	Luke 6:45-49	Genesis 17:1-8	Galatians 3:18-29

FREEDOM AND THE LAW

ADULT TOPIC:	BACKGROUND SCRIPTURE:
RECEIVING A GOOD INHERITANCE	GALATIANS 3

GALATIANS 3:18–29

King James Version	New Revised Standard Version
FOR if the inheritance be of the law, it is no more of promise: but God gave it to Abraham by promise.	FOR if the inheritance comes from the law, it no longer comes from the promise; but God granted it to Abraham through the promise.
19 Wherefore then serveth the law? It was added because of transgressions, till the seed should come to whom the promise was made; and it was ordained by angels in the hand of a mediator.	19 Why then the law? It was added because of transgressions, until the offspring would come to whom the promise had been made; and it was ordained through angels by a mediator.
20 Now a mediator is not a mediator of one, but God is one.	20 Now a mediator involves more than one party; but God is one.
21 Is the law then against the promises of God? God forbid: for if there had been a law given which could have given life, verily righteousness should have been by the law.	21 Is the law then opposed to the promises of God? Certainly not! For if a law had been given that could make alive, then righteousness would indeed come through the law.
22 But the scripture hath concluded all under sin, that the promise by faith of Jesus Christ might be given to them that believe.	22 But the scripture has imprisoned all things under the power of sin, so that what was promised through faith in Jesus Christ might be given to those who believe.
23 But before faith came, we were kept under the law, shut up unto the faith which should afterwards be revealed.	23 Now before faith came, we were imprisoned and guarded under the law until faith would be revealed.
24 Wherefore the law was our schoolmaster to bring us unto Christ, that we might be justified by faith.	24 Therefore the law was our disciplinarian until Christ came, so that we might be justified by faith.
25 But after that faith is come, we are no longer under a schoolmaster.	25 But now that faith has come, we are no longer subject to a disciplinarian,
26 For ye are all the children of God by faith in Christ Jesus.	26 for in Christ Jesus you are all children of God through faith.
27 For as many of you as have been baptized into Christ have put on Christ.	27 As many of you as were baptized into Christ have clothed yourselves with Christ.
28 There is neither Jew nor Greek, there is neither bond nor free, there is neither male nor female: for ye are all one in Christ Jesus.	28 There is no longer Jew or Greek, there is no longer slave or free, there is no longer male and female; for all of you are one in Christ Jesus.

MAIN THOUGHT: If you belong to Christ, then you are Abraham's offspring, heirs according to the promise. (Galatians 3:29, KJV)

GALATIANS 3:18–29

King James Version	New Revised Standard Version
29 And if ye be Christ's, then are ye Abraham's seed, and heirs according to the promise.	29 And if you belong to Christ, then you are Abraham's offspring,heirs according to the promise.

LESSON SETTING
 Time: AD 46–48
 Place: The Roman Province of
  Galatia

LESSON OUTLINE
 I. The Purpose of the Law
  (Galatians 3:18–22)
 II. God's Children through Faith
  (Galatians 3:23–29)

UNIFYING PRINCIPLE

Laws are provided to govern and ensure a functioning society. If there were no laws, what would guide human behavior? Paul taught that God's Law served a purpose, but when Christ came, grace made it possible for all people to become children of God and heirs of God's promises.

INTRODUCTION

In Galatians 3, Paul starts his letter with a discussion about justification through faith. He repeated his teaching because, as he mentioned, they had forgotten what he taught them.

Galatians 3 starts with Paul explaining his argument about how they have been justified by faith. He probed them to remember how they received the Holy Spirit and from whom. Paul's most significant concern was that they had been misled into believing that they received the Spirit by the works of the Law.

In a continuation of his argument on justification by faith, Paul pointed out in Galatians 3, the example of Abraham, whose righteousness was determined by faith. Also, he emphasized that God would prove the nations by faith. Paul prompted the Galatians to remember that whoever lived by the works of the Law was cursed.

However, through Christ, they had been liberated from such a curse. According to Paul, the priority of the promise over the Law was quite evident, given that the Law was given 430 years after God made His promises to Abraham.

EXPOSITION

I. THE PURPOSE OF THE LAW (GALATIANS 3:18–22)

There is yet another reason why salvation cannot be gained through the Law. The words law and promise are opposites in nature. Like oil and water, they cannot be united in nature. Like oil and water, they cannot be combined. Inheritance refers to believers' enjoyment of what they receive through the promise: salvation, eternal life, and removal of the curse. Thus, if our salvation and enjoyment of God's gift depend on obeying the Law, then they cannot depend on a promise, for it cannot be both ways. People do not need to work to attain what has been promised to them.

Instead, God, in His grace, hands it to Abraham. Grace means "undeserved and unearned favor." God gave the promise because He loved Abraham, not because Abraham deserved it. God "gave" the promise-the verb implies something that is both free (or unearned) and permanent. God gave Abraham the inheritance through a promise. That way of salvation was still in effect in Paul's day, as well as in our faith alone. He graciously and generously, (not reluctantly) gave us His promise in love with compassion (not in judgment), abundantly, and without reservation. We have an advantage over Abraham; we "know whom we have believed" in a way that Abraham did not know. We have been given the record of how God secured our salvation.

In the previous verses, Paul made four distinct observations about the law: the Law could not give the Holy Spirit (Galatians 2:1–5); the Law could not give righteousness (Galatians 3:6–9); The Law could not justify, it could only condemn (Galatians 3:10–12); the Law could not change the fact that righteousness always comes by faith in God's promise (Galatians 3:15–18).

God's assurance to Abraham dealt with Abraham's faith whereas, the Law's focal point was on actions. Abraham's covenant shows that faith is the only way to be saved; the Law revealed how to obey God in grateful response. Faith does not declare that the Law has no legal right, but the more we know God, the more we will see how sinful we are. Then we will be driven to depend on Christ alone for our salvation.

The Law was put into place through angels as a mediator to show the inherent inferiority of the Law. Paul explained that while God personally gave Abraham the promises, the Law was put into effect through angels and by a mediator. This was not a new idea made up by Paul; it was already a Jewish belief. Although it is not detailed in Exodus, Jews believed that the Ten Commandments had been given to Moses by angels. In his speech before his death, Stephen said, "You who have received the law that was put into effect though angels" (Acts 7:53). The writer of Hebrews called the Law "the message spoken by angels" (Hebrews 2:2). The "mediator" was undoubtedly Moses, who acted as the mediator between God and his people (Exodus 19:1–20;21; Deuteronomy 33:2).

Now a mediator involves more than one party. A mediator works between two or more parties to aid in communication, effect an agreement, or settle a dispute.

Moses, implied in Galatians 3:19, was the mediator who communicated between God and Israel. God (through angels) mediated the Law to Moses, who then gave it to the people. The Law could be compared to a contract, which is valid only as long as both sides keep their sides of the agreement. While God kept him, the people of Israel could not keep theirs.

However, when God gave the promises to Abraham, He did so directly, without any mediator. The promises were given and would be kept by God, regardless of the actions of people. Thus, the promise is superior to the Law because the promise is from God alone, meant for eternity, and would not be broken. The Law and its mediator, Moses, were temporary, preparatory arrangements designed to confirm the truth of God's ultimate desire to relate directly with His creatures. Paul did not put down Moses but showed the primacy of Christ's way of faith over the Law.

We were held prisoners by the Law, that means that the Law held people in bondage, it made the whole world "a prisoner" (Galatians 3:22). This phrase could also be interpreted to mean that the Law guarded us or held us in protective custody. In a sense, it kept us out of trouble, kept us away from the evil into which our natures might otherwise have led us, until faith in Christ would be revealed. That faith then sets us free from the Law and leads us into the desire to obey God wholeheartedly out of love for him.

II. GOD'S CHILDREN THROUGH FAITH (GALATIANS 3:23–29)

Therefore, the Law was our disciplinarian until Christ came so that we might be justified by faith. The NIV renders the word as "put in charge," and the NKJV says the Law was a "tutor," while the NRSV best translates it, "disciplinarian." In Greek culture, a "pedagogue" was a slave who had the critical responsibility for the children in a family.

A wealthy family might have one pedagogue for each child. This slave strictly disciplined the child, transported the child to and from school, cared for the child, taught the child manners, and gave the child moral training. He or she reviewed "homework" but was not a teacher as such. Alternatively, to put it another way, the ancients understood better than we—that a child needs far more direct instruction in life skills than merely learning educational content. The pedagogue's role was temporary. He or she was responsible for the child until the child reached adult age (probably age 16).

Now that faith has come, we are no longer under the supervision of the Law. The supervision of the Law is like the pedagogue's supervision of the young child (Galatians 3:34). Once the child came of age, they no longer needed the preparatory service of the pedagogue. After Christ arrived, offering salvation by faith alone, people no longer needed the Law's supervision. The Law teaches the need for salvation; God's grace offers us that salvation.

The Old Testament still applies today. In it, God has revealed His nature, will for humanity, moral laws, and guidelines for living. The Law still serves as a demanding instructor to those who have not yet believed. However, we cannot be saved by keeping that Law. Alas, now that faith has come, we must trust in Christ.

The Law supervised us until Christ came; but now Christ has come, so we can now respond to God through faith. We are no longer bound by legalism or guilt-ridden by perfectionism.

As Paul will immediately demonstrate, the arrival of faith was not a static experience. Living does not come to an end when we are no longer under the authority of the Law. Faith comes first. Then we lay aside the supervision of the Law. Many would like to do away with the Law's supervision, but they also do not want the requirements of faith. Now we must live by faith in Christ. Paul had already addressed this issue in Galatians 2:20–21.

Faith had its most essential work in our being "crucified with Christ," but it immediately pursues its ongoing task: "the life I live in the body, I live by faith in the Son of God" (Galatians 2:20). This living by faith will be the theme of much of the remainder of this letter.

For in Christ Jesus, we are all children of God through faith. The change to you shows Paul's return to focusing on the Galatian believers. They did not need to be children under the care of the pedagogue (the Law); instead, they are all children of God. They received this status in Christ Jesus and through faith. Those who are indeed God's children have been justified by faith in Christ and receive a new relationship with God, that of adopted children.

Moreover, if you are Christ's, then you are Abraham's Seed and heirs according to the promise. Besides becoming God's children (Galatians 3:26), and one in Christ (Galatians 3:28), believers (those who are Christ's) also become Abraham's Seed.

Abraham was the prime element in Jewish thought about salvation. Jews believed that they were automatically God's people because they were "Abraham's seed." Paul concluded that Abraham's spiritual children are not the Jews, nor are they merely those who have been circumcised. Abraham's children are those who respond to God in faith, as Abraham had done. The only difference is that our response is to Christ as Savior.

Because we have responded, we are heirs according to the promise. The original promise (Galatians 3:16), though given to the Seed (Christ), was fulfilled in the believers, who are "in Christ." Since they are "the body of Christ," they are heirs to God's eternal kingdom.

By responding to Christ in faith, we have followed Abraham's old way, one of the early ones justified by faith. He trusted God, and so do we. Nevertheless, to us has been added the opportunity to appreciate the great price Christ paid to ensure our share in the promise.

LESSON APPLIED

We should love the church, and we should love our Christian brothers and sisters worldwide. I know not all of them feel the same way about us, but we should not let that bother us. We are called to love people (Christian and non-Christian), not judge them or find a difference between them and us.

The Bible says we are "all one in Christ Jesus" (Galatians 3:28). We should love to see people giving their lives in the service of God, despite their flavor of church or stable of theology.

So we should choose today to honor and remember all people of faith who have gone before us, and we should praise God for their gifting. We should pray they (and us) never feel discouraged and that they will continue to "live a life worthy of the calling they have received." That we all will "be completely humble and gentle; be patient, bearing with one another in love. Making every effort to keep the unity of the Spirit through the bond of peace" (Ephesians 4:1–3).

We are all called to preserve unity wherever we are, whether in a small, rural church in Tennessee, in a mega-church in Texas, or in the bush somewhere. We must speak well of our brothers and sisters and make every effort to show them godly kindness.

LET'S TALK ABOUT IT

Why did God give the Law? Moreover, what purpose does the Law serve?

Paul's arguments could sound as though

he believed the Law had no purpose whatsoever and that he was opposed to it. So, Paul explained the real purpose behind God's giving of the Law and its place in the plan of salvation.

The Law was added because of transgressions, till the Seed should come to whom the promise was made. The Law had two functions. First, it had a negative function: it was added because of transgressions (meaning that God had given the Law to punish sin). Second, it had a robust positive function: the Law reveals God's nature and will, and it shows people how to live. Thus, it had been given to restrain transgressions by helping people recognize wrong behavior and thus refrain from them. Negatively, the Law points to our people's sins and shows them that it is not possible to please God by trying to comply with all His Laws completely. It was given to reveal transgressions, causing people to realize their sinfulness and desperate need for a Savior. God intended that by starkly spotlighting sin, the Law would drive us toward Christ (Galatians 3:23). This is a positive function. Elsewhere Paul writes, "Where there is no law there is no transgression" (Romans 4:15), for "through the law, we become conscious of sin" (Roman 3:20). The phrase "it was added" implies that the Law was supplementary to God's promise because it came into effect after the promise made to Abraham.

The little word "till" indicates that the Law was meant as a temporary measure and certainly not as the permanent and final means of salvation. The Law was in place until the Seed should come to whom the promise was made. When Jesus Christ ("the Seed") came, the Law was finally fulfilled (Matthew 5:17).

What is the significance of the phrase God is one?

Paul seems to have intentionally used a double meaning. On the one hand, "God is one" refers to the unity of His person. He is one being, and that truth is the theological foundation for both Jews and Christians. Nevertheless, also, "God is one" refers to His unity in dispensing his sovereign will. He needs no auxiliaries to accomplish His decrees in the world.

Christ is indeed called a mediator between God and people: "there is one God; there is also one mediator between God and humankind, Christ Jesus." The phrase "God is one" was part of the great Hebrew creed (Deuteronomy 6:4), essential to their belief about God. No Jew would argue with Paul here.

We who live today must not separate the Father, Son, and Holy Spirit, our Triune God worked in flawless harmony to bring about our salvation by grace. When God saved us, He acted on His own—alone.

HOME DAILY DEVOTIONAL READINGS
MAY 16–22, 2022

MONDAY	TUESDAY	WEDNESDAY	THURSDAY	FRIDAY	SATURDAY	SUNDAY
Children and Heirs through God	Authentic Circumcision Philippians	Press toward the Goal	Let Us Love One Another	Love and Pray for Your Enemies	Avoid Strive; Love Always	Faith Working through Love
Galatians 4:1-7	Philippians 3:1-8	Philippians 3:1-14	1 John 4:7-13	Matthew 5:43-48	Proverbs 17:13-17	Galatians 5:1-15

THE NATURE OF CHRISTIAN FREEDOM

ADULT TOPIC:	BACKGROUND SCRIPTURE:
FREED TO LOVE	GALATIANS 5:1–15

GALATIANS 5:1–15

King James Version

STAND fast therefore in the liberty wherewith Christ hath made us free, and be not entangled again with the yoke of bondage.

2 Behold, I Paul say unto you, that if ye be circumcised, Christ shall profit you nothing.

3 For I testify again to every man that is circumcised, that he is a debtor to do the whole law.

4 Christ is become of no effect unto you, whosoever of you are justified by the law; ye are fallen from grace.

5 For we through the Spirit wait for the hope of righteousness by faith.

6 For in Jesus Christ neither circumcision availeth any thing, nor uncircumcision; but faith which worketh by love.

7 Ye did run well; who did hinder you that ye should not obey the truth?

8 This persuasion cometh not of him that calleth you.

9 A little leaven leaveneth the whole lump.

10 I have confidence in you through the Lord, that ye will be none otherwise minded: but he that troubleth you shall bear his judgment, whosoever he be.

11 And I, brethren, if I yet preach circumcision, why do I yet suffer persecution? then is the offence of the cross ceased.

12 I would they were even cut off which trouble you.

New Revised Standard Version

FOR freedom Christ has set us free. Stand firm, therefore, and do not submit again to a yoke of slavery.

2 Listen! I, Paul, am telling you that if you let yourselves be circumcised, Christ will be of no benefit to you.

3 Once again I testify to every man who lets himself be circumcised that he is obliged to obey the entire law.

4 You who want to be justified by the law have cut yourselves off from Christ; you have fallen away from grace.

5 For through the Spirit, by faith, we eagerly wait for the hope of righteousness.

6 For in Christ Jesus neither circumcision nor uncircumcision counts for anything; the only thing that counts is faith working through love.

7 You were running well; who prevented you from obeying the truth?

8 Such persuasion does not come from the one who calls you.

9 A little yeast leavens the whole batch of dough.

10 I am confident about you in the Lord that you will not think otherwise. But whoever it is that is confusing you will pay the penalty.

11 But my friends, why am I still being persecuted if I am still preaching circumcision? In that case the offence of the cross has been removed.

12 I wish those who unsettle you would castrate themselves!

MAIN THOUGHT: The whole law is summed up in a single commandment, "You shall love your neighbor as yourself." (Galatians 5:14, KJV)

GALATIANS 5:1–15

King James Version	*New Revised Standard Version*
13 For, brethren, ye have been called unto liberty; only use not liberty for an occasion to the flesh, but by love serve one another.	13 For you were called to freedom, brothers and sisters;only do not use your freedom as an opportunity for self-indulgence, but through love become slaves to one another.
14 For all the law is fulfilled in one word, even in this; Thou shalt love thy neighbour as thyself.	14 For the whole law is summed up in a single commandment, 'You shall love your neighbour as yourself.'
15 But if ye bite and devour one another, take heed that ye be not consumed one of another.	15 If, however, you bite and devour one another, take care that you are not consumed by one another.

LESSON SETTING
Time: AD **46–48**
Place: The Roman Province of Galatia

LESSON OUTLINE
I. **Protecting Freedom (Galatians 5:1–6)**
II. **Exposing the False Teachers (Galatians 5:7–12)**
III. **Ethical Appeal (Galatians 5:13–15)**

UNIFYING PRINCIPLE

Sometimes people feel bound by laws and desires that keep them in chains. Where can we find the freedom to experience life in transforming ways? According to Galatians, God calls us to a freedom that is guided by love for others.

INTRODUCTION

Paul's primary concern is to demonstrate the total worthlessness of legalism as a means of attaining salvation. The specific point of the controversy revolves around the observance of circumcision as the Judaizers advocated. From Paul's standpoint, the adoption of this practice would lead to several tragic consequences.

First, the Galatians would become obligated to observe the whole Law, not just circumcision. Secondly, The Galatians would be seeking justification through the observance of the Law rather than through Christ. In addition, the sacrifice of Christ would be of no effect for them. Finally, they would fall away from the grace of God as the means of salvation.

Paul proceeds to remind the Galatians that they have made a good beginning but are now in danger of completely losing the race. They cannot continue as they are going; they must turn from the Judaizers' false teachings. He does not, however, view the situation as hopeless. He encourages believers to remain faithful to Christ and to not be led astray.

One thought comes through strongly: the false teachers leading the Galatians away from the truth and distorting Paul's preaching, will not go unpunished for their deception. The judgment of God is sure to fall upon them.

EXPOSITION

I. PROTECTING FREEDOM (GALATIANS 5:1–6)

Paul starts chapter 5 by telling his

readers to stand in the grace they have received, to avoid backsliding into previous ways, not to lose the gift of freedom that they have obtained.

At this point, Paul demonstrates with force his apostolic authority, and clarifies his unique ministry and role in salvation history. In effect he says: "I, Paul, the teacher of the Gentiles, whose work you are in Christ, say to you quite clearly that Christ will be of no advantage to you if you are circumcised." The Lord Himself said: "the law and the prophets were until John, since then the kingdom of heaven is preached" (Luke 16:16). Before the new preaching began, it was necessary to be circumcised. However, now that the Law of faith has replaced it, we must do what the plain truth requires. On the authority of the Lord, the old means of salvation must not be mixed with the new. Jesus says: "No one sews a patch of unshrunk cloth on an old garment, for the patch will pull away from the garment, making the tear worse." (Matthew 9:16; Mark 2:21).

Therefore, not only will circumcision not be advantageous to a believer, but it will also actually stand in our way. It is worse to become a slave after having been free than to be born into slavery.

Some people can keep the Law to some extent without being circumcised, and there were many Romans in Judea who did just that. This is why the apostle Paul says to King Agrippa of Judea, "I know, King Agrippa, that you believe the prophets. I know you do" (Acts 26:27). There was also the centurion whose servant was on the point of death, who sent a word to Jesus, inquiring him to come and heal that servant, to whom the Jews bore witness when they said to Jesus, "He is worthy of your assistance because he loves our people and even built our synagogue himself" (Luke 7:4–5). There is nobody who had been circumcised who must not keep the whole Law, for he is bound to it because the Law was given to those who are circumcised. Paul said this because the Galatians were so full of themselves that they claimed that they could bear all the burdens of the Law.

The Galatians had been full of grace, but they rejected it, and so lost it all. Paul said this because after they had accepted God's grace, they had chosen to be circumcised.

The righteousness of the Law is dependent on keeping what had been given in it. So, whoever wants to be justified by the Law after believing Christ loses their grace because they in effect have opted out of the free grace—gift of righteousness (justification) in Christ.

Paul is saying the hope of justification is accepted in faith, as a work of the Spirit and not through the adherence to the Law. By faith, we are servants of God spiritually. We serve God by offering Him loyal minds, and clean hearts. This is why the Lord said to the Samaritan woman in John 4:24, "God is spirit, and his worshipers must worship in the Spirit and in truth." Consequently, circumcision is not of any value, but what counts is having the faith and love required for justification. Faith must be kept in the company by brotherly love if the believer is to be perfected.

Finally, the Savior answered the scribe, who asked what the most important commandment was, "You shall love the Lord your God with all your heart and with all your soul and your neighbor as yourself"

(Matthew 22:27, 39–40). Everything else is excluded and imperfect because perfection is contained in these two commandments.

II. EXPOSING THE FALSE TEACHERS (GALATIANS 5:7–12)

Paul testifies that their progress in the work of faith had been right, however, they had been prevented by the wickedness of evil men from finishing the race with perseverance. This is why he calls on them to repent, so that in the future they would not believe anyone who would cause them to betray the truth of the Gospel.

The Jews were indeed acting in their human wisdom by trying to subject them to the yoke of the Law. Moreover, they were unknowingly subjecting the Galatian saints to the judgment of God, who was calling them by the apostle away from legalism to Himself through grace. Paul says this because the slightest addition to the Law of faith corrupts that faith and makes it fruitless and unacceptable. Paul put this in so that the Galatians would not think that they could keep the grace of faith pure and still observe the Law's commands.

Paul says this hoping that he can trust the Galatians in these matters because they had initially embarked upon the Christian journey with excellence. Therefore, he was confident that once the true pathway was pointed out to them, it would be easy for them to return to it.

The reward for someone who manages to convert a person who had fallen into error is spelled out by the apostle James in his epistle (James 5:20). In the same way, someone who forces a person who is walking in the right way to deviate from that path will obtain damnation, whom-

ever they may be. Paul added this because of those who defended their actions with their identity as children of Abraham according to the flesh. Those who boasted of this said to Jesus, "We are the children of Abraham too" (John 8:33).

In addition, Paul says clearly that he was still considered an enemy by the Jews, who did not stop persecuting him, because he thought circumcision was no longer valid. At the end, when the Jews forced the issue and laid innumerable charges against him, Paul realized that he had no chance of a fair trial and so appealed to Caesar (Acts 25:10–11).

The preaching of the cross was a scandal to the Jews because it nullified the Sabbath and circumcision. However, if Paul had accepted circumcision, there would have been no scandal, and we would have lived in peace with the Jews (John 9:16).

This is what Paul said in 1 Corinthians 16:22, "Whoever does not love the Lord Jesus, let him be accursed." They belonged to the same tainted flock and shared the same condemnation that they should be cut off from the mercy of God as those who took the Galatians away from the grace of God. Paul curses them not only spiritually but also in the flesh. Because they forced the Galatians to be circumcised, they would be cut off so that the pain of their body might be increased.

III. ETHICAL APPEAL (GALATIANS 5:13–15)

They were called to freedom because when they were still bound in sin, they received the forgiveness of their wrongdoings and were set free by the grace of God. Paul says this because he was afraid that the flesh would seize the opportunity to take it away. This was why the false apostles wanted the saints to be circumcised and to come under the Law's restrictions.

Paul, therefore, warns them not to give them an opportunity by agreeing to what they say. He exhorts them, saying that they should not love each other carnally but, in the Spirit, and so be subject to one another.

The fact that in Galatians 5:13, Paul warns that the flesh is the danger to freedom in Christ, instead of slavery to the Law, has led many to suppose that Paul begins to attack libertarianism and lawlessness in Galatians 5:13, the description of warfare between the flesh and the Spirit in the verses which follow is understood to confirm this supposition.

Nevertheless, in the allegory which precedes this section, Paul identifies slavery with both the Sinaitic covenant and the flesh. According to the flesh, like Ishmael, are those who identified with the proponents of the Sinaitic covenant. Moreover, in a subscription which follows this section, those who campaign for circumcision boast in the flesh. So it seems best to interpret Galatians 5:13–6:10 as a polemical attachment against the works of the flesh and a continuation of his attack against dependence on the Law for salvation.

LESSON APPLIED

God gives a simple rule that can turn the people in your family into some of your best friends: Love your neighbor—your mom, dad, sisters, brothers, whoever else lives in your house—just as you love yourself.

The family is a collective of relationships from which you cannot escape. It forces you to learn to love, forgive, talk about what hurts, put God and others first, and get help when the family breaks. What you refuse to learn in the family home will become problems that will hurt all your relationships until you learn to solve them.

If you want your family to work well, you have to work hard at working together. This is true not just for family households, in truth our closest neighbors share the same community roof too. Remember, the purpose of the whole Law is summed up in a since command: "Love your neighbor as yourself" (Galatians 5:14).

LET'S TALK ABOUT IT

What does it mean to "fall from grace"?

In Galatians 5:4, Paul's warning against mixing the Law and the Gospel to attain justification is the context. Paul says, "to those who let themselves be circumcised" (Galatians 5:2) "Mark my words! I, Paul, tell you that if you let yourselves be circumcised, Christ will be of no value to you at all." It should be eminent that there is no mention of salvation or the security of the believer. He is telling those who have subjected themselves to the rites and rules of the Law, that Christ will be of "no benefit" to them.

Paul warns the saints about the danger of setting aside the grace that comes from Christ. Those who do so, have declared the grace procured by Calvary null and voided, and instead, have attempted to justify themselves by their labor of the Law. The motive of Paul's letter to the Galatians was to warn them against the Judaizers because they tried to lure born-again Christians back to justification through the Law, which is impossible

(Galatians 2:16). He reminded them of the freedom they have in Christ. For Paul says, "It is for freedom that Christ has set us free. Stand firm, then, and do not let yourselves be burdened again by a yoke of slavery" (Galatians 5:1).

Who were the Judaizers?

There have always been those who balk at the idea of God's salvation being offered freely to those who believe. They reasoned that such a gift as grand as forgiveness from a holy God, must require some sacrifice. We should thank God for His grace, but we should also understand that thankfulness and gratitude birth action. No, we can not work to gain God's grace through Law, but we are obligated to God because we owe our lives to God.

In the early church, the people who taught a combination of God's grace and human effort were called "Judaizers." The word Judaizer comes from the Gauls, a Celtic people, and it is derived from a phrase that means "to live according to Jewish customs." The word phrase also appears in Galatians 2:14, where Paul recounts how he challenged Peter for influencing Gentile Christians to "Judaize."

A Judaizer taught the gentles that, in order for a Christian to be indeed right with God, he or she must conform to the Mosaic Law. The male must be circumcised. Gentiles had to become Jewish converts first, and then they could come to Christ.

The Bible is transparent that the attempt to add human works to God's grace overlooks the very meaning of grace. Grace is an "undeserved blessing." As Paul says, "And if by grace, then it cannot be based on works; if it were, grace would no longer be grace" (Romans 11:6). Praise the Lord, "It is for freedom that Christ has set us free. Stand firm, then, and do not let yourselves be burdened again by a yoke of slavery" (Galatians 5:1).

What is Christian freedom?

Christian freedom is not living under the Law, which the Apostle Paul compared to slavery (Galatians 5:1). We cannot earn righteousness through the Law; the Law's purpose was to define sin and show our need for a Savior. Christian freedom involves living under God's grace (Romans 6:14) not the burdensome obligations of legalism. In Christ, we are freed from the obligation of the Law.

We are free from the punishment and authority of sin. Christian freedom is not a permit to sin. We are not free to live however we want, indulging the flesh (Galatians 5:13). Believers are free to live holy lives in Christ. True freedom means becoming a slave to Christ, which happens through a relationship with Christ.

HOME DAILY DEVOTIONAL READINGS
MAY 23–29, 2022

MONDAY	TUESDAY	WEDNESDAY	THURSDAY	FRIDAY	SATURDAY	SUNDAY
The Righteous Yield Their Fruit	Abide in Christ and Bear Fruit	Wisdom's Harvest of Righteousness	The Spirit Produces a Fruitful Field	Known by Their Fruits	God's Presence Brings Forth Healing Fruit	Live by the Spirit
Psalm 1	John 15:1-8	James 3:13-18	Isaiah 32:9-20	Matthew 7:15-20	Ezekiel 47:1-7, 12	Galatians 5:16-26

THE SPIRITUAL FRUIT OF FREEDOM

ADULT TOPIC:	BACKGROUND SCRIPTURE:
CHOOSING WELL	GALATIANS 5:16–26

GALATIANS 5:16–26

King James Version

THIS I say then, Walk in the Spirit, and ye shall not fulfil the lust of the flesh.

17 For the flesh lusteth against the Spirit, and the Spirit against the flesh: and these are contrary the one to the other: so that ye cannot do the things that ye would.

18 But if ye be led of the Spirit, ye are not under the law.

19 Now the works of the flesh are manifest, which are these; Adultery, fornication, uncleanness, lasciviousness,

20 Idolatry, witchcraft, hatred, variance, emulations, wrath, strife, seditions, heresies,

21 Envyings, murders, drunkenness, revellings, and such like: of the which I tell you before, as I have also told you in time past, that they which do such things shall not inherit the kingdom of God.

22 But the fruit of the Spirit is love, joy, peace, longsuffering, gentleness, goodness, faith,

23 Meekness, temperance: against such there is no law.

24 And they that are Christ's have crucified the flesh with the affections and lusts.

25 If we live in the Spirit, let us also walk in the Spirit.

26 Let us not be desirous of vain glory, provoking one another, envying one another.

New Revised Standard Version

LIVE by the Spirit, I say, and do not gratify the desires of the flesh.

17 For what the flesh desires is opposed to the Spirit, and what the Spirit desires is opposed to the flesh; for these are opposed to each other, to prevent you from doing what you want.

18 But if you are led by the Spirit, you are not subject to the law.

19 Now the works of the flesh are obvious: fornication, impurity, licentiousness,

20 idolatry, sorcery, enmities, strife, jealousy, anger, quarrels, dissensions, factions,

21 envy, drunkenness, carousing, and things like these. I am warning you, as I warned you before: those who do such things will not inherit the kingdom of God.

22 By contrast, the fruit of the Spirit is love, joy, peace, patience, kindness, generosity, faithfulness,

23 gentleness, and self-control. There is no law against such things.

24 And those who belong to Christ Jesus have crucified the flesh with its passions and desires.

25 If we live by the Spirit, let us also be guided by the Spirit.

26 Let us not become conceited, competing against one another, envying one another.

MAIN THOUGHT: If we live by the Spirit, let us also be guided by the Spirit. (Galatians 5:25, KJV)

LESSON SETTING
Time: AD 46–48
Place: The Roman Province of Galatia

LESSON OUTLINE
I. **Walking in the Spirit (Galatians 5:16–21)**
II. **The Fruit of the Spirit (Galatians 5:22–23)**
III. **The Freedom of the Spirit (Galatians 5:24–26)**

UNIFYING PRINCIPLE

In the world, many opposing forces influence our lives. When we feel conflicted, what can we do? Paul reminds us that choosing to be guided by the Spirit will result in good fruit.

INTRODUCTION

It is easy to forget when we read passages like Galatians 5:16–26, that Paul was writing to Christians, persons who have received the Spirit of God. Paul is aware of the potential relapse into fleshly existence and the ever-present possibility of falling from grace. For Paul, the flesh refers to our whole selves, not to a part of us that is dirty and distasteful. To live in the flesh is to live as a member of human society in a physical body. The flesh also denotes a domain of power, a sphere of influence in which one lives. The miracle of justification is that fleshly persons are transformed into Spirit-persons.

From the beginning of Christian history, it seems that every claim about the Holy Spirit has seemingly led to disputes. Nonetheless, disputes should not cause us to avoid one of the most vital messages conveyed in the Bible here in Galatians 5:16–26.

Paul and countless Christians bear witness to the truth that the Holy Spirit is so real, and through fellowship, the Spirit can become a far more intimate part of our being than some dimensions of the flesh. This is what happened to Paul (Galatians 2:20).

Paul is urging the Galatians to remember that, as Christians, they have received the Spirit and they are to walk in the Spirit. The Spirit is the supreme energizing and regulative force in their lives. If they walk in the Spirit, there is no danger that their Christian liberty will become an opportunity for the flesh.

For Paul, the Spirit is more than the manifestation of supernatural power, more than the giver of dramatic gifts, and much more than an explosive force erupting in the believer every now and then. The Spirit is the daily sustaining, inspiriting, and guiding power of the Christian's life. The Spirit is the domain of power and the sphere of influence that replaces the flesh as our lives' energy force.

EXPOSITION

I. WALKING IN THE SPIRIT (GALATIANS 5:16–21)

Verse 17, echoes Romans 4:14. But more is being said here. In the Romans passage, Paul deals with human psychology, the helplessness of our ideals divorced from the saving power of Christ. Paul says, "For I do not do what I want, but I do the very thing I hate" (Romans 7:15). There is no reference in that passage to the Spirit. Here, the power of the Spirit is the dominant note. Paul is not concerned with human psychology as such, but about the divine work of sanctification. The Spirit is shaping us into the kind of persons who can overcome and rise above the flesh's desires. This verse is not a description of equal forces combating each other, with the outcome indecisive. True, the flesh will always continue to assert its desires in opposition to the Spirit; nevertheless, the Spirit who indwells every Christian, declares opposition to the flesh and Paul is confident the Spirit will emerge triumphantly. We can be sure too, if we walk in the Spirit.

All across the land, growing numbers of Christians have allowed the Spirit to have the center of their lives. They are often called "Spirit-people" or members of the "Spirit-movement." Taking a cue from the experience of the spontaneous visit by the Spirit on Pentecost, they are often called Pentecostals. Because the Spirit brings gifts, "charismata" in the New Testament Greek language, they are referred to as "charismatics."

As has always been the case, controversy has accompanied the movement. Congregations have experienced schisms, church leaders have been frightened, and responded bureaucratically and institutionally, rather than pastorally. In some quarters, the movement has produced more heat than light, more ecstasy and enthusiasm, than genuine Spirit-energy and ministry. Even so, many are convinced that the movement has genuine depth and is a response of God to the spiritual hunger of a materialistic, pleasure-oriented, flesh-surfeited people. People are receiving help, being spiritually transformed, experiencing reconciliation in relationships, receiving physical and emotional healing. Time will tell whether we are on the verge of another Great Awakening. Noteworthy however, is that in the meantime, some of us are discovering (some a fresh and some for the first time) that we can walk in the Spirit. The Spirit who helps us avoid the lust of the flesh, and helps us avail ourselves by His power for ministry.

Verse 19–21, we should never forget the terrible menace of the flesh. The struggle is not an overnight one. Though we may win the victory in an initial, sincere, and complete commitment of our lives to Christ, the war continues because we must continue living "in the flesh."

We are always exposed to that domain of power. The struggle may be extended and indecisive. For many, the flesh will achieve supremacy until the believer yields to the Spirit's domination.

So Paul catalogs the work of the flesh. This is not an exhaustive list, but it is concrete and personal. Adultery is a breaking of the marriage vows and more often than not leads to the breaking of hearts, the breaking of homes, and the multi-faceted breaking of persons.

Fornication is primarily sexual intercourse between two people who are not married to each other. Uncleanness is about "moral impurity" that soils our lives and separates us from God, it defiles us. It detracts us from right relation with God, thus from right living. Licentiousness is often used for lewdness and sensuality.

It applies to unrestrained violence, a calloused, runaway passion for pleasure at any cost, desire and lust that care nothing for what others think. Idolatry is a "work of the flesh" in which we create God in our image, according to our desires, it is also constructing our theology to rationalize and justify the way we want to live. Sorcery means the use of drugs. It is the root word from which pharmacy comes. It designated the beneficent use of drugs as a doctor would prescribe them and the poisoning of drugs. It came to be specially connected with witchcraft and magic, of which the ancient world was full of, because witches and sorcerers used drugs extensively.

The next series of words can profitably be lumped together because they describe sins in human relationships, the sins of self-assertion and pride which both destroy the community. Paul minces no words in concluding his exhortation about works of the flesh (Galatians 5:21).

II. THE FRUIT OF THE SPIRIT (GALATIANS 5:22–23)

Over against the works of the flesh, Paul contrasts, "the fruit of the Spirit is love, joy, peace, longsuffering, kindness, goodness, faithfulness, gentleness, self-control" (Galatians 5:22–23).

Fruit of the Spirit is the outward expression of Christ dwelling within. This fruit grows and is expressed in any person that willingly dies with Christ and is born again of the Spirit, who brings new life. The Spirit works powerfully, sometimes dramatically, sometimes slowly, and almost imperceptibly in our lives to repeat the miracle of new creation in Christ Jesus.

Like the proceeding list of evils, Paul's cataloging of the fruit of the Spirit is not exhaustive. The infinite variety by which the indwelling Christ expresses Himself through our unique personalities defies any description, as the outburst of undisciplined passion is also beyond our ability to label.

Love leads the list, naturally. Love is the summation of the Law and of all true spiritual life. Paul tried and rose to eloquent heights in 1 Corinthians 13. Even there, all is not said about love. Jesus did more to teach about love with pictures, (a shepherd braving the wilds for a lost sheep and a father embracing in total acceptance a prodigal son who has finally come home) but, the ultimate dynamic of love Jesus expressed in John 15:13. As was always the case, it was not enough for Jesus to say it; He lived and died it on the Cross.

Joy is a gift that is strength overflowing into all the other facets of our lives. Joy cannot be self-created. Real joy is something else, and its only source is obedience. Peace is to live in harmony with God and with each other. Not only did God send His Son to make peace, God calls His followers to preach peace and to be peacemakers. This peace includes right relations with God and justice between persons. It is far more than freedom from strife. Longsuffering is generally used as patience regarding people, not to things or events. Kindness is sometimes translated as gentleness. Kindness verifies the integration of the inner character and the outward expression of our lives as we grow up into the full stature of Christ. We become patient, kind, good, and gentle.

Goodness is a goodness that is "good for something." For example, Christ's goodness expressed itself prophetically, demanding a change, requiring a response, bringing the fruit of the Spirit to fruition.

With faithfulness we can be steadfast in word and deed, reliable in our discipleship. Our response to God in faith evokes His gift of the Spirit, and the Spirit makes us faithful. Gentleness describes how we, in whom the love of Christ is growing, treat others. We excercise gentleness and tenderness, with respect, and consideration. Self-control has to do with the mastery of the self. This is the Christian's ability to overcome the "flesh-works" Paul has already listed.

III. THE FREEDOM OF THE SPIRIT (GALATIANS 5:24–26)

Paul closes his fruit of the Spirit list with a word that catches us off guard; in fact, it almost takes our breath away. It does not take great imagination, knowing what we know about Christ, and Paul grasp the reality of this fruit flowing from the Spirit. We have seen their fruitful walk highlighted in Scripture. There are no big surprises in that list-knowing Christ and knowing Paul.

But here it comes-the surprise as Paul tosses in that extra line. Against the fruit of the Spirit, there is no law. You can throw the book away. Forget about codes to regulate your life. However, do not think the list of the fruit of ever exhausted.

When you are in Christ and are moved by the Spirit, the unexpected and the unlisted will come. Gifts and fruits you never thought of will be expressed in you. If we fill our lives with "flesh-works," there will be no room for the Spirit. Freedom is yours, and the Spirit is free, so who can tell how He may express Himself in you?

LESSON APPLIED

There is much misunderstanding about the Holy Spirit. Many Christians do not know how the Holy Spirit fits in with God and Jesus. The Trinity has always existed as God the Father, God the Son, and God the Holy Spirit. You receive the Holy Spirit at the same moment you are saved. Jesus told His disciples that He would send the Holy Spirit to take His place, to comfort them, to guide them, to help them fulfill God's purpose for our lives, and fulfill the Great Commission to spread the Gospel. Each day as you begin your day, ask the Holy Spirit to fill you with His presence. He will produce the fruit of the Spirit, which Paul listed in Galatians 5:22–23. Seek to stay filled so that you can stand against all the weapons of Satan and be a victorious warrior. Every day we should ask the Holy Spirit to fill us again with His love, His peace, His truth. Every day, we should ask the Holy Spirit to fill us up to an overflowing status with His compassion for others. When He does, you will experience joy unspeakable and peace that passes all understanding.

LET'S TALK ABOUT IT

What will we allow to dominate? Flesh or Spirit?

So long as we are in our bodies, there will be a conflict between flesh and Spirit, which is what Paul is dealing with here in our lesson. Remember that our very physical existence is "flesh" insofar as we give ourselves over to the determined by it. That means that we can never withdraw from "the flesh" in our earthly lives, but we do not have to succumb to the flesh. We can fight against its controlling power. We can do this by walking in the Spirit.

What are the works of the flesh?

Galatians 5:19-21 declares of the works of the flesh, saying they are "sexual immorality, impurity and debauchery; idolatry and witchcraft; hatred, discord, jealousy, fits of rage, selfish ambition, dissensions, factions and envy; drunkenness, orgies, and the like." Paul then warns his readers "that those who do such things will not inherit the kingdom of God" (Galatians 5:21).

When the Bible states "of the flesh," it is often referencing our natural sin tendencies. We are all born with a sinful nature (Roman 5:12). Our natural liking is to please ourselves any way we see fit.

We can be educated to behave in more socially acceptable methods and even find enjoyment in bringing others' kindness; however, without the power of God, we continue to be self-centered. We do what we do, even morally good things, because we receive some egocentric reward.

Anything that is not done from faith or love for God, any deed not empowered by the Holy Spirit, is a "work of the flesh" (Romans 8:8).

The works of the flesh are not always as obvious as the ones listed above. Sometimes they can even be found within the confines of ministry, as people try to gain popularity or self-worth under the guise of serving Christ. Diotrephes was rebuked for this in 3 John 1:9.

Diotrephes shows us that trying to please God motivated from selfishness leads to unhealthy competition, slander, bitterness, and eventual burnout (Galatians 1:10).

What does Paul say about those who belong to Christ?

In verse 24, the apostle Paul declares, "those who belong to Christ have crucified the sinful nature along with its passions and lusts." Triumph is presented here as an accomplished fact: the sinful nature was crucified (past tense). Victory belongs to the Christian because of our relationship to the Lord Jesus Christ. When one puts their faith in Jesus, they become spiritually united to Christ in His death and Resurrection (note Galatians 2:20).

This verse's truth must cause the Christian to view her relationship to her old sinful nature in a radically new and different way. She must no longer consider herself as a helpless victim of the sinful nature who must inevitably yield to its demands. She must recognize that she now shares in the victory the Lord Jesus won over the sinful nature.

Note: the victory of Christ should progressively transform the Christian's attitudes and actions as we yield ourselves to the Holy Spirit, allowing the Spirit to apply the victory of Jesus to every part of our lives. This process is known as "sanctification." Sanctification is a process that will not be fully and finally accomplished until we enter into glory.

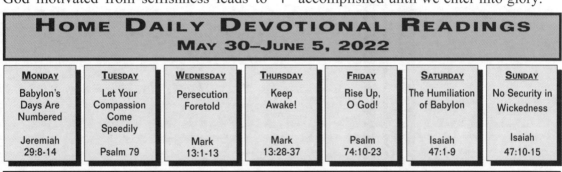

HOME DAILY DEVOTIONAL READINGS
MAY 30–JUNE 5, 2022

MONDAY	TUESDAY	WEDNESDAY	THURSDAY	FRIDAY	SATURDAY	SUNDAY
Babylon's Days Are Numbered	Let Your Compassion Come Speedily	Persecution Foretold	Keep Awake!	Rise Up, O God!	The Humiliation of Babylon	No Security in Wickedness
Jeremiah 29:8-14	Psalm 79	Mark 13:1-13	Mark 13:28-37	Psalm 74:10-23	Isaiah 47:1-9	Isaiah 47:10-15

FOURTH QUARTER

June

July

August

GOD FORETELLS DESTRUCTION

ADULT TOPIC: NOWHERE TO RUN	BACKGROUND SCRIPTURE: ISAIAH 47

ISAIAH 47:10–15

King James Version	*New Revised Standard Version*
FOR thou hast trusted in thy wickedness: thou hast said, None seeth me. Thy wisdom and thy knowledge, it hath perverted thee; and thou hast said in thine heart, I am, and none else beside me.	YOU felt secure in your wickedness; you said, 'No one sees me.' Your wisdom and your knowledge led you astray, and you said in your heart, 'I am, and there is no one besides me.'
11 Therefore shall evil come upon thee; thou shalt not know from whence it riseth: and mischief shall fall upon thee; thou shalt not be able to put it off: and desolation shall come upon thee suddenly, which thou shalt not know.	11 But evil shall come upon you, which you cannot charm away; disaster shall fall upon you, which you will not be able to ward off; and ruin shall come on you suddenly, of which you know nothing.
12 Stand now with thine enchantments, and with the multitude of thy sorceries, wherein thou hast laboured from thy youth; if so be thou shalt be able to profit, if so be thou mayest prevail.	12 Stand fast in your enchantments and your many sorceries, with which you have laboured from your youth; perhaps you may be able to succeed, perhaps you may inspire terror.
13 Thou art wearied in the multitude of thy counsels. Let now the astrologers, the stargazers, the monthly prognosticators, stand up, and save thee from these things that shall come upon thee.	13 You are wearied with your many consultations; let those who study the heavens stand up and save you, those who gaze at the stars and at each new moon predict what shall befall you.
14 Behold, they shall be as stubble; the fire shall burn them; they shall not deliver themselves from the power of the flame: there shall not be a coal to warm at, nor fire to sit before it.	14 See, they are like stubble, the fire consumes them; they cannot deliver themselves from the power of the flame. No coal for warming oneself is this, no fire to sit before!
15 Thus shall they be unto thee with whom thou hast laboured, even thy merchants, from thy youth: they shall wander every one to his quarter; none shall save thee.	15 Such to you are those with whom you have laboured, who have trafficked with you from your youth; they all wander about in their own paths; there is no one to save you.

MAIN THOUGHT: Thus shall they be unto thee with whom thou hast laboured, even thy merchants, from thy youth: they shall wander every one to his quarter; none shall save thee. (Isaiah 47:15, KJV)

LESSON SETTING
Time: Mid 5th Century BC
Place: Babylon

LESSON OUTLINE
I. Blinded!
(Isaiah 47:10–11)
II. Tragedy of Self-Deception
(Isaiah 47:12–13)
III. Lost Beyond Hope
(Isaiah 47:14–15)

UNIFYING PRINCIPLE

Humans trust in their own abilities and the systems they develop to control their lives and the lives of others. How does this confidence shape us? Isaiah affirms that God, the Creator of all, humbles the proud and the powerful.

INTRODUCTION

The book of Isaiah spawns Israel's growth as a nation through its post-exilic years, raising the question of authorship and its overall purpose. Isaiah 47 is an Old Testament oracle presented to us in the form of a poem. It is an oracle against one of the major powers in the ancient world, and a part of a larger unit of Scripture called Second or Deutero-Isaiah (Isaiah 40–55). Some scholars also break the book up further into a composition known as Trito-Isaiah, highlighting chapters 56–66). For the most part, some scholars see Deutero-Isaiah as pertaining to events after the death of the prophet Isaiah, and after the fall of Jerusalem in 587 B.C. They believe it was dictated by an unknown disciple of Isaiah, who took the role of the prophet Isaiah seriously, and wanted to continue his message to Israel. Others, however, see the entire book as a single composition with the latter portion of the book credited to prophetic insight under divine inspiration (see Claus Westermann, *Isaiah 40-66: A Commentary.* The Westminster Press, Philadelphia and John D. W. Watts, *Word Biblical Commentary,* Word Books, Waco, TX; see also, Gene M. Tucker, *The New Interpreter's Bible: A Commentary in Twelve Volumes, Vol. 1–39,* Abingdon Press, Nashville, TN).

Nevertheless, Isaiah's message of salvation rings clear in this book. God would use the nation of Israel to bring about its salvation as well as the salvation of the world (see Isaiah 9:6–7). However, salvation included both deliverance from sin and God's rebuke for committing it. In this pericope of Scripture, the prophet addresses the issue of sin, not Israel's but Babylon's sin. Her sin was the elevation of herself irrespective of God's position as Creator, Sustainer, and Redeemer. Often the way we see ourselves can be totally different from how we are perceived by others. That is why it is important for one to constantly evaluate one's perspectives of self so that one might correct any delusion of perfection. Because she was at the top of the world order—in terms of economic prosperity and military power—and was used by God to discipline Israel, Babylon erroneously considered herself to have arrived. God sets the record straight by reminding Babylon that she had totally deceived herself, and would have to answer to Him for her lofty ideas about herself. God also exposed her claim to have arrived by calling her into divine judgment. It's His reminder to us that God alone stands at the top of the arch. He alone evaluates our deeds and determines whether or not they are consistent with His will. This lesson examines three things in relationship to this text. First, it analyzes

Babylon's inability to see her condition of blindness (vv. 10–11). Second, we will examine the text to witness the tragic outcome of Babylon's self-deceit (vv. 12–13). Finally, we will look at Babylon's inability to change the outcome of this divine oracle (vv. 14–15).

EXPOSITION

I. BLINDED! (ISAIAH 47:10–11)

The destruction of the Northern Kingdom (Israel) and the subsequent Exile of Judah (the Southern Kingdom) was the Hebrew people's punishment for their refusal to refrain from idol worship. God withdrew His hand of protection from Israel and allowed them to be destroyed by the Assyrians in 721–22 B.C. Judah was subsequently taken into captivity by the Babylonians in 587 B.C. Foreign powers often took smaller and more vulnerable nations under their control during times of siege and war. Many of the captured were forced to integrate into the culture of their oppressors and lost their identity and heritage.

This oracle is a rebuke against Babylon for her self-elevation (vv. 6–7), for her hostility against Judah, more specifically, for abusing her role as the answer to Judah's sin against God. At the height of her military and economic superiority, Babylon snorted her lofty attitude and internally expressed her self-achieved acclaim before the Lord. It was the height of disrespect and dishonor. God had elevated Babylon to international supremacy, yet she disregarded God's role in her climb to worldwide fame. She had become blind to her responsibility to give credit to and acknowledge God for her development, and as a consequence of her neglect was called

on the red carpet by the Lord. God read the nation's innermost thoughts and motives and flagged her ingratitude. He exposes her silent thoughts about herself and denounces her self-elevation publicly. It was a case of what was done in secret being brought to light (vv. 2–3). It was ratification that God sees not only our outward deeds, but He also peers into the deep dark crevices of the human heart. Notice verses 1–9 of the contextual chapter. They serve as a precursor to the prophet's prediction of the nation's impending demise. The prophet declares Babylon's days of sitting high and mighty upon the pinnacle of power have ended. It points to God's judgment upon Babylon's abuse of her privileged situation. God had used her to discipline Israel, but Babylon had taken it a bit too far. She oppressed the elderly and had subjected the lowly to wickedness.

Yet, at the height of her power, she refused to see the folly of her ways (v. 10). She deceived herself into believing that she was both judge and jury. "No one sees me," she said. The truth is that she did not even see herself, at least not the way God saw her. Babylon marveled in her own wisdom and because of it she lost her way. The voice of God speaks resoundingly to the situation and brings Babylon back to reality from her erroneous self-perception. The word "*but*" used here establishes a contrast between Babylon's perspective of herself and God's true knowledge of her and of her future. Verse 11 predicts evil in the nation's immediate future, an evil that would not be susceptible to her charisma. "But the evil shall come upon you, which you cannot charm away; disaster shall fall upon you, which you will not be able to ward off; and ruin shall come on you suddenly, of which you know nothing" (v. 11, NRSV). It was a case of the blind being blinded by her own self-centered wickedness. The failure to see the reality of our sin is the ultimate definition of what it means to be blind. In Matthew 7:14, Jesus illustrated this tragic disposition of the Pharisees. He contended the blind cannot lead the blind, if so both will fall into the ditch. Babylon's fall will be great because she has lived from an inflated ego far too long and the time for reckoning had come.

II. TRAGEDY OF SELF-DECEPTION (ISAIAH 47:12–13)

Babylon is summoned to appear before God. The King James Version uses an imperative to reveal the action here. She is commanded to stand and to bring her twin cousins of sorcery and enchantments with her. Babylon has trusted in these activities from her youth and she is challenged to test their power and ability to help her escape divine judgment. It is the equivalent of the Psalmist's conclusion of those who worshiped Baal. He rhetorically asked in Psalm 115:2 (KJV), "Where is now their God?" Psalm 114:5–8 declares the emptiness of those who worship idol gods.

Babylon is challenged by the prophet to put her gods to the test. The end results, however, are already revealed. They cannot save her from her public demise for the Lord has already spoken it into being. Consultations with her astrologers, sorcerers, and those who practiced black magic, and the like, would be a futile effort on her part (v. 13). The prophet declared these consultations might make Babylon feel better, but it would only be a short temporary resolution for nothing would save Babylon from the destruction that awaited her. Notice the imperative addressed to Babylon, and to her partners in crime, to stand up and thwart this divine-orchestrated act of destruction (v. 12–13). God openly challenged Babylon to a showdown. In 1 Kings 18, we read of a similar challenge put before the people of Israel. Elijah put forth the question of who the people should worship. When the prophets of Baal presented their offerings to Baal there was no response. Elijah mocked them by inquiring about Baal's "whereabouts." He taunted Baal to show up and erase any doubt of his authenticity as a divine rival of the Lord God. Elijah was asserting that Baal was unable to stand up and therefore would be useless when needed by the people to act in their behalf. Babylon's gods would also come up short of delivering the nation from God's just verdict (vv. 12–13).

III. LOST BEYOND HOPE (ISAIAH 47:14–15)

In verse 14–15, the fan hits the fire as Babylon's destruction is readily declared. Behold as used in the King James Version is a declaration of what will take place. Babylon must and should prepare herself to hear and receive the truth of God. Her destruction is imminent. "The fire will burn them," the prophet notes. Fire is one of the elements used both to reveal the glory of God and to execute God's judgment. In 1 Kings 18, God sends fire from heaven to drink up the water-drenched sacrifice. Also, in Exodus 3, God reveals Himself to Moses in a burning bush that is not consumed by the fire. Similarly, He is seen walking in the fire as the three Hebrews are protected from the fiery furnace (see Daniel 3:15–20). In each of these examples, God's presence nullified the destructive force of the fire, and illuminated His superiority over it. However, not only does God use fire to glorify Himself, but He also uses it to administer judgment. For example, in Genesis 18:20–19:29, God destroyed Sodom and Gomorrah by fire for its failure to hearken unto His will. Revelation 19–20 speaks of the lake of fire where all who deny God will be cast into, including death and Hades. In this text (v. 14), fire is used to punish Babylon for her atrocities against the people of God. This fire is distinguished from one that provides comforting heat. It is destructive in nature and the prophet promised it will be totally devastating in its effect.

Babylon's punishment would also include her partners in crime. Verse 15 says, "Thus shall they be unto thee with whom thou hast laboured, even thy merchants, from thy youth: they shall wander every one to his quarter; none shall save thee" (KJV). They who helped to make Babylon into the aggressive and oppressive empire that she became would be held accountable to God as accessories, to the fact, of her criminal and immoral activities. Our willingness for whatever reason to support subversive activities leave us holding the blame as well. Babylon's partners in evil are not let off the hook.

In Matthew 18:15–20, Jesus warned the disciples not to be a party to the sinful indulgences of others and encouraged them to withdraw the hand of fellowship from those who refused to listen to their righteous preachments. The author of Deutero-Isaiah prophesied that each group will be so self-absorbed in their own punishment that they will not have time or energy to assist others. The end result is doom for Babylon and her ungodly supporters.

THE LESSON APPLIED

There is an old saying which goes, "You can't do wrong and get by." This would apply appropriately to the nation of Babylon. Over and above each powerful and successful nation stands God, the One to whom all national powers must answer (see Romans 13). Babylon had conquered the world with her military might and God had used her to teach His people a lesson. But Babylon abused Judah's elderly. She went too far and flaunted her authority. Now she would suffer the same fate as the Lord God called her on the red carpet of righteousness, to answer for her many atrocities against God's people. God was preparing the Persian-Median Empire to show her the result of her cruelty. Even more striking was Babylon's assertion that she was untouchable. Just when she thought she had arrived her end would be forthcoming.

This text conveys that one should walk humbly before the Lord, and not be too quick to wield the whip upon others. It informs us that God observes our every thought, word, and deed. He peers into the heart to examine our every motive. Also, the text bears out that we never can become too powerful for God to deal with us. Babylon erroneously conceived within herself that she was untouchable. She was sadly mistaken. God called her on the red carpet of His divine judgment. He also calls contemporary people to give an account of themselves and to attest to their activities, in relationship to His standards for human life. Babylon came up way short of God's expectations for her and, therefore, incurred His wrath. Her doom was sealed as a consequence of her self-deception that she stood above all others, even God. This text affirms and confirms that God alone is Judge, Jury, and the Enforcer. He evaluates and hold us accountable for our individual and collective responses to His commandments.

Therefore, let us humbly submit ourselves to complete our assigned task by not abusing the privilege we have to partner with Him. Let us remember that what we dish out to others, we can be sure will in turn be dished out to us. God has the final word!

LET'S TALK ABOUT IT

If God is forgiving, why does He judge us for our actions?

God is forgiving, we can see that in His dealings with the first parents and all people thereafter. After the first parents disobeyed Him, although He sent them out of the garden and away from the Tree of Knowledge of Good and Evil, He yet sustained their living and also sent One to redeem them from sin.

In this text, Babylon refused to be remorseful for how she treated the elderly. She also refused to recognize God's sovereignty. In fact, the failure to obey God's command to treat others as we desire to be treated is the equivalent of refusing to acknowledging Him as Lord. To Babylon she was her own god. She had reigned over the entire region, but failed to submit to God as the Creator. He requires us to live righteous and blameless lives. The failure to live accordingly requires us to repent of our sinful thoughts, words, and/or deeds. When we do so we seek out His presence and power to forgive us, and to give us another opportunity to align ourselves in accordance with His will. Yet, that does not mean that we escape His judgment for the things we have done. His judgment is to discipline us so we will learn a lesson from our mistakes. However, forgiveness is God's divine prerogative. Babylon's refusal to acknowledge God as her Lord prohibited her from seeking His forgiveness by repenting of her sin.

What does it mean to deceive one's self?

In this text, Babylon suffers from self-deception. She elevated herself into believing that she was her own Creator and Lord, and was free to do whatever she pleased. She was soon to discover however, that she had totally deceived herself into believing an untruth. The Bible clearly states that God created the world and everything therein (Psalm 24:1), and that we are accountable to Him for the deeds done in this life. To believe otherwise is to open ourselves up to total and complete destruction (2 Corinthians 5:10).

HOME DAILY DEVOTIONAL READINGS
JUNE 6–12, 2022

MONDAY	TUESDAY	WEDNESDAY	THURSDAY	FRIDAY	SATURDAY	SUNDAY
God's Redemption Defies Human Wisdom	Righteousness, Sanctification, and Redemption	Redemption to God's People	Christ Brings Eternal Redemption	Pardon My Guilt, O Lord	Redeem Israel, O God	The Lord Will Have Compassion
1 Corinthians 1:1–25	1 Corinthians 1:26–31	Psalm 111 God Sent	Hebrews 9:11–14	Psalm 25:1–11	Psalm 25:12–22	Isaiah 49:1–17

GOD FORETELLS OF REDEMPTION

ADULT TOPIC: A MISSION TO SAVE	BACKGROUND SCRIPTURE: ISAIAH 49:1–17

ISAIAH 49:1–13

King James Version	*New Revised Standard Version*
LISTEN, O isles, unto me; and hearken, ye people, from far; The Lord hath called me from the womb; from the bowels of my mother hath he made mention of my name.	LISTEN to me, O coastlands, pay attention, you peoples from far away! The Lord called me before I was born, while I was in my mother's womb he named me.
2 And he hath made my mouth like a sharp sword; in the shadow of his hand hath he hid me, and made me a polished shaft; in his quiver hath he hid me;	2 He made my mouth like a sharp sword, in the shadow of his hand he hid me; he made me a polished arrow, in his quiver he hid me away.
3 And said unto me, Thou art my servant, O Israel, in whom I will be glorified.	3 And he said to me, "You are my servant, Israel, in whom I will be glorified."
4 Then I said, I have laboured in vain, I have spent my strength for nought, and in vain: yet surely my judgment is with the Lord, and my work with my God.	4 But I said, "I have labored in vain, I have spent my strength for nothing and vanity; yet surely my cause is with the Lord, and my reward with my God."
5 And now, saith the Lord that formed me from the womb to be his servant, to bring Jacob again to him, Though Israel be not gathered, yet shall I be glorious in the eyes of the Lord, and my God shall be my strength.	5 And now the Lord says, who formed me in the womb to be his servant, to bring Jacob back to him, and that Israel might be gathered to him, for I am honored in the sight of the Lord, and my God has become my strength—
6 And he said, It is a light thing that thou shouldest be my servant to raise up the tribes of Jacob, and to restore the preserved of Israel: I will also give thee for a light to the Gentiles, that thou mayest be my salvation unto the end of the earth.	6 he says, "It is too light a thing that you should be my servant to raise up the tribes of Jacob and to restore the survivors of Israel; I will give you as a light to the nations, that my salvation may reach to the end of the earth."
7 Thus saith the Lord, the Redeemer of Israel, and his Holy One, to him whom man despiseth, to him whom the nation abhorreth, to a servant of rulers, Kings shall see and arise, princes also shall worship, because of the Lord that is faithful, and the Holy One of Israel, and he shall choose thee.	7 Thus says the Lord, the Redeemer of Israel and his Holy One, to one deeply despised, abhorred by the nations, the slave of rulers, "Kings shall see and stand up, princes, and they shall prostrate themselves, because of the Lord, who is faithful, the Holy One of Israel, who has chosen you."

MAIN THOUGHT: Thus saith the Lord, In an acceptable time have I heard thee, and in a day of salvation have I helped thee: and I will preserve thee, and give thee for a covenant of the people, to establish the earth, to cause to inherit the desolate heritages. (Isaiah 49:8, KJV)

ISAIAH 49:1–13

King James Version	*New Revised Standard Version*
8 Thus saith the Lord, In an acceptable time have I heard thee, and in a day of salvation have I helped thee: and I will preserve thee, and give thee for a covenant of the people, to establish the earth, to cause to inherit the desolate heritages;	8 Thus says the Lord: In a time of favor I have answered you, on a day of salvation I have helped you; I have kept you and given you as a covenant to the people, to establish the land, to apportion the desolate heritages;
9 That thou mayest say to the prisoners, Go forth; to them that are in darkness, Shew yourselves. They shall feed in the ways, and their pastures shall be in all high places.	9 saying to the prisoners, "Come out," to those who are in darkness, "Show yourselves." They shall feed along the ways, on all the bare heights shall be their pasture;
10 They shall not hunger nor thirst; neither shall the heat nor sun smite them: for he that hath mercy on them shall lead them, even by the springs of water shall he guide them.	10 they shall not hunger or thirst, neither scorching wind nor sun shall strike them down, for he who has pity on them will lead them, and by springs of water will guide them.
11 And I will make all my mountains a way, and my highways shall be exalted.	11 And I will turn all my mountains into a road, and my highways shall be raised up.
12 Behold, these shall come from far: and, lo, these from the north and from the west; and these from the land of Sinim.	12 Lo, these shall come from far away, and lo, these from the north and from the west, and these from the land of Syene.
13 Sing, O heavens; and be joyful, O earth; and break forth into singing, O mountains: for the Lord hath comforted his people, and will have mercy upon his afflicted.	13 Sing for joy, O heavens, and exult, O earth; break forth, O mountains, into singing! For the Lord has comforted his people, and will have compassion on his suffering ones.

LESSON SETTING
Time: Mid 5th Century BC
Place: Babylon

LESSON OUTLINE
I. A Call to Serve
   (Isaiah 49:1–4)
II. Salvation is Near
   (Isaiah 49:5–12)
III. A Reason to Praise the Lord
   (Isaiah 49:13–17)

UNIFYING PRINCIPLE
Individuals and nations aspire to accomplish great things even in the midst of great challenges. How can we make a difference? Creator God covenants with us to redeem us—even when we don't realize it—for a higher purpose and important mission.

INTRODUCTION
Deutero–Isaiah contains unique passages of Scripture called Servant Songs. Isaiah 49 is one of those types of passages (see Isaiah 42:1–4; 49:1–6; 50:4–9; 52:13–53:12). Servant Songs answer the following questions: "How is Israel to go forward to serve God after her exile?" "What is Israel's role in salvation history?" "What type of Messiah will come to save God's people?" The Servant is the chosen One endowed with the Spirit of the Lord to usher in justice and righteousness. In this particular text, the Servant is dismayed because of what He perceives as His failure. However, God proclaims to Him that it is through Him that the Lord will be glorified. Thus, His work is

not just to restore Israel, but to also be a light to the nations. God's salvation through Him will be spread to all people of the earth (see C. R. North, "Servant of the Lord," in The *Interpreter's Dictionary of the Bible, Vol. R–Z*, Abingdon Press, Nashville, p. 292). Three things are important in this passage. First, Deutero–Isaiah examines in verses 1–4 the Servant's call and commission to represent God. Second, the Servant's failure is evaluated by God Himself and leads the Lord to appoint the Servant's to a higher mission, the salvation of the Gentiles (vv. 5–12). Finally, the appointment to bring the Gentiles into the divine fold is a cause for praise and celebration by the Servant (vv. 13–17). The point is that God takes the role of the believer seriously and even in the midst of perceived failure, God can use us for His higher purpose when we are faithful in our initial assignment.

I. A Call to Serve (Isaiah 49:1–4)

The first four verses here make up part of the second servant song in this book. In the first song, Isaiah 42:1–4, the Lord God presents the Servant and declares His mission to address the Gentiles. Here in the second servant song, it is the Servant Himself who boldly announces His selection as God's Servant. It begins with an announcement for the people to give heed to His cry. "The Lord has called me from the time of my conception in the womb to a special task" (paraphrase of v. 2). The Servant's articulation of His appointment by the Almighty God is closely akin to the prophetic call made by Jeremiah and Deutero–Isaiah's counterpart, the writer of Isaiah 1–39 (see Jeremiah 1:4–5 and Isaiah 6:1–8). It also bears a striking resemblance

to Gabriel's announcement to Mary in Matthew 1:20–23, and Jesus' reference to Himself to be the fulfillment of God's Word in John 10:36. The Servant comes in the historical tradition of the prophets. Now, the writer gives us a hint of humanity's pending salvation through the Servant, who will speak the message of salvation to Israel, and spread it to the Gentile nations as well. The reference in verse two concerning the sharp and piercing sword refers to the words and activities the Servant has to deliver to and carry out before the people. Although the sword is depicted normally as an offensive weapon of war, here it is declared to be an agent of God. It is used by the writer to express the judgment and will of God to the people (see Unger, p. 254).

As God's Servant, His goal and objectives are not to please His hearers, but to speak the words and do the bidding of God. The Servant is to apply the Word of God, along with the consequences for disobeying it. In the New Testament, the sword is often referred to as a two-edged sword. This means it is applied to deliverers of God's message as well as to its hearers (Luke 2:35; Ephesians 6:17; Revelations 1:16; 2:12). The sword cuts both ways and none are exempt from following its divine mandates. One cannot miss the metaphoric intent of the writer here. It is the Word of God to which both prophet and the people are accountable. The Contemporary English Version is more emphatic here, "He made my words pierce like a sharp sword or a pointed arrow; he kept me safely hidden in the palm of his hand." The latter part of v. 2 focuses on God's protection of the Servant for doing His bidding. The Lord claims and identifies the Servant as His own. He hides Him. Hiding in God is an important concept within Scripture. King David confessed God was his refuge, a place of hiding from his enemies. Refuge is used over 80 times in the Old Testament and is found mostly in the Psalms (see Psalm 14:6; 46:1; 59:16; 62:7–8). The Apostle Paul said in Colossian 3:3 that He was hid in Christ with God, the ultimate place of safety and security (see Colossians 1:2–2:3).

Verse three reidentifies Israel as the Servant of God. In this verse, the Servant informs His hearers that God has appointed Him and will be glorified through Him. In the New Testament, we have a similar instance where a voice from heaven identifies Jesus as the Son of God and expresses approval in Him (Matthew 3:17; Mark 1:11; Luke 3:22; John 1:32). Also, in John's Gospel, Jesus acknowledged that God will be gloried in Him and He in the Father (John 12:23; 13:31; 17). Glorification is verification that the divine call rested upon the Servant and God would use Him to accomplish His purpose. God's presence and power would be manifested in the words and deeds of the Servant. The Servant's call would be validated by the divine activity that would follow in the wake of His work. However, the Servant does not have the same perspective as the Lord God in relationship to His work. The Servant saw Himself as a dismal failure. Verse 4 is a record of the Servant's dismay: "Then I said, I have laboured in vain, I have spent my strength for nought, and in vain: yet surely my judgment is with the Lord, and my work with my God" (KJV). Apparently, His message was rejected by the people and it disturbed Him greatly (see v. 5). He took the rejection personally and it impacted Him negatively. But as the next section will point out, it is God's evaluation that matters most. The names Jacob and Israel are used interchangeable throughout the Servant Songs and refer to the people of Hebrew heritage. The Servant's work, however viewed by Him, will bring glory to God and He will persevere because His faith and strength is in the Lord (v. 5).

II. SALVATION IS NEAR (ISAIAH 49:5–12)

In contradistinction to the Servant's analysis of His work, stands the verdict of the all-seeing God. It is a contrast of immense proportions. The Servant in His self-assessment concluded that His work has been in vain. Moses, Isaiah, and Jeremiah expressed their unworthiness to carry out the divine mandate to do the work of God (Exodus 3:11–4:17; Isaiah 6:5, and Jeremiah 1:6). However, the Servant is not reluctant in accepting the initial call. He expressed reluctance to proceed because of His past failure to accomplish God's purpose. However, from God's perspective the Servant did succeed in His mission. God speaks to the Servant in verse 6 to confirm the Servant's success and to articulate to Him a new mission, a more expansive one. Thus verse 5 becomes an introduction to the Servant promotion and granting of a much greater responsibility. Actually verse 5 gleans back to verse 1. It reminds us that the Servant has been called to minister, while in the womb of His mother, and reaffirms the divine continuity of His call to restore Israel and to bring the Gentiles into the divine–fold. The greatest affirmation that we are doing God's will is for Him to call us to a higher mission. The Servant's notification of His promotion was evidence to Him of divine acknowledgement that He had succeeded, where He initially perceived He had failed. The truth of the matter is that human failure when cradled in the effort to do God's bidding always equates to success. The crucifixion is a case in point. The crucifixion of Jesus was perceived as failure by the Jews and the Greeks, but God gave this perceived failure His stamp of divine approval and it resulted in Jesus' resurrection from the dead (I Corinthians 1:22–30), and being given all power in heaven and in earth (Matthew 28:18–20).

Verse 6 also adds God's commentary on the Servant's declaration of failure in verse 5. It shows the Servant operating from a limited perspective, but God is revealed as the omniscient One. In the New Testament (Acts 1:6–8) the disciples asked Jesus if He would at this time "restore the kingdom to Israel." Jesus informs them that, "It is not for you to know the times or the seasons, which the Father hath put in his own power" (KJV). The Servant's acknowledgement of God's omniscience and omnipotence here is in contrast to His own limited perception. The Servant has not failed, rather God will restore Israel within His own configuration of time. In fact, the restoration of His people is the main focus of this section. Verse 6 anticipates the forthcoming good news that is revealed in detail in verses 7–12. God's salvation is a clear demonstration of His divine activity which is given in gracious and bold terms. First, the writer describes God as the Holy One and as the Redeemer of Israel. The Holy Redeemer then speaks to the one who is oppressed, "to him whom man despiseth, to him whom the nation abhorreth, to a servant of the ruler, Kings shall see and arise, princes also shall worship, because of the Lord that is faithful, and the Holy One of Israel, and He shall choose thee" (v. 7, KJV). Verse 8 repeats the traditional prophetic summons initially given in verse 7 for one to hear what "Thus saith the Lord." This phrase is used over 400 times in the Old Testament and means to pay attention to a specific statement or activity of God. Israel should give an enormous amount of weight and consideration to this statement for it means God is about to act decisively on her behalf.

The statement reminds the reader that God is not ignorant of the human predicament. In Exodus 3, the Lord tells Moses from the burning, but unconsumed bush, that He is cognizant of His people's condition. He used four verbal statements to indicate His awareness, "I have seen," "I have heard," "I have known," and "I have come down" (see Exodus 3:7–12; 23–25). These statements signify and reaffirm God's acute awareness and total displeasure with sin and human oppression as denoted in His engagement with the people's unfortunate situation. Verse 8 is a rearticulation of divine oversight of the contemporary oppression and the continuity of God's displeasure with it, "I have heard thee… and I will preserve thee…(v. 8, KJV). God assures the people that their oppression will end and their legacy as His people will continue. Their deliverance will be a testimony to others who are oppressed and residing in darkness, that help is on the way (vv. 9–10). God promises nourishment, protection from foreign military might, and starvation. He shall renew them and restore them to prosperity. Verse 10 underscores that He shall lead them to "springs of water." That is to say they shall be comforted and well-nourished as denoted in Psalm 23:2–3. Divine promise is the thread that binds together this message of restoration and salvation. The word *"shall"* indicates movement from that which is an atrocity to that which is salvific. Hunger and thirst, heat and sun are threatening to one's survival. However, God assures Israel of its deliverance from threatening situations. Israel shall be guided on their journey to the place where abundant life reigns (vv. 9–10).

III. A REASON TO PRAISE THE LORD (ISAIAH 49:13–17)

Verses 13–17 call for the heavens and the earth to rejoice in the salvific activity of God. He will comfort them and have mercy upon the afflicted (v. 13). Even though Zion reacts in skepticism, she is reassured of God's love for her based upon an analogy of the eternal bond of a child with its parent (vv. 14–15).The child may for some reason forget, but the parent cannot easily discharge the child she birthed into the world. Their image is firmly established in His heart. The term *"graven upon the palms of My hands,"* suggests that Israel is forever within the sight view of God and that His hands are continually working for the people's good. They are always on His mind (see Exodus 13:9). Just because they are undergoing a tough time, does not mean God has forgotten about them.

THE LESSON APPLIED

We should offer praise unto God in spite of the challenges we have to face. Our shortcomings will not cause Him to forget us. He ratified the Servant's call even though the Servant believed he had failed. The text confirms that God can use human failure for His glory. The ministry and service of Abraham, Jacob, Moses, Elijah are cases in point. God always remembers His own. He has you on His mind.

LET'S TALK ABOUT IT

Who is the Servant of God?

The Servant in the Servant Songs is believed by scholars to be a variety of individuals and people. In Isaiah 49 the Servant is Jacob/Israel. In Isaiah 51 the Servant is Cyrus the Great. Some scholars believe that the Servant of the Lord has messianic tendencies and is a description of Jesus (see Isaiah 53). Even though each of these perspectives are relevant in terms of helping us to understand God's message to us, we cannot afford to focus only what it meant then, the Word of God has relevance for us today. This passage challenges us to see ourselves as servants of the Lord, who at various times need our calling and mission to be ratified and clarified as well. We are the ones called to proclaim His Word today.

HOME DAILY DEVOTIONAL READINGS
JUNE 13–19, 2022

MONDAY	TUESDAY	WEDNESDAY	THURSDAY	FRIDAY	SATURDAY	SUNDAY
God Puts Down and Lifts Up	God Protects a Restored, Holy People	Blessings upon God's People	God Has Turned Mourning into Dancing	God Gives Good Gifts	Blessings for Obedience	Wait for the Lord
Psalm 75	Leviticus 26:3–13	Luke 6:20–26	Psalm 30	James 1:13–18	Deuteronomy 28:9–14	Isaiah 49:18–23

GOD'S RESTORED PEOPLE SHALL PROSPER

ADULT TOPIC:	BACKGROUND SCRIPTURE:
ALL THINGS PUT RIGHT	ISAIAH 49:18–26

ISAIAH 49:18–23

King James Version

LIFT up thine eyes round about, and behold: all these gather themselves together, and come to thee. As I live, saith the Lord, thou shalt surely clothe thee with them all, as with an ornament, and bind them on thee, as a bride doeth.

19 For thy waste and thy desolate places, and the land of thy destruction, shall even now be too narrow by reason of the inhabitants, and they that swallowed thee up shall be far away.

20 The children which thou shalt have, after thou hast lost the other, shall say again in thine ears, The place is too strait for me: give place to me that I may dwell.

21 Then shalt thou say in thine heart, Who hath begotten me these, seeing I have lost my children, and am desolate, a captive, and removing to and fro? and who hath brought up these? Behold, I was left alone; these, where had they been?

22 Thus saith the Lord God, Behold, I will lift up mine hand to the Gentiles, and set up my standard to the people: and they shall bring thy sons in their arms, and thy daughters shall be carried upon their shoulders.

23 And kings shall be thy nursing fathers, and their queens thy nursing mothers: they shall bow down to thee with their face toward the earth, and lick up the dust of thy feet; and thou shalt know that I am the Lord: for they shall not be ashamed that wait for me.

New Revised Standard Version

LIFT up your eyes all around and see; they all gather, they come to you. As I live, says the Lord, you shall put all of them on like an ornament, and like a bride you shall bind them on.

19 Surely your waste and your desolate places and your devastated land—surely now you will be too crowded for your inhabitants, and those who swallowed you up will be far away.

20 The children born in the time of your bereavement will yet say in your hearing: "The place is too crowded for me; make room for me to settle."

21 Then you will say in your heart, "Who has borne me these? I was bereaved and barren, exiled and put away—so who has reared these? I was left all alone—where then have these come from?"

22 Thus says the Lord God: I will soon lift up my hand to the nations, and raise my signal to the peoples; and they shall bring your sons in their bosom, and your daughters shall be carried on their shoulders.

23 Kings shall be your foster fathers, and their queens your nursing mothers. With their faces to the ground they shall bow down to you, and lick the dust of your feet. Then you will know that I am the Lord; those who wait for me shall not be put to shame.

MAIN THOUGHT: And kings shall be thy nursing fathers, and their queens thy nursing mothers: they shall bow down to thee with their face toward the earth, and lick up the dust of thy feet; and thou shalt know that I am the Lord: for they shall not be ashamed that wait for me. (Isaiah 49:23, KJV)

LESSON SETTING
   Time: **Mid 5th Century** BC
   Place: **Babylon**

LESSON OUTLINE
   I. Homeward Bound
      (Isaiah 49:18–20)
   II. Life Begins Anew
       (Isaiah 49:21–23)
   III. No Longer Prey
        (Isaiah 49:24–26)

UNIFYING PRINCIPLE

When freedom from oppression is realized, it is hard to believe. From where do freedom and blessings come? Creator God will restore relationships between God's people, nations, the land, and the next generation in ways that confirm God's Lordship.

INTRODUCTION

This section of chapter 49 actually has its actual beginning in v. 14 (which was basically covered in the last lesson). It is the start of Israel's lament about her deplorable condition. Her expression of anguish and despair in this pericope of Scripture is immediately answered by God in what scholars call the dispute-proclamation sequence. Israel reveals her disputes and laments concerning her physical condition and God responds to counteract them.

The first dispute comes as Israel charges God with the complaint of erasing her from His memory. "The Lord has forsaken me and My Lord has forgotten me," she said (v. 14). The Lord rhetorically asked, "Can a mother forget her nursing child? And if by chance she does facing human limitations, I will never forget" (v. 15). He then turns to a Babylonian illustration that the people of Israel would be aware of to further His

point of constant love for the Daughters of Zion. Images of the Babylonian god were tattooed on the palm of the hand to indicate constant loyalty to the Babylonian deity. It was also something men, within the culture, did to show their sustaining love for a specific woman. God pledges His abiding love by drawing a parallel between His loving remembrance of Israel with images of her suffering etched on His palms. It is an awesome metaphor signifying the tragic condition of her plight, and the agony and pain it has caused Him. In response to her condition, God proclaims to Israel she will indeed be set free (v. 17).

The second dispute comes after the Lord reassures His people that He will gather them from all parts of the world for the journey back to their homeland for a reunion of sorts. This is where an examination of this pericope of Scripture begins.

I. HOMEWARD BOUND (ISAIAH 49:18–20)

Verses 18–19 is a call for Israel to stop wallowing in self-pity and see the glory of her new beginning. God has given her a new start and it is based upon His identity and life as the Lord God, the Creator of heaven and earth. The call to lift up her eyes and see is an imperative. The evidence of what God is doing is right in front of her. Gathering before her from the four corners of the world are multitudes of people from the diaspora. The comparison given here is that of a "bride who looks up the aisle and beams with love as she sees the bridegroom coming to her." As a bride wears her wedding ornaments, those who are coming home "will be the jewels that Israel will adorn." Israel's new family will be a massive gathering of new sons and daughters, so plenteous that the boundaries of the tiny nation will be stretched beyond its limits. The people are encouraged to put Babylon in their rear view mirror and allow the distance between the two nations to see Babylon's image shrink all the more. It is further evidence that the Lord God has not forgotten His people (see McKenna, p. 516).

Yes, Israel is forced to admit, and does so quite readily in this section with her question of divine forgetfulness, that her demise was at the hand of the Lord Himself for her idolatry. The Assyrians and Babylon were simply instruments of His wrath. But these belong to former times. Now they who were once the objects of His wrath and judgment are now the objects of His grace and mercy. A change has taken place and their period of punishment and destitute are over. Old things have passed away and Israel must not be blinded by her past situations (see Watts, p. 189).

The prophet declares Israel's restoration is totally underway. It is a new beginning for God's people, to start all over again. Being homeward bound is another opportunity for the people to redevelop their relationship with God and live according to His Covenant.

II. Life Begins Anew
(Isaiah 49:21–23)

These verses address the second lament from God's people. The lament is similar in tone with the laments found in the book of Lamentations (see 1:5, 20; 5:3). The Exiles lament because they perceive themselves to be childless. That is to say they are depressed over the condition of the nation and cannot see any way forward or beyond their suffering, and perceived barrenness. She asked the question, "Whence have these come?" (v. 21). Yet, because of Israel's lingering doubts coupled with years of exile, she felt humiliated and withdrew from life "like a widow who had lost her children, her home and her relatives" (McKenna, p. 516). She felt as if God's promise to Abraham to multiply his descendants, to be as numerous as the stars of the sky and the sands of the seashore, for generations to come, had been vacated by Him. As Israel continues her dispute concerning her lot she decries a picture of death. Her children are gone, her homeland lie in waste, and she is isolated and barren. Like Cain in Genesis 4:13–14, Israel believes her punishment for idolatry is more than she can bear. Even with the sight of children in the distance she asks, "Who has begotten these for me?" and Who has brought these up?" (v. 21, KJV). Although the answer is obvious for all to see, Israel fails to understand that she continues to be on the mind and heart of God. Her experience has blinded her to see that God had never truly abandoned her, even though, He allowed Babylon to chastise and discipline her.

But now her time of discipline was behind her. It is a new day with a new beginning. The Almighty hand of God has moved toward Israel and has intervened in her behalf. He has restored her children. It is divine confirmation once again that the Lord has not forgotten Israel and is, therefore, innocent of the charges laid against Him. Despite her dispute against God and expressions of doubt about her future, God promises Israel that she will become the progenitor of faith for all nations, generationally speaking (vv. 22–23). Even royalty will bow in humiliation and homage to Israel They must see Babylon as an afterthought and no more. It is time for them to refocus their attention on divine providence and care. The salvation that God promises Israel is a message of hope to the despairing and despondent.

III. No Longer Prey (Isaiah 49:24–26)

The last dispute in this section comes in vv. 24–26. It is a lament emerging from Israel's concern about her enemies. Assyria and Babylon had dominated her life since 721 B.C., (roughly the past 250 years) and Israel continued to be concerned and weary about her enemies. She relived her fears of being prey and articulated this fear to the Lord God. "Can the prey be taken from a strong man? or the captive be rescued from the tyrant?" (v. 24). In a real sense Israel sees herself as being both consumed and fed as fodder and subjected to the evil whims of her more powerful opponents.

Her outlook for the future paints a dismal picture of hopelessness. The psalmist expressed a similar lament in Psalm 74:22 and Psalm 35:1. It is significant that Yahweh speaks affirmatively at this point in a personal tone contrasting His might over that of Israel's enemies (v. 24–25). The Lord God acknowledged their status as captives and prey, but He informs them that even captors and those who prey upon the unfortunate can themselves be taken captive and preyed upon too. His point is, Israel is not alone in this struggle. God is with her. Therefore, those who contend with Israel will find they are actually contending with God. The Lord's assertion is that her opponents are powerless against the mightier hand of God (v. 25).

God establishes His identity here. He reaffirms who He is just as He declared Himself to Moses at the burning bush (see Exodus 3). Israel's oppressors shall devour themselves when contested against the Almighty, the Lord God declares to His people, who are drowning in self–pity. "I make your oppressors eat their own flesh, they drink their blood like wine (Bible verse from Isaiah 49:26; the author's translation of the a and b portion of the biblical text. (See Westermann, p. 218.). This great work of God will be broadcasted to the world. God will make it happen.

Finally, the passage closes with a reference back to v. 23, "For thus, says Yahweh." The Almighty Lord has spoken. His speech here is meant to be declarative, revealing His dual role as Sovereign Lord and as Redeemer. It outlines His holy purpose for Israel and Israel's role in sharing His salvific work throughout the world. His self-declaration of affirming the Covenant relationship is make use of the "I AM" statement that we see used in Exodus 3, and throughout John's Gospel account. Here the claim is more emphatic because God Himself asserts His name in between the Noun and the Verb, "I, *Yahweh*, am …" (v. 26). He further personalizes it by identifying Himself as "Your Saviour" and so that there would be no doubt of their salvation, He also refers to Himself as "the Mighty One of Israel."

These verses speak volumes about God's concern for Israel. They have no reason to lament because their time of suffering is past and their redemption is come.

THE LESSON APPLIED

This pericope of Scripture is important because it shows the faithfulness of God. Even though Israel deserved her chastisement, God remembered her and forgave her of her worship of idol gods. He maintained His side of the Covenant promise, to be her God. She was the one who failed to be His people.

Even though her demise was all her fault, Israel laid three charges against Him; He had forsaken her, she had been abandoned, and was being consumed as prey. Yet, God reassured her that her salvation was imminent. He comforted Israel by emphasizing His Covenant relationship, that He was indeed her God and had not forgotten her. This reassurance would remind Israel that she was the one who failed Him. It also illustrated that the Lord's was indeed gracious. Often after our struggle with sin and disciplinary action from God, we feel abandoned and left alone. It is a natural consequence that follows our chastisement. But God's discipline does not remove us from the list of the ones that He loves. We will undergo punishment to help teach us the lessons we need to learn, but we must never conclude that discipline means or results in divine abandonment.

Israel made three charges against God, however God refuses to side-step any one of them. He admits to the reality of Israel's punishment for her sin of idolatry, but offers comfort by turning the page to a more glorious day that is on the horizon for Israel. God dealt with Israel's sin problem, but over against the problem of sin stands the willingness of God to forgive it. But forgiving sin is not the same thing as ignoring it and letting it run rampant. Sin is something God cannot easily dismiss, since sin is totally anathema to Him, and will result in our total ruin. However tough it might be for Israel to distinguish between punishment for sin and God's enduring love for her, she must know and understand the difference, and so must we.

In fact, divine chastisement for human wrongdoing must always be viewed as an aspect of divine love and never as abandonment on God's part. Chastisement does not mean God is out to get us rather, it means God is seeking to save us from total destruction by teaching us the error of our ways. Chastisement then has to be viewed as a part of God's redemptive plan to win us back and to help us come to repentance, and to return to Him again. Israel found it hard to accept her sin, yet God reassured her the page had turned and had moved toward her again. He reassured her that she was the apple of His eye, and that even if a mother forsook her young that He could never do so. When she asked about her growth and development and expressed concern about her homeland, God reassured her that He would gather her from all parts of the world, allow her to grow again, and be nurtured by Him. When she expressed concern about being overridden by her enemies, God promised that her enemies would have to come through Him first. And that is no small order as Babylon discovered.

The key to our restoration to the Kingdom is to be repentant of our sin, by acknowledging our faults and failures before Him. We must also distinguish between divine chastisement and abandonment. Punishment for sin does not mean we are permanently removed from seeking God's face or Him seeking us. When our period of punishment is over we should gladly welcome God's loving arms of protection and providential care. Finally, we must pledge to never dishonor God again by seeking after idol gods. The people of Israel had participated in a foolish trade. They exchanged the living God to worship idols that could not move. It turned out to be a disaster for them. It will also be a disaster for us. We serve the Living God of heaven and earth. Any trade or exchange to serve another is the equivalent of running down a slippery slope.

LET'S TALK ABOUT IT

Should God ignore our sin?

No! God cannot ignore our sin. Sin is anathema to Him, because it distorts His purpose for our lives by offering us a way that leads to our total destruction. Sin is like a cancerous sore that festers and infects everything it touches. The more we sin the more it spreads and distorts and deceives us into believing that it is good for us, when it is not. His chastisement does two things: It hold us accountable for our actions and then it teaches us to guard against giving into our fleshy desires, and to follow His commandments. When we depend on God and allow him to guide our steps we are sure not to fall prey to sin. Rather than seeing God's discipline as hurtful, we must come to understand and accept it as a teaching moment where we learn better to live according to God's Holy and righteous standard.

Does forgiveness of our sin mean we can do whatever we desire?

Again the answer is "No!" God forgives us of our sin because He is loving and gracious. He does not want us to perish because we are His children. However, God has given us freewill and He respects our ability to chose which way we will go. He will not force us to live according to His good and perfect will, but when we refuse to follow His wise counsel and guidance we must be willing to pay the price, or to suffer the consequences of our decision.

Israel had to pay the price for her flirtation with idol gods. She broke her part of the Covenant and God withdrew from her, allowing the nations around her to use her as fodder. God will likewise withdraw Himself from us when we willingly travel the path of sinful rebellion against Him. The good news is God does not withdraw from us permanently. The moment we repent of our sin God will restore us unto Himself.

HOME DAILY DEVOTIONAL READINGS
JUNE 20–26, 2022

MONDAY	TUESDAY	WEDNESDAY	THURSDAY	FRIDAY	SATURDAY	SUNDAY
God Will Vindicate God's Servant	Remember God's Mighty Deeds	God Defends Israel's Cause	God Rescues Us from Peril	Jesus Rescues Us from Wrath	Deliverance Belongs to the Lord	God's Deliverance Is Coming
Isaiah 50:4–9	Isaiah 51:9–16	Isaiah 51:17–23	2 Corinthians 1:7–14	1 Thessalonians 1:6–10	Psalm 3	Isaiah 51:1–8

GOD OFFERS DELIVERANCE

ADULT TOPIC: BACK TO BASICS	BACKGROUND SCRIPTURE: ISAIAH 51

ISAIAH 51:1-8

King James Version

HEARKEN to me, ye that follow after righteousness, ye that seek the Lord: look unto the rock whence ye are hewn, and to the hole of the pit whence ye are digged.

2 Look unto Abraham your father, and unto Sarah that bare you: for I called him alone, and blessed him, and increased him.

3 For the Lord shall comfort Zion: he will comfort all her waste places; and he will make her wilderness like Eden, and her desert like the garden of the Lord; joy and gladness shall be found therein, thanksgiving, and the voice of melody.

4 Hearken unto me, my people; and give ear unto me, O my nation: for a law shall proceed from me, and I will make my judgment to rest for a light of the people.

5 My righteousness is near; my salvation is gone forth, and mine arms shall judge the people; the isles shall wait upon me, and on mine arm shall they trust.

6 Lift up your eyes to the heavens, and look upon the earth beneath: for the heavens shall vanish away like smoke, and the earth shall wax old like a garment, and they that dwell therein shall die in like manner: but my salvation shall be for ever, and my righteousness shall not be abolished.

7 Hearken unto me, ye that know righteousness, the people in whose heart is my law; fear ye not the reproach of men, neither be ye afraid of their revilings.

New Revised Standard Version

LISTEN to me, you that pursue righteousness, you that seek the Lord. Look to the rock from which you were hewn, and to the quarry from which you were dug.

2 Look to Abraham your father and to Sarah who bore you; for he was but one when I called him, but I blessed him and made him many.

3 For the Lord will comfort Zion; he will comfort all her waste places, and will make her wilderness like Eden, her desert like the garden of the Lord; joy and gladness will be found in her, thanksgiving and the voice of song.

4 Listen to me, my people, and give heed to me, my nation; for a teaching will go out from me, and my justice for a light to the peoples.

5 I will bring near my deliverance swiftly, my salvation has gone out and my arms will rule the peoples; the coastlands wait for me, and for my arm they hope.

6 Lift up your eyes to the heavens, and look at the earth beneath; for the heavens will vanish like smoke, the earth will wear out like a garment, and those who live on it will die like gnats; but my salvation will be forever, and my deliverance will never be ended.

7 Listen to me, you who know righteousness, you people who have my teaching in your hearts; do not fear the reproach of others, and do not be dismayed when they revile you.

MAIN THOUGHT: Hearken to me, ye that follow after righteousness, ye that seek the Lord: look unto the rock whence ye are hewn, and to the hole of the pit whence ye are digged. (Isaiah 51:1, KJV)

ISAIAH 51:1-8

King James Version

8 For the moth shall eat them up like a garment, and the worm shall eat them like wool: but my righteousness shall be for ever, and my salvation from generation to generation.

New Revised Standard Version

8 For the moth will eat them up like a garment, and the worm will eat them like wool; but my deliverance will be forever, and my salvation to all generations.

LESSON SETTING
   Time: Mid 5th Century BC
   Place: Babylon

LESSON OUTLINE
 I. Listen!
    (Isaiah 51:1–3)
 II. Listen Again!
    (Isaiah 51:4–6)
 III. Listen Again and Again
    (Isaiah 51:7–8)

UNIFYING PRINCIPLE
   People of integrity find it difficult to ignore criticism. Where do they find affirmation in the face of adversity? God delivers the righteous from the judgment of others when they are faithful to God's teachings.

INTRODUCTION
   Isaiah 50:1–52:12 is the larger pericope of Scripture that includes our text for study today, Isaiah 51:1–8. The entire passage denotes the activity of the Servant of God. Previously, we saw that the Servant was given an expanded mission to be a light to the Gentiles. Ultimately, God's address to the Servant, in Isaiah 49, was to proclaim salvation to the world through God's chosen people, Israel. God decided to restore Israel after her years of exile and barrenness because of her sins of idolatry, greed, and oppression of her own people. He comforted Israel by reaffirming His Covenant to be her God. Of course, there were some things Israel must do in order for her to feel the full effect of her salvation. They are listed and expounded upon in Isaiah 51. Previously, the nation had failed to pay close attention to the warnings given to her by the prophets. She had ignored God's call upon her life and ended up paying the consequences of her ill-proned action. However, she could not afford to continue ignoring the prophetic warnings to her to remain faithful. If she was to be truly redeemed then she must give heed to the lingering voice of the divine, calling her to duty.

   The pericope for study today is that call to duty. Three things are important in this examination of the text. These three points make up the instructive curriculum that God desires the Servant to teach the people, both those who have remained in Jerusalem, and those who are products of the Babylonian Exile.

   First, the Servant cries out to Israel, "Listen to God." In this sense, listening is different from mere hearing. Listening takes on the concept of learning from what is heard. Israel must listen with an effort to learn. It is active participation in the learning process, which is precisely the type of listening the Servant has mind for the nation. It is to listen to the Lord for the purpose of learning what it is she must do to experience the Lord's salvation, both her salvation and the world's. This first call to listen is a call to listen so that one can seek and follow the Servant's instruction (vv. 1–3). It is rudimentary in nature and refers to those who more likely than not are babes and inquirers of the faith. They seek out God's presence to enhance their understanding and knowledge of Him.

Second, Israel must listen again to what she is being told to do. This time she must listen and give heed to justice and keeping God's Law. It is God's Law that will be "a lamp unto the nation's feet and a light to her pathway" (vv. 4–6; see also Psalm 119:105). It is a progressive movement from infancy to a deeper level of theological understanding and doing.

Third, the people who know what righteousness is and practice it are once again instructed to listen to the words and teachings of the Servant of the Lord. In Isaiah 49, the writer identifies the Servant as Israel. But here we see an evolution taking place, the Servant is Israel and she is to display the salvific acts of God to the world. It is the role she will play in leading other nations to God. In Isaiah 50 and beyond, the Servant is not only Israel in the broader sense as a nation, but also includes a particular One who comes in the name of the Lord and speaks on God's behalf.

In other words, the Servant as revealed in this pericope has messianic overtones as the One God will use to deliver Israel and her counterparts to renewed fellowship with Him. God's Law abides in His heart and He therefore calls upon those practitioners of the faith to exemplify maturity as they apply His words to their lives (vv. 7–8). The Servant calls for deliberate action, a type of faith practice that reveals a deep seeded belief in the goodness of God.

I. Listen!
(Isaiah 51:1–3)

The main verses of this pericope of Scripture begins with an imperative, a call to listen (see vv. 1, 2, 4, 6, and 7). The first major directive is for Israel to listen to the words of the Servant. Listening is an important directive in Scripture. Deuteronomy 6:4–6, a passage commonly called the *Shema*, commands the Hebrew people to listen attentively to the Word of the Lord God. They are also commanded to tie the Words of the Lord to their physical person, to repeat it constantly, and to carry it with them wherever they went. Listening to the Lord's words leads to practicing it, wholeheartedly.

In I Samuel 1, the youthful figure Samuel hears the divine voice twice, but fails to understand who is calling him. After hearing the voice of the Lord a third time, he received instructions from Eli the priest to answer the Lord's summons by saying, "Speak Lord for I am listening." Samuel listened attentively to what the Lord had to say and informed Eli of the forthcoming downfall of his family.

In the book of Proverbs, readers are continuously cautioned to listen to good advice and to seek divine counsel (see Proverbs 1:5; 5:7; 7:24; 8:32–34; 12:15; 15:31). The emphasis on listening to the voice of God continues in the New Testament as well. Jesus often called upon His disciples to hear and listen to what He was saying to them. He begins His ministry at 12 years old by listening to the spiritual advice of the elders (Luke 2:46). In His Baptism and at other points in His ministry, a voice from heaven demanded that the disciples and others listen to His gracious words (see

Matthew 17:5; Mark 9:7; Luke 9:35; and John 10:27).

The Servant's call for the people to listen is directed to those who follow after righteousness and who seek the Lord (v. 1). It is a call to remember from where the people have come. They are ordered to take a step back in time to relive their experiences on memory lane and to review their humble beginnings. They must bring to mind their historical development. They who were not a people were selected by God from their humble and meager beginnings to demonstrate God's power (see Genesis 12). David McKenna said, "The children of Israel had come from the poorest of the poor and the weakest of the weak to be chosen as God's covenant people. On this fact they can build their case" (McKenna, p. 530).

Those who seek after God are then given a second imperative to look back and observe the lives of Abraham and Sarah. As the father of the Hebrew faith the writer wants the religious seekers to "go back to the old landmark," back to where it all began for the war-torn nation, back to God's revelation of Himself to Abraham. From their barrenness, God had brought life to the aged couple, which was the result of His promise to Abraham to make his seed as numerous as the stars in the sky and as the sands on the seashore (Genesis 12). Remembering these sobering and historical facts would encourage the current group of Hebrew seekers to put their faith in God, for He was the same One who had made their original barrenness fruitful (see Genesis 12), the One who brought life from nothing. Remembering their history would spur them on to a greater faith, where they would look beyond the dismal state of their enslavement and bondage by the Babylonians. Looking at and remembering their past beginnings would lead them to sing songs of thanksgiving, joy, and melody. They would find great comfort in doing so. Westermann points out that comfort means "turning toward a person that definitely alters a stressful situation, and not just words of sympathy" (see Westermann, p. 237). The comparison with Eden is that her new experience will be one of joy, similar to the joy that the first parents enjoyed in their first home (Genesis 2). The joy will be so overwhelmingly expressed that all will see it and hear it.

II. LISTEN AGAIN! (ISAIAH 51:4–6)

The note of joy the Servant is calling the people's attention to is worth repeating. He calls upon the people a second time to listen, to give heed, and bend their ear to conceptualize His teaching. God's justice goes forth as a light to the people and His salvation is near (see Isaiah 42:3–5). His salvation is inclusive of the Gentile community. The reference to justice corresponds to obedience to God's Law. The proof God is at work among them is for them to carry out His will. Micah 3:8 comes to mind here, "What the LORD doth require of thee: only to do justly, and to love mercy, and to walk humbly with thy God." The phrase "do justly" means to treat others as one desires to be treated. One might also look at the Servant's call in relationship to I John 4:20–21. "If a man say, I love God, and hateth his brother, he is a liar: for he that loveth not his brother whom he hath seen, how can he love God whom he hath not seen? And this commandment have we from him, That he who loveth God love his brother also" (KJV). That is to say that social justice must be a part of one's willful desire and practice. The text affirms God's bent toward the disenfranchised and the lowly in life.

In fact, the entire corpus of the minor prophets addresses the issue of social justice and one of the reasons for the Exile lay in the sin of greed and oppression upon the lowly by Israel's elite. The reference to justice here is to remind Israel that justice remains an important matter to God. God cannot stomach oppression and will deliver Israel from the brunt of Babylonian oppression, and will also forbid Israel's practice of it upon her own people. To do or to treat others justly require that one's heart be attuned to the heart of God. Therefore, the Servant's call for justice comes from one's apprehension of the spiritual. Being attuned to doing things God's way is essential.

Verses 5 and 6 recognize the nearness of God's salvation. Israel must look attentively to the heavens from whence she will obtain clues for living out her life. God's Law will stand before her as a guiding light. His Word is eternal and will not pass away. It is equivalent to the New Testament's declaration of the eternal stability of God's Word (see Matthew 24:35; Mark 5:18; Luke 21:33). Based upon this fact, the Servant declares the eternal deliverance of God. His salvation cannot be shaken by others, nor will any other natural cause lead to its falling apart. God's salvation is sure and enduring.

III. LISTEN AGAIN AND AGAIN (ISAIAH 51:7–8)

For a third time the Servant calls upon Israel to listen. This call is for the mature believer to hearken to His words. McKenna

said, Here "the seekers have become knowers and those who are keepers of the Law have become lovers of the Law. For them the Servant has the lesson of faithfulness" (McKenna, p. 531). This passage relates to the affirmation of the Psalmist who boldly declared, "Thy word have I hid in mine heart that I might not sin against thee" (Psalm 119:11). God's Law abides within them. They are the faithful few who cling to God as they travel on the narrow road that leads to abundant life. Lovers of the Law are lovers of God. They are those who keep His commandments as pointed out by Jesus to His disciple (John 14:15). The Law is not an end within itself, rather it is the guide to righteous living. They are not to fear the reproach of others, nor be frighten away from doing what is good and right before God because others complain to the contrary. The others are expendable and will meet their end, but the righteousness invoked by God is everlasting (v. 8).

This third encouragement to listen is given to the mature and devout believers, who have resisted criticism and complaint. The Servant alludes to their reward while pointing out the miserable end of those who offer only criticism and resistance. They shall be as a cloth that will be eaten by moths and like wool that is silently consumed by worms. They will be devoured and not fully realize it. These verses have a striking resemblance to Isaiah 40:31, "They that wait upon the Lord...."

THE LESSON APPLIED

Israel is encouraged to listen attentively to the voice of the Servant of God. Those who seek to carry out the concepts of God's righteousness, abide by His Laws, and take the lead in encouraging others to joyfully await His promised salvation are the original people to whom this proclamation was addressed. The people had undergone tremendous challenges during their period of exile in Babylon. But now the hand of God was offering them abundant forgiveness and renewal. The Servant calls upon them to heed to His voice and to be assured their time of suffering and remorse is over. He teaches them to become lovers and keepers of God's justice and Law, and not to return to their old ways of idolatry and rebellion. Their salvation is on the horizon and assured if they would have patience and be faithful.

The Servant's Word for them then is also a meaningful Word for contemporary believers. Our salvation is likewise on the horizon and assured if we seek after God's righteousness, abide in His Word, and lead others to faithfulness (see Matthew 6:33; John 10:1–11; and John 14:6–20).

LET'S TALK ABOUT IT

Who is the Servant of the Lord?

According to Deutero-Isaiah the Servant is Israel in the broadest sense, but the Servant can also be an individual person working within the frame of fulfilling the will of God.

In the Old Testament, Cyrus the Great is often depicted as a servant of God and Cyrus was not a believer. The point is God can use whoever He so desires to accomplish His purpose. He does not need the person to be a believer. God as the Sovereign Lord can also use time, events, nature, circumstances, and/or any creature to accomplish His purpose. He alone is God!

Consequently, in the New Testament, Jesus certainly sees Himself as the Servant who brings about the salvation of the world through redemptive suffering. The Servant Songs prophesied many of the experiences Jesus went through to fulfill the Messianic hopes that One would come to restore Israel to a level of prominence in world history. As the Messiah, Jesus not only did this as the definitive Representative of God, but also assured that salvation would come through Israel, just as God had promised.

Today each believer becomes the servant of God in his/her own community to call attention to the need for His presence and power in human life. Servants of the Lord must call others to repentance and faith. They must also demonstrate in their own lives what it means to worship God, and how to live according to His purpose. In other words, we must render ourselves as servants to share His message of love and forgiveness for our sins.

HOME DAILY DEVOTIONAL READINGS
JUNE 27–JULY 3, 2022

MONDAY	TUESDAY	WEDNESDAY	THURSDAY	FRIDAY	SATURDAY	SUNDAY
God Created the World through Wisdom	In Christ All Things Hold Together	Christ, the Head of All Things	God's Well-Ordered Creation	Praise God for Creation	The Son Reflects God's Glory	The Word Became Flesh
Proverbs 8:22–31	Colossians 1:13–17	Colossians 1:18–22	Psalm 104:1–15	Psalm 104:24–35	Hebrews 1:1–4	John 1:1–14

THE CREATING WORD BECOMES FLESH

ADULT TOPIC:	BACKGROUND SCRIPTURE:
THE REASON FOR IT ALL	JOHN 1:1–14

JOHN 1:1–14

King James Version	*New Revised Standard Version*
IN the beginning was the Word, and the Word was with God, and the Word was God.	IN the beginning was the Word, and the Word was with God, and the Word was God.
2 The same was in the beginning with God.	2 He was in the beginning with God.
3 All things were made by him; and without him was not any thing made that was made.	3 All things came into being through him, and without him not one thing came into being. What has come into being
4 In him was life; and the life was the light of men.	4 in him was life, and the life was the light of all people.
5 And the light shineth in darkness; and the darkness comprehended it not.	5 The light shines in the darkness, and the darkness did not overcome it.
6 There was a man sent from God, whose name was John.	6 There was a man sent from God, whose name was John.
7 The same came for a witness, to bear witness of the Light, that all men through him might believe.	7 He came as a witness to testify to the light, so that all might believe through him.
8 He was not that Light, but was sent to bear witness of that Light.	8 He himself was not the light, but he came to testify to the light.
9 That was the true Light, which lighteth every man that cometh into the world.	9 The true light, which enlightens everyone, was coming into the world.
10 He was in the world, and the world was made by him, and the world knew him not.	10 He was in the world, and the world came into being through him; yet the world did not know him.
11 He came unto his own, and his own received him not.	11 He came to what was his own, and his own people did not accept him.
12 But as many as received him, to them gave he power to become the sons of God, even to them that believe on his name:	12 But to all who received him, who believed in his name, he gave power to become children of God,
13 Which were born, not of blood, nor of the will of the flesh, nor of the will of man, but of God.	13 who were born, not of blood or of the will of the flesh or of the will of man, but of God.
14 And the Word was made flesh, and dwelt among us, (and we beheld his glory, the glory as of the only begotten of the Father,) full of grace and truth.	14 And the Word became flesh and lived among us, and we have seen his glory, the glory as of a father's only son, full of grace and truth.

MAIN THOUGHT: All things were made by him; and without him was not any thing made that was made. (John 1:3, KJV)

LESSON OUTLINE

UNIFYING PRINCIPLE

People are often curious about how things began. How do we understand the origins of life? John begins by explaining that Jesus, the Word, was God's creating and redeeming agent in the world.

INTRODUCTION

Matthew, Mark, and Luke are called the Synoptic Gospels because they *"see"* (Greek: o*ptic*) *"together"* (Greek: *syn)*, or follow a similar path in laying out the course of events and proclamations in Jesus' life. The one remaining Gospel account is the Gospel composed by the Fourth Evangelist, the Gospel of John. Although it is written from a Jewish perspective, it is radically different in tone and scope than the other three accounts. First, it is important to note that there is no birth narrative in John's account. The Word is the Pre-existent Logos, who became flesh (vv. 1–3, 14, 18). Therefore, as the One who brought life into existence and empowers it, there is no need for a birth narrative. He is life and not one who is merely the recipient of it (v. 4). Second, the Word's identification with God is there from the beginning (see vv. 1–3; also see vv. 14–18). Third, the idea or concept of witness is prevalent in this account as well.

John the Baptist is the initial person bearing witness to the ministry of Jesus in this Gospel (Greek: *marturia/martureo*), but he is just one among many, who will validate the activity and Words of Jesus as those approved by the Father (see. vv. 19; 3:11, 32; 4:44; 5:31–32, 37; 7:7; 8:13–15, 18; 10:25; 13:21; 15:26; 18:37; 19:35; 21:24). Taken together these three things make up what scholars call the "Prologue" in John's Gospel account (vv. 1–18).

In these verses, the writer introduces the book and reveals in skeletal form the essence of the book's contents. This examination observes three things. First, we shall look at the Pre–existent Word. What does John mean when he writes "In the beginning was the Word. " (vv. 1–3). Second, we shall explore the Word as Life and Light, His relevance and meaning in relationship to humanity (vv. 4–5). Also worthy of note, the text thrives on the concept of bearing witness to the Word, who gives the gifts of Life and Light to others (vv. 6–9). Third, we are told that this Light, which should have been recognized as the Giver of life, was not recognized. In fact, John reveals the Light as the essence of life was utterly rejected. Verses 12–13 offer us some sense of comfort in that the Word *"was"*, however, accepted by many through faith and they reveal faith as an important commodity in the salvific process. Finally, we will observe that "the Word was made flesh and dwelt among us" (v. 14).

EXPOSITION

I. THE PRE–EXISTENT WORD (JOHN 1:1–3)

It is not by accident that John informs us that "In the beginning was the Word"… (v.

1). Taking the reader back to the beginning serves his purpose, which is to establish the pre-existence of the Word (Greek: *Logos*). It is a theological statement of faith the writer makes in accordance with his beliefs and experience (see Genesis 1:1). He takes his que from two things. First, he wants to show the eternal existence of the Word as a part of the Godhead, and second, that this Word was made flesh (Greek: *egeneto*) to inaugurate human salvation. Clearly John borrows from Genesis 1:1 to establish a relationship between the two texts. Genesis 1 tells us that in the beginning God created the heaven and the earth. It establishes God as the Creator of all things. But John asserts here that was not all that was taking place in the beginning. The *Logos* was there too. *Logos* means word, speech, to express an opinion. For the Johannine author, the *Logos* or Word has a concept of a personal pre-existence (see John 1:1, 14; Revelations 19:13; and I John 1:1; also see Hebrews 4:12 for a possible personification of these terms).

The writer points out that "In the beginning was the Word and the Word was with God".… This statement denotes equality in the Godhead and that the Word accompanied God before the creation process begin. The Word is eternal in every aspect of life. Therefore, the Johannine author carries our thoughts concerning time to a previous period when only deity lived. The idea expressed is that of continuous existence without any regard to origin or birth (see Robertson, p. 3).

There is a vivid contrast between the opening verses of John 1:1–3 with John 1:14. That contrast lay in the pre-existent Word who was made flesh. The latter, "was made flesh," was an intentional action for an intentional purpose and flows out of that which "*was*" and "*is*" always eternal in nature. Jesus implicitly claimed this pre–existent status on at least two occasions. The first occasion took place when He disputed with the Jews saying, "before Abraham was I Am" (John 8:58). I AM (Greek: *Eimi*) means here a timeless existence. There is no beginning or ending. The second occasion was when He rebuked Philip who asked Him to "shew us the Father" (John 14:6–11). Jesus replied with a rhetorical question, "Have I not been with you for so long and you don't' know who I AM." Jesus was alluding to His affinity with God, to God's eternal existence and creative power. His claim verifies the One made here in the prologue of this Gospel account of His eternal existence (v. 1). The writer was also refuting the heretical claims of religious deviants and opponents of the Early church such as the Docetic and Cerinthian Gnostics, who believed that Jesus was only spirit and not human or they separated the aeon Christ from the man Jesus (Ibid., p. 4). They believed to be human was to be made of filthy and sinful matter and therefore argued erroneously that Christ could not have been human.

In this opening statement, the writer firmly declares the *Logos* (Word) was in perfect harmony with God (Greek: *pros ton theon*). Not only was the Word with God, but he emphasized, "and the Word was God" (Greek: *kai theos en ho logos*). He meant here that the totality of God was expressed in the Word, thereby, making the terms interchangeable. The Word then is the definitive expression of all that God is. Thus, when the Word became flesh nothing was lost in the action that would result in human salvation. Verse two doubles down on what has been previously stated in v. 1. This redundancy is emphatic and serves to underline the importance and significance of equating the Word with God and as God. Before the measurement of time came into being the "Word was with God" and "the Word was God." After the development of time the Word came to be a Man" (Ibid, p. 5).

He picks up again the Genesis text to add clarity to the creation story. All things (Greek: *panta*) came into being through Him (Greek: *di' autou*). John leaves no doubt about creation. It did not just happen automatically. It was a decisive act of God and the Word was the Agent that was responsible for its becoming (see Hebrews 1:2 and Colossians 1:16 as supportive statements to John's assessment here). We also have here in this verse the first personification of the Word. The pre-existent Word or *Logos* was germane to the act of creation. After informing his readers that all things were created by Him, the writer again emphatically points out "and without him was not anything made that was made" (v. 3, KJV). The Word, the intermediate Agent, is construed as being essential to the creation process. Nothing was made without Him!

II. THE LIFE, THE LIGHT, AND A WITNESS (JOHN 1:4–9)

The *Logos* gave life. The power to bring things into being belonged essentially to Him as noted in v. 3. John called this coming into being life (Greek: *zoe'*). The term life as used here goes beyond the meaning of spiritual life, but includes life of every form (physical, personal intellectual power, spiritual, etc.). The *Logos* emits (creates, sustains, and redeems) life in its totality. Life itself resides in Him. All life emerges or comes out of Him. In John 11:25, Jesus claimed and accepted the fact that He is the source of life when He encountered Lazarus' grieving sister, Martha. Also in Luke 8:45–46, Jesus acknowledged that virtue had gone out from Him and asked, "Who touched me?" The life force that went forth from Him resulted in the healing of the woman from her infirmity. The life that resided in Him was the light (Greek: *phos*) of people. The writer used the two terms interchangeably to denote Jesus as being both the Light and the Life of humanity. He is the source of its existence and the motivating force that make persons living souls (see Genesis 2:7). Light and Life describe not only who He is, as the Word, but also His relationship to those He has called into being. The Light shines brilliantly, both before time was developed into measurable units, and afterwards.

In other words, the Word is the Light that keeps on shining. The darkness (Greek: *skotia*) cannot and will never overtake it. The darkness here is sin, death, or any opposition that seeks to quell the brilliance of the Light. Rather than overtake the Light, the Scriptural hint here is that darkness will run away and give up its secret hiding places when confronted by the Light. This verse certainly alludes to the resurrected Christ's victory over death. Not even humanity's worst enemy can stop Him. In I Corinthian 15:55, the Apostle Paul boldly asked, "O death where is your sting?" and "O grave where is your victory?"

In the Old Testament, witnesses were required to testify to the actuality of an event to authenticate it (see Vine, pp. 292, 680). This Gospel fulfills that requirement as witness is one of the key themes in this book. The first notable witness is introduced in the prologue. His name is John. The Synoptic Gospels give support to this as John the Baptist's ministry is noted in all three books (see Matthew 3; Mark 1:1–14; and Luke 1:57–63). John the Baptist's role as witness to the Word takes on a major role after the prologue in John 1:19–37. He literally pushed his disciples to follow after the Christ. He also confessed as noted in the prologue that He was not the Light, but he was merely a witness to the Word of God that came from above, and was made flesh (see John 3:22–36). John was to call men and women to faith (Greek: *pistis*), to see what he had been privileged to see. Preachers and others who proclaim the Christian message of salvation must always be careful to distinguish themselves from the One who they proclaim to be the Word of God, the Light and Life of the world. The true Light preceded John as the Pre-existent *Logos* and would continue on in the Word made flesh, the Light of the World (see John 1:14; 8:12).

III. Unrecognized, Rejected, but Gracious (John 1:10–14)

Verses 10–11 are a sad commentary on creation. The One, who was fundamentally essential to the creation of the world (v. 3–4, 10), and filled it with His presence (Colossians 1:16), went unrecognized, and therefore, unappreciated as its Maker (v. 11). These verses quietly point to another theme that will be covered in this Gospel account, the theme of grace. Although the term grace is only used in the prologue (vv. 14, 16, and 18), one cannot and should not underestimate its presence in this Gospel. The Light that provided life to creation was utterly rejected by the very ones He created. The first parents and their offspring bear out the extent of this rejection and rebellion, not to mention the choice of God's chosen people, Israel, to repeatedly seek after those who were no gods. The Word, the *Logos*, came to His own, to His own home, to the house that He built, but faced and found only bitterness and constant rejection. Indeed, we can safely say that the Creator took a big risk that the creature would go against the Creator (see Genesis 3), and that John 1:10–11 illustrates it amply. In reciting the old saying that a prophet is not without honor save in his own country, Jesus hit the nail straight on its theological head (see Mark 6:4; John 4:44; Luke 4:28ff; and Matthew 13:58). Also, the parable where the tenants rose up in defiance of the owner's son and killed him illustrates the magnitude of this rejection of the divine Word (see Matthew 21:34–38; Luke 20:14). However, the text points to a remnant that remains faithful in the worst of times and in the best of times. These are the ones the text refers to "as many as received him to them he gave power ..." (v. 12, Greek: *exousian)*. That is to say He gave them the gift to become His spiritual offspring. He beget (Greek: *hoi egennethesan*) them means spiritual generation, to become children of God. The regeneration process is faith-based and is more akin to them being born by the Spirit of God through faith (see v. 12).

Verse 14 says, "And the Word became flesh" (Greek: *kai ho logos sarx egeneto*)....

Notice there is no regeneration process revealed by the text in relationship to the *Logos* (Word). Verse 14 is a reference back to v. 1. The *Logos* that pre-existed, before the development of time, was made flesh. John is saying the pre-existent Word who entered into the historical/human frame of reference, and was made flesh. Hence, the Incarnation is declared within the Johannine corpus (see II Corinthians 8:9; Galatians 4:4; Romans 1:3; 8:3, also Matthew 1:18–25 and Luke 2:1–14). Not only did the Word become flesh, but the text affirms the Word made flesh pitched its tent with humanity (Greek: *skenos*, *skene*). That is to say, The Word tabernacled with humankind. It is a continuation of the presence and power of God to abide, live with and within His creation. The word tabernacle is an allusion back to the Old Testament's Ark of the Covenant that accompanied the Hebrew people as they journeyed. It later was established in a more permanent worship facility called the tabernacle. The glory of the Lord's presence shone brightly in the tabernacle and John applies a similar meaning in reference to the Word made flesh. The glory of the Lord shone brilliantly in the Man, Christ Jesus. John gives testimony to the same and exclaims He is the only begotten of the Father (Greek: *hos monogenous para patros*). Begotten here means the only One

of its kind. Jesus is uniquely the Word made flesh. This Word manifests the full glory of the Father, full of grace and truth.

THE LESSON APPLIED

The lesson shows the pre-existence of the Word before time came into play. The Word was the essential Person in creating the world. Apostle Paul confirms this in the book of Colossians (see Colossians 1:14–18). The Word has total equality with God. The Word came into the human frame of reference to provide salvation to a world darkened by sin. John 1:14-18 tells the story of the Word's purpose. To dwell among humans to reveal the glory and the salvation of God.

Like John the Baptist, contemporary Christians are to witness to the Word's presence to give and guide others to the abundant life He offers.

LET'S TALK ABOUT IT

Can John 1:14 read that "flesh became the Word?"

No! The article before *Logos* in John 1:14 prohibits a reversal of this sentence. The intent of the writer is to show that He who Pre–existed before time, entered into time for a particular purpose, and that purpose was to reveal the glory of God. John 1:14 is the Christmas story in this Gospel.

HOME DAILY DEVOTIONAL READINGS
JULY 4–10, 2022

MONDAY	TUESDAY	WEDNESDAY	THURSDAY	FRIDAY	SATURDAY	SUNDAY
Jesus Reveals His Glory	O Lord, Heal Me!	Jesus Heals a Centurion's Servant	Jesus Heals a Paralyzed Man	Jesus Heals a Blind Man	God Heals Their infirmities	Jesus Heals a Royal Official's Son
John 2:1–11	Psalm 6	Matthew 8:5–13	John 5:1–9	John 9:1–7	Psalm 41	John 4:46–54

The Word Heals

Adult Topic: Never Too Far Away	Background Scripture: John 4:46–54

John 4:46–54

King James Version

SO Jesus came again into Cana of Galilee, where he made the water wine. And there was a certain nobleman, whose son was sick at Capernaum.

47 When he heard that Jesus was come out of Judaea into Galilee, he went unto him, and besought him that he would come down, and heal his son: for he was at the point of death.

48 Then said Jesus unto him, Except ye see signs and wonders, ye will not believe.

49 The nobleman saith unto him, Sir, come down ere my child die.

50 Jesus saith unto him, Go thy way; thy son liveth. And the man believed the word that Jesus had spoken unto him, and he went his way.

51 And as he was now going down, his servants met him, and told him, saying, Thy son liveth.

52 Then enquired he of them the hour when he began to amend. And they said unto him, Yesterday at the seventh hour the fever left him.

53 So the father knew that it was at the same hour, in the which Jesus said unto him, Thy son liveth: and himself believed, and his whole house.

54 This is again the second miracle that Jesus did, when he was come out of Judaea into Galilee.

New Revised Standard Version

THEN he came again to Cana in Galilee where he had changed the water into wine. Now there was a royal official whose son lay ill in Capernaum.

47 When he heard that Jesus had come from Judea to Galilee, he went and begged him to come down and heal his son, for he was at the point of death.

48 Then Jesus said to him, "Unless you see signs and wonders you will not believe."

49 The official said to him, "Sir, come down before my little boy dies."

50 Jesus said to him, "Go; your son will live." The man believed the word that Jesus spoke to him and started on his way.

51 As he was going down, his slaves met him and told him that his child was alive.

52 So he asked them the hour when he began to recover, and they said to him, "Yesterday at one in the afternoon the fever left him."

53 The father realized that this was the hour when Jesus had said to him, "Your son will live." So he himself believed, along with his whole household.

54 Now this was the second sign that Jesus did after coming from Judea to Galilee.

MAIN THOUGHT: So the father knew that it was at the same hour, in the which Jesus said unto him, Thy son liveth: and himself believed, and his whole house. (John 4:53, KJV)

LESSON SETTING
Time: Approx. AD 100–110
Place: Judea

LESSON OUTLINE
I. A Return to Cana
(John 4:46)
II. A Visit and a Request from a
Nobleman
(John 4:47–49)
III. Healed by the Word
(John 4:50–54)

UNIFYING PRINCIPLE

When we or our loved ones are sick, we seek restoration and healing. When all efforts fail, what can we do? Jesus invites our active, faith–filled participation with his power to create new life through healing—even at a distance.

INTRODUCTION

Faith (Greek: *pisteuo*) is an important aspect of salvation in the Gospel of John. This lesson picks up the theme of faith in the Word (Greek: *Logos*) that was introduced in verses 10–13 of the Prologue, and hammered home by Jesus in His conversation with Nicodemus in John 3:1–18. Not only is faith mentioned explicitly, but it runs silently as a major theme of this book implicitly as well. One can observe it in rudimentary stages in the actions of the disciples to follow Jesus (John 1:34–51), in his mother's comment to Jesus that the wine has run out at the wedding in Cana and in her subsequent instructions for the servants to do whatever Jesus tells them to do (John 2:1–11). In John 4:1–43, we see the Samaritan woman and her community coming into a growing and ever-increasing faith in Jesus as the Messiah of God. Because of their faith in Him, this community that was on the fringes of life

because of its mixed ancestry received salvation, and became children of God, just as it was promised in the Prologue (see John 1:12–13). John 4:46–54 continues this examination into faith as a precursor to experiencing wholistic salvation or life as denoted in John 3:16.

Three things are important in this examination. First, the text reveals Jesus' return to Cana where He performed His second miracle in as many days. It is evident from the miracle where He turned the water into wine that Jesus had gained a bit of notoriety there. It would be fertile ground for His second miracle and lay in stark contrast to those who would reject Him. Rejection or unbelief prevented Jesus from working miracles in His hometown, Nazareth (Mark 6:5–6; see also John 1:10–11; 5:15–6:59). Additionally, it shows that Jesus is accepted by those who live outside of His immediate home area (by Samaritans and Galileans), but will be rejected by the Jews.

Second, while in Cana, Jesus received a request from one of the officials in King Herod's court for Him to come and heal his sick son. This request is the first of its kind in the Gospel of John, even though the Samaritan woman asked Jesus for Living Water (John 4:1–44). It illustrates that faith has broad reaches and its appeal may take various forms of expression to supply a variety of needs.

Third, the text shows the power of Jesus to heal just by speaking the word. The beginning of this book (John 1 :1) referred us back to Genesis 1:1. The Hebrew word (*Bara*) is an account of God speaking creation into existence. Here Jesus does the same thing. He speaks wellness, wholeness, and newness into the life situation of the official's son. With a word, the "Word made flesh," brings healing and renewal.

These three things point to faith as a necessary commodity for healing and salvation. It is important to point out that some scholars see this part of John as being misplaced. They argue that chapter 6 should come before chapter 5 and would allow for a natural reading of the text, but it does not alter or change our interpretation of the text. (For more information concerning this order please see, William Barclay. *The Daily Study Bible Series: The Gospel of John. Volume 1*. Philadelphia: Westminster Press, 1975, p. 156; Gerard S. Sloyan. *John: Interpretation: A Bible Commentary for Teaching and Preaching*. Atlanta: John Knox Press, pp. 61–62).

I. A RETURN TO CANA
(JOHN 4:46)

Cana was the place, according to John's Gospel, where Jesus performed His first miracle, where He turned the water into wine. Jesus returned to an area familiar to Him and where He evidently gained inroads and a level of prominence. It is believed that the royal official is a Gentile, but we cannot know for certain. This miracle story is a story of a request for healing from a member of the court of King Herod, the Tetrarch. He has journeyed approximately 20 miles from Capernaum to meet Jesus, to make a serious request for healing. Similar requests for healing are made of Jesus in the Synoptic Gospels (see Matthew 8:5–13; Luke 7:2–10 for a centurion and his son; and Matthew 15:21–28; Mark 7:24–30 for a Canaanite woman and her daughter). With the emphasis placed on the journeys of both Jesus and the nobleman we can rightly call this small pericope of Scripture

a travel narrative similar to those beginning in Luke 9:51. Verse 46 serves as a transitional verse and closes the previous story of Jesus' visit with the Samaritan woman and her community.

II. A VISIT AND A REQUEST FROM A NOBLEMAN
(JOHN 4:47–49)

The contrast in this story is quite significant. The two characters are as opposite as opposites can be. On the one hand, there is an itinerant preacher and former Carpenter from the small town of Nazareth, and on the other hand, there is a member of the king's court, a palace office. The other dichotomy is the fact that it is the royal personality making a request of the community carpenter (see Barclay, Ibid. p. 174). As auspicious as it sounds that is precisely the point the writer is seeking to make. Word about the turning of the water into wine has spread all over the countryside and made Jesus a household name and the talk of the town. Word had spread by-word-of mouth, even as far as Capernaum and convinced a royal official who lived there, that there was hope for his sick son. Therefore, the scene composed of opposite figures is the right one for the Johannine writer to make his point about faith. The unnamed royal official (Greek: *basilikos,* meaning petty king) approached Jesus and asked Him to heal his son, who was at the point of death (v. 47). Jesus responded to him in an unlikely manner probably to test the level of his faith. Jesus said to him, "Except ye see signs and wonders, ye will not believe" (v. 48, KJV). "Jesus is not discounting his sign and wonders"… (Robertson, pp. 74–75). Jesus had come to earth to transform the hearts of human beings and turn them toward

God. He had not come merely to perform miracles and did not want to gain the reputation of being desired only because of His powers to heal people, physically. Rather, He has more to offer them than a temporary healing. He had come to set people in a right relationship with God. As the Antidote to the sin problem that haunted every human being, He had therefore, come to restore their spiritual relationship with their Creator. Jesus makes this plain in His rebuke of the multitude in John 6:26–71. In this passage, Jesus questioned the motive of the multitude, who followed Him across the sea, after He had fed them, and challenged it to look for more than temporary satisfaction or fulfillment, but to "Labor not for the meat which perisheth, but for that meat which endureth unto everlasting life, which the Son of Man shall give unto you:"… (John 6:27, KJV). After they asked for additional signs to authenticate Himself as the Bread of Life, "Jesus said unto them, Verily, verily, I say unto you, Except ye eat the flesh of the Son of man, and drink his blood, ye have no life in you" (John 6:53, KJV). It is clear that Jesus was upset with the crowd's limited desire to grasp hold of the real meaning for His coming into the world (v. 48).

However, the man proved that he was not there just because he had heard of Jesus' ability to perform miracles. He was not intimidated by Jesus' question. He reaffirmed his request for Jesus to heal his son. He expresses belief in Jesus' power to heal, but at this point he sees the power as effective only before death, like Mary and Martha expressed in John 11:21–32. His growing faith caused him to make the long journey from Capernaum, to plead for his son's healing. But there are things he has yet to conceive of in relationship to Jesus.

III. HEALED BY THE WORD (JOHN 4:50–54)

Having passed the test of possessing an authentic yet growing belief, the man hears six words that stirs his faith to a higher level. Jesus said unto him, "Go thy way; Thy son liveth"… (John 4:50, KJV). The text says the man believed the words Jesus had spoken and went his way. The "Word made flesh" had spoken words of life to the desperate nobleman. His acceptance of Jesus' words are the equivalent to the expression Peter gave when Jesus asked the Twelve in John 6:67 "Will ye also go away?" (KJV). Peter responded saying, "Lord, to whom shall we go? Thou hast the words of eternal life. And we believe and are sure that thou art the Christ, the Son of the living God" (John 6;68–69, KJV). The man had come to Jesus as his last hope and received words too good to be true, "Thy son is living and will not die." (v. 50, Robertson, Ibid, p. 76). His son is healed without Jesus making the journey to Capernaum. Robertson called this healing the "absent treatment." Speaking the divine Word of authority and renewal, Jesus healed the boy from a distance. The fact that the man went his way is indicative of instantaneous faith. The man had no further need to plead. His faith had been rewarded with sustained life for his son. While on the way home he was met with the good news that his son's condition had turned for the better. The servants repeated Jesus' healing words, that his son was alive, therefore, confirming Jesus' ability to give life. The repetition further confirmed Jesus' promise and the writer's words in the prologue that "in Him was life and this life was the light of men" (see John 1:4; also see Gail R. O'Day, *The Gospel of John. The New Interpreter's Bible: A Commentary in Twelve Volumes, Volume IX*, Abingdon Press: Nashville, p. 575).

The man asked his servant's when did his son's condition change for the better, and to his delight discovered the healing occurred at the same time Jesus spoke the words. This discovery contributed to salvation for the man and his entire household. The man's faith in Jesus is concretized. The pericope ends with a declaration of faith on part of the nobleman. The passage is careful to note that this faith is not in the miracles Jesus performed, but in Him. The miracles serve as a window to authentic faith. Gail O'Day raises question of the purpose of the Cana miracles. She argues that ... "they allow us to see the glory of the Word made flesh and to see the Word's ability to give life. The miracle of the water being turned to wine revealed Jesus' glory, the second miracle reveals his ability to give life." (O'Day, p. 576).

THE LESSON APPLIED

The lesson focuses on the ability of God to give life. The nobleman comes to Jesus seeking to have his son restored to health. However, through Jesus he comes to faith that leads him and his household to abundant life. The miracle Jesus had performed earlier in Cana caught the attention of the royal official and caused him to desperately come to Jesus with hope in hand for his son.

However, when questioned by Jesus the nobleman held firm to his rudimentary faith that Jesus could heal him. As it turned out, his faith secured the boy's healing, but much more than what he bargained for. It resulted in him and his entire household being saved. God can bless our small steps of faith and grow them into blessings that benefit us on more than a temporary basis.

LET'S TALK ABOUT IT

Why is faith so important in John's Gospel?

Faith is not only important for John, but it is essential for human salvation. Faith is the mechanism God has chosen to justify humanity. Faith in Jesus allows God to impute His righteousness into us and to provide spiritual regeneration thereby putting us in a right relationship with Him.

Justification by faith is a major Christian doctrine articulated by Paul, to explain God's acceptance of human beings even though we fail in our endeavor to live as He has commanded us. Through faith in Jesus, we are redeem unto God and cleansed from sin. Faith puts one in the right relationship with the Lord God.

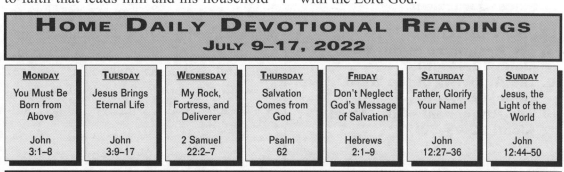

HOME DAILY DEVOTIONAL READINGS
JULY 9–17, 2022

MONDAY	TUESDAY	WEDNESDAY	THURSDAY	FRIDAY	SATURDAY	SUNDAY
You Must Be Born from Above	Jesus Brings Eternal Life	My Rock, Fortress, and Deliverer	Salvation Comes from God	Don't Neglect God's Message of Salvation	Father, Glorify Your Name!	Jesus, the Light of the World
John 3:1–8	John 3:9–17	2 Samuel 22:2–7	Psalm 62	Hebrews 2:1–9	John 12:27–36	John 12:44–50

THE WORD SAVES

ADULT TOPIC:	BACKGROUND SCRIPTURE:
BRINGING THE LIGHT	JOHN 12:27–50

JOHN 12:44–50

King James Version

JESUS cried and said, He that believeth on me, believeth not on me, but on him that sent me.

45 And he that seeth me seeth him that sent me.

46 I am come a light into the world, that whosoever believeth on me should not abide in darkness.

47 And if any man hear my words, and believe not, I judge him not: for I came not to judge the world, but to save the world.

48 He that rejecteth me, and receiveth not my words, hath one that judgeth him: the word that I have spoken, the same shall judge him in the last day.

49 For I have not spoken of myself; but the Father which sent me, he gave me a commandment, what I should say, and what I should speak.

50 And I know that his commandment is life everlasting: whatsoever I speak therefore, even as the Father said unto me, so I speak.

New Revised Standard Version

THEN Jesus cried aloud: "Whoever believes in me believes not in me but in him who sent me.

45 And whoever sees me sees him who sent me.

46 I have come as light into the world, so that everyone who believes in me should not remain in the darkness.

47 I do not judge anyone who hears my words and does not keep them, for I came not to judge the world, but to save the world.

48 The one who rejects me and does not receive my word has a judge; on the last day the word that I have spoken will serve as judge,

49 for I have not spoken on my own, but the Father who sent me has himself given me a commandment about what to say and what to speak.

50 And I know that his commandment is eternal life. What I speak, therefore, I speak just as the Father has told me."

MAIN THOUGHT: I am come a light into the world, that whosoever believeth on me should not abide in darkness. (John 12:46, KJV)

LESSON SETTING
Time: AD 100–110
Place: Jerusalem

LESSON OUTLINE
I. The Assurance of the Word (John 12:44–46)
II. The Authority of the Word (John 12:47–48)
III. The Attainment of the Word (John 12:49–50)

UNIFYING PRINCIPLE
Most people acknowledge a sense of a higher, spiritual power that exceeds our human capabilities. How do we understand the mysteries of the universe, the world, and our lives? Jesus' mission is to save the world so that the world can live in an eternal relationship with His Father, the Creator God.

INTRODUCTION

One of the greatest joys in life is to know that we are on mission and in the center of God's purpose for our lives. Functioning by faith and seeing the Word of God active in our daily walk brings peace and a sense of fulfillment; it's a day well spent in focus and service. This method of existence would be great if only there didn't exist so much distraction in our days.

In today's lesson, Jesus gives us encouragement to stay focused on our Christian witness and mission amidst "turmoil" by overcoming the unnecessary distractions of life. There can be so much unnecessary noise and activity in our daily life; not to mention the recovery from a global pandemic situation with its losses and death, racial upheaval, and the rise of "hate" groups and extremists in our world today. Any continued focus on these types of concerns may easily sway us from God's purpose for our living. One of my mentor's, a fellow pastor said, "the main thing is to keep the main thing the main thing."

Amidst the confusion caused by the Pharisees, the beginning stages of the betrayal of Judas, and the questioning of the people, Jesus stayed focused and again reaffirmed His identity, His connection to the Father and the purpose (Greek: *telios*) of His mission. This idea of divine mission being tied to getting persons to believe is a major theme in John's Gospel. John 20:31 announces the complete summation of John's strand and theme – "these things were written that you may believe and that in believing you may have eternal life."

John's emphasis is to push the reader to reflect and embrace the urgency of keeping "the main thing the main thing" by receiving the revelation of who Jesus is, believing that Jesus is who He claims to be, and therefore, receiving the eternal life that only Jesus can provide.

EXPOSITION

I. THE ASSURANCE OF THE WORD (JOHN 12:44–46)

Jesus has been anointed at Bethany, the decision has been made to assassinate Lazarus, the triumphal entry has happened, the Greeks have come to worship, and the rejection of the rulers now mark the conclusion of the public ministry of Jesus. Jesus returns to the "hiding" place or the obscurity from which He originally came (12:36). Jesus will no longer engage the public nor entertain public discourses; rather, Jesus will be in conversation with the disciples and the Father.

The unbelief of Judaism was not beneficial to their supposed salvation because although they had seen signs (the Gospel of John records seven) they still couldn't believe. Interestingly, signs won't help one's belief if God has not provided the eyes for them to see. This is explained in John's utilization of the passages from Isaiah 53:1 and Isaiah 6:10. This backdrop issue of Judaism's unbelief is paramount if one is to grasp the importance of the necessity of correct belief in Jesus.

Verses 44–46 contain Jesus' separate summation of His ministry and its motives, results, and themes. Note the repeated emphasis here on the (a) mission of Jesus from His Father; (b) the revelation of His Father; (c) the Light of the Word; (d) judgment; and (e) eternal life. The content and substance of Jesus' assurance roots in these two particular aspects: it derives from the

Father and it is sure. Jesus gives the reason for His entrance into the world, the source by which He operates, and the result of believing in Him (see Matthew 10:40).

Jesus as God's ambassador or envoy is obedient and He comes to do the bidding of His Father. Jesus clearly articulates that to believe in Him, see Him or hear Him is to do the same with the Father. This close identification is reminiscent of John the Baptist's statement that "he who has come after me was before me" (John 1:30). Jesus is clear that the Father identifies with Him and Jesus identifies with the Father.

"Believing", *"seeing"* and *"sent"* are critical threads through John's Gospel account (John 13:20). In these verses, John presupposes and presents the collective unity that has been previously introduced in the Prologue (John 1:1–18). John reminds us that Jesus has also been sent on this mission by God to reveal and to "make God known" (John 1:8). The verb forms for the word *"sent"* are repeated no less than thirteen times. John wants us to have the assurance that this Jesus is the ambassador and agent of His Father, carrying out the express purpose of the Father's will.

In verse 46, we see John's next important reason for delivering the message of divine salvation to us, so we can possess the assurance of the Word. Jesus is the Light and has entered into the world as penetrating Light in order that those who believe in Jesus will not have to continue or abide in darkness. This summation has also been noted before in John 1:4–5:9.

This announced Light is presented as the cure and remedy for darkness and blindness (8:12; 9:1–5). The function of the Light is to prevent one from stumbling and being paralyzed by walking in the darkness of sin and evil.

The element of abiding has been added to these verses. Although here it is attached to the idea of darkness, it is normally used as an aspect and reference of discipleship.

II. THE AUTHORITY OF THE WORD (JOHN 12:47–48)

During the Festival, the Words of Jesus were heard and many of His statements were debated by the Jews. The Scripture here asserts that apparently just hearing the Words of Jesus is insufficient. What is necessary is the application of what one has heard. Hearing Jesus must be accompanied by "keeping" His Words.

We must be ever so mindful that "keeping" His Word can be a risky and dangerous enterprise. Although the disciples heard Jesus over and over, they still struggled to understand, accept, and follow Him. Even more simply, their struggle as Jesus' followers is shown when the disciples are confronted by the Jewish leaders with their inherent danger and threats bought to them by "keeping" their identity tied to Jesus and His teachings. We are told that even Peter, who refused to leave Jesus (John 6:68), denied Jesus in the death pericope (18:27). What to some people may seem such an easy task, will require of others their very lives. It raises a great and an important question, "If obeying Jesus' message was difficult for the close disciples, what about others? Indeed, what about us today?"

Jesus says that His coming into the world was not for judgment, however, it was for the salvation of God's world and people (John 3:17). Yet, although Jesus comes to save the world as Savior and Light (4:42), the failure of rejecting Jesus by not believing, receiving Him and His Words can mean nothing else other than to be given over to divine judgment and the loss of eternal life.

III. THE ATTAINMENT OF THE WORD (JOHN 12:49–50)

In these verses, we note a return to the major themes and strands previously presented earlier – "*sent one*" or "*agent*." Jesus is the only Son of God, sent by God to provide the means for the attainment of abundant and eternal life (see John 3:16; 20:31). As such an Agent, Jesus cannot or will not speak or act upon His own will, but the will of the One who sent Him (5:19). He, as the faithful and definitive representative of the Father, acts in complete conformity to the Father's will (5:30; 7:16–17).

Jesus' Words should not be interpreted as just mere human speech. These words of Jesus should not be considered shallow or empty. At this point, John brings the word command or commandment to the forefront. While often seen and interpreted as connected to legalism, John uses "command" to reference the teachings of Jesus and as the major principles of life (Deuteronomy 23:46–47).

The centerpiece of this Gospel is that the New Moses has come to the world (1:21; Deuteronomy 18:15) and has been sent from the Father. He speaks and does what is the will of the Father for the revealing and saving of God's creation and humanity. In the Gospel of Matthew, Jesus is not only the New Moses, but He is superior to Moses in every way. He reissued the commandments and insisted that one must go farther than just keeping the Law, "You have heard that it was said by them of old time, thou shalt not commit adultery: But I say unto you,

That whosoever looketh on a woman to lust after her hath committed adultery with her already in his heart" (see Matthew 5:19-48). Several times in the former pericope of Scripture, Matthew reminds us that Jesus' Words surpasses the words of Moses.

One can also see His superiority to both Abraham and Moses in John 6-8. In a dispute with the Jews, they bluntly asked Him if He was greater than Moses, who gave them manna, while they were in the desert. Jesus answered them immediately by first correcting their misconception of who gave them manna, telling them the manna came not from Moses, but from God. Then He went a step further to remind them that manna sustained their ancestors' lives only temporarily. Jesus further explained that He is the Bread sent from above that would sustain them eternally. Jesus told them "I am the Bread of life" (see John 6:48). Additionally, when the Jews claiming to be the descendants of Abraham, asked Him if He was greater than Abraham, Jesus told them that Abraham was glad to see His coming. When they expressed disbelief to what He said to them, Jesus told them "'Before Abraham was, 'AM'" (see John 8:59).

The Lesson Applied

Jesus has come to the world to provide assurance, authority and attainment for our new lives with the Father. Jesus is the Messenger or Agent of God sent with the Father's Word and following the Father's commands. He has not come for condemnation or judgment, rather Jesus has come to reveal the Father and provide the means for creation and humanity to be saved.

We are challenged to receive Jesus and His words; if we do not accept His words, we reject the One who sent him and therefore, we bring upon ourselves our own judgment and miss the salvation that the Father has prepared for us. As Light, Jesus keeps us from being blind and stumbling in the darkness. He gives us abundant life and renews our fellowship and relationship with our Creator, Sustainer, and Redeemer. However, the text is clear. This abundant Light and Life are ours only if we believe and trust in his gracious Words. He invites all of us to receive Him as the Word made flesh so that we can be a part of His eternal Kingdom.

LET'S TALK ABOUT IT

Which way is the right way to get to God and enjoy Heaven forever?

We live a syncretistic culture that is post-Christian, post-Church and post-modern. The message is to do what's right for you and don't try to give or force upon me what you believe.

Another major sentiment of this culture is that we don't have to go to church to be spiritual or Christian. Jesus, as God's sent Agent and Ambassador came in the authority of His Father with the Word of the Father to provide salvation for all those who would accept, believe and keep His commandments. Jesus says that it is not enough to just hear the Word; we must "*keep*" His Word. His Word advises us that He is the Way, the Truth and the Life; no one comes to the Father except through the Son (John 14:6). The Word teaches that there is no other name whereby we can be saved, but the name of Jesus and the word reminds us that if we confess with our mouth the Lord Jesus and believe in our hearts that God raised Him from the dead we can be saved (Romans 10:9).

Why does John make Jesus the Centerpiece of His Gospel?

Jesus is the Centerpiece not only of John's Gospel account, but He is the Centerpiece of all of life. The message from John reveals that Jesus is indeed the Pre-existent Word of God, who was God, and was in the beginning with God. Through Him all things were made. In Him was life and this life was the light of humanity (John 1:1–4). Paul said in Colossians 1:14–19 that the fullness of God dwelt in Jesus and it was through Him that all things came into being and through Him that redemption came.

Therefore, it is abundantly clear from the perspective of Scripture that Jesus Christ is the centerpiece of life. However, the objective of Scripture is for Him to become the centerpiece of your life. This means it is up to each individual to accept Him as Lord and personal Savior through faith. In Jesus, we are justified before the Lord God.

HOME DAILY DEVOTIONAL READINGS
JULY 18–24, 2022

MONDAY	TUESDAY	WEDNESDAY	THURSDAY	FRIDAY	SATURDAY	SUNDAY
Awake, O Dead, and Sing!	The Dead Shall Be Raised	In Christ All Are Made Alive	Wake Up!	The Dead Will Hear Christ's Voice	Jesus Travels to Lazarus	The Raising of Lazarus
Isaiah 26:12–19	1 Corinthians 15:12–19	1 Corinthians 15:20–28	Daniel 12:1–4	John 5:25–29	John 11:1, 3–16	John 11:20–27, 38–44

THE WORD RESURRECTS THE DEAD

ADULT TOPIC:	BACKGROUND SCRIPTURE:
CONQUERING THE ULTIMATE ENEMY	JOHN 11:17–44

JOHN 11:17–27, 38–44

King James Version	*New Revised Standard Version*
THEN when Jesus came, he found that he had lain in the grave four days already.	WHEN Jesus arrived, he found that Lazarus had already been in the tomb four days.
18 Now Bethany was nigh unto Jerusalem, about fifteen furlongs off:	18 Now Bethany was near Jerusalem, some two miles away,
19 And many of the Jews came to Martha and Mary, to comfort them concerning their brother.	19 and many of the Jews had come to Martha and Mary to console them about their brother.
20 Then Martha, as soon as she heard that Jesus was coming, went and met him: but Mary sat still in the house.	20 When Martha heard that Jesus was coming, she went and met him, while Mary stayed at home.
21 Then said Martha unto Jesus, Lord, if thou hadst been here, my brother had not died.	21 Martha said to Jesus, "Lord, if you had been here, my brother would not have died.
22 But I know, that even now, whatsoever thou wilt ask of God, God will give it thee.	22 But even now I know that God will give you whatever you ask of him."
23 Jesus saith unto her, Thy brother shall rise again.	23 Jesus said to her, "Your brother will rise again."
24 Martha saith unto him, I know that he shall rise again in the resurrection at the last day.	24 Martha said to him, "I know that he will rise again in the resurrection on the last day."
25 Jesus said unto her, I am the resurrection, and the life: he that believeth in me, though he were dead, yet shall he live:	25 Jesus said to her, "I am the resurrection and the life. Those who believe in me, even though they die, will live,
26 And whosoever liveth and believeth in me shall never die. Believest thou this?	26 and everyone who lives and believes in me will never die. Do you believe this?"
27 She saith unto him, Yea, Lord: I believe that thou art the Christ, the Son of God, which should come into the world.	27 She said to him, "Yes, Lord, I believe that you are the Messiah, the Son of God, the one coming into the world."
• • • • • •	• • • • • •
38 Jesus therefore again groaning in himself cometh to the grave. It was a cave, and a stone lay upon it.	38 Then Jesus, again greatly disturbed, came to the tomb. It was a cave, and a stone was lying against it.
39 Jesus said, Take ye away the stone. Martha, the sister of him that was dead, saith unto him,	39 Jesus said, "Take away the stone." Martha, the sister of the dead man, said to him, "Lord,

MAIN THOUGHT: Jesus said unto her, I am the resurrection, and the life: he that believeth in me, though he were dead, yet shall he live: And whosoever liveth and believeth in me shall never die. Believest thou this? (John 11:25–26, KJV)

King James Version	*New Revised Standard Version*
Lord, by this time he stinketh: for he hath been dead four days.	already there is a stench because he has been dead four days."
40 Jesus saith unto her, Said I not unto thee, that, if thou wouldest believe, thou shouldest see the glory of God?	40 Jesus said to her, "Did I not tell you that if you believed, you would see the glory of God?"
41 Then they took away the stone from the place where the dead was laid. And Jesus lifted up his eyes, and said, Father, I thank thee that thou hast heard me.	41 So they took away the stone. And Jesus looked upward and said, "Father, I thank you for having heard me.
42 And I knew that thou hearest me always: but because of the people which stand by I said it, that they may believe that thou hast sent me.	42 I knew that you always hear me, but I have said this for the sake of the crowd standing here, so that they may believe that you sent me."
43 And when he thus had spoken, he cried with a loud voice, Lazarus, come forth.	43 When he had said this, he cried with a loud voice, "Lazarus, come out!"
44 And he that was dead came forth, bound hand and foot with graveclothes: and his face was bound about with a napkin. Jesus saith unto them, Loose him, and let him go.	44 The dead man came out, his hands and feet bound with strips of cloth, and his face wrapped in a cloth. Jesus said to them, "Unbind him, and let him go."

LESSON SETTING
Time: AD 100–110
Place: Judea

LESSON OUTLINE
I. The Arrival
(John 11:17–19)
II. The First Conversation
(John 11:20–27)
III. The Resurrection of Lazarus
(John 11:38–44)

UNIFYING PRINCIPLE

When people experience tragic situations, they long for comfort. Where can we find hope and strength for the future? Our faith in Jesus releases the power of God to bring resurrection and new life.

INTRODUCTION

As mentioned in an earlier lesson, one of the major themes of the Gospel of John is life. The Pre-existent Word embodied the totality of life (see John 1:4). This life was the light of [men]. Although, we see instances where Jesus, the Word made flesh renews and restores life to the sick and the ailing, nothing trumps His ability to give life and to define Him as God in the flesh like the resurrection of Lazarus. Other than Jesus' own resurrection from the dead, Lazarus' resurrection holds center stage in this Gospel account and leads of course to Jesus' death on the cross and to His subsequent resurrection to new life.

Three things are important as we analyze this pericope of Scripture. First, we will review Jesus' arrival in Bethany. He had received the news that His friend Lazarus was quite ill several days before his death (John 11:1–3). Yet, Jesus intentionally delayed going to Bethany immediately, in order to bring glory to God (v. 4, 6). When He put His disciples on notice that He intended to go to Bethany, they reminded him of the danger of going back to the place where the Jews had previously sought to stone Him (vv. 7–8). However, Jesus would not be deterred and told the disciples that He needed to go to Bethany to awaken Lazarus, who had fallen asleep. The disciples initially misunderstood what Jesus meant by awakening Lazarus and He had to plainly state to them that their friend Lazarus was dead (vv. 11–15).

In telling them that Lazarus was indeed dead, Jesus was revealing to them His dual purpose for the journey to Bethany (Greek: *hina exupniso auton*), "That I may awake him out of sleep" (v. 11) and (Greek: *hina pisteusete*), "that you may come to believe (more than you do)." Thomas' utterance of blind devotion expresses "more than he realizes: for Jesus the journey will be for death, but one that will mean life for the world" (see v. 15; also see Robertson, *Word Pictures in the New Testament. Volume V, The Fourth Gospel, The Epistle to the Hebrews.* Nashville: Broadman Press, 1932, pp. 195–197).

A third purpose for the journey to Bethany was to precipitate events that would result in His subsequent death and resurrection to bring ultimate glory to the Father and salvation to all who came to believe in Him (see v. 16). That is to say, Jesus knew why He had responded to the news that Lazarus was sickness and had delayed His trip there for a much higher purpose than the disciples could have possibly imagined (see George Beasley–Murray. *Word Biblical Commentary: John. Volume 36,* Word Book Publishers: Waco, 1987, p 187–188). His arrival in Bethany, kicked off a series of events which emphasized the need of a strong and enduring faith in Him.

Second, the text records His first conversation with one of the bereaved sisters, who questioned His late arrival in Bethany, but confessed she knows that God hears Jesus' prayers. It is a roundabout way of asking Jesus to put in a good word for her brother's return to life. Although the passage concerning the response of Mary to Jesus' coming is not included in our study, it is important to note that her response mirrors her sister's and leads us to the third portion of our study which is Jesus' raising Lazarus to new life. It is a case of the Word made flesh speaking to the dead and death responding positively to His command and producing life.

EXPOSITION

I. THE ARRIVAL (JOHN 11:17–19)

After four days, Jesus arrived in Bethany (fifteen furlongs was about two miles from Jerusalem). His friend Lazarus was dead. It was the custom of the Jews during this period of time to bury the dead on the day of death (Robertson, Ibid., p. 197). The Jews were in mourning with Mary and Martha, which indicates that the family had received some level of prominence and affluence in the community. The Greek word *paramutheomai*, meaning to offer comfort and consolation bears this out (v. 19). When the news came to Martha that Jesus had arrived she went out to meet Him. Mary, on the other hand, remained in the house. The two women, though sisters appear to be on the opposite sides of the spectrum. One runs out to meet Jesus, while the other sits in the house in deep concentration. In Luke 10:38–42, the two sisters are also seeming at odds because Martha is busy making preparations for Jesus, while Mary sits at His feet in a position of learning.

II. THE FIRST CONVERSATION (JOHN 11:20–27)

Martha is the first to approach Jesus to express her faith in Him. She leads off with an "*if*" statement (v. 21–22). The "*if*" expresses a level of belief, but it also expresses or includes limitations. She said, "Lord, if you had been here my brother would not have died." Her faith had not yet reached the level of faith expressed by the nobleman in John 4:50–54. Jesus told him, "Your son will live." The nobleman took Jesus at His word and headed back to his sick son who resided in Capernaum, approximately twenty miles away. This healing proved Jesus did not have to make the journey to Bethany. He could have spoken the words of resurrection and new life from a distance, but He went in order to glorify God and to grow the faith of His disciples. Yet, she to her credit confessed her belief that whatsoever Jesus asked of God would be granted unto Him (v. 22).

It is ironic, however, that both of the sisters responded to Jesus' arrival after the fact of death with the same statement although it came much later from Mary (see vv. 21–22 and 32). This would suggest that the two sisters though opposites in some ways, nevertheless possessed a similar, but firm belief in Jesus as the Word, who had come from above. It is also highly probable that they had witnessed Jesus healing others, and based upon the quality of their relationship with Him, believed He would likewise act in their behalf as well.

Jesus' words to Mary were meant to be applied to her current situation (and parenthetically) as something the disciples needed to comprehend in their own ministries), "Thy brother shall rise again" (v. 23). However, she took them as applicable only in the future, "I know that he shall rise again in the resurrection at the last day," she responded (v. 24). To her amazement, Jesus' words of assurance were not just futuristic, but were meant for the current day believers as well. "I am the resurrection, and the life: he that believeth in me, though he were dead, yet shall he live: And whosoever liveth and believeth in me shall never die. Believest thou this?" (v. 25, KJV). John Beasley–Murray said, "It can relate to the recall of Lazarus to life about to take place or to his resurrection in the end time… It signifies not so much a rejection of Martha's faith as an extension of it and a setting of it on a sure foundation" (*Word Biblical Commentary,* Ibid, p. 190). Jesus' use of these words, mimics God's statement to Moses in Exodus 3.

There are a total of seven "I AM" statements in this Gospel account [I AM the Bread of life (John 6:35); I AM the Light of the World (John 812); I AM the Door (John 10:9); I AM the Way, the Truth, and the Life (John 14:6); I AM the Vine (John 15:5); I AM the Resurrection and the Life (John 11:25–26)]. "I AM" denotes God's eternal existence and Sovereign power. Jesus, as the Word, uses the phrase to identify His union with God (v. 1–2). The question to Martha is actually an examination of her faith. Her response is crucial for her to see the full scope of Jesus' power and sovereignty as the Word sent from above. It is a confession of faith that Jesus is who He says He is, that He is not only the Resurrection and the Life, but that He is the Truth also (see John 14:6). In her acknowledgement of Him as the Messiah (Greek: *Christos*) she joins others in this and the Synoptic Gospel accounts, who confess Him as the One sent from above (see John 1:42, 49; Matthew 11:3; John 3:31; 6:33, 51; 12:13).

III. THE RESURRECTION OF LAZARUS (JOHN 11:38–44)

Although John 11:28–37 are not a part of this study, they are important for us to review albeit, but briefly. In these verses, we have one of the three instances in the New Testament where it is recorded that Jesus wept (John 11:35; Luke 19:41; Hebrews. 5:7–9). In each of these instances Jesus revealed His compassion for humanity and identification with His people. In other words, Jesus lived out the purpose of John 1:14, "And the Word was made flesh "...and dwelt among us..." This is important because they record Jesus doing something that is expressly denoted as a human emotion. He wept. In the face of Greek and Roman gods, the Christian concept of divinity carries with it the idea of a personal and loving relationship with the human creature. Human beings are not toys to be played with or abstract figures created for the amusement of the gods as noted in Greek and Roman mythology. Neither are they creatures to be scorned and tortured as in the case of Baalism. In Jesus Christ, the Word of God came close to humanity to save it from the darkness of sin and destruction (see Mark 1:14–15; John 1:14–18). Just as God appeared in the burning bush that was not consumed and held a personal encounter with Moses defining who He was, Jesus came to Bethany and definitively identified who He was to Martha. It was a personal and public display of His concern and compassion for her, and for all of those believers who would one day, likewise, stand in her shoes.

However, some of the Jews who came to offer comfort to the grieving sisters complained that Jesus should have arrived earlier and done more than show up after the fact of Lazarus' death. Little did they realize that they were about to witness the grandest display of God's power in human history. They were content with seeing Jesus as a mere miracle-worker rather as the Savior of the world to which Jesus expressed anger and displeasure (see vv. 37–38). "Here we have the most profound aspect of John's treatment of the miracles. It places Jesus poles apart from the mere wonder-workers, and seeks to penetrate into the mystery of how he, though to all outward appearance an ordinary (or perhaps extraordinary) human being, is the one in whom is disclosed God's presence and his very self in saving action" (Beasley-Murray, Ibid, p. 195).

At any rate, Jesus' displeasure with the Jews did not cause him to lose focus of what He had come to Bethany to do. He had come to give glory to God by allowing the glory of God to shine through Him. When He came to the site where Lazarus was buried He commanded the stone to be taken away. Martha reminded Jesus that Lazarus had been dead for four days, and therefore, his body had begun to decay. Her confession that "He stinketh" put the whole narrative in perspective. The purpose of the Word being made flesh was to deal with humanity's stinking stuff, the stinking stuff of sin and darkness, the stinking stuff of humanity seeking to go its own way, albeit, but blindly (John 1:4–9, 11–12). Jesus reminded Martha of His promise to reveal to her the glory of God is a reiteration of vv. 23–26, and a reference to His own death and subsequent resurrection. Afterward, Jesus prayed. His prayer is a prayer of thanksgiving and was predicated on a previous prayer that had already taken place before this time. This prayer reaches back to v. 22 to confirm the truth of Martha's acknowledgement of His unique relationship with God. The term "know" (Greek: *yinosko*) carries the understanding of intimate knowledge. Jesus uses the same term (in the past tense) when He publicly prayed at Lazarus' tomb. He had prayed to God previously about Lazarus' situation and now He prayed that others might believe that God had sent Him. In this prayer, Jesus put the focus on God and on God's response to His cry. With a loud cry for Lazarus to come forth, the dead man heard the voice of the Creator and Word of Life, and in complete obedience left the darkness of the cave and came forth to new life. Jesus issued a second command for the cloth that bound his feet and hands, and the napkin that secured and covered his face, to be loosed in order to set him free. They were no longer needed for the dead man was now alive and living. John 1:4 had come full circle. In the Word was life, and that life was the light that shined brilliantly in Lazarus as he left the domain of the dead. What happened to Lazarus will happen eternally for all who profess faith in Jesus, the Word made flesh.

THE LESSON APPLIED

This lesson confirms the narrator's opening statement in v. 4 that the Word was the Light of men (people). It is the climax of Jesus' earthly ministry. Jesus, the Word made flesh, came to dwell with human beings to illustrate God's love, compassion, and concern for them. He came to rekindle the fellowship of God with humanity and to bring it salvation. The resurrection of Lazarus was the greatest sign that God chose to disclose Himself through the Word made flesh. Lazarus came forth from the dead when He was called by the Creator.

LET'S TALK ABOUT IT

Did Lazarus' resurrection lead to Jesus' crucifixion?

Yes! The Jewish leaders were upset that so much attention was going to Jesus. They thought by killing Him they would rid themselves of Jesus once and for all. They were wrong. The glory of God shone through Him at Lazarus' resurrection and pointed to His own rising from the dead.

HOME DAILY DEVOTIONAL READINGS
JULY 25–31, 2022

MONDAY	TUESDAY	WEDNESDAY	THURSDAY	FRIDAY	SATURDAY	SUNDAY
Seek Peace and Pursue It	Rest for the Weary	Jesus Has Conquered the World	Peace for the Upright	Unmovable Covenant of Peace	Don't Let Your Hearts Be Troubled	Peace to the Disciples
Psalm 34:4–14	Matthew 11:25–30	Psalm 119:161–176	Isaiah 54:6–10 God's	John 14:1–14	John 14:15–29	John 16:23–27, 32–33

THE WORD GIVES PEACE

ADULT TOPIC:	BACKGROUND SCRIPTURE:
PRESENT FOREVER	JOHN 14:15–31

JOHN 14:15–29

King James Version	New Revised Standard Version
IF ye love me, keep my commandments.	"IF you love me, you will keep my commandments.
16 And I will pray the Father, and he shall give you another Comforter, that he may abide with you for ever;	16 And I will ask the Father, and he will give you another Advocate, to be with you forever.
17 Even the Spirit of truth; whom the world cannot receive, because it seeth him not, neither knoweth him: but ye know him; for he dwelleth with you, and shall be in you.	17 This is the Spirit of truth, whom the world cannot receive, because it neither sees him nor knows him. You know him, because he abides with you, and he will be in you.
18 I will not leave you comfortless: I will come to you.	18 "I will not leave you orphaned; I am coming to you.
19 Yet a little while, and the world seeth me no more; but ye see me: because I live, ye shall live also.	19 In a little while the world will no longer see me, but you will see me; because I live, you also will live.
20 At that day ye shall know that I am in my Father, and ye in me, and I in you.	20 On that day you will know that I am in my Father, and you in me, and I in you.
21 He that hath my commandments, and keepeth them, he it is that loveth me: and he that loveth me shall be loved of my Father, and I will love him, and will manifest myself to him.	21 They who have my commandments and keep them are those who love me; and those who love me will be loved by my Father, and I will love them and reveal myself to them."
22 Judas saith unto him, not Iscariot, Lord, how is it that thou wilt manifest thyself unto us, and not unto the world?	22 Judas (not Iscariot) said to him, "Lord, how is it that you will reveal yourself to us, and not to the world?"
23 Jesus answered and said unto him, If a man love me, he will keep my words: and my Father will love him, and we will come unto him, and make our abode with him.	23 Jesus answered him, "Those who love me will keep my word, and my Father will love them, and we will come to them and make our home with them.
24 He that loveth me not keepeth not my sayings: and the word which ye hear is not mine, but the Father's which sent me.	24 Whoever does not love me does not keep my words; and the word that you hear is not mine, but is from the Father who sent me.
25 These things have I spoken unto you, being yet present with you.	25 "I have said these things to you while I am still with you.
26 But the Comforter, which is the Holy Ghost, whom the Father will send in my name, he	26 But the Advocate, the Holy Spirit, whom the Father will send in my name, will teach you

MAIN THOUGHT: And I will pray the Father, and he shall give you another Comforter, that he may abide with you for ever. (John 14:16, KJV)

JOHN 14:15–29

King James Version	New Revised Standard Version
shall teach you all things, and bring all things to your remembrance, whatsoever I have said unto you. 27 Peace I leave with you, my peace I give unto you: not as the world giveth, give I unto you. Let not your heart be troubled, neither let it be afraid. 28 Ye have heard how I said unto you, I go away, and come again unto you. If ye loved me, ye would rejoice, because I said, I go unto the Father: for my Father is greater than I. 29 And now I have told you before it come to pass, that, when it is come to pass, ye might believe.	everything, and remind you of all that I have said to you. 27 Peace I leave with you; my peace I give to you. I do not give to you as the world gives. Do not let your hearts be troubled, and do not let them be afraid. 28 You heard me say to you, 'I am going away, and I am coming to you.' If you loved me, you would rejoice that I am going to the Father, because the Father is greater than I. 29 And now I have told you this before it occurs, so that when it does occur, you may believe.

LESSON SETTING
Time: Approx. AD 100–110
Place: Judea

LESSON OUTLINE
I. Expressions of Concern
(John 14:15–19)
II. A Promise Made
(John 14:20–24)
III. The Role of the Comforter
(John 14:25–29)

UNIFYING PRINCIPLE

People seek trustworthy guidance for their lives. How can we find guidance? Our love for Jesus, shown through our obedience to His words and the Holy Spirit's teachings, creates an incredible peace.

INTRODUCTION

John 14:15–31 is a part of a larger pericope of Scripture (John 13:1–17:20), that provides an extended farewell discourse of Jesus with His disciples. The discourse is followed by the only elongated prayer of Jesus recorded in the Bible. The purpose of this discourse was meant to prepare the disciples for the course of events that would result in Jesus being tried, found guilty of blasphemy, and sentenced to death on a Roman cross. Because He was leaving to return to the Father, Jesus wanted His disciples to understand the ministry they were about to undertake, without the benefit of His physical presence. Having set an example of humility in the washing of feet, Jesus told His disciples of His pending departure. He then commanded them to love one another as He had loved them (John 13:34–35).

Real and true discipleship must be strong in the face of opposition, especially when the Teacher is absent. It must operate from a basis of love for the Teacher and respect for His teachings. What follows then in John 14–16 is a set of teachings or instructions that are important for the disciples to recognize and obey if they are to move from being mere disciples into their new roles as "distributors of the faith." It leaves open the question "What are they to do after He has gone?" As a segway into the answer to this question the text includes important questions from two of His disciples. The first questions came from Thomas who seeks to understand where Jesus is going and how do the disciples find their way (see John 14:5). The next question comes from Philip for Jesus to reveal to them the Father. For three years Jesus had walked and taught among them about the Kingdom of God and the disciples had failed to put the two things together. Jesus had alluded to their need to grow and develop their faith (see John 11:15). Their faith must grow from their just observing him to committing themselves to carry out His mandates. That is to say, rather than for them to focus on His whereabouts and seeing the Father, they must learn to take care of the matter at hand, increasing their faith. This session of preparation must be harnessed by their hearts if they were to become the distributors of the faith He had called them to be.

This study is divided into three parts. First, we observe Jesus' expressions of concern for them that guided this set of teachings. He defined loving Him as keeping His commandments. He also expressed concern for them that the Advocate that He would send would abide with them.

Second, Jesus promised that the Father's love would abide in them and keep them. It would be a triangular union and bond composed of them, Jesus, and the Father.

Finally, Jesus defined the role of the Spiritual Advocate that would help them to comprehend and call to mind His teachings. The presence of the Advocate in their hearts would be the granting of His blessing of peace upon them. However, these three things required them to be faithful. Faith is pertinent to the success of the mission they are about to embark upon. Without this type of faith, they would be unable to complete their mission.

EXPOSITION

I. EXPRESSIONS OF CONCERN (JOHN 14:15–19)

Jesus expressed concern for His disciples, repeatedly in John 14-16. He was going away to return to the Father and instructed them on how to carry on in anticipation of His physical absence. He assured them that whatever requests they made to the Father, in His name, that He would supply them (John 14:12–14). It is the "first mention of his name as the open sesame to the Father's will" (see also John 14;26; 15:16; 16:23, 24 26; also see, Archibald Thomas Robertson, *Word Pictures in the New Testament*. Volume V. *The Fourth Gospel. The Epistle to the Hebrews*. Broadman Press: Nashville, 1932, p. 251). These verses served as evidence of His concern for them and were based on His love for them as He seeks to eradicate any feelings of abandonment and uncertainty they may be experiencing concerning His departure. But this love is a two-way street. He loved them and expected them to demonstrate their love for Him as well. Loving Him is the equivalent of keeping His commandments. Love as used here is not a mere feeling of warmth, but is an action that transforms His words into purpose for their lives.

Notice the "*if*" in v. 15. "If you love me then this is the action that you will take (Greek: *ean agapate me*)." This statement also carries with it the sense of continuation (Greek: *teresate*). "Not only will you keep My commandments, but you will keep on keeping them." Robertson notes here that "Continued love prevents disobedience" (Ibid.). Their obedience and conformity to His recommendations for their lives will result in Jesus making supplication to the Father in their behalf (v. 16). He seems to be saying there is no greater or better way for me to show my concern for you other than to pray for you. These powerful words were meant to paint a picture of long-term divine care. Any sense of abandonment was erased as He promised to send Another (of a like kind) to walk by their side (Greek: *allon parakleton*).

Here Jesus introduces the Holy Spirit as their personal Advocate. The *Paracleton* is composed of two words: Para, meaning with and *kleton*, meaning walk. Taken together it is a legal term, such as an attorney, who accompanies one in a court of law. Gail O'Day suggests that whereas Jesus is specifically identified in the text as a *Paraclete* (see I John 2:1), the Holy Spirit as another *Paraclete* will continue the work of Jesus and walk beside the disciples as their Advocate (see Gail O'Day, *The New Interpreter's Bible : A Commentary in Twelve Volumes: Volume IX. Luke. John.* Abingdon Press: Nashville, 1995, p. 747). The word *paraclete* describes the work of the Spirit, which is a continuation of Jesus' work.

The Holy Spirit is also named the Spirit of Truth (Greek: to *pneuma tes aletheia*s; Robertson, Ibid. p. 251). Verse 17 is a throwback to John 1:10–13. Jesus issued a sad commentary of the world's inability and refusal to recognize its Creator, Sustainer, and Redeemer. The world could not receive the Spirit of truth and therefore, rejected Him because it did not have, nor did it desire to possess the spiritual acumen to distinguish His presence, just as it had rejected Jesus (v. 17). His point is clear, rejecting Him is the equivalent of rejecting the Father and the Holy Spirit. The converse is also true, to accept Him is to know the Father and the Holy Spirit, and to experience the indwelling of the same. Jesus' point is that the disciples will not be orphaned. Soon His earthly mission will be completed, and through their faith they will continue to experience His presence and power to go forth in His name. He will continue to be by their side and is their written guarantee that they will share with Him, for He lives forevermore.

II. A PROMISE MADE (JOHN 14:20–24)

The reference, "In that day" in v. 20 points to the New Dispensation of the Holy Spirit that will be unleashed at the resurrection of Jesus and more fully at Pentecost (see Acts 1–3). He will seal Jesus' promise to the disciples to create a triune relationship between them, Him, and the Father. This relationship is to be predicated on them loving Him and showing it through their keeping of His commandments (vv. 20–21). The risen Christ of God will be an authentic presence to the obedient and faithful believer. The key word that reflects the quality of this relationship is expressed in the term "know" (Greek: *yinosko*). Know, as used here (v. 20), means to have intimate knowledge of another, much like a husband knows his wife. To know Jesus is to be intimately involved with Him and to own (adopt) His vision for ministry to others. Jesus is the key link that places one in a similar relationship with the Father. Earlier in this chapter, Jesus scolded Philip for failing to realize the significance of His portrayal of the Father and the inseparable union between Father and Son (see John 14:8–11). The equation formula for this union is knowing and loving Jesus is to know the Father and the Holy Spirit, and to be known by them.

Jesus' comments here provoked a question from one of the disciples named Judas. It is the fourth time Jesus has been interrupted in this discourse (by Peter, 13:36; by Thomas, 14:5; by Philip, 14:8; by Judas 14:22; Ibid. p. 254). The writer is careful to point out that there are two people named Judas in the list of disciples. This Judas was better known as Thaddaeus, the brother of James (see Mark 3:17; Matthew 10:3; John 6:15; Acts 1:13). Judas asked Jesus about manifesting Himself to the world. The question is similar to one of the temptation narratives in Matthew 4:5–6 and Luke 4:9–10.

In these verses, Satan tempted Jesus to show His Sonship by encouraging Him to publicly reveal or manifest His power by throwing Himself down from the pinnacle of the temple. Jesus refused this temptation and He also refused to comply with Judas' suggestion. Jesus seemed to be saying that if the world did not receive Him during the time He ministered unto them as the Word made flesh, then it would likewise refuse to receive Him in any other time period or capacity. The key to receiving the spiritual manifestation is to love Jesus and to demonstrate that love through obedience to His commandments. Keeping His commandments, as a result of loving Him, is the mechanism that invites or welcomes the Father and the Son to abide in the heart through the coming of the Spirit (v. 23).

On the contrary, those who do not keep His words do not love Jesus and their actions prove it (v. 24).

III. THE ROLE OF THE COMFORTER (JOHN 14:25–29)

This section describes Jesus as the One who yet abides with the disciples. His instructions to them in this pericope of Scripture is His way of tying together the various emphases of this farewell discourse (see v. 25). He is the departing One, who currently walks besides (Greek: *Paraclete*) them giving them information that will be vital to their spiritual development as they make the transition. His departure is imminent as He makes way for the Holy Spirit (the other *Paraclete*) that is coming. The Holy Spirit will focus on helping them to recollect the teachings of Jesus.

Once again we can see continuity between Jesus and the Spirit. As such, the Holy Spirit will be sent by the Father, in the name of the Son, to reinforce and bring to mind Jesus' teachings. The Holy Spirit will do what Jesus did. His role is to keep the teachings of Jesus alive in the post-resurrection world. Beasley-Murray said, "Constantly in this Gospel Jesus is represented as the sent One of God, having His origin in God, a mission from God, and an authority from God [(John) 5:23, 24, 30, 37; 6:38–40; 7:16; 8:16, 18 26: 12:44–49]." "That the Spirit is sent by the Father carries similar implications" (George Beasley–Murray, *Word Biblical Commentary. Volume 36. John,* Word Book Publishers, Waco, p. 261).

Jesus gives the disciples His peace (Greek: *eirenen ten emen*). It is His bequest ("My peace") to the disciples before He departs to be with the Father. It is a spiritual peace that provides inner joy based upon a fuller understanding of His purpose (see Isaiah 9:6–7; 52:7; 57:19 Acts 10;36; Romans 14:17).

Jesus' act of self–sacrifice and pending resurrection and their faith in them will seal this sense of peace for them. His gift of peace lay in contrast to the promise of the world to provide a lasting peace, which is at most merely an apparition. The disciples can be assured that the God who sent Jesus with the mission to bring salvation to the world, remains in control of events, even though Jesus' departure is imminent. Although He is leaving, yet shall He be with them in terms of the sending of and prevalence of the Holy Spirit. Therefore, they should rejoice at His departure for it results in salvation for all who come to express faith in Him. Jesus remarked that the Father is greater than He. He bases this on being sent and directed to perform His tasks by the Father. He comes at the Father's command and is fully obedient to the Fathers directions. It is this same type of faithfulness that Jesus encourages the disciples to have, as they proceed in the ministry He has laid out for them.

The purpose of Jesus' discourse was to prepare His disciples for His physical departure and to assure them of His abiding presence with them. The discourse comes to its conclusion on the same note, "a word of assurance… to have faith" (Beasley-Murray, Ibid, p. 262). He has forewarned them of events that shall come to pass. They have received His assurance of His continued presence with them by way of the Spirit. He has done these things to propagate and strengthen their faith.

THE LESSON APPLIED

Jesus gives us Peace. We can see it clearly expressed in His discourse with His disciples. His earthly ministry is coming to an end. It is now their time to step out on the path He has laid out before them. If they keep His commandments and persevere in His Word, He promised to be with them and to send another *Paraclete* to walk besides them. He has laid the foundation for ministry that they are to build upon. He will likewise dwell with us as we carry His word of salvation to others.

LET'S TALK ABOUT IT

Why must our ministry be a continuation of the ministry of Jesus?

Simply put, we cannot save any one from sin and evil. Jesus is the Light of the world that dispels the darkness of sin and leads us to renewed fellowship with the Father. Therefore, faith in His work as the Word made flesh infuses us with His presence and power to keep His commandments, and qualifies us to extend the abundant and glorious life to others.

HOME DAILY DEVOTIONAL READINGS
AUGUST 1–7, 2022

MONDAY	TUESDAY	WEDNESDAY	THURSDAY	FRIDAY	SATURDAY	SUNDAY
The Lord, Our Dwelling Place	To Love God Is to Know God	Faith Is the Victory	God Will Do a New Thing	Come, You Who Thirst	More Than Conquerors	God Will Dwell with God's People
Psalm 90:1–12	1 John 2:12–17	1 John 5:1–5	Isaiah 43:14–21	Isaiah 55:1–5	Romans 8:31–39	Revelation 21:1–9

A NEW HOME

ADULT TOPIC:	BACKGROUND SCRIPTURE:
NO MORE TEARS	REVELATION 21:1–9

REVELATION 21:1–9

King James Version	*New Revised Standard Version*
AND I saw a new heaven and a new earth: for the first heaven and the first earth were passed away; and there was no more sea.	THEN I saw a new heaven and a new earth; for the first heaven and the first earth had passed away, and the sea was no more.
2 And I John saw the holy city, new Jerusalem, coming down from God out of heaven, prepared as a bride adorned for her husband.	2 And I saw the holy city, the new Jerusalem, coming down out of heaven from God, prepared as a bride adorned for her husband.
3 And I heard a great voice out of heaven saying, Behold, the tabernacle of God is with men, and he will dwell with them, and they shall be his people, and God himself shall be with them, and be their God.	3 And I heard a loud voice from the throne saying, "See, the home of God is among mortals. He will dwell with them; they will be his peoples, and God himself will be with them;
4 And God shall wipe away all tears from their eyes; and there shall be no more death, neither sorrow, nor crying, neither shall there be any more pain: for the former things are passed away.	4 he will wipe every tear from their eyes. Death will be no more;mourning and crying and pain will be no more, for the first things have passed away."
5 And he that sat upon the throne said, Behold, I make all things new. And he said unto me, Write: for these words are true and faithful.	5 And the one who was seated on the throne said, "See, I am making all things new." Also he said, "Write this, for these words are trustworthy and true."
6 And he said unto me, It is done. I am Alpha and Omega, the beginning and the end. I will give unto him that is athirst of the fountain of the water of life freely.	6 Then he said to me, "It is done! I am the Alpha and the Omega, the beginning and the end. To the thirsty I will give water as a gift from the spring of the water of life.
7 He that overcometh shall inherit all things; and I will be his God, and he shall be my son.	7 Those who conquer will inherit these things, and I will be their God and they will be my children.
8 But the fearful, and unbelieving, and the abominable, and murderers, and whoremongers, and sorcerers, and idolaters, and all liars, shall have their part in the lake which burneth with fire and brimstone: which is the second death.	8 But as for the cowardly, the faithless, the polluted, the murderers, the fornicators, the sorcerers, the idolaters, and all liars, their place will be in the lake that burns with fire and sulfur, which is the second death."

MAIN THOUGHT: And God shall wipe away all tears from their eyes; and there shall be no more death, neither sorrow, nor crying, neither shall there be any more pain: for the former things are passed away. (Revelation 21:4, KJV)

REVELATION 21:1–9

King James Version

New Revised Standard Version

9 And there came unto me one of the seven angels which had the seven vials full of the seven last plagues, and talked with me, saying, Come hither, I will shew thee the bride, the Lamb's wife.

9 Then one of the seven angels who had the seven bowls full of the seven last plagues came and said to me, "Come, I will show you the bride, the wife of the Lamb."

LESSON SETTING
Time: AD 95
Place: Aegean Isle of Patmos

LESSON OUTLINE
I. **Fulfillment of Heaven and Earth (Revelation 21:1–3)**
II. **Fulfillment of Believers (Revelation 21:4–8)**
III. **Fulfillment of New Jerusalem (Revelation 21:9)**

UNIFYING PRINCIPLE
People long for a place and time when life's stresses and death will not exist. Where can we find such a peaceful existence? The vision in Revelation 21 foretells that God will create a new heaven and earth where life's challenges will be banished forever.

INTRODUCTION
In this chapter, we are told that John sees a "new world," which he expresses as the new heaven and a new earth. This "new world" replaces the old one that has been marred by sin and that has disappeared (20:11). This description of the New Jerusalem will run from Revelation 21:9–22:5.

John, as a leader of the churches of Asia Minor, has been banished to the Aegean Isle of Patmos (a Roman political prison), as a sociopolitical and religious prisoner by the Roman ruler Domitian Caesar. It is in this pitiful prison context that John receives and writes his Apocalypse. Scholars suggest that John may have been put at the bottom of the mines to dig, given scanty clothes, limited water and food, and soon expected to die. Interestingly enough, John is the only disciple to die a natural death around the age of one hundred years old.

This type of Roman banishment was a very rigid penalty that included being held in caves, hard labor in rock quarries and being held in heavy chains. Domitian and other emperors seem to have no problem with this form of punishment. Domitian, according to early records, even banished his own wife Flavia Domitilla to the Isle of Patmos because of her Christian convictions and belief.

James Blevins, Greek and New Testament scholar notes that "God's people need to be freed from the 'gloom and doom' of Revelation and be challenged with the relevant message of victory and overcoming." It is to be clearly stated that John writes to Christians in very difficult circumstances. These first century Christians are in a setting of political turmoil and persecution for believing and confessing Christ Jesus as Lord. The Roman emperor Domitian, AD 81–96, desired worship and the Christian assertion that "Christ Jesus is Lord," was a grave offense and affront to Domitian. Scholars further note that Domitian even believed that he was divine and placed statues of himself all through the Roman Empire. This Caesar worship was utilized as a means to hold the distanced Roman Empire together and to procure loyalty to the Caesar.

Another aspect of persecution faced by the first century Christians was the demand of the Romans to curse the name of the Christ and declare, "Caesar is Lord." Some specific marking or tattoo was often placed on the person's hand upon participating in Caesar's worship and it appears that the marking or tattoo permitted people to buy food in the marketplace (Revelation 13).

Finally, it is important to note that Domitian, among other emperors, intended to abolish Christianity through organized means. So we must read and interpret Revelation as being written from a prison to people who were facing either prison or execution because of their refusal to compromise and bow down to Roman pressure and persecution. Revelation is a message of hope from a beloved disciple to other disciples seeking to remain true to their Christian beliefs in the midst of horrible persecution, pressure and horrific mistreatment.

When studying apocalyptic literature it must be remembered that this type of literature must be distinguished from other biblical genres and that there are a few important features that one must keep in mind. Apocalyptic literature arises from the exilic and post-exilic experience of the Jews. The word apocalyptic derives from the Greek word *apokalupsis* meaning to uncover, reveal or open up.

One of the characteristics of apocalyptic literature is its duality perspective as it relates to time. There exists the "present time" which normally is evil and under the control of evil (ruled by) and carries a fatalistic perspective in that not much can be done to redeem the time. Believers are afflicted and persecuted and some are condemned to death. Destruction, sorrow and death increase until the end of the age.

The next phase of time is what may be called the "golden period" or time. It is the time God will move to rid his people of this destruction and inaugurate this new age. This golden time is vividly described and displayed in apocalyptic literature. There will be a glorious depiction of heaven or a heavenly-like city and vision.

Another interesting facet of apocalyptic literature is the dualism of good and evil. There is a struggle between the good and the lesser power of evil. We see this aspect in Revelation 12 and Revelation 19. Satan is never on the level of God but fights to overturn and thwart the vision and plans of God.

Another aspect of this kind of literature is its dependence on visions. These visions are usually imparted to pseudonymic persons such as Abraham, Enoch, or Elijah. This reasoning and usage of these names serve to give the vision and the visionary experience authority. The content of these visions may be warfare concerning angels and the demons fighting against one another.

A major focus in apocalyptic literature is water, winds, location, and specific geography (places). Water is important because it symbolizes evil, barriers or hostile forces. The beast emerges from the water (sea). Locations are also symbolic and have meaning for instance the abyss (bottomless pit) is the residence of evil spirits, fallen angels. Both plagues and beasts seem to have their origin in the pit. Mountains are the place where visions occur; the New Jerusalem is the center of hope and promise in Revelation; the temple in Revelation is the center of action for many of the visions and the dwelling place of God. It is of critical significance as we examine the text to be familiar with and understand the codes in Revelation.

EXPOSITION

I. FULFILLMENT OF HEAVEN AND EARTH (REVELATION 21:1–3)

Here in these verses, we now enter into the third vision of John, which is directed to the redeemed and the righteous from the face of the earth. John speaks of a new heaven and a new earth. Because of the earth having fallen from humanity's sin, the earth will now share in humanity's judgment. John sees that the old earth will be transformed and rid of all its evil. The earth is redeemed just as humanity is redeemed.

The description of God's throne is given in chapter 5 and now we note that its beauty and peace encompass the complete universe. The sadness, sorrow, persecution and pain the believers have endured are now gone and the new age of overwhelming joy has come to the believers. The great harlot has perished, the beast has been destroyed, and Satan has been cast into the lake of fire. It is as though sunbeams are shining out of the dismal clouds of gray. Peace has begun to be the ruler of the day and there will be no more disasters such as earthquakes, floods, tornadoes, hurricanes, hail, storms, or drought. Creation will now exist as God originally intended from its beginning.

The New Jerusalem, the Holy City descends from heaven and represents the power and presence of God in his new creation. Similar to Genesis, God will once again walk in the midst of His people. Further, scholars note that the New Jerusalem may well represent the last of the temple themes. This temple theme has appeared in each of the seven sections of Revelation, and now has reached its completion. We see this idea in the fact that John tells the reader that there is now no need for a temple because God is in the midst of His people. The Holy of Holies coming to earth brings the realization that no fantastic temple facility is needed: "Behold, the dwelling of God is with men. He will dwell with them, and they shall be his people, and God himself will be with them" (21:).

II. FULFILLMENT OF BELIEVERS (REVELATION 21:4–8)

John's fourth vision comes in the shape of a series of personal assurances provided to the believers who will soon inherit the world. The first assurance is that pain, the old enemy of humanity, will cease or be no more. We all know the great physical and psychological affect of pain that accompanies disease or the pain and anguish associated with watching someone grapple and struggle with a terminal illness with which we can do nothing to aid them. The early believers experienced the horrible torment and pain that accompanies being burned alive, thrown to wild animals, and enduring accumulated afflictions.

Not only were these Christian martyrs persevering through physical pain, but also the mental pain and anguish of mourning the deaths of many believers, family and friends. In ancient Palestine, the process of mourning could last months and mourning responsibilities were assigned to the women (since they reasoned sin entered the world through women). Also Jewish women were often asked or in some instances hired to mourn publicly and to follow the deceased to the grave or tomb.

Paradise is such a grand promise because of what it does not have and because of the resolution and conclusion of humanity's pain and brokenness. This paradise contains our God who has from the beginning desired the redemption of both creation and humanity. God is seeking to redeem and restore the universe and create a world in which there remains no more pain and brokenness. Death itself has been conquered.

Thirst during biblical times was a great concern. Water has always been very difficult to come by in the region of Palestine. One should note the importance of water and that Revelation carries this theme emphasis throughout the book (rivers and springs of water). John presents God as the Alpha and Omega. As such, God is able to be the source of "living water" and quench forever all thirst.

Verse 8 contains a repeated assurance that all evil will be absent from the city. Note that all these listed evils are the results of following the beasts. John has at the top of the list "cowardly." Interestingly, those who celebrate with God in paradise are those who were not afraid to stand up to the beast and resist its evil influence. John calls on the believers to have the courage to stand up for their convictions and persevere. It has been stated that the coward is hated in every society. Those who do not shrink back from any risk related to discipleship populate the eternal paradise of God and they are willing to die for God's kingdom.

III. FULFILLMENT OF NEW JERUSALEM (REVELATION 21:9)

The center of attention in this fifth vision is the city itself, the New Jerusalem. The jasper make-up of the New Jerusalem has been previously mentioned in chapter 4, now we see that the city comes down from heaven with jasper being used as a symbol of God's glory and magnificent presence. Be reminded that the New Jerusalem is the Holy of Holies, God's dwelling place. God will "tabernacle" with us. This description of the city is intended to lift and sensitize God's people to His presence among them. So often after the storms of life are over, believers may have a tendency to "take His presence for common or for granted." This should never be the case for believers who have come through the difficulties of life by only His divine power.

LESSON APPLIED

As believers, we can only proceed through this Christian struggle by counting on the promises and assurances provided to and for us by our conquering God. Things are not going to be easy for us just because we are Christians. We have no exemption from the pain and brokenness of life. In fact, often the very reason we experience afflictions and tribulations is because we are believers. Many of our struggles will come because of what we speak and how we live, and we are required to step up and stand by courage for the convictions and confidence of our faith.

The early Christians needed a word of hopeful assurance that brought help and encouragement to them in the midst of their adversity and sorrow. Watching friends, family, and loved ones tortured, persecuted, boiled in vats of hot oil, fed to wild animals and torn asunder would be sufficient reason for the early martyrs to throw in the towel. Yet, God gives to John a word of fulfillment and encouragement about the new age, the new believers and the New Jerusalem.

This word of hope encapsulated in the visions of John is not for everyone. These visions are for the redeemed, who despite trouble and sorrow, continue to stand and persevere. The lavish picture of the new earth and New Jerusalem is one of peace and tranquility. Satan is a defeated foe. The earth has been purged of all its evil and transformed. Even as humanity has been redeemed, so has the earth. No more earthquakes, floods, tornadoes, hurricanes, hailstorms, or drought. Creation is as it was created to be.

Another much needed assurance is that humanity's old enemy pain will be no more. Pain, mental anguish, weeping and thirst shall all be done away with. What a great encouragement to know that the reward for faithfulness is the banishing of all that would disturb our peace in paradise. Although a broad assurance, it is also a narrow assurance. John warns that the cowardly won't be in the number of those who persevered and won the prize. We must be ever so careful not to allow external circumstances to derail our faith in God.

The next vision is the climax of the "temple ideology." The New Jerusalem is coming down and the appearance is of clear jasper, having the glory of God. The Holy of Holies, the dwelling place of God is now among His people. There will be no need for a temple because God tabernacles with His people. God's presence is promised among His people.

LET'S TALK ABOUT IT

We often talk of the perfect vacation and what that would do for our bodies and minds. Have you ever contemplated what paradise with God would be like?

Death will be destroyed and there will be no more decay, sorrow, sadness, and mourning. Renewal, restoration, peace, and unabated intimacy with our King will be the feature of our new existence. We will live in complete victory and the joy of His presence. We are rewarded with tranquility because we didn't cower, but stood boldly for what we believe and whom we serve. As you contemplate paradise, please know that it will be a much better than a vacation. It will be living in the joy of the Lord's presence and power for eternity.

HOME DAILY DEVOTIONAL READINGS
AUGUST 8–14, 2022

MONDAY	TUESDAY	WEDNESDAY	THURSDAY	FRIDAY	SATURDAY	SUNDAY
You Shall Be Comforted in Jerusalem	God's Glory Revealed in Jerusalem	City of the Living God	Jerusalem, Joy of All the Earth	The Faithful City, the Holy Mountain	God, Who Dwells in Unapproachable Light	The Holy City
Isaiah 66:6–14	Isaiah 66:18–22	Hebrews 12:18–29	Psalm 48	Zechariah 8:1–8	1 Timothy 6:11–16	Revelation 21:10–21

A NEW CITY

| ADULT TOPIC:
NO PLACE LIKE IT | BACKGROUND SCRIPTURE:
REVELATION 21:10–27 |

REVELATION 21:10–21

King James Version	*New Revised Standard Version*
AND he carried me away in the spirit to a great and high mountain, and shewed me that great city, the holy Jerusalem, descending out of heaven from God,	AND in the spirit he carried me away to a great, high mountain and showed me the holy city Jerusalem coming down out of heaven from God.
11 Having the glory of God: and her light was like unto a stone most precious, even like a jasper stone, clear as crystal;	11 It has the glory of God and a radiance like a very rare jewel, like jasper, clear as crystal.
12 And had a wall great and high, and had twelve gates, and at the gates twelve angels, and names written thereon, which are the names of the twelve tribes of the children of Israel:	12 It has a great, high wall with twelve gates, and at the gates twelve angels, and on the gates are inscribed the names of the twelve tribes of the Israelites;
13 On the east three gates; on the north three gates; on the south three gates; and on the west three gates.	13 on the east three gates, on the north three gates, on the south three gates, and on the west three gates.
14 And the wall of the city had twelve foundations, and in them the names of the twelve apostles of the Lamb.	14 And the wall of the city has twelve foundations, and on them are the twelve names of the twelve apostles of the Lamb.
15 And he that talked with me had a golden reed to measure the city, and the gates thereof, and the wall thereof.	15 The angel who talked to me had a measuring rod of gold to measure the city and its gates and walls.
16 And the city lieth foursquare, and the length is as large as the breadth: and he measured the city with the reed, twelve thousand furlongs. The length and the breadth and the height of it are equal.	16 The city lies foursquare, its length the same as its width; and he measured the city with his rod, fifteen hundred miles; its length and width and height are equal.
17 And he measured the wall thereof, an hundred and forty and four cubits, according to the measure of a man, that is, of the angel.	17 He also measured its wall, one hundred forty-four cubits by human measurement, which the angel was using.
18 And the building of the wall of it was of jasper: and the city was pure gold, like unto clear glass.	18 The wall is built of jasper, while the city is pure gold, clear as glass.
19 And the foundations of the wall of the city were garnished with all manner of precious	19 The foundations of the wall of the city are adorned with every jewel; the first was jasper,

MAIN THOUGHT: And the wall of the city had twelve foundations, and in them the names of the twelve apostles of the Lamb. (Revelation 21:14, KJV)

REVELATION 21:10–21

King James Version	New Revised Standard Version
stones. The first foundation was jasper; the second, sapphire; the third, a chalcedony; the fourth, an emerald;	the second sapphire, the third agate, the fourth emerald,
20 The fifth, sardonyx; the sixth, sardius; the seventh, chrysolyte; the eighth, beryl; the ninth, a topaz; the tenth, a chrysoprasus; the eleventh, a jacinth; the twelfth, an amethyst.	20 the fifth onyx, the sixth carnelian, the seventh chrysolite, the eighth beryl, the ninth topaz, the tenth chrysoprase, the eleventh jacinth, the twelfth amethyst.
21 And the twelve gates were twelve pearls: every several gate was of one pearl: and the street of the city was pure gold, as it were transparent glass.	21 And the twelve gates are twelve pearls, each of the gates is a single pearl, and the street of the city is pure gold, transparent as glass.

LESSON SETTING
Time: AD 95
Place: Aegean Isle of Patmos

LESSON OUTLINE
I. **The City Described (Revelation 21:10–14)**
II. **The City Described Further (Revelation 21:15–21)**

UNIFYING PRINCIPLE

It is difficult for people to imagine living in a place that is totally different from the one in which they presently live. What will the new place be like? Revelation 21 uses figurative language to describe the brilliant new city God will create.

INTRODUCTION

In the previous lesson on Revelation 21:1–9, the reader gets a clear glimpse of the Christian believers' destiny as the redeemed of God. Ray Summers, notes that this was the main thing that the Christians of the first century as a whole and those who in subsequent days desired to know.

Summers continues further by asserting that the believer's destiny is shown to us in three symbols to reveal the perfect condition of the redeemed. Heaven is depicted from three different perspectives. There is the Fellowship with God (21:1–8), Protection from God (21:9–26) and Provisions from God (22: 1–5). Our lesson today will focus on the protection we have from God.

This section of Revelation gives an extended discussion on the aspects of the New Jerusalem as the eternal dwelling place of God with His people. Proverbs strengthens this discussion by asserting, "God's delight is with the sons of men" (Proverbs 8:31). As we examine this section of Revelation, we are challenged to view this section in light of God's desire for His people and the love God has, which results in God bringing them back to the original status of undeterred communion and fellowship. We readily see the continuation of this theme in Revelation 21:3. Three times the phrase *with men* is used in one verse. God is revealing His love that surpasses all understanding to His creation by positioning them again to share transcendent, unbothered, and joyful fellowship with their Creator and God.

Another aspect of the theme of fellowship is the symbolic usage of the tabernacle. The tabernacle is the first symbol noted and is symbolic of perfect or complete fellowship. Ray Summers makes the comment that God's place of abode was with His people in the wilderness, so the new heaven and the new earth will be His abode with them throughout eternity.

Another faucet of this revealed fellowship consists of the divine intimacy noted by John in that he sees that "the sea is no more." Here John is articulating that the divide that has caused separation is no longer existent and there can now be no separation between God and His people. The New Jerusalem is the place where the tabernacle has become the place of translucent intimacy.

John lifts a particular mode of action to signify the level of care God generously shares with His people. Tears are wiped away and He erases forever crying, mourning, pain, and death. God then instructs John to encourage the readers by reminding the readers who it was that spoke these words to him. God through John reminds the first century readers of Who it was that made these promises—the Alpha and Omega who has the power to perform them.

EXPOSITION

I. THE CITY DESCRIBED (REVELATION 21:10–14)

One of the messengers with the seven bowls again comes in (21:9–10) to give a detailed description on Jerusalem, the Holy City. The physical features are given first (21:11–21). Then (21:22–27) we are told of the lighting of the New Jerusalem as it influences the nations. Finally, John concludes with the description of the inner workings of the city as it involves all who now inhabit the city. There are three things we know about this heavenly Jerusalem: it is a literal city, it has an object of attraction and affection along with a destiny, and it has relational continuity with the earth.

With these verses, we now turn our attention to the city, which John symbolically uses to represent perfect protection. One of the angels of the seven last plagues approaches John to provide him with a more detailed description of the New Jerusalem. This lengthy section is a continuation of the prior announcement of her arrival in 21:2. The description of the bridge here may be considered as a possible description of the millennial kingdom. Robert Thomas asserts that this description made it much easier to harmonize certain features of the city with assumed conditions in the eternal state.

In verse 9, John says that the angel guide, who had one of the seven bowls, which were full of the seven last plagues, came, and spoke with him. The similarity of these statements (17:1 and 21:9) reveals the parallelism between this passage about the bride and the earlier one. The idea is that a person cannot inhabit both cities; a choice must be made between them.

Scholars disagree as to if this angel is the same messenger that John speaks of in 17:1. Some scholars affirm that this angel is the same angel who guided John previously in 17:1; others disagree. While we are not completely sure on this matter, the point of the passage is that there is a continuation of the bowl visions occurring in 16:1–22:5.

One point of note in this final vision of the bride is the comparison to the great harlot city of the beast. God's people are both the bride and wife of the Lamb. As bride, the church is pure and lovely, and as wife enjoys the intimacy of the Lamb.

This is in drastic contrast to the great city of the beast, Babylon. Verses 10–14 are one compound sentence in the Greek text. John seems to be in a spiritual or prophetic trance and is transported by the angel. This is a fresh vision with a new transport of ecstasy (Ezekiel 3:14).

John's new destination is " a great and high mountain" as opposed to the wilderness as in John 17:3. This is not Mt. Zion because the New Jerusalem is visible from this mountain; rather it appears to be a high vantage point in John's visional experience from which he is able to see the site and the buildings of the city. This speaks to the need for John to have an appropriate vantage point from which he can see the descent of the eternal order. John was taken to the wilderness (desert) to behold the wicked Babylon, but it is from a high mountain that he views the New Jerusalem. Mountains have always been an important part of Jewish thought. Moses receives the commandments on Mt. Sinai and Ezekiel's vision of the temple and land restoration was provided to him "on a very high mountain" (Ezekiel 40:1–2).

In the verses that follow, we are given the physical features (appearance, structure, dimension, and construction materials) of the New Jerusalem. John says that the city was arrayed with God's glory. This brilliance of glow (light) was like a precious stone, as a crystal. This is not a divinely caused splendor, but rather it is the splendor of the presence of God Himself, the *Shekinah*. His very presence dwells in the Holy City, which is the bride of the Lamb. Other references to the radiant splendor of God in Scripture are Exodus 40:34; Numbers 9:15–23, 1 Kings 8:11; 2 Chronicles 5:14; Isaiah 24:33; 60:1; John 12:42; Acts 26:13.

The city wall and gates are described next. It is a massive high wall that is not for the purpose of imminent protection for the city because there are no enemies from which to defend it. Rather, the wall then is a symbol of the eternal security of the city's population. Verse 18 tells us that wall is made of jasper as is the first foundation (19), making it resemble the glory of God. Next, we encounter the twelve gates or "gate towers." In Revelation 21–22 we note references to "gate towers" of the city walls eleven times. These twelve gates in the plural designate access and entrances to the city. The twelve angels are positioned at the twelve gates as watchmen to reinforce the idea of security. They are posted at the gates to "keep watch" and to keep all impurity from the city. The names of the twelve tribes of Israel are inscribed on the gates according to the plan in Ezekiel 48:31–34 and there is one name on every gate. The inscription is a reminder of the description on the high priest's breastplate in Exodus 28:9, 29: 39:14. This inscription is an explicit notice of the distinction of Israel's role in the eternal city in fulfillment of their role in history throughout the centuries of their existence.

John sees twelve gates with each section of the city having three gates (v. 13). Through these gates the tribes go out to their allotted possession (land). John's vision is that the gates bear the names of the twelve tribes and are entrances for all the peoples of the earth whose names are written in the Lamb's Book of Life (Revelation 24–27). There are twelve gates in this city and the number twelve here is symbolic of abundant entrance. The reference to the twelve tribes here is a continuation of the theme that the New Testament church with God's people is connected to the Old Testament times.

Similarly, the wall of the city has twelve foundations, and the twelve names of the Lamb's apostles are on them. A perfect foundation cannot be shaken. We are reminded in Ephesians 2:20 that the household of God is built upon the foundation of the apostles and prophets. The church rests upon the labor and faith of those who first proclaimed the Gospel message. The connecting of the twelve tribes and the twelve apostles points to the unity of ancient Israel and the New Testament church.

II. THE CITY DESCRIBED FURTHER (REVELATION 21:15–21)

Verses 15–17 are descriptive of the measuring of the heavenly city. In Revelation 11 John is told to measure the temple, but in the passage the angel uses a golden reed (staff) slightly more than ten feet in length to measure the city (Ezekiel 40–41; Zechariah 2:1–5). The measuring of the city seems to portray the vast size and completed symmetry of the eternal dwelling place of the faithful.

The city is "foursquare" or "four cornered." The city is perfectly square, height, breadth, and length measures 12,000 furlongs (v. 16). This could mean that the city was laid out in a square pattern, but it is more likely that this refers to a three-dimensional form similar to a cube with equal dimensions. This shape is reminiscent of the shape of the inner sanctuary of the temple in 1 Kings 6:20. The angel measured the city and found it to be 12000 stadia or 1400–1500 hundred miles in each direction. The number 12000 is the multiple number of two complete numbers 12 and 1000. Here the implication is that of perfection and completeness. There will be perfect room for all the redeemed. This description of the city presents a spacious, beautiful and complete city, where God's redeemed will dwell with Him in undeterred fellowship.

In Revelation 21:17, the angel measures the wall and finds it to be 144 cubits; scholars differ on if this measurement is thickness or height, but it most likely refers to the width. The point here is 144 is a multiple of twelve and has to do with the people of God and their sanctuary. The angel measures the wall, but utilizes a human standard in doing so.

In the next verse, John addresses the materials used to construct the city. The wall had jasper built in and the city was pure gold like glass. Here we are to note the splendor and worth of the wall. In Revelation 4:3, the One who sits on the throne appears like jasper and earlier in Revelation 21 the Holy City is glistening with the glory of God and the radiance is as of jasper (v. 11). The implication in verse 18 is that even the wall of the city speaks of the glorious presence of God.

In Revelation 21:19–20, John returns to the city foundations and advises that the foundations of the city are "adorned" or that each foundation consisted of one of the twelve stones. There are twelve precious stones mentioned ranging in general colors from white, blue, green, topaz, red, and yellow. Most, if not all of the "precious stones," correspond to those in the breastplate of the high priest (Exodus 28:17–20; 39:10; Isaiah 54:11–12; Ezekiel 28:13).

This symbolism points to the reserved right given only to the high priest alone now being freely given to the entire people of God. The picture being presented here is of a city of brilliant gold surrounded by a wall inlaid with jasper and resting upon twelve foundations adorned with precious gems of every color and complexion. This city of God is beautiful beyond description. As the eternal dwelling place of God and His people, it is described in language that continually attempts to break free from its own limitations to do justice to the experience it describes.

Finally, we have the description of the twelve gates mentioned in vv. 12–13, each gate is inscribed with the name of a tribe of Israel. These gates were carved from a single pearl. Among the ancients pearls were ranked highest among the precious stones, because their beauty originated from nature. In the New Testament, pearls were for the wealthier demographic (Matthew 7:6; 1 Timothy 2:9; Revelation 18:12), and was one of the great valuables in the Roman culture. The street of the city is said to be pure gold, like transparent glass. The street (streets or public square) is constructed of gold so pure that it seemed transparent. Similar to the priests of the Old Testament (1 Kings 6:30) who ministered in the temple, the servants of God will walk upon gold.

THE LESSON APPLIED

Being a Christian does not exempt the believer from the worst that life has to offer. Christians often go through additional trials because of their beliefs. This lesson is a vision to be shared for the encouragement and edification of those who need beauty in the midst of ashes. The early church needed a word of help, hope, and healing in the midst of martyrdom, persecution and punishment for wedding the Christ. John is carried to a high mountain to see the city coming down from heaven with its brilliant glory and radiance. We as believers have to possess a perspective and mentality that is "from above" and not below. The Spirit of God can only give this mentality or attitude to us. Faith and trust in Him through suffering will redeem the Church and make her beautiful and acceptable to Him.

LET'S TALK ABOUT IT

How can we buttress our faith and convictions to stay in the Christian race and receive His grace?

When life rips us it is good to have a vision beyond the present pain and anguish we suffer and it is good to know that we will be received there not by merit but by mercy. John encourages us to remember that our labor is not in vain and one day we will dwell with God undeterred in that New Jerusalem.

HOME DAILY DEVOTIONAL READINGS
AUGUST 15–21, 2022

MONDAY	TUESDAY	WEDNESDAY	THURSDAY	FRIDAY	SATURDAY	SUNDAY
My Soul Thirsts for You	Living Waters Shall Flow from Jerusalem	Jesus Promises Living Water	Worship God in Spirit and Truth	Rivers of Living Water	Water on the Thirsty Land	For the Healing of the Nations
Psalm 63	Zechariah 14:6–11	John 4:4–14	John 4:15–26	John 7:37–40	Isaiah 44:1–8	Revelation 22:1–9

THE RIVER OF LIFE

ADULT TOPIC:	BACKGROUND SCRIPTURE:
NO BETTER REFRESHMENT	REVELATION 22:1–7

REVELATION 22:1–7

King James Version

AND he shewed me a pure river of water of life, clear as crystal, proceeding out of the throne of God and of the Lamb.

2 In the midst of the street of it, and on either side of the river, was there the tree of life, which bare twelve manner of fruits, and yielded her fruit every month: and the leaves of the tree were for the healing of the nations.

3 And there shall be no more curse: but the throne of God and of the Lamb shall be in it; and his servants shall serve him:

4 And they shall see his face; and his name shall be in their foreheads.

5 And there shall be no night there; and they need no candle, neither light of the sun; for the Lord God giveth them light: and they shall reign for ever and ever.

6 And he said unto me, These sayings are faithful and true: and the Lord God of the holy prophets sent his angel to shew unto his servants the things which must shortly be done.

7 Behold, I come quickly: blessed is he that keepeth the sayings of the prophecy of this book.

New Revised Standard Version

THEN the angel showed me the river of the water of life, bright as crystal, flowing from the throne of God and of the Lamb

2 through the middle of the street of the city. On either side of the river is the tree of life with its twelve kinds of fruit, producing its fruit each month; and the leaves of the tree are for the healing of the nations.

3 Nothing accursed will be found there any more. But the throne of God and of the Lamb will be in it, and his servants will worship him;

4 they will see his face, and his name will be on their foreheads.

5 And there will be no more night; they need no light of lamp or sun, for the Lord God will be their light, and they will reign forever and ever.

6 And he said to me, "These words are trustworthy and true, for the Lord, the God of the spirits of the prophets, has sent his angel to show his servants what must soon take place."

7 "See, I am coming soon! Blessed is the one who keeps the words of the prophecy of this book."

MAIN THOUGHT: And he shewed me a pure river of water of life, clear as crystal, proceeding out of the throne of God and of the Lamb. (Revelation 22:1, KJV)

LESSON SETTING
Time: AD 95
Place: Aegean Isle of Patmos

LESSON OUTLINE
I. The Character of the City
   (Revelation 22:1–5)
II. Confirmation of His Blessing
   (Revelation 22:6–7)

UNIFYING PRINCIPLE
Rivers give life and nourishment to the things that exist around them. How do rivers nourish our lives? In God's new creation, God's power will be in the river, nourishing and healing people and nations in the New Jerusalem.

INTRODUCTION

Today's lesson is a reminder that the Lamb and the Father have supplied all we shall need to sustain eternal life. It is a word for those longing to know about the restoration of their future and the lesson encourages us to be assured and know that Heaven is a place of perfect fellowship, perfect protection, perfect provision, and perfect service. Note in this passage that there is great distinction between the destiny of the wicked and the destiny of the redeemed.

The first five verses lift the idea that through God's loving redemption the new creation will return to the Garden of Eden experience; to the Creator's original design and humanity will return to the original purpose of God. These verses will encourage the reader to remember that God promises to nurture and sustain His redeemed as they are in His presence serving Him.

The last two verses confirm the truth of verses 1-5 and verify that God will make all of His blessed action transparent to the faithful. Then the writer confirms the necessity of keeping the words of this prophecy. They are blessed if they maintain their faithfulness.

EXPOSITION

I. THE CHARACTER OF THE CITY (REVELATION 22:1–5)

Verses 1–5 cover thematically and symbolically the fulfillment of the divine life seen and recorded by John. In this seventh vision, we note John's dependence on the Garden of Eden narrative in Genesis, Ezekiel's river vision, and the focus and utilization of the river of life. In this final discourse about the Holy City, we have a perspective that focuses on the attributes of the city as they relate to the city's occupants. The unimaginable blessings of Eden have been restored to its original purpose and purity.

John is shown a pollution-free sparkling river that flows from the throne of God and of the Lamb. It is a throwback to Ezekiel 47:1–12. In these verses, Ezekiel has a vision of the sacred river. This river flowed from under the threshold of the temple eastward beyond the altar and eventually into the Dead Sea. As a result, the Dead Sea was healed and made less salty such that many fish could again live in its waters. There are also other passages which denote a similar theme (see Zechariah 14:8 and Joel 3:18. In Joel 3:18, there is a fountain in the midst of the house of the Lord that is to provide water for Shittim).

This theme "springs of water of life" is the first feature we are given and are listed in 7:17; 21:6 and 22:17. "Springs of water of life" has been a constant theme in revelation as an important element in the blessings of the destiny of the redeemed. Scholars in a variety of ways have interpreted the imagery of "flowing water." Some of the scholars interpret "flowing water" as symbolizing the Holy Spirit. Others have noted it as the promise of immortality. Still others have leaned more toward seeing "flowing water" as a reference to abundant life that God has provided and now gives to His people. All these are true in some capacity, however, the central or core affirmation of the verse is that in the eternal state the faithful will be provided for, and live at the source of the life-giving stream which originates from the presence of God. Those who lived in hot and dry Palestine would relish this reality. Water, in such areas, was hard to come by and a precious commodity of renewal, refreshing and life survival.

John also describes the water as "clear as crystal" (v. 1). There is no contamination from the Source or its flow. The two words used here in the Greek *lampos* and *krystallos* are never used together except in this passage. Together they denote that the river as a type sparkling and shimmering stream of water passing over the mountains and rocks. It is unpolluted and the river rushes pure from its Source. The river's Source is the throne of God in 7:15 and 12:5, but here in verse 1, the sacrificial Lamb has been given a place of honor to share and because of His sacrificial death He is worthy of heavenly praise (see Revelation 5:9–15).

The River of Life flows down the middle of the main street and on either side of it is the Tree of Life, which bears twelve kinds of fruit every month and whose leaves are good for healing the nations. The phraseology here of the location of the water and the tree are not clear but denotes the centrality of eternal life in the New Jerusalem. We see this verse and immediately reference the tree in the Garden of Eden, which was lost to humanity as the result of the sin that was committed (Genesis 2:9; 3:22). In Ezekiel 47:12, we further note the vision there of healing water originating from the temple to form a river along the banks where the trees bring forth new fruit each month and their leaves are used for healing. It appears that the Tree of Life was a regular component of Jewish portrayals of paradise and to eat the Tree of Life fruit mentioned earlier would cause an individual to live forever. In John's vision, this tree produces twelve kinds of fruit, yielding a fresh crop monthly. What are we to take from this passage? The passage is trying to express that God's provision is always new and fresh and always more than adequate for any un-met needs.

John describes the leaves of the tree as being good for the healing of the nation. This healing seems to be for those who have entered the city with maladies suffered prior to entry. This healing is for the perpetuation of good health. The healings indicate the complete absence of physical and spiritual want. Even in health, the life to come will be a life of abundance and perfection.

In verses three and four, John continues his description of Paradise and its contents. John's next descriptive item is not what is present, but what is absent. As John continues the contrast between the life in this age and the age to come, he says there will no longer be any curse (Zechariah 14:11). Because of the presence of God, a tremendous transformation has taken place. The previous age was characterized by evil, sin, and other issues that reside under the category of cursed. This phrase "the throne of God and of the Lamb will be in the city" is here again repeated (21:3) because it most likely is the central theme of this new age.

John reports that as a result of the new age being without distraction and the accursed, His servants will serve Him. This is because the chief joy of the redeemed is the Redeemer. As a result of their experiencing the chief joy as God's servants, they now are caught up in the service of worship they render to their Redeemer.

Verse 4 is clear that they (the redeemed believers) shall see His face. The fulfillment of their hope and one of the objectives of one's salvation throughout the Scriptures has now been realized. This is an incredible word because throughout biblical record one is reminded that God mediated His presence to humanity in several different ways.

In the Old Testament, God used dreams, theophanies, the prophetic Word, and angels to meet with humanity. For humanity, to meet with God face to face would be certain death (see Exodus 33:20). In the New Testament, the Incarnation fleshes out the presence of God in the person of Jesus (Matthew 1:23). Jesus says that to know and see Him is to know and see the Father (John 14:7, 9; 17:3). Scholars agree that although this is a "perfect" manifestation of God, it is still a mediated one and could only be received by faith. However, according to the text in the age to come, faith will give way to sight (Psalm 17:15; Matthew 5:8; 1 John 3:2), and we shall behold His face. Not only will we see Him, but His stamp of ownership will identify us as His children. "His Name shall be on their foreheads" is a phrase that indicates the believers' affinity and full or perfect possession by God. As those who follow the beast were marked, so then will the faithful bear the name of God upon their foreheads (Revelation 13:16).

As the depiction of the "paradise restored" closes, verse 5 contains a previously repeated promise that the presence of God will illuminate the city. This seems to point back to Isaiah 60:19, 20 where the sun and moon are replaced with the eternal light of the glory of God (Revelation 21:23). It is not clear over who the believers will reign, but the text clearly points out like the martyrs of Revelation 20:4, 6, these inhabitants of the Holy City will share the office of Christ and reign eternally (Daniel 7: 18, 27; Revelation 5:10).

II. CONFIRMATION OF HIS BLESSING (REVELATION 22:6–7)

The closing words of this text are verifications of the truth that the aforementioned things in Revelation 22:1–5 will take place. The holy One of God speaks to the Johannine writer and demonstrates divine activity to reinforce His words. God revealed to the servants the procedural actions that must take place in order for the vision to be enacted. The holy One then announces He is coming quickly. The idea expressed here is that of preparation. Believers do not have time to waste; the Lord Jesus will act and act decisively. He will be coming to receive those to whom He promised to prepare a place for as noted in John 14:6, and others who have climbed up the rough side of the mountain (see Revelation 14:13). However, there is an additional thing believers are compelled to do as they prepare for and await His coming. They must keep the "sayings of the prophecy of this book" (v. 7). In the Gospel of John, in Jesus' Farewell Discourse, the disciples are strongly encouraged to keep Jesus' commandments, if they are to receive the Father and to be known by Him. Here the text expresses the same type of sentiment. Keeping His words are the equivalent of loving Him and His Spirit abiding in the believers' heart.

THE LESSON APPLIED

As believers, we are often faced with the disappointments of life. We are often told one thing, but given something completely different. The world and all its fallen humanity make believe that things change and that things work out very differently. How many times have we gotten our hopes up only for them to be shattered? Promises made and promises broken have been the story of many believers. The good news for our journey and encouragement is found in Revelation 22.

As the Revelation closes, the divine providence of God is shown by restoring all that have missed the mark back to its original purpose. We are to be encouraged by examining the contents of the Holy City. There in the Holy City is a river of living water, a tree that bears twelve manners of fruit every month, and the leaves of which are good for the therapeutic healing of nations. Believers are encouraged to see that God and the Lamb who sit on the throne have satisfied every need they may have.

We are also told that the Holy City will be a pollution and sin free environment and nothing there will be accursed. The believers will be marked on their foreheads, symbolizing that they are fully possessed by God. They will not need the sun or the moon because John says, "that Lord God will provide their light and they shall see Him face to face." What an astonishing reality they will experience, the glory of God wrapped in the truth of His presence for all to enjoy and partake of. Revelation 22:6–7 confirms the validity this vision that it will happened as prophesied. The one thing the believer must do is to prepare by keeping these words and holding them dear to the heart.

Let's Talk About It

What is the significance of God's satisfying presence in the midst of down times.

Someone has said, "One moment in God's Kingdom will pay for it all." This is a true statement. What John describes in this chapter is a city that is above all other cities. It is a heavenly city made for the Christ of God, filled with those who have forsaken all other allegiances to commit themselves to worship and praise the Lord their God.

We have here a description of beauty, holiness, and splendor. Human sin and its evil twin will be totally abolished. Not only will the city be a marvelous sight to behold, but we can look forward to inhabiting it because God has promised our complete healing, fulfillment, and restoration. Believers will not need the sun or the moon because the Lord God's holy presence will light the city. We will be able to fellowship with God, not by meditated means, but rather directly face-to-face. Our restoration is definitely worth the wait.

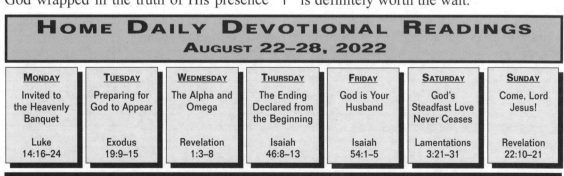

HOME DAILY DEVOTIONAL READINGS
AUGUST 22–28, 2022

MONDAY	TUESDAY	WEDNESDAY	THURSDAY	FRIDAY	SATURDAY	SUNDAY
Invited to the Heavenly Banquet	Preparing for God to Appear	The Alpha and Omega	The Ending Declared from the Beginning	God is Your Husband	God's Steadfast Love Never Ceases	Come, Lord Jesus!
Luke 14:16–24	Exodus 19:9–15	Revelation 1:3–8	Isaiah 46:8–13	Isaiah 54:1–5	Lamentations 3:21–31	Revelation 22:10–21

COME AND ENJOY

ADULT TOPIC: NO SUBSTITUTE	BACKGROUND SCRIPTURE: REVELATION 22:8–21

REVELATION 22:10–21

King James Version

AND he saith unto me, Seal not the sayings of the prophecy of this book: for the time is at hand.

11 He that is unjust, let him be unjust still: and he which is filthy, let him be filthy still: and he that is righteous, let him be righteous still: and he that is holy, let him be holy still.

12 And, behold, I come quickly; and my reward is with me, to give every man according as his work shall be.

13 I am Alpha and Omega, the beginning and the end, the first and the last.

14 Blessed are they that do his commandments, that they may have right to the tree of life, and may enter in through the gates into the city.

15 For without are dogs, and sorcerers, and whoremongers, and murderers, and idolaters, and whosoever loveth and maketh a lie.

16 I Jesus have sent mine angel to testify unto you these things in the churches. I am the root and the offspring of David, and the bright and morning star.

17 And the Spirit and the bride say, Come. And let him that heareth say, Come. And let him that is athirst come. And whosoever will, let him take the water of life freely.

18 For I testify unto every man that heareth the words of the prophecy of this book, If any man shall add unto these things, God shall add unto him the plagues that are written in this book:

New Revised Standard Version

AND he said to me, "Do not seal up the words of the prophecy of this book, for the time is near.

11 Let the evildoer still do evil, and the filthy still be filthy, and the righteous still do right, and the holy still be holy."

12 "See, I am coming soon; my reward is with me, to repay according to everyone's work.

13 I am the Alpha and the Omega, the first and the last, the beginning and the end."

14 Blessed are those who wash their robes, so that they will have the right to the tree of life and may enter the city by the gates.

15 Outside are the dogs and sorcerers and fornicators and murderers and idolaters, and everyone who loves and practices falsehood.

16 "It is I, Jesus, who sent my angel to you with this testimony for the churches. I am the root and the descendant of David, the bright morning star."

17 The Spirit and the bride say, "Come." And let everyone who hears say, "Come." And let everyone who is thirsty come. Let anyone who wishes take the water of life as a gift.

18 I warn everyone who hears the words of the prophecy of this book: if anyone adds to them, God will add to that person the plagues described in this book;

MAIN THOUGHT: For I testify unto every man that heareth the words of the prophecy of this book, If any man shall add unto these things, God shall add unto him the plagues that are written in this book: And if any man shall take away from the words of the book of this prophecy, God shall take away his part out of the book of life, and out of the holy city, and from the things which are written in this book. (Revelation 22:18–19, KJV)

REVELATION 22:10–21

King James Version

19 And if any man shall take away from the words of the book of this prophecy, God shall take away his part out of the book of life, and out of the holy city, and from the things which are written in this book.

20 He which testifieth these things saith, Surely I come quickly. Amen. Even so, come, Lord Jesus.

21 The grace of our Lord Jesus Christ be with you all. Amen.

New Revised Standard Version

19 if anyone takes away from the words of the book of this prophecy, God will take away that person's share in the tree of life and in the holy city, which are described in this book.

20 The one who testifies to these things says, "Surely I am coming soon." Amen. Come, Lord Jesus!

21 The grace of the Lord Jesus be with all the saints. Amen

LESSON SETTING
Time: AD 95
Place: Aegean Isle of Patmos

LESSON OUTLINE
I. Remain As You Are!
(Revelation 22:10–13)
II. Identifying Who's Who
(Revelation 22:14–16)
III. The Testimonies
(Revelation 22:17–21)

UNIFYING PRINCIPLE
Everything has a beginning and an end. What is the source and ultimate purpose of human life? Revelation affirms that God, who is the Alpha and Omega, creates and controls all things.

INTRODUCTION
The drama is now coming to an end and the final curtain has come down. We have learned of God's providential care for the believers, the assurance of the believer's triumph in terrible existent conditions and conflict, and the abiding glory, which is stationed beyond the grave marker and grave.

The scene is set for the Redeemer to step forward and conclude the pageant with a final address. Revelation 22:10-21 contains the final message of John to his reader and is where this study begins.

EXPOSITION
I. REMAIN AS YOU ARE (REVELATION 22:10–13)
The angel who has previously spoken to John in 19:9; 21:9 again speaks to him here and in verse 11. He tells John do not seal up the words of this prophecy, for the time is near. Previously John had received a vision of the scroll sealed along the edges with seven seals showing that the contents of the scroll weren't accessible to humanity. When earlier prophets received revelations that were not for their present times or persons, but for future revealing, they were commanded to seal the prophecy (see Isaiah 8:16; Daniel 8:26; 12:4, 9). This prophecy is of immediate importance for the people of God. It has been purposed to remain open to meet the immediate need of those facing the churches of Asia Minor. This is a distinguishing mark for Revelation from other apocalyptic literature (Daniel 12:4). This vision of John is prophetic and needs to be heard and understood because "the time is near." We are mindful here of the tension in the New Testament as it

relates to the *parousia* of the Christ (His second coming). Jesus may return at any moment and this was the belief of the early church and should be our belief as well. Yet, we are aware that His coming speaks of the future as well. So the believer should be ready and possess a character that is acceptable to Him when He does return. When He returns there won't be time to get ready (see Matthew 24-25, the Parables of the Nations).

Those who practice wrong will continue to practice wrong and those who are morally filthy will continue in their unclean ways. The point here is that since the time is ready, people will reap the consequences of the kinds of lives they lived. There comes a juncture in time where change is impossible because character has already been determined by a lifetime of habitual action. The coming of the end closes all possibility of better or change. We are warned here that the two possible results of our outcome depend on what one has done in their present life.

In verse 12, once again Jesus announces His soon return, but in verse 7 the announcement accompanies a beatitude. Here the announcement comes with a reward. The reward is located in the actions and works one has done. The giving of rewards according to works is also pronounced in the Scripture in Jeremiah 17:10; Romans 2:6; and 1 Peter 1:17.

Jesus' impending return comes with the judgment of human life behaviors. There will be a division of the right from the wrong and the unrighteous from the righteous. Jesus comes as a rewarder in both the negative and positive sense according to this verse. The language here suggests that Jesus is coming with the reward that is His to give (Isaiah 40:10; 62:11). Here the point of the passage is that Jesus will come as a judge to reward the individuals for their continuous work and responsibility, whether it was good or bad.

Jesus is qualified to grant these rewards based on His position as the Lamb of God. Verse thirteen denotes the great assurances of Jesus' right and qualifications to reward each person with what they rightfully deserve. He appropriates three titles for Himself that may be considered the highest attribution of divine power. The first is "Alpha and Omega", which is the title noted for God the Father in 1:8; 21:6. The translation might go – "I am He from whom all being has proceeded and to whom it will return."

The second title, "the first and the last" is applied to Christ in Revelation 1:17; 2:8. It is also noted in Isaiah 44:6; 48:12 and refers to the LORD. It may be translated as, "I am the primal cause and the final aim of all history." The title "the beginning and the end" applies to the Father in 21:6 (see Hebrews 12:2) and refers to "the author and finisher of our faith." The translation would be "What the Lord starts, He also finishes (Philippians 1:6). The idea here is that He is the One who has created the world and He is the One who will perfect it.

II. IDENTIFYING WHO'S WHO (REVELATION 22:14-16)

Having given the three titles of qualification; Jesus pronounces the seventh final beatitude of Revelation (1:3; 14:13; 16:15; 19:9; 20:6; 22:7). Here Jesus is dealing with the ultimate issues of life, which are access to the Tree of Life (22:2) and entrance to the Holy City (12:25).

This blessed group (not just the martyrs) has "washed their robes and made them white in the blood of the Lamb" (Revelation 7:14, NKJV). This need for washing came because the people have defiled themselves (or spiritual clothes) through sin similar to the church at Sardis (3:4). The believers mentioned in this verse have repented and clothed themselves in the pure white linen that stands for the just deeds of the saints. Jesus says these aforementioned persons will have the authority over or the right to eat from the tree of life. Another way of saying or understanding the latter portion of Jesus' statement is that the believers will enter the city freely and have access to the tree of life because it is within the city. When we reverse the order it would read "and so they will have the right to go through the gates into the city and eat the fruit from the tree of life."

Whereas verse 14 details the blessing of being in the city, verse 15 delineates all those who will be denied entrance into the city. Jesus continues His discussion of eternal life and destiny by elucidating to all those who will be outside the city and realize their final destiny in the lake of fire (20:15; 21:8). The "dogs" here is a metaphor for those who are morally impure. This idea flows throughout Scripture. Dogs, as scavengers and objects of great contempt in the Orient, were used to represent the morally impure and different genre of impure persons such as male prostitutes (Deuteronomy 23:18), Gentiles (Matthew 15:26; and Judaizers (Philippians 3:2–3).

As in 21:8, fornicators, murders, and the idolaters are also listed, but are outside of the city. Again, note the eternal destiny of those outside the city and their resulting eternal rejection and the denial of fellowship with the Father and the Lamb. Jesus spoke of their eternal home as "outer darkness" or outside the lighted house (Matthew 8:2; 22:13; 25:30).

The phrase "whosoever loveth and maketh a lie" (v. 15, KJV) is an elaboration of Revelation 21:8 and 21:27. Satan, as the father of lies, also has an eternal home and it is the future residence of those who love and practice lying (2 Thessalonians. 2:12).

In v. 16, Jesus switches the subject and moves to discuss His role in the production of this letter. This "I Jesus," emphatic self –designation, is not located anywhere else, but here in this passage. It serves to place final weight on this last attestation of His role in revealing the contents of the Revelation. This is the only time that the Lord announces Himself by this personal name. This announcement will serve to demonstrate that this letter is not the result of just any individual (1 Peter 1:21). This word assists in lifting the case being raised by John in competition with the "other" prophets and professing prophets in Asia Minor (2:2; 20–21). The angel was "sent" by Jesus to attest these things. "Sent" here is translated as being sent to represent with a special commission. Here Jesus says, "He sent His angel." This is a continuation of the sending (1:1). My angel is the same here as His angel in 22:6. What God does, Jesus does also.

Jesus identifies himself as the Root and the Offspring of David, the Bright and Morning Star. Jesus' claim to authority here is tied to His claim to Messiahship and His right to inaugurate the kingdom promised to David. Also Jesus calls himself the Bright and Morning Star. Jesus is implicating that He is explicitly the brightest star in the complete galaxy.

III. THE TESTIMONIES (REVELATION 22:17–21)

There are four invitations extended in this verse. All those in the seven churches are invited to receive this free offer. It also extends to those who hear and accept the invitation who thirst for the water of life. It is also extended to those coming generations until history is closed and no further option is available.

Revelation closes with a stern warning: don't add or take away from the book. This severe warning is against the willful distortion of the message (Galatians 1:6, 7). This was not an uncommon plea. See Deuteronomy 4:2 when Moses tells the Israelites not to add or take away from what he has instructed them to do. We can take away from this that God considers it a serious issue to distort the Word of God.

Once again, we have the Savior saying that He will be coming soon and John the seer replying, "Come, Lord Jesus." This confession is noted as the earliest confession of the church. This book closes with the answer to all of the problems of life and the realization that the answers do not lie in people to necessarily create a better world, rather the answer lies in the Creator returning to right human affairs. Redemptive history is incomplete until Christ returns.

In verse 21, John ends his apocalypse with a transforming word that will strengthen the churches of Asia Minor and encourage them to be faithful in both their witness and message. Although this is an unusual ending, yet as an epistle it is appropriate to close remembering God's gracious provision for His people in heaven and on earth.

THE LESSON APPLIED

When we think about the second coming what ideas and pictures cross our minds? When considering all the benefits of the Holy City, what most would you like to see? Chapter 21:10–21 provide a glimpse of all that will be received and rejected and an encouragement to the churches of Asia Minor and to us that God has providentially provided for us both in heaven and on earth.

LET'S TALK ABOUT IT

What makes the struggle easier to persevere?

John reminds us we have receive grace on top of grace (John 1:16). All that we have to succeed in this Christian struggle has been granted to us by God's grace. We are challenged to live by faith in the grace that God provides. We can depend on God to see us through all of our difficulties.

HOME DAILY DEVOTIONAL READINGS
AUGUST 29–SEPTEMBER 4, 2022

MONDAY	TUESDAY	WEDNESDAY	THURSDAY	FRIDAY	SATURDAY	SUNDAY
The Faith of Abraham	How Lovely Is Your Dwelling Place!	God Reckons Righteousness Apart from Works	A Promised Inheritance	Abraham Rejoices in Christ	First Steps of Faith	Called to Be a Blessing
Hebrews 11:8–19	Psalm 84	Romans 4:1–12	Romans 4:13–25	John 8:51–59	Genesis 11:27–32	Genesis 12:1–7; 15:1–7

BIBLIOGRAPHY

Ambrosiaster, and Gerald Bray. Commentaries on Galatians-Philemon. Downers Grove, Ill: IVP Academic, 2009.

Anders, M. E., Martin, G., Butler, T. C., Gangel, K. O., & Lawson, S. J. (2001). Holman Old Testament commentary. Nashville, TN: Broadman & Holman.

Augsburg, Myron S., and Lloyd John. Ogilvie. The Preacher's Commentary Matthew. Nashville: Thomas Nelson, 1982.

Barton, Bruce B., David Veerman, and Neil S. Wilson. Life Application Commentary Romans. Wheaton, IL: Tyndale House Publishers, 1992.

Barclay, William. The Daily Study Bible Series: The Gospel of John. Volume 1. Philadelphia: Westminster Press, 1975.

Barton, Bruce B. Life Application Commentary Galatians. Wheaton, IL: Tyndale House, 1994.

Beasley-Murray, George. Word Biblical Commentary: John. Volume 36, Word Book Publishers: Waco, 1987.

Blevins, James L. , Revelation.:Knox Preaching Guide, Atlanta, Ga: 1984 John Knox Press

Bratcher, Robert G. & Howard A. Hatton, A Handbook on the The Revelation to John, United Bible Society: New York: New York, 1993

Brueggemann, W. (2008). Abingdon Old Testament Commentary Deuteronomy. Nashville, TN: Abingdon Press.

Bruner, Frederick Dale. The Gospel of John: a Commentary. Grand Rapids, MI: William B. Eerdmans Publishing Company, 2012.

Dunnam, Maxie D., and Lloyd John. Ogilvie. Galatians, Ephesians, Philippians, Colossians, Philemon. Nashville, TN: Thomas Nelson, 1982.

GotQuestions.org. "Home." GotQuestions.org, June 20, 2013. https://www.gotquestions.org/Judaizers.html.

Hamm, Lydia. Matthew 26 Questions and Answers, May 10, 2014. http://www.growingdisciples.org/Studies/Mt26QA.htm.

"John 8:12,31-36,51-59 Exploring the Passage." BIBLE STUDY COURSES. Accessed January 13, 2021. http://biblestudycourses.org/john-bible-study-courses-section-1/john-8-12-31-36-51-59-exploring-the-passage/.

Keller, Jack A. Immersion Bible Studies: Deuteronomy. Nashville, TN: Abingdon Press, 2012.

Ladd, George Eldon. A Commentary on the Revelation of John, Eerdmans Publishing, Grand Rapids, Michigan; 1972.

Larson, Knut, Max Anders, and Kathy Dahlen. Ezra, Nehemiah, Esther. Nashville, TN: Broadman & Holman, 2005.

Lawrence, John W. The Six Trials of Jesus. Grand Rapids, MI: Kregel Publications, 1996.

"Matthew Chapter 26." Enduring Word, July 22, 2019. https://enduringword.com/bible-commentary/matthew-26/.

Maxwell, John C. The Preacher's Commentary. Edited by Lloyd J Ogilvie. 05. Vol. 05. Deuteronomy. Nashville, TN: Thomas Nelson INC, 1987.

McKenna, David L. The Communicator's Commentary: Isaiah 40–66, Word Books Publisher: Waco.

Moody, Josh. "Devotionals." God Centered Life. the Bible Teaching Ministry, August 4, 2020. https://godcenteredlife.org/devotional/ezra-6-a-joyful-ending/. "Passage: Ezra 5:1-6:22." Enter the Bible - Passages: Ezra 5:1-6:22. Accessed January 12, 2021. https://www.enterthebible.org/resourcelink.aspx?rid=716.

Mounce, Robert. The Book of Revelation: The New International Commentary on the New Testament. Eerdsmans: Cambridge, U.K., 1977

Newell, Wm R. The Book of the Revelation, Grace Publishing, Chicago,ILL 1935

North, C. R. "Servant of the Lord," in The Interpreter's Dictionary of the Bible, Vol. R–Z, Abingdon Press, Nashville.

O'Day, Gail R. The Gospel of John. The New Interpreter's Bible: A Commentary in Twelve Volumes, Volume IX, Abingdon Press: Nashville.

Roberts, Mark D. The Preacher's Commentary Series. Edited by Lloyd J. Ogilvie. 11. Ezra, Nehemiah, Ester ed. Vol. 11. Nashville, Tennessee: Thomas Nelson, INC., 1993.

Robertson, Archibald Thomas. Word Pictures in the New Testament. Vol. V, The Fourth Gospel. The Epistle to the Hebrews

Rowley, H. H. An Outline of the Teaching of Jesus. London: Lutterworth Press, 1945.

Sloyan, Gerard S. John: Interpretation: A Bible Commentary for Teaching and Preaching. Atlanta: John Knox Press.

Summers, Ray. Behold The Lamb, Broadman Press, Nashville, Tn 1951

Thomas, Robert L. Revelation 8-22: An Exegetical Commentary, Chicago, Ill, Moody Press, 1995.

Throntveit, Mark A. Interpretation A Bible Commentary for Teaching and Preaching Ezra-Nehemiah. Louisville, KY: John Knox Press, 1992.

Tucker, Gene M. The New Interpreter's Bible: A Commentary in Twelve Volumes, Vol. 1–39, Abingdon Press, Nashville, TN

Unger. Merrill. Vine's Complete Expository Dictionary of the Old and New Testament.

Westermann, Claus. Isaiah 40-66: A Commentary. The Westminster Press, Philadelphia

Watts, John D. W. Word Biblical Commentary, Word Books, Waco, TX